BRITAIN AND EUROPEAN
RESISTANCE, 1940–1945

By the same author

FROM ANARCHISM TO REFORMISM:
THE POLITICAL ACTIVITIES OF PAUL
  BROUSSE 1870–1890

BRITAIN AND EUROPEAN RESISTANCE, 1940–1945

A survey of the Special Operations Executive, with Documents

DAVID STAFFORD

UNIVERSITY OF TORONTO PRESS
TORONTO AND BUFFALO

First published 1980 by
THE MACMILLAN PRESS LTD
London and Basingstoke

*First published in Canada
and the United States by
University of Toronto Press,
Toronto and Buffalo, 1980*

Printed in Great Britain

Library of Congress Cataloging in Publication Data

Stafford, David.
    Britain and European resistance, 1940–1945.

    Bibliography: p.
    Includes index.
    1. World War, 1939–1945 – Secret service –
Great Britain.   2. Great Britain. Special
Operations Executive – History.   3. World War,
1939–1945 – Underground movements – Europe.
I. Title.
D810.S7S76   940.54'86'41   79-19224
ISBN 0-8020-2361-4

In memory of my father

Contents

	Preface	ix
	Introduction	1
1.	The origins of SOE, 1939–1940	10
2.	Secret armies and the detonator concept	28
3.	A lean year	50
4.	Survival and consolidation	79
5.	A year of troubles	103
6.	Invasion, liberation, and order	144
7.	Epilogue	199
	Conclusion	205

Documentary appendices:

1. *Probable state of readiness and ability of certain countries to rise against the Nazi régime, 4 September 1940* — 213
2. *Subversive activities in relation to strategy, 25 November 1940* — 219
3. *Interference with German oil supplies, 8 January 1941* — 225
4. *The distant future, 14 June 1941* — 234
5. *Special Operations Executive, 9 August 1941* — 240
6. *SOE collaboration in operations on the continent, 12 May 1942* — 246
7. *Special Operations Executive directive for 1943, 20 March 1943* — 248
8. *SOE activity in the British zone of Austria, 22 November 1945* — 258

	Notes	260
	Sources and Bibliography	279
	Index	286

Preface

This book is designed to provide a general overview of the activities of the Special Operations Executive as they concerned Europe during the Second World War. The study is focused at the policy-making level and is concerned primarily with demonstrating how SOE and its activities related to the strategic and diplomatic objectives of the British government. It is not, therefore, a compendium of SOE exploits in Europe, and the reader who seeks detailed accounts of individual SOE missions and agents, or indeed of such matters as SOE's clandestine currency operations or involvement in escape work, will look in vain. A multitude of postwar memoirs and reminiscences by SOE agents and others exists already, and it has been no part of my intent to compete with their many graphic and colourful accounts of SOE activities at the operational level. Nor is this book a comprehensive history of the full range of British relations with European resistance movements. Such a book needs to be written, but its scope would have to include, in addition to the activities of SOE, the propaganda activities of the Political Warfare Executive (PWE) and the BBC, as well as the intelligence and escape activities of other clandestine organisations such as SIS and MI9. It is probably true to say that the single most important link between Britain and occupied Europe in the Second World War was the BBC, and Britain's most important contribution to European resistance the simple fact of continuing to fight after Dunkirk, so that the history of SOE and Europe is no more than one small part in the total story of Britain and European resistance. On the other hand, the study is focused more broadly than on SOE alone. SOE was an anomaly, an executive agency with its own Minister. The Minister—especially Hugh Dalton—claimed the right to make his own policy, yet simultaneously SOE was instructed to confine itself to the *execution* of policy decisions made by others, in particular by the Chiefs of Staff and the Foreign

Office. As these in turn embodied 'short-term' strategic objectives and 'long-term' (that is postwar) foreign policy objectives, the debates over SOE policy often throw light upon the operational assumptions and the differing or even conflicting requirements of British strategy and diplomacy in the Second World War.

Recently, a distinguished historian writing in the *Times Literary Supplement* referred to the perils facing the historian who dared venture to deal with the 'Serbonian bog' of European wartime resistance. Much the same warning might be given to the historian rash enough to deal with SOE, whose task it was to execute plans of sabotage, subversion, and resistance in occupied Europe. I have certainly been made aware of the complexities, and as this book has been completed without access to any of the official SOE records, such as they may still be, the dangers are obvious. Much about SOE will remain unknown, and many of its secrets taken to the grave. There have been those kind enough to intimate that my energies might be better spent elsewhere than in attempting to reconstruct the story from incomplete records, and occasionally I have been aware of an implicit and understandable scepticism about the wisdom of a historian born after Pearl Harbour and the fall of Singapore writing about the subject at all. But a historian cannot accept that history should be written only by those who took part in it, and if we are to wait for the release of the SOE archives, the wait will be long, if not infinite. So far, no general survey of SOE policy in Europe of this kind has been published, and yet at perhaps no other time has the academic interest in clandestine operations and the Second World War been so great. An attempt to place SOE in context is needed, and if in producing what must of necessity be a general and provisional survey I have occasionally lost my footing, so be it.

An official history of SOE activities in France was published about ten years ago, and recently two non-official and scholarly studies of SOE activities in the Balkans have appeared. I have made considerable use of these in places, as I have also of the official histories of Grand Strategy and British foreign policy. The former, especially, contain a fair amount of material relating to SOE, although the earlier published volumes reflect the circumspection about its activities common for the period of their publication, and they need to be supplemented by the archives. Some of the personal recollections of SOE members which have been published are also of value. Above all, however, I have been able to consult much of the 'raw material' through an examination of documents now available in the Public Record Office in London. This has been supplemented by documentary material available elsewhere, and by the recollections of some of those involved in SOE.

I am only too conscious of the shortcomings of my sources, and of the limits imposed by them on this study. We all have selective memories, and discussions with participants about events which took place thirty to thirty-five years ago are bound to carry severe limitations. Churchill himself once observed that 'memories of the war may be vivid and live, but should never be trusted without verification', and Sir Llewellyn Woodward, the official historian of British foreign policy in the Second World War, once observed that 'the memories of persons who have held positions of power tend . . . to be unreliable . . . they nearly always exaggerate and antedate their own importance, forget the number of their mistakes, overrate their own foresight'. Nonetheless, interviews can, if used with care, add to the story, and they have proved useful to me on occasion. As far as the available documentary sources are concerned, a special word needs to be said. The sources mainly relied upon here are the files of the Prime Minister, Chiefs of Staff and related committees, and, to a lesser extent, the Foreign Office. At the best of times, documents have to be treated with scepticism and caution, and any historian who accepts them at their face value is in for trouble. However complete a documentary collection is, it represents only part of any story. People do not record all that they say or do, least of all in a bureaucracy, and what they do record is not necessarily an accurate representation of what they in fact do or say. Official documents such as the Chiefs of Staff or War Cabinet minutes are usually designed to record agreement and unanimity, and, literally, to paper over disagreements and disguise the influences at work in the decision-making process. In times of war, moreover, who would have committed defeatist thoughts to paper— who would have had time to do so if engaged in actually conducting it? The limitations of documents have always existed, but perhaps more so in the twentieth century than previously, and it makes the path of the contemporary historian particularly perilous. The speed and ease of oral communications means that major decisions are often made with no written record being left, save perhaps the *ex post facto* justification carefully drafted to bestow legitimacy and maintain order in the files. The historian, unless he gives up altogether, can only take the documentary material as one item in the total body of evidence, compare it with all the rest, and reach a conclusion which on balance seems to make sense. With such a subject as SOE, all these problems are compounded by others. It was a secret organisation whose existence was not acknowledged until after the war, when it had already been wound up. The 'SOE archives' are still unavailable for public inspection, as are those of other secret agencies with which it often came into close contact, such as the Secret Intelligence Service. While some of its former members are willing to give their recollections, others are not. In the documentary sources which are available, this lack of consistency is also evident. SOE material found its inevitable way into the papers of the Chiefs of Staff, Foreign Office, and Prime Minister's Office, and before these were released for public inspection, an arbitrary hand removed some, but by no means all, of it. It appears to be assumed by many that because of this there is no point in looking through what has been released for information about SOE. This is not the case. Material removed from the minutes and memoranda of the Chiefs of Staff has in many cases not been removed from the papers of the Joint Planning Staff, thus rendering the 'weeding' exercise useless. The removal of papers in some volumes has been more thorough than in others, with the result that by careful cross-referencing the content of removed documents can in some cases easily be deduced. As a recent study of SOE in the Balkans has shown, moreover, large amounts of SOE-related material still remain embedded in the Foreign Office papers. Indeed, the removal of SOE material has been so imperfectly and arbitrarily done, with no apparent criterion underlying it, that one can only marvel at the collective mind responsible for it. Over ten years ago, when Bickham Sweet-Escott wrote the foreword to the excellent personal account of his SOE career, *Baker Street Irregular*, already held up for ten years by the official censor, he noted that those who still opposed its appearance 'must be sadly out of touch with what the public has been told about SOE and its work since 1945'. Now that material is available in the Public Record Office and participants are speaking more freely than ever before, one can only add that continued government secrecy about SOE matters perpetuates an absurdity. The obsession with secrecy is perhaps the true English disease. It pervades all levels of society, and is particularly acute in Whitehall. It is more, however, than simply an occupational disease of the bureaucracy. Malcolm Muggeridge, who served in the wartime Secret Intelligence Service, once noted that 'secrecy is as essential to [SIS] as vestments and incense to a Mass, or darkness to a spiritualist séance'. The cult of secrecy is one of the rituals in a wider sociodrama whereby powerful and informal élite groups exercise and protect their influence in British society. Georg Simmel, the sociologist, pointed out that 'the purpose of secrecy is above all protection. Of all protective measures, the most radical is to make oneself invisible.' Secrecy is maintained less to secure the safety of the state than to protect those who rule it from the scrutiny of the ruled, and helps perpetuate the hierarchical structure of British society in the age of democracy. The secrecy surrounding SOE must long since have lost any 'rational' justification, at least if the evidence of documents which have clearly escaped the weeders by mistake is any guide. In the meantime, however, and until more liberal attitudes prevail, this volume might be of some use to those interested in the subject.

Many people have helped me one way or another in the course of my research. In particular, I wish to thank Ian Armour and Jeanne Cannizzo who helped considerably in the voluminous task of reviewing the various series of documents in the Public Record Office, and without whom the material could not have been covered. Others who have helped me at various times and in various ways over the last five years are: Phyllis Auty, Elisabeth Barker, John Cairns, Richard Clogg, F. W. Deakin, Josef Garlinski, the late Lawrence Grand, the late Sir Colin Gubbins, Michael Howard, W. J. M. McKenzie, H. N. Sporborg, Bickham Sweet-Escott, George Taylor and Donald Watt. Theodore Zeldin and the Warden of St Antony's College provided me with the opportunity, as a Senior Associate Member of the College, to enjoy the ruminative and placid backwaters of Oxford where a substantial first draft of the book was prepared. Special thanks must go to James Joll, who encouraged me at a difficult stage and whose support, interest, and comments have, as always, been positive and helpful. Finally, for the invaluable financial support without which the essential research visits to the United Kingdom would not have been possible, I wish to thank the Canada Council which provided me with both a Leave Fellowship and a Research Grant, the University of Victoria for a Faculty Research Grant, and the American Philosophical Society for a grant from the Penrose Fund. The secretarial staff of the Department of History at the University of Victoria must be thanked for their skill and patience in preparing the manuscript. Quotations from Crown Copyright material appear with the permission of the Controller of Her Majesty's Stationery Office.

David Stafford
Victoria, British Columbia
June 1978

Introduction

This study originated with an interest in the European origins of the Cold War. It soon became apparent however that if Europe was to be regarded as more than simply the passive object of ideological conflict and division imposed by the two postwar superpowers, in terms of which it is still too often exclusively discussed, then the social, political, and ideological struggles within occupied wartime Europe were crucial originating elements in the story. The political dimensions of European resistance therefore came into focus. From there, it was a small step to the issue of British participation in their affairs. The British were deeply involved in many aspects of European wartime resistance, and it was Churchill, not Stalin, who first called for Europe to be set ablaze with the flames of revolt. In some cases, the British were so involved that historical discussion about particular national movements was conducted almost solely in the context of the British role, and even where this was not the case the strategic, tactical, or political dimensions of resistance led almost inevitably back to the requirements of Allied and therefore British strategy and diplomacy. But how and why did Britain become involved, what were her motives and objectives, and what were the results? These were questions far more easily asked than answered, and it soon became apparent that for all the volumes of literature on the Second World War there was not one that sought to explore the question in any detail or even considered it of particular significance. The memoirs of Britain's war leaders were singularly disappointing or reticent. This was partly the result of the secrecy which surrounded the Special Operations Executive, the main operational link between Britain and European resistance. Secrecy in excessive proportions was the bane of SOE's existence, hindering its effective functioning in wartime as well as subsequent discussion of its performance in peacetime. Its early derivation from and association with the Secret Intelligence

1

Service undoubtedly accounted for the fact that high-ranking officials of SOE itself never even saw the charter which laid down its functions as approved by the War Cabinet in July 1940, still less were theatre commanders or other British representatives abroad fully informed of its tasks and of their responsibilities to assist it. This caused it many unnecessary problems and undoubtedly hindered its work, especially when many professional soldiers and diplomats were sceptical and unreceptive to the basic concepts surrounding SOE's activities in the first place. But continued postwar reticence about SOE was due to more than simply a concern with secrecy; it also reflected the interpretive structure which for so long dominated British historical writing about the Second World War. The foundations for this were laid by Churchill in his *History of the Second World War* which provided the central narrative and interpretive core around which the other leading participants constructed their own individual contributions, and which achieved almost semi-official status. Yet Churchill's account is less than generous in its acknowledgement of the importance attached to SOE by the wartime government, especially in its beginnings, and fails completely to mention his own part in creating and sustaining it. It is a classic example of the filtering process, conscious or unconscious, of a selective memory. As the first chapter of this book shows, SOE was founded in July 1940 as a desperate attempt to plug the gaping hole in British strategy caused by the collapse of France, and wildly unrealistic hopes were pinned upon it at the very highest levels—as they also were on other 'indirect' methods of defeating the Germans such as economic warfare and strategic bombing. Indeed, at this early stage of the war, European uprisings fomented by SOE were envisaged as replacing the need for any mass land invasion of the European Continent. SOE was very much a product therefore of the period when Britain 'stood alone'. In writing his *History*, however, Churchill was anxious to dispel the widespread suspicions which had been voiced particularly in the United States over his so-called Mediterranean, or 'indirect' strategy. According to these, Churchill had preferred a Balkan or Mediterranean strategy to that of a direct cross-Channel attack by massive Allied armies on *Festung Europa*. The realities of the controversy and the puncturing of many myths on this issue have subsequently been admirably illuminated and accomplished by Michael Howard in Britain and Richard Leighton in the United States. But when Churchill wrote his history the controversy was at its height, and in order to defend himself he went out of his way to stress that he had always favoured a Normandy-type invasion in a direct confrontation with the German armed forces. In so doing, he implied that he had favoured this course even *before* US entry into the war, in other words during the period immediately after the collapse of France, when Britain 'stood alone'. Yet it is clear from the context of the various memoranda produced by Churchill in his defence that when he talked in 1940–2 of the invasion of Europe he was thinking primarily in terms of landings to assist prior European uprisings after Germany had been substantially weakened by blockade, bombing, subversion and propaganda. SOE (in both its branches—SO1 for propaganda and SO2 for operations) was an element in this strategy. But the strategy was superseded after American and Russian entry into the war, and those responsible for pinning their hopes upon it were no doubt eager to forget the largely illusory assumptions upon which it was founded. Churchill's work became a conscious or unconscious model for his associates when writing their own memoirs, but they were even less forthcoming. The comment of General Sir Leslie Hollis on Ismay, the crucial intermediary between Churchill and the Chiefs of Staff— that 'he knew everything and said little'—is as true of his memoirs as of the man. Hollis's own recollections are not much more helpful. Dill wrote no memoirs, and the published Alanbrooke Diaries contain only scarce references to subversion, especially for the early period of the war. The reader will find only incidental and unenlightening reference to SOE and the hopes pinned on European resistance in Anthony Eden's volume on the war years, while the memoirs of the commanding generals rarely mention SOE at all, and, like Churchill's own work, mostly adopt a teleological approach which has each campaign leading to the next in an inexorable chain culminating in the invasion of Normandy, as though the use of mass Anglo-American armies in a direct confrontation with the German Army had always been envisaged in their strategy. The tendency to fill out the basic narrative provided by Churchill, and in particular to slide over the very expansive claims made in this period for subversion as a weapon of war, is still to be found. A recent book which traces the war history from Dunkirk to Alamein using the newly released War Cabinet and Chiefs of Staff papers makes no reference to SOE except passingly, without explanation or comment, to refer to its creation in 1940.[1] Dalton's memoirs were practically the sole exception to this general pattern, and this for the obvious reason that he was the Minister responsible for SOE during the period 1940–2.

If these memoirs were mostly reticent or silent about SOE and relations with wartime resistance, the volumes of official history were only marginally more informative, and it was clear that the censor's hand lay heavily upon all except the latest volumes of the *Grand Strat-*

egy series. An official history of SOE and Europe was written but never published, while the official history of *SOE in France* which appeared in 1966 caused so much controversy that it was decided that no further volumes should appear. As for the work of independent professional historians, few broached the subject for understandable reasons, and although a valuable and informative conference on Britain and European resistance took place in Oxford in 1962 its papers and proceedings were not published and were severely restricted in circulation.

Where SOE did figure more prominently in the published literature it was only too frequently (with a few notable exceptions) either the object of allegations or counter allegations about its worth and efficiency, or the subject of highly spiced, melodramatic, or exculpatory memoirs and accounts which often served merely to fuel the flames of controversy further. Dimly perceived through the smoke such polemics and controversies generated there emerged three images, largely contradictory although in some cases overlapping. The first was most strongly etched by an anonymous writer in the *Times Literary Supplement* who, in reviewing the record of SOE involvement with the left-wing resistance in Greece, laid down a wider indictment of SOE as an organisation drastically out of step with its own government, and 'among whose higher executives many displayed an enthusiasm quite unrestrained by experience, some [of whom] had political backgrounds which deserved a rather closer scrutiny than they ever got, and a few [who] could only charitably be described as nutcases'.[2] The image has been perpetuated. The author of a history of the British secret service has said of SOE that 'in achievements, in professionalism, and in organisation it never matched up to SIS; in many respects it was downright inefficient, wasteful, and even damaging to the war effort', while in a recent work on wartime strategic deception 'departmental muddle, overwork at headquarters, inefficiency of wireless and security staffs, and amateurishness' are invoked to describe SOE.[3] Implicit in these and similar criticisms was the suggestion that SOE was unique in such characteristics and that it was at cross purposes with the more rational objectives and disciplined behaviour of the British war leadership, the regular armed forces, and the professional Secret Intelligence Service. The postwar Cold War climate contributed to the criticisms of SOE for having become entangled with radical and revolutionary resistance movements. There was much wisdom after the event here, and Basil Liddell Hart, the *doyen* of writers on British strategy, issued a typical indictment when, writing at the height of the Cold War in 1950, he con-

demned British support for armed resistance in wartime Europe both
on account of its relative strategic and tactical ineffectiveness and for
'its wider amoral effect on the younger generation as a whole [for teach-
ing them] to defy authority and break the rules of civic morality'.[4]
Although Liddell Hart did not suggest that SOE had acted independently of the war leadership represented by Churchill himself, others
were less careful. There were those who were also eager to continue wartime interbureaucratic rivalries, and the image of SOE as an irresponsible, amateurish, and uncontrollable organisation, only too
often consorting with foreign and certainly undesirable radicals and
revolutionaries, became firmly established.

The second view contains features of the first, but is fundamentally
opposed to it. Here too on occasion is the bumbling amateurishness
of the British public school tradition, the muddling through, the inefficiency, the eccentricity. This is presented, however, as the strategic
disguise for what was in reality the clandestine arm of a determined attempt to further British interests in Europe. Some of those who
worked for SOE encountered this view themselves during the war.
C. M. Woodhouse, whose superb memoirs of his experiences in Greece
deserve close reading by any reader interested in the Second World
War, later recalled how the Greeks only too often interpreted apparent
contradictions in British policy: 'If three British officers say three different things, that does not mean that any of them is wrong; it does not
even mean that any of them is confused; it only means that it is more in-
tricate and far-reaching than has hitherto been supposed.'[5] Jasper
Rootham, who served as a liaison officer for SOE with the Yugoslav
Chetniks in Serbia, likewise remembered the incredulity with which the
Serbs received his explanation that limitations of aircraft availability,
overwork in Cairo, and priorities elsewhere accounted for delays in supplies: '. . . at that moment, unobserved by any of those present, there
slipped quietly down the chimney and into the room a well-known historical character . . . Perfidious Albion was with us, and had come to
stay . . . she was there, on our backs, like an Old Man of the Sea, stran-
gling us slowly but surely.'[6] Here, too, the recipients of British support
perceived a Master Plan of machiavellian proportions. Such perceptions were confined neither to the Balkans nor to the immediate pas-
sions of wartime Europe. That British policy towards European
resistance was motivated by considerations deeper and more long term
than purely military objectives and that consistent if devious pursuit of
political gain was the hallmark of SOE policy in Europe was a theme
readily picked up by others. The House of Commons was the scene of

heated debates in early December 1944 following action by British troops against EAM-ELAS, the left-wing Greek resistance forces. Several Members of Parliament charged that Britain was seeking to suppress the democratic forces of the resistance not only in Greece but throughout Europe. 'The attitude of the Government in regard to many European countries,' claimed one, 'appears to be that of opposing . . . the forces in those countries which have been the backbone of the resistance movements and who fought by our side so gallantly, [and] reserving all their sympathy for the representatives of the old social order.' It was criticism such as this which stung Churchill to his famous retort that 'democracy is no harlot to be picked up in the street by a man with a tommy gun'.[7] The critics were unimpressed. It was the then youthful Major Denis Healey who told the Labour Party Conference in May 1945 that British policy was designed to protect the interests of Europe's ruling class who 'in every country look to the British Army and the British people to protect them against the just wrath of the people who have been fighting underground against them for the past few years. There is very great danger, unless we are very careful, that we shall find ourselves running with the Red Flag in front of the armoured car of Tory imperialism and counter-revolution.'[8] A Britain opposed to the struggles of the European resistance was an image whose contours were more deeply etched in the following year by Basil Davidson, who had himself served in important positions for SOE in Hungary, Cairo, Yugoslavia, and Greece. He too condemned the British relationship with the resistance for its conservatism. Davidson argued

> Instead of accepting the movements of resistance and liberation . . . as logical and desirable allies, the British Government of the war years preferred to treat with the runaway kings and ministers of small-power-cliques whose interests were as much against as they were for us. Time and time again British policy launched in a direction which ran contrary to the success, and sometimes even the very existence of these movements for resistance and liberation.

Twenty-five years later the same author attributed a good part of this to the 'nabobs of SOE London [who were] men of banking or commercial experience interested in restoring the *status quo ante bellum*'.[9] Similar views have become commonplace in Soviet and left-wing interpretations of British policy. Kim Philby, who worked for SOE in its early phase, later noted the implicit contradiction in the conservative objectives of British foreign policy and the declared aims of SOE, with the inevitable subordination of the latter to the former;[10] a Soviet historian addressing the 1961 Milan Conference on European Resistance Movements explicitly charged the British and Americans with seeking to limit the scale of resistance through fear of their challenge to existing regimes in Europe;[11] and Gabriel Kolko has argued at length in *The Politics of War* that 'everywhere they looked the British and Americans saw political dangers on the left, and they had to prepare for the worst or else risk political defeat after their military triumphs', and for this reason became involved in containing and manipulating resistance movements.[12]

Between the view of SOE as in effect the saboteur of the British rather than the German war effort on the one hand, and that which sees SOE as the expression of Perfidious Albion's deeper political purposes in Europe on the other, there is a third view, or group of views, which has largely been propounded by those involved in or associated with SOE, anxious to clear the organisation of charges against it and to justify the courageous activities of those who volunteered to operate inside Nazi-occupied Europe. In this view, SOE functioned efficiently with the limited resources made available to it by the regular armed forces and within the often paralysing limits imposed by the Foreign Office and the Secret Intelligence Service. It had no other objective than to help pursue the military war against the Germans, and here it accomplished its task at least as well as, if not even more efficiently than, other branches of the British war effort. If indeed it had been given the resources it needed, it is sometimes argued, it could have done more damage to the German war effort and with considerably less expense than Bomber Command with its thousands of deaths for the sake only too often of implanting large holes in German fields.[13] The debate about the strategical and tactical contribution of SOE, and, by extension, of the European resistance movements, is a continuing one. In the view of Henri Michel, one of Europe's most distinguished experts on the resistance, Allied support was essential to its success, while their task would have been far more arduous without its assistance. But how many opportunities, he asks, did the Allies squander by failing to make the best use of resistance, by arming it too little and too late?[14] Unfortunately, such generalisations still remain largely unsubstantiated, and Professor Alan Milward is right to criticise many historians of the resistance for failing to move much beyond opinion when it comes to discussing the economic and strategic effectiveness of resistance movements. So far as the economic value of resistance is concerned, Professor Milward's own conclusion is that in France at least it was very small, in Norway it had practically no impact on the Germans at all, and that generally 'on a co-ordinated level it [resistance] seems to have been seldom effective, sometimes stultifying, frequently dangerous, and almost always too costly'.[15] Here, too, therefore, there is little consensus, and the detailed work upon which more valid general conclusions might be drawn has yet to be done.

It would be an impossible task for any one historian even to attempt to reach definitive conclusions about all of these issues and controversies, even if they merited the effort. Too many echo interprofessional jealousies and resentments which thirty-five years after the war have little more than a titillating interest for the connoisseur of bureaucratic interfamilial feuding, although they still mean much to those involved. Others raise questions which still remain unanswerable; while others, even if they were answerable, do not advance us very far. Even if all higher executives of SOE in London had been miners or schoolteachers instead of bankers or 'nabobs' from the City (which in any case they were not) this would not, in isolation, tell us much about the intent, pattern, and direction of SOE operations in Europe. Nonetheless, there remains as a profitable and plausible area for further exploration the question of SOE's relationship both to the higher direction of the war and to the European resistance itself. Was SOE an organisation concerned solely with military objectives, or was it, on the contrary, an instrument for the political oppression and containment of left-wing resistance in Europe? Was it part of a wider strategy by the British war leadership to contain communism and restore the social and political *status quo* in Europe? At one level, of course, such an approach is trite. The British government had the responsibility of pursuing what it perceived to be British interests, and no obligation to pursue those of the Soviet Union or of the communist parties of Europe. Not surprisingly, British interests were not always compatible with those of the Soviet Union or of the communist parties of Europe. Britain was neither a communist nor a revolutionary power and only the naive would express shock or dismay at discovering this. To write a book to prove it would not be of much interest. What is of interest, however, is to examine SOE in its relationship to British wartime strategy and diplomacy, and to break down 'grand strategy' into its component parts. When and in what circumstances—if at all—for example, did concerns about the future political shape of Europe begin to affect SOE relations with resistance in each of the European countries, and did this necessarily mean the abandonment of communist or left-wing resistance movements? If not, why not, and what part did Anglo-Soviet relations play in the question? If left-wing resistance forces were not supported, was this for political or other reasons, and did SOE seek to preserve and restore the prewar governments of Europe? Can any broad comparative conclusions be reached and can a general pattern in SOE relations with the forces of European resistance be discerned? These are the questions which this book attempts to answer, and in doing so it is hoped to make a contribution not only to an understanding of SOE but also to the study of British strategy and diplomacy in the Second World War.

1 The Origins of SOE, 1939-1940

Even before the outbreak of war in September 1939 Britain had established secret agencies to conduct clandestine operations in Europe going beyond the scope of mere intelligence gathering. Their job was to carry out various forms of subversion and propaganda. It was only in July 1940, however, that these activities were brought under the control of one central organisation, the Special Operations Executive (SOE). What did the British expect these subversive organisations to achieve and why, in July 1940, did they create a new organisation to control clandestine activities? What does this tell us about British expectations of European resistance to Nazism and the potentialities of SOE? This chapter, in describing the origins of SOE, will suggest answers to these questions. To begin with, something needs to be said about the assumptions underlying British strategic thinking on the eve of the Second World War.

British strategic planning in the 1930s had taken for granted that Britain's main contribution in a war against Germany would be on the sea and in the air. Only very late in the day, in February 1939, had the Cabinet agreed to the creation of an expeditionary force for use in Europe—and this was mainly as a gesture to the French, whose much larger army, it was assumed, would bear the main burden. The basic British strategy, once any initial enemy advance had been halted, would, in the words of the Chiefs of Staff Committee, 'be directed to weakening Germany and Italy by the exercise of economic pressure and by intensive propaganda, while at the same time building up our major strength until we can adopt an offensive strategy. Command of the sea would then confer freedom of choice in striking at the enemy's most vulnerable points.'[1]

In short, British strategic planning did not foresee the defeat of Germany as resulting from the application of a massive exterior force, such

10

as eventually took place in the Normandy landings of 1944. Large land armies, and certainy British ones, were not going to be used in major offensives against the enemy's defences. Instead, more indirect means were to be steadily applied to weaken the enemy from within. The finale envisaged by Britain's official strategists was one in which Germany finally crumbled under the impact of consistent and sustained economic pressure. Britain's strength, it was believed, lay in her ability to wage economic warfare and to cause economic collapse in Germany. It was on this underlying and often unarticulated assumption that the British placed such faith on the strategic bombing offensive as a weapon against German power. Equally, it was as an outgrowth of the fundamental doctrine of the undermining of Germany by indirect means that Britain's policies toward European resistance were first formulated, as we shall see later.

The search for indirect means of defeating Germany undoubtedly owed much to the traumatic memories of the First World War. Hundreds of thousands of men had died in fruitless land offensives against the enemy's defences, and revulsion against this experience deeply affected the attitudes and policies of British governments and their planners in the 1930s. It was widely believed that in the end Germany had only succumbed as a result of a collapse of morale and economic disintegration caused by the British blockade. Why should not this weapon now play an even more important role? As one of Britain's official historians has put it, the blockade of Germany, 'adorned and transmogrified with a new name and an ill-defined promise . . . had become in 1939 Britain's secret weapon'.[2] But instead of a simple blockade, as in the First World War, there was now 'economic warfare', a concept which in addition to the conventional devices of the blockade embraced the air bombing of industrial targets, sabotage, and psychological warfare; in other words, economic pressure carried directly behind the enemy lines. Throughout the 1930s various committees of the Committee of Imperial Defence had laid the plans for the setting up of a Ministry of Economic Warfare, and this was duly constituted on 3 September 1939. Neville Chamberlain himself had taken an active share in the work of the interdepartmental Economic Pressure on Germany Committee, and firmly shared the expectations which characterised thinking and planning about economic warfare in the first nine months of the war. Combined with his own loathing for war and his fundamental misconceptions of the nature of the enemy, it led him to hope that Germany would be defeated without the employment of the British army. He wrote in September 1939:

I have a feeling that it [the war] won't be so very long. There is such a widespread desire to avoid war, and it is so deeply rooted, that it must surely find expression somehow. Of course the difficulty is with Hitler himself. Until he disappears and his system collapses, there can be no peace. But what I hope for is not a military victory—I very much doubt the feasibility of that—but a collapse of the German home front. For that, it is necessary to convince the Germans that they cannot win.

Thus, Chamberlain rejected the bombing of German towns and military targets: 'What we ought to do is just throw back the peace offers and continue the blockade . . . I do not believe that holocausts are required.'³ He thus still held, even after the outbreak of war, to one of the basic assumptions which had underlain his appeasement policy— the belief that Hitler might be overthrown by moderate forces in Germany under the impact of economic pressure. It was a belief not confined to Chamberlain. As Gladwyn Jebb later recalled 'we all more or less subscribed to the famous doctrine "nous vaincrons parce que nous sommes les plus forts" . . . it all sounds a little unrealistic now.'⁴ Economic warfare as the primary instrument of war and the means to victory was the conventional wisdom of the day, and the mainstay of official strategy. Combined with this, it was common to find a belief that the inherent contradictions of the Nazi régime had produced a political fragility which was profoundly vulnerable to the strains of war. The idea that the monolithic unity of the Nazi régime was a façade concealing conflicting factions which could be manipulated effectively for British purposes was a comforting one. Divisions amongst Nazi leaders were seized upon, and signs of popular indifference in Germany exaggerated, in the usually unarticulated belief that totalitarianism could not accommodate, and therefore could not survive, such phenomena. Looking for 'cracks' in the Nazi régime became a popular pastime. At its most extreme, this led to the belief, common in London and Paris, that Hitler was bluffing in his threats against Poland, and that if Britain and France stood up to him, his bluff would be called; and that if he persisted, and declared war, he would quickly seal his own political fate. At the end of August 1939 the French Commander-in-Chief Gamelin expressed the view in its most excessive form: 'Hitler will collapse the day war is declared on Germany. Instead of defending the frontiers of the Reich, the German army will be forced to march on Berlin to suppress the trouble that will immediately break out.'⁵

Given these kinds of assumptions, even if they were not all as absurdly expressed as was Gamelin's, the prospect of short-term German military victories was not in itself a matter for total despair. Quick German victories could only be partial and superficial. They must, by definition, be meretricious. This view was best expressed four days after the outbreak of war by Air Commodore Slessor, then Director of Plans of the Royal Air Force: 'We are now at war with a nation which possesses an imposing façade of armed might, but which, behind that façade, is politically rotten and weak in financial and economic resources, and already heavily engaged on another front. The lessons of history prove that victory does not always go to the big battalions.' Well might Slessor have noted in his postwar memoirs 'how amazing [it is] to look back upon the illusions and miscalculations of that twilight period.' His view was echoed by another important military observer, the then Chief of Staff to the Commander-in-Chief of the British Expeditionary Force in France. On 29 October 1939 Lieutenant-General Sir Henry Pownall noted that

Both we and the French have weak elements but surely we can outlast a nation which starts with so many early disadvantages—a leader who has considerable, if latent and intimidated, opposition. A leader who is *très nerveux* too. A population that has been dragooned and living at war pressures for years already and who start on a VERY low scale of nourishment. If we can't last out on morale we don't even deserve to survive.

Oliver Harvey, private secretary to Lord Halifax, the British Foreign Secretary, confided identical sentiments to his diary on 22 September, and five days later Halifax himself informed Lord Lothian, the Ambassador in Washington, that 'economic pressure may eventually induce a collapse in Germany . . . Time is on our side.' Similar complacency was expressed by many ministerial spokesmen in the 'phoney war' period, and R. H. Cross, the Minister for Economic Warfare, said on 17 January 1940 that Germany, after four months of war, was in the same economic straits as she had been in after two years of the First World War. Official optimism was such that in March 1940 a critic dubbed the Ministry of Economic Warfare as the 'Ministry of Wishful Thinking.'[6] Such a description would have aptly described government thinking as a whole. It was not only Chamberlain who believed in the spring of 1940 that 'Hitler had missed the bus'. For the Chamberlain government indeed, there was nothing phoney about the phoney war. In

Chamberlain's view—and in this he was largely reflecting the views of his military advisers—the way for Britain to win the war was by convincing the Germans that they could not win. Once they saw that, Chamberlain believed, the forces within Germany hitherto supporting Hitler would turn against him. Victory would therefore be achieved politically, not by military force; all that Britain and France needed to do was to stand firm. If any one belief characterised British policy from September 1939 to May 1940, it was the belief that 'time is on our side'. This was reinforced by the various secret contacts which Britain had with opposition forces inside Germany. These stressed Germany's financial and economic weakness, and lent credence to the mistaken belief that an effective anti-Hitler faction existed, ready to take action and remove Hitler from power.[7]

In so far as the British conceived that positive action was required, it should take the form of careful diplomacy and selective action to bring home to Germans their economic vulnerability. The Balkans—and Italy—should be kept neutral, while the German economy should steadily be weakened. It was these guiding principles which shaped British policy between the collapse of Poland and the collapse of France. The plans for assistance to Finland and the projected action in Norway which Churchill so doggedly favoured were designed more to strike at Germany's supplies of vital iron ore from the Swedish ore fields and thereby cripple the German war economy than to inflict a military defeat on Germany. Similarly, the diplomatic attempts to create a neutral *bloc* in the Balkans were aimed at preventing Germany from obtaining control of important raw materials. In particular, the British were worried about Rumanian oil supplies to Germany. As we shall see later, extensive efforts were made through subversion and sabotage to stop these supplies.

If a complacent optimism characterised official assumptions about the course of the war with Germany prior to and during the phoney war period, it was in large part because of a confident belief in the defensive strength of Britain's ally, France. What, however, happened when France collapsed suddenly in May 1940, and Britain was forced to evacuate its continental expeditionary force? Did this not shatter all the confident assumptions upon which British strategy had been based? And how did the British now expect to defeat the Germans, who controlled the European continent from Northern Norway to the Mediterranean?

The fact that Churchill became Britain's new war leader at the beginning of the May Crisis is sometimes taken as evidence that the British from then on approached the war with a new strategy. Churchill was an inspiring war leader, and he infused a sense of strength, determination and ruthlessness into the execution of the war which had been absent under Chamberlain. More than any other single individual, he remains the symbol of Britain standing alone in the dark days following the collapse of France and the humiliation of Dunkirk. The Churchill government was a coalition, and Labour now shared power with the Conservatives. Churchill reorganised the entire war machinery, and, above all, saw clearly that Britain could only survive with the help of the United States. Nonetheless, for all these important and vital changes, the strategy of the new government was limited by necessity, and continuity as much as innovation characterised the strategic sphere. There was continuity in that when looking ahead to the eventual defeat of Germany, the blockade and the strategic air offensive were still seen as the two major weapons in the war. Indeed, it was believed that these weapons could now be more effectively applied. But what could replace the armies of Britain and France to administer the *coup de grâce* to Germany once she had been fatally wounded by these traditional weapons? In this context, the British Chiefs of Staff found a new weapon forged by the very victories of Hitler which had eliminated their continental ally. This third weapon was subversion, the encouragement of and aid to popular resistance within the occupied countries of Europe.

Before discussing the measures taken to implement this third arm of British strategy in 1940 it is essential to recapture some of the mood of the period and some of the assumptions upon which the British war leadership operated. The rapid collapse of France had in many ways not seriously disturbed confidence about the fundamental weakness of Germany. On the surface at least, almost the contrary was the case. Germany's victories, it was now argued, had overextended Nazism, which was now more vulnerable than before to internal pressures. This argument was combined with a certain belief that now Britain 'stood alone', she could act more effectively than she could when tied to her former ally. There is ample evidence to suggest that these reactions were quite widespread, and that they were to be found within as well as outside the government. The various sources of information open to the Foreign Office, for example, pointed, or perhaps more accurately, were made to point, in a direction encapsulated in a report sent to the Prime Minister on 30 May 1940, entitled *Present Conditions in Germany*. This diagnosed low German civilian morale, attributed serious results to the bombing of Germany, and concluded that if Britain could hold out for a few more weeks 'the spearhead of the Nazi attack may be successfully blunted and . . . if this occurs there is a very real prospect of disorganization spreading on the German home front'.[8] Churchill, while rejecting the more extreme and fatuous forms of this optimism, was nonetheless inclined to share the view that in the near future Hitler was likely to suffer rather than benefit from the occupation of Western Europe. It was on the basis of assumptions such as these that there developed the belief in the post-Dunkirk period that within a short while the occupied European nations would be in a state of revolt and that this could be turned to good account. Again, this assessment depended partly on economic predictions. Hugh Dalton, the Minister of Economic Warfare, who was put in charge of special operations in July 1940, predicted on the eve of the Dunkirk withdrawal that within six months Europe would be faced with 'famine, starvation and revolt, most of all in the slave lands which Germany had overrun'. Two weeks later he had not changed his view: 'Nazidom will be like a dark pall over all Europe, but, after only a few months, it may dissolve like the snow in spring.' Dalton was merely echoing what was common currency in Liberal and Labour circles. The widely circulated newsletter published by Sir Stephen King-Hall told its readership on 28 June that there was good reason to suppose that 'in due course Field Marshall *Famine* may knock at Hitler's door'. George Orwell had recorded the same sentiments in his diary only four days previously, and on 11 August Harold Nicolson predicted starvation in Germany in 1941.[9] But such views were to be found deeply entrenched elsewhere, and perhaps particularly so in the clubs of St James's, Pall Mall, and Piccadilly, where the world was often perceived through the warm afterglow of postprandial port. Raymond E. Lee, the American military attaché in London, whose contacts were cultivated in such circles, noted on 8 July 1940 that 'famine in Europe is predicted on every hand here . . . the British, of course, regard this as their greatest weapon against Hitler'.[10] Indeed, as Lee also wryly noted, it had reached the point where the British were beginning to feel sorry for Hitler. It went beyond economic prediction, however, to judgements about the nature of a European response to Nazi occupation. If Nazism was evil and maintained itself in power by force, and moreover, if it was also a German phenomenon, then clearly the response of the Europeans must be to reject it. Left, Right and Centre could find some common ground here, the Left and Centre on the basis of the virtues of European democracy, the Right on the basis that patriotism would reject German Nazism, and all by appealing to what amounted to a nineteenth-century radical view of Europe with Hitler and Nazism as latter-day versions of the Pope, despotism, and

Catholicism. Dalton's view perhaps best portrays this Left and Centre view. In July 1940 he described the potential arising from the combination of democracy and nationalism in Europe in the following terms:

> No doubt in the earlier part of the war the prospect of a revolution in Germany was remote. The organisation of any widespread subversive movement there was likely to encounter great difficulties. The position in Europe is now completely different. We have on our side not only the anti-Nazi elements in Germany and Austria, not only the Czechs and the Poles, but also the whole of the democractic and liberty-loving elements in Norway, Denmark, Belgium, France, Holland and Italy. Moreover, in each of these countries except Italy, there will be a Nationalist appeal which can be linked with the ideals of democracy and individual liberty. I am convinced that the potentialities of this war from within are really immense. It is even today one of our best offensive weapons if only we can learn to use it, and it will be an absolutely essential part of any land counter-offensive which we must eventually undertake.[11]

Judgements about the capacity and the will of the Europeans to resist were inevitably based at this stage not on empirical evidence, but primarily on *a priori* assessments of how Europeans would behave when faced with the tangible evil represented by Nazi occupation, and here there were deep psychological foundations in a common fund of historic British attitudes towards Europe. The natural insularity of temperament formed by geographical isolation from the European continent could produce a sense of superiority, of optimistic insularity, and of a romanticism which had enthusiastically espoused democratic movements in Europe both in the nineteenth and twentieth centuries, often with little or no understanding of the particularities of national cultures.[12] It could also produce distrust of foreigners and foreign governments, and this too emerged in the post-Dunkirk atmosphere. Dunkirk quickly became mythologised as in some senses a victory, not a defeat, and as a sign of strength, not weakness. King George VI confided that 'personally I feel happier now that we have no allies to be polite to and pamper', while Churchill told Lord Swinton that following the French surrender Britain would be alone; but added, 'I find that rather inspiring'. The parliamentary correspondent of *The Fighting Forces* found solace in the littered Dunkirk beaches—'No longer do we rely on others . . . alone we bear the honour of shouldering the responsibility', while the more

august *Journal of the Royal United Services Institute* echoed his relief
by remarking that 'Now that we are alone in the fight we have a sense
of freedom and a feeling that we can concentrate on British interests'.
Maurice Hankey, the ubiquitous *éminence grise* of British governments
since the First World War, told Sir Samuel Hoare, the British Ambassador in Spain, on 19 July that it 'was almost a relief to be thrown back on
the resources of the Empire and of America'. Finally, and perhaps most
characteristically of all, Baldwin informed Halifax that a voice had
spoken to him in a vision, saying 'Have you not thought there is a purpose in stripping you one by one of all the human props on which you
depend, that you are being left alone in the world? You have no one
upon whom to lean and I have chosen you as my instrument to work my
will. Why then are you afraid?'[13] Sir Joseph Mainwaring, the elderly
confidant of Lady Seal in Evelyn Waugh's novel of 1940, *Put Out More
Flags*, presented a parodied version of such thinking when he pon-
derously pronounced after Dunkirk that 'seen in the proper perspective I regard this as a great and tangible success'. The continental commitment distrusted by so many had been ended by Dunkirk, and Britain
was the stronger for it. Sea power, moral force, and economic strength
were back in the saddle. Britain was, therefore, in a paradoxical way, all
the more able to lend assistance to the oppressed peoples of the Continent. Isolation gave the illusion of strength.

It might be argued that the kinds of view illustrated here were merely
wishful thinking, and that they should not be taken too literally; that
no-one seriously believed that victory could be achieved in this way, and
that statements to that effect were a compound of wishful thinking and
a conscious or unconscious attempt to maintain personal and collective
morale in a time of great crisis; and that in July 1940 the need for immediate survival precluded serious thought about the long-term future
and about the shape of victory. While part of this argument can be
accepted—clearly, a belief in ultimate victory and in one's own inherent
superiority was essential for the maintenance of morale—three points
should be borne in mind. First, wishful thinking is merely thinking that
in retrospect turns out to be wrong, it is not thinking that is not believed.
If actions and decisions are based on it, as they were, then it hardly matters whether it was wishful or not. The fact that so much of it turned out
to be mistaken is not an argument against it having played an important
part in shaping decisions and attitudes in 1940. It seems clear from all
the available contemporary evidence that SOE was established within a
context receptive to the concept of an eventual strong and effective
European resistance to Nazism, however mistaken in retrospect that

may have turned out to be. Secondly, it should be transparent that these beliefs about the future were remarkably consistent with the past assumptions upon which British policy had been based throughout the 1930s and in the first year of the war. Belief in fundamental Nazi weakness, its economic vulnerability, and its political brittleness, did not suddenly develop following the collapse of France and the defeat of Dunkirk. They had been there all along. Britain's isolation after June 1940 certainly lent an air of necessity to the strategy of the future. But this strategy did not emerge from a vacuum. It had its roots deep in traditional British assumptions. Thirdly, it is simply not true that Dunkirk and the fall of France focused people's attention exclusively on the immediate question of survival. Almost the contrary was the case. The shock of the June defeats led to demands for the removal from office of the 'guilty men' responsible for or associated with Britain's prewar policy of appeasement. These were, almost by definition, Conservatives. Dunkirk and all it symbolised pushed the state of feeling in Britain sharply to the left. As a recent historian of Britain's domestic politics from 1939 to 1945 has noted, Dunkirk gave the first clear impetus to the consideration of future social and economic reconstruction. What indeed is striking is how *early* in the war planning began for postwar Britain. Planning for reform in the social, economic and educational spheres all began in 1940 or 1941. Ten days after the opening of the Battle of Britain the War Cabinet set up a War Aims Committee whose job it was to make suggestions for the shape of postwar Britain, Europe, and the world. Thus, concern for the present raised urgent questions about the future. If this was true for domestic strategy, it was equally true for Britain's military strategy and foreign policy planning. The shape of victory in all its guises was a real (if relatively minor) concern in the aftermath of Dunkirk and the collapse of France.[14]

Given this background to British assumptions about the weaknesses of Germany and the potential strength of European resistance, what had been done in the field of sabotage and subversion, and in the building up of relations with groups and movements in Europe opposed to Nazism and prepared actively to resist it? Three main organisations in the subversive field had been established in 1938, shortly after Hitler's annexation of Austria.[15] The first was a section of the General Staff at the War Office, known as GS(R), and later as MI(R), which concentrated on studying techniques of irregular warfare. It had some contacts with, although it was separate from, the second organisation, Section D of the Secret Intelligence Service (SIS). SIS itself was a pre-First World War organisation and it had been active ever since, even if, as Kim

Philby later described it, it was in a ramshackle state by the end of the 1930s. But its function was the gathering of intelligence, and it was not suited or inclined to take action, through sabotage or subversion, against German influence in Europe. It was for this reason that Section D was created early in 1938, under the charge of Colonel Lawrence Grand. Grand was a colourful figure, whose personality perhaps unfortunately stamped itself indelibly on Section D and its successor, SOE. Bickham Sweet-Escott remembered him as follows: 'He was tall and thin, with a heavy black moustache. He never wore uniform, always had a long cigarette holder in his mouth, and was never without a red carnation in his buttonhole'. Philby, who was also a member of Section D, said that Grand's mind 'ranged free and handsome over the whole field of his awesome responsibilities, never shrinking from an idea, however big or wild', while Gladwyn Jebb disapprovingly described his leadership as 'theatrical and James Bond-ish'.[16] It all meant that Section D fitted uneasily into SIS, and undoubtedly contributed to the suspicion with which 'that old-established racket' subsequently regarded SOE. Section D's purpose was to 'investigate every possibility of attacking potential enemies by means other than the operations of military forces'. About the same time that GS(R) and Section D were established, a third organisation, a Department of Propaganda, was also set up, one of whose functions was to specialise in 'black' (or unattributable) propaganda to Europe. This was known as EH, after Electra House, its London headquarters.

From the very beginning it became clear that sabotage and subversive activities raised difficult problems for other activities of the British government. These problems were never entirely resolved, and it is doubtful they could have been by the very nature of things. First, it soon became clear that the activities carried out by Section D risked disturbing intelligence networks carefully prepared by SIS. Sabotage drew the attention of foreign authorities, whereas the essential condition for the effective functioning of intelligence was normally the exact opposite. This exacerbated conflicts between Section D and its parent body, and in 1940, as we shall see, they were separated. Nonetheless, the conflict of interest remained, with rivalry and hostility characterising the relations between SIS and SOE throughout the war. In the second place, sabotage and subversion threatened British diplomacy, especially in the Balkans, where the British were attempting to create a neutral *bloc* in 1939–40. It was feared by the Foreign Office that subversive and sabotage operations might either damage relations with friendly neutrals, or, alternatively, provoke German intervention. Either way, the attempt to preserve neutrality would be damaged. From the first, therefore, the Foreign Office kept a close eye on all such activities, and for the most part vetoed them in this early period.

Although it is not the intention of this study to go into any great detail about the functioning and operations of Britain's clandestine organisations something needs to be said at this stage about each of the three which have been mentioned. GS(R) concentrated on the study of guerrilla warfare and paramilitary operations of all kinds. By the summer of 1939 its studies had concluded that if coordinated with regular operations, guerrilla operations could cause major diversions of enemy strength and thus significantly help the main regular forces. The Department of Propaganda, or EH, was headed by Campbell Stuart, a Canadian, who had worked with a similar organisation in the First World War. Its accomplishments in this period were undistinguished, and Stuart was pensioned off when the Department was merged with the other two to form SOE in the summer of 1940. Of the three organisations, Section D was the main nucleus of what later became SOE. It was, as we have seen, an offspring of the Secret Intelligence Service, and as such came, like SIS, under the nominal control of the Foreign Office. For the first year or so of its existence it consisted of merely a handful of men, somewhat haphazardly recruited from the informal social networks centred upon the gentlemen's clubs of St James's and Piccadilly, where members of the City, the military, and government maintained and refined the friendships and acquaintances first made in the public schools and at Oxbridge. It concentrated in these first months of its existence on building up as many contacts as possible with anti-German and pro-British elements in Europe in order to lay the groundwork for future action which was often, as the personality of its leader indicated, of an imaginative and dreamlike quality.

Although the *Anschluss* had prompted the creation of Section D and the other clandestine organisations, activity in their first year was restricted to preparation. Hitler's occupation of Prague in March 1939 led in this sphere as in so many others to action. Only a week after Hitler's first open defiance of his own claims to be interested exclusively in German-speaking territory, Section D was authorised to take active steps to resist Nazi influence in states threatened by Germany. In May 1939 it received its first order for sabotage operations—the Rumanian oil fields, Germany's main source of oil. Unsuccessful attempts were made to carry out these instructions, and for the next two years Rumania was to be a main focus of Section D's activities. Indeed, the Balkans occupied much of Section D's attention throughout the years

1939 and 1940.[17] Apart from the hope of destroying Germany's access
to Rumanian oil—identified by British intelligence experts as an important Achilles' heel of the German economy—the main objective in
the sabotage field became that of blocking traffic on the Danube. Several schemes were devised. One was to 'blow up' the Iron Gates; another
was to block the river by sinking barges. The plans involved such
devices as forming dummy shipping companies, and all failed, or were
prevented from proceeding, either by Balkan governments anxious not
to offend the Germans, or by the Foreign Office which was worried
about the effects on diplomatic relations with these governments.

Section D also went beyond sabotage to subversion. Sabotage—the
physical dislocation of supplies useful to the Germans—often involved
making contact with individuals or groups in various countries willing
to lend assistance. In this way, the British were led inevitably into contact with political groups who were often in opposition to their own
governments. The support and encouragement they found themselves
obliged to give these groups in exchange for cooperation therefore extended Section D's activities into the area of political subversion. (It
appears that Section D carried out no activities at this stage in Germany
or Italy, although it was in touch with dissident fascist elements in Italy;
Italy in any case was a neutral state until June 1940.) Subversion, however, immediately created problems for the conduct of official foreign
policy, and for this reason also many of Section D's activities were discouraged or curtailed. They appear also to have been limited by the
rivalry with SIS which had an extensive Balkan network and was dis-
inclined to see it damaged by the activities of Section D. SIS, moreover,
still controlled the communications of its offspring, and was able to use
this on occasion to limit its activities.

The concern with Rumania and the Balkans in general in 1939–40
reflected the importance the British government attached within the
general strategic plan of the war to economic warfare.[18] Indeed, Lawrence Grand, Section D's head, often received instructions for the selec-
tion of targets from committees concerned primarily or exclusively with
industrial and economic intelligence. Within this area of economic concern there was, in addition to Rumanian oil, Swedish iron ore. In 1939
Section D prepared plans for the destruction of German ore supplies in
Oxelsund, but all were vetoed by the Foreign Office. Finally in March
1940, it was agreed that they could proceed. Unfortunately the British
agent in charge of the operation was shortly thereafter arrested by the
Swedish authorities, and within a month it was too late anyway; in April
1940 the Germans occupied Norway and Denmark and further action

became for the time being impossible. Indeed the German victories of May and June 1940 broke practically all of the contacts made by Section D in northern and western Europe. It was almost exclusively in the Balkan states that links still existed when SOE was formed in July 1940, and, as will be seen, the Balkans were a main preoccupation until they too succumbed to Germany in 1941.

British sabotage and subversive activities before and during the phoney war were, therefore, seen as playing a part within the strategy of economic warfare, but they were given only a low priority, the level of activity was minimal, and they achieved very little. The collapse of France and the German victories in the West in May and June 1940, with all the results this had for British thinking about the future, were to throw the importance of this kind of activity into sharp relief. On 19 May 1940, when the defeat of the French army could be seen looming on the horizon, the British Chiefs of Staff met to consider both the threat of invasion and the implications of French defeat for future British strategy. Discussion centred on a paper entitled 'British strategy in a certain eventuality'—this being a euphemism for French collapse.[19] It included in its recommendations for immediate action measures against 'fifth column' activities, especially the danger allegedly represented by aliens, and asserted that provided American economic and financial support could be assured Britain could survive and through economic pressure bring about the eventual defeat of Germany. The blockade should be complemented by a bombing offensive on economic targets. The consequent stimulation of economic discontent in the occupied territories would bring about a situation of revolt. 'In the circumstances envisaged,' continued its authors, 'we regard this form of activity as of the very highest importance. A special organisation will be required and plans to put these operations into effect should be prepared, and all the necessary preparations and training should be proceeded with as a matter of urgency.' It was from this recommendation, with which the War Cabinet concurred on 27 May, that there began the reorganisation of the agencies dealing with subversive activities which led ultimately to the formation of SOE, later to be described by one of its senior officials as 'no more than a hopeful improvisation devised in a really desperate situation'.[20]

The close juxtaposition of recommendations for action against the alleged German Fifth Column in Britain with recommendations for intensified British subversive activities abroad to stimulate revolt in occupied Europe was more than coincidental. It was widely—and mistakenly—believed that Germany's victories in the West could be explained by the presence of fifth columns in the defeated countries, in other words, by internal subversion.[21] If the Germans could benefit from this phenomenon, the argument went, why not Britain? Was there not now a democratic fifth column in the occupied territories which could in turn be used against the Germans? The belief, or hope, that there was such a fifth column ready to subvert the Nazi empire from within was the converse of explanations current in the post-Dunkirk period to explain the unexpectedly rapid German victories. The close correlation of fifth column fears and the demand for firmer British action in the subversive sphere in Europe was widespread both in government and public circles, as were the assumptions about long-term German vulnerability and the potential strength of European resistance. They were not always clearly articulated, and were often obscured by concern with the measures to be taken against invasion, the outcome of the Battle of Britain, and later, the effects of the Blitz. They were, however, of decisive importance for a whole range of decisions taken in the summer of 1940, in particular for SOE.

Steps towards bringing some coherence into the field of British subversive organisation and activities took place within the Service ministries both in response to the Chiefs of Staff recommendations and to the constant pressure from Churchill for counter offensive measures against the Germans. The Service ministries, in particular the War Office, hoped to control the new organisation, and on 5 June 1940 the Director of Military Intelligence produced a draft plan to this effect. This effort, however, was to be thwarted. Both the Foreign Office, and the Ministry of Economic Warfare under the leadership of Hugh Dalton, a dynamic and ambitious man, put in claims for control. A lengthy and complicated behind-the-scenes struggle took place, and was eventually resolved on 11 July 1940 when it was decided by Churchill that Dalton should head the new organisation.[22] Dalton had lobbied hard for the position and had pleaded eloquently at a meeting in the Foreign Office on 1 July that subversive warfare was a matter better handled by civilians than by regular soldiers. As he put it in a letter to Attlee, the leader of his party, 'regular soldiers are not men to stir up revolution, to create social chaos or to use all those ungentlemanly means of winning the war which come so easily to the Nazis'.[23] He had also used his extensive contacts within and without Whitehall to plead his case by emphasising the importance of European resistance and subversion as a means of defeating the Nazi régime. Depending upon the nature of the audience this could be described as either an anti-German fifth column or as a prelude to a European revolution, the latter being a theme sparking a ready response on the left. A back-bench Parliamentary committee calling itself the Guerrilla Warfare Committee was set up by Sir Stephen King-Hall to pressure the government into adopting stronger measures of subversive warfare, and newspaper articles began to appear on the same theme. These and other measures strengthened Dalton's hand, and as Mininster of Economic Warfare he was in a position to use a major secret session on 9 July to stress to the Commons that economic warfare was a crucial adjunct 'to naval, military and air action, and to the flame of revolt in the enslaved lands of Europe which we must seek to kindle and fan'.[24] The political and parliamentary base ensured, the decisive factor then became the firm stand of Attlee, who demanded a Labour appointment to offset Conservative control of the Foreign Office and Home Security. The post-Dunkirk climate of opinion made Attlee's claim hard to resist. The demand for the removal of the 'guilty men' and the appointment of new blood was at its peak. It would have been difficult for Churchill not to make a Labour appointment in such a context. Moreover, it made great sense to place the new organisation within the purview of a ministry which had as its main objective the waging of economic warfare, and moreover, a ministry which was under the control of a Labour minister; it was a reasonable assumption that it would be mainly the European Left which would form the nucleus of resistance. It was certainly Dalton's view that SOE would be a 'revolutionary' organisation, just as it was his opinion that SOE had as its field of operations a Europe potentially open to revolt. There is a well-known passage in his published memoirs in which Dalton quoted from a letter he wrote in July 1940 setting out the kind of activities with which SOE would be concerned:

> We must organise movements in every occupied territory comparable to the Sinn Fein movement in Ireland, to the Chinese guerrillas now operating against Japan, to the Spanish Irregulars who played a notable part in Wellington's campaign or—one might as well admit it— to the organisations which the Nazis themselves have developed so remarkably in almost every country of the world. We must use many different methods, including industrial and military sabotage, labour agitations and strikes, continuous propaganda, terrorist acts against traitors and German leaders, boycotts and riots.[25]

This was a programme of action which SOE never fulfilled for a number of reasons which will emerge in the course of the study. It should be sufficient at this stage to say that the reasons had less to do with SOE than with the inability of the European resistance forces to accomplish organisation and effective action until a time when the Allied regular armies themselves were able to intervene, thereby to a large extent undercutting the role originally assigned to them. The British underestimated the effectiveness of German control of the occupied countries and overestimated the ability of the Europeans to resist. It was a case once more of 'optimistic insularity'.

Dalton received official confirmation of his position on 17 July, and the organisational details were confirmed at a meeting of the War Cabinet on 22 July when the so-called 'SOE Charter' which laid down SOE's tasks was approved. It was at this meeting that Churchill turned to Dalton, who was present for the occasion, and reportedly uttered his famous and laconic injunction—'now set Europe ablaze'. The new organisation, christened the Special Operations Executive, brought under its wing all existing organisations whose function was sabotage, subversion, and propaganda, i.e. MI(R), Section D, and EH, although MI(R) was not in fact disbanded until November 1940. Its function was defined by the SOE Charter (which is still a classified document), as being to 'co-ordinate all action, by way of subversion and sabotage, against the enemy overseas'. Sir Robert Vansittart, the former head of the Foreign Office, was appointed as Dalton's assistant, and Dalton was empowered to call on other departments for additional staff. The Charter concluded by saying that 'the general plan for irregular offensive operations should be in step with the general strategic conduct of the war', and Dalton was instructed to keep the Chiefs of Staff informed of his plans, and, in return, it was promised he would be kept informed of the broad strategic picture. Similarly, he was instructed to consult with the Foreign Office and other ministries when their interests were likely to be affected. The Charter was vague, however, about the precise relationship of SOE to the Foreign Office, the Chiefs of Staff, and SIS, and rivalries with these three organisations, as well as with the Ministry of Information which was in charge of overt propaganda, were soon to emerge.[26]

The inflammatory image contained in Churchill's injunction to Dalton clearly appealed to the Prime Minister's belligerent nature. Shortly afterwards he gave the House of Commons a review of the first year of the war in the course of which he outlined the meaures being undertaken for the defence of Britain and its Empire. This was important, he told the Commons, not only because it demonstrated that Britain could stand alone, but because the 'fact that the British Empire stands invincible, and that Nazidom is still being resisted, will kindle again the spark of hope in the breasts of hundreds of millions of down-trodden or despairing men and women throughout Europe, and far beyond its bounds, and that from these sparks there will presently come cleansing and devouring flame'.[27] It was a theme he was to repeat throughout the next eighteen months. Churchillian rhetoric and imagery is a misleading guide, however, to the strategy those actually involved in turning SOE into a functioning organisation envisaged for the resistance movements in Europe. As the next chapter reveals, far from setting Europe ablaze in some spectacular conflagration, they were determined to ignite a carefully controlled fire whose embers would be kept dampened and fanned into flames only when desired by Britain. The development and formulation of concepts defining the role of European resistance in the framework of British strategy, the clarification of SOE's relationship with other branches of government and the war leadership, and the creation of the necessary administrative and logistical machinery to implement SOE's targets, were tasks yet to be confronted. As Lord Selborne later summarised the position facing SOE at this time:[28] 'Underground warfare was an unknown art in England in 1940; there were no text-books for newcomers, no old hands to initiate them into the experiences of the last war . . . lessons had to be learned in the hard school of practice.'

2 Secret Armies and the Detonator Concept

The minister responsible for SOE, Hugh Dalton, was a man of energy and ambition. He had held a Foreign Office post in the 1929–31 Labour Government, and had been the Labour Party spokesman on foreign affairs before the war. He undoubtedly saw his tenure of office at the Ministry of Economic Warfare and his control of SOE (which he dubbed the 'Ministry of Ungentlemanly Warfare') as a stepping stone to his eventual appointment as Foreign Secretary. Widely referred to as 'Dr Dynamo', his drive and enthusiasm undoubtedly played a large part in the relative speed with which SOE passed from being no more than a bright idea to becoming an operational organisation—a period which very roughly coincided with Dalton's own tenure of office. On the other hand, Dalton's personality was not the best of assets in SOE's inevitable conflicts with existing organisations and interests. Gladwyn Jebb, his personal assistant, later recalled that many people found him heavy-handed and a bore. He had, Jebb said, 'a rather elephantine way of endeavouring to ingratiate himself with people', his voice was penetrating and deafening, and 'his eye used to roll round in rather a terrifying way'.[1] The sins of his personal presence were compounded by a lack of tact and abrasiveness which quickly alienated those who crossed Dalton the wrong way. A man who on arriving late to receive his seal of office from the Lord President, Neville Chamberlain, could say, 'Sorry, Mr Lord President, have I missed the bus?' was a man unlikely easily to endear himself to his colleagues. And it was undoubtedly unfortunate that he thought of Eden, who became Foreign Secretary in December 1940, as 'that wretched Eden, posing before the looking glass'.[2] He was ever suspicious, too, of Conservative plots to outmanoeuvre Labour within the Coalition, and never enjoyed Churchill's close confidence. Nonetheless, his virtues probably outweighed his vices in this early period, and the conflicts which characterised SOE's childhood and adolescence were real enough. Dalton's personality was a secondary rather than a primary factor.

One thing which Dalton certainly did not lack was an ambitious idea of what SOE could achieve in Europe and a belligerence of spirit attuned to the times. On 17 August he told his Cabinet colleagues that 'we must learn, for the duration of this war at least, to shed many inhibitions and to act on the assumption that the end justifies the means . . . We must beat the Nazis at their own game.' Two days later, in a proposal to the Chiefs of Staff entitled *The Fourth Arm* he put forward the claim that 'Subversion should be clearly recognized by all three Fighting Services as another and independent Service.'[3] By subversion Dalton meant not only propaganda but 'subversive activities in the widest sense', by which he was thinking particularly of the kinds of activities upon which he had focused a month earlier while lobbying for his position—the use of 'many different methods, including industrial and military sabotage, labour agitation and strikes, continuous propaganda, terrorist acts against traitors and German leaders, boycotts and riots.' What he contemplated for the most part was not, as he recalled later, primarily a military job at all, but 'concerned Trade Unionists and Socialists in enemy and enemy-occupied countries, the creation of Fifth Columns, of explosions, chaos, and revolution.'[4] Although Dalton was very soon forced to modify these ideas quite radically, as we shall see shortly, the broad concept of subversion as primarily the task of the left and the trade unions in Europe was a theme to which he returned with regularity. In November 1940 he was to be found telling his senior officials that 'if the Germans were in occupation of Great Britain, and he were trying to organise a movement against them, he would choose people like his own constituents, the Durham miners,'[5] and he was quick on occasion to suspect that his senior officials in SOE, many of whom came from banking and the legal profession, were prejudiced against mobilising left-wing and Labour elements in Europe. There was a particularly acrimonious internal row in 1941 over the apparent reluctance and then failure of SOE French section to persuade Leon Jouhaux, the *doyen* of French syndicalism, to co-operate with SOE. Dalton was convinced that political prejudices were responsible.[6] Only the month before he relinquished his position as Minister of Economic Warfare in the government reshuffle of February 1942 he was again to be found expounding enthusiastically, this time to Mountbatten, the Head of Combined Operations, the view 'that it was the French industrial working class on whom we must count'.[7] There is no need to doubt Dalton's sincerity in holding this view, and even Philby, one of

his temporary employees, accepted it as genuine. Yet even the most enthusiastic admirer of Dalton would have had to admit that his description of 'subversion' lacked precision, and its wide-ranging scope left it
unclear how, even if more closely defined, it could be mobilised to the
advantage of the British war effort. Leaving aside the fundamental assumption that the European population would be prepared to strike,
riot, boycott, assassinate, and in other ways make life miserable for the
Germans, it had to be shown that this would be of use to British purposes, which in the short term were the defeat of Hitler. The nature and
power of subversion and its relationship to British strategic requirements had still to be defined, and the heady flights of Dalton's rhetorical
and ideological vision translated into practicable working guidelines.

Dalton's view as expressed in the summer of 1940 was virtually that of
Europe in a state of 'permanent revolution', that is, of constant open
unrest of both a military and civil kind against German occupation.
This vision, with its assumptions about the willingness of European
Socialist parties and Trade Unions to behave in this way, and,
moreover, to do so at the behest of the British government, was soon
superseded by another which became SOE orthodoxy and guided its
strategy towards European resistance for most of the rest of the war.
This was the concept of the 'secret armies' in Europe, which it would be
SOE's job to supply and to mobilise when the invasion of Europe
eventually took place.

The 'secret army' concept was the development of senior officials
within SOE such as Gladwyn Jebb and George Taylor, and it was enthusiastically adopted by Major Colin Gubbins. Gubbins was a professional soldier with a distinguished career. He had won an MC as a
gunner in the First World War, had served under Ironside at Mur-
mansk, and as a member of MI(R) in 1938–39 had been responsible for
producing pamphlets on guerrilla warfare. In September 1939 he had
headed an MI(R) mission to Poland which had subsequently only nar-
rowly escaped the Germans; he had then commanded the Independent
Companies in Norway, and on his return was placed in charge of
organising the Auxiliary Units, the nucleus of the British resistance
movement in case of German invasion. (The task had originally been
given to Grand and Section D, but they had produced only chaos and
criticism, and in July 1940 it was given over to the War Office and Gubbins.) In October 1940 Gubbins, with part of MI(R), joined SOE with
the prime responsibility of taking over liaison with the Polish and
Czech secret armies. In addition he was soon put in charge of training
and operations, and appears also to have retained his responsibility for

the Auxiliary Units. He was a major figure, who exercised strong influence on SOE organisation and doctrine, and eventually in 1943 he became its executive director. His contribution in 1940–41 was to give military precision to the vague ideas about subversion. However unconventional a soldier he may have appeared in his willing espousal of guerrilla warfare and other irregular operations, he nonetheless remained a military man who thought in military terms. He was crisp, efficient, and monosyllabic, and for him resistance in Europe meant the resistance of the secret armies. And for Gubbins, the model was provided by the secret armies of the Poles and the Czechs.[8] For all the differences in national tradition and character between them, the Poles and the Czechs shared some common characteristics. They had both fallen victim to Nazi aggression before the nations of Western Europe, and had had more time to organise resistance to the Germans. Their governments-in-exile in London, had, likewise, had more time to establish clandestine contact with the home country, and each had started with a more developed and sophisticated intelligence network than that of most Western European states in the first place—the contributions of the Polish and Czech intelligence services to the Allied cause were immense. Each claimed to be in contact with, and in control of, large underground resistance organisations—secret armies—in their own country, and these claims were accepted.[9] The Poles in particular impressed British observers. The gallant Polish resistance in September 1939, the presence in Britain of large numbers of Polish soldiers and airmen only too keen to fight against the Germans, the feeling of guilt that such an ally could not have been helped more, and the strong personality and presence of General Sikorski as leader of the government-in-exile, contributed their part in creating an image in British eyes of Polish internal and external resistance as the ideal model for other European nations. Gubbins's influence was particularly important here, as at the time of the German attack he had taken part in discussions with the Polish General Staff about post-occupational resistance planning, and he maintained close personal links with the Poles in London. Shortly after the war, in 1948, he told one audience that whereas the shock of German victories in 1940 had stunned the peoples of Western Europe, 'only the Poles, toughened by centuries of oppression, were spiritually uncrushed'.[10] This view strongly influenced his thinking about plans for the secret armies of Europe. Dalton, too, was impressed by the Poles, and recalled warmly in his memoirs how he had spent the Christmas of 1940 inspecting Polish forces in Scotland.[11] It is not surprising therefore that both the Poles and the Czechs were granted privileges by SOE not granted to other nationalities. They had, for example, control of their own communications to their resistance forces, and were responsible for planning missions and selecting their agents—SOE limited itself to trying to provide them with the means of carrying out their task.[12] It is not surprising either, that, in the absence of any substantial empirical evidence it was assumed that given the same amount of time and effort resistance in Western Europe would take the same form and scope as in Poland and Czechoslovakia: that is, in the creation of organised and disciplined secret armies. Their role would be to grow steadily in strength, but to refrain from overt action against the Germans until the moment of liberation. Then, in conjunction with Allied invasion, they would rise up and liberate their homeland.

The idea that SOE's major effort should be directed towards the encouragement and supply of secret armies, and that this in turn would contribute substantially to British strategy, was developed within SOE in the months following its formation. It gradually superseded Dalton's original idea of the constant fomentation of civil unrest and guerrilla warfare; sabotage was not ruled out, but it was to be encouraged sparingly, and only for tasks of immediate strategic significance. More important than that, premature uprisings were to be strenuously discouraged and guerrilla warfare was implicitly ruled out. Dalton himself explained the new doctrine in these terms:

> The underground fighters should show sufficient active resistance to cause constant embarrassment to the occupying forces, and prevent any reduction in their numbers. But they should keep their main organisations underground and avoid any attempt at large-scale risings or ambitious paramilitary operations which could only result in severe oppression and the loss of our key men. They should do all they can to prepare a widespread underground organisation ready to strike hard later, when we give the signal.[13]

It was a vast and well-ordered concept well-suited to appeal to the military mind. And as we shall see in the next chapter, SOE—primarily Gubbins—based its demand to the Chiefs of Staff for a substantially increased number of aircraft in 1941 on the need to supply and organise these secret armies.

The replacement of Dalton's vision of a Europe in revolutionary ferment by that of the slow and patient construction of secret armies whose uprisings would be detonated only when British forces were ready to return to the Continent was the result less of personalities than of certain harsh realities which confronted SOE as it sought to implement the tasks of its Charter. The first 'reality' was that it would take far greater time and effort than originally anticipated to make effective contact with Europe. Preliminary attempts to infiltrate agents by sea into Europe proved only its virtual impossibility, and as Sweet-Escott later recalled 'the revolutionary belief was thus gradually forced on us that the only hope we had of doing our job in Western Europe lay in the parachute'.[14] This immediately made SOE dependent upon aircraft (as well as eventually providing it with its unofficial symbol), and as aircraft were in very limited supply it meant that ambitions had accordingly to be scaled down. The second and in many respects more fundamental reality was that operations in and plans for Europe could not be carried out without close liaison with the various European governments-in-exile. Operationally it proved difficult for SOE to work without or against these governments, and politically the fact that their legitimacy was recognised by Britain meant that their wishes could not simply be ignored. For most of these governments, the prospect of a 'Daltonian' resistance was disturbing, and they rejected it. Invariably, they expressed their views in terms of wishing to avoid a resistance strategy which would lead to savage reprisals by the Germans against the civilian populations. But they were not unaware that a more activist strategy would probably lead to invidious comparisons being made between conditions in Europe and their own relatively comfortable and safe existence, and thereby risk opening a breach with the home population, thus threatening the possibilities of restoration. This link between resistance strategy and political objective was explicitly recognised by SOE in an appreciation of the factors governing its operations written in 1943. 'In countries where resistance is directed by SOE in conjunction with a refugee government,' it acknowledged, 'that government is often reluctant to encourage open resistance for fear of reprisals and the risk of their organisation which they hope to conserve for an eventual rising, and, to a lesser extent, to facilitate their own return home.'[15] And that Britain was committed to assisting their return home was incontrovertible. To say that the British government was committed to the restoration of the European governments, however, is not to deny the pragmatic nature of British foreign policy, nor to overlook that the need for some change in the European states' system was accepted in the Foreign Office. On the contrary, it was accepted in the area of foreign policy almost as quickly as it was in the domestic sphere. Just as plans for the postwar economic and social reconstruction of Britain began (at superficially the least likely moment) in the grim days and weeks following Dunkirk and through the Battle of Britain, the same can be shown for foreign policy. On 23 August 1940 the Minister of Information, Duff Cooper—one of Dalton's greatest rivals—persuaded the War Cabinet to set up a subcommittee on war aims. Its first term of reference was 'to make suggestions in regard to a postwar European and world system, with particular regard to the economic needs of the various nations, and to the problem of adjusting the life force of small countries in a durable international order'.[16] Although this concern was inevitably only a minor preoccupation of the government at the time and Churchill himself was opposed to discussion of such issues, the creation of such a committee and the subsequent discussions which took place within the Foreign Office reveal that even at official levels it was recognised that change would have to come. But it was not necessarily accepted enthusiastically, neither was it conceived as radically altering the political *status quo*. The Foreign Secretary, Lord Halifax, showed little sympathy for a suggestion by Attlee in October that reactionary elements in the governments-in-exile and amongst the Free French should make way for left-wing elements more actively committed to democratic ideals,[17] and although personnel changes in the governments-in-exile were sometimes welcomed by the Foreign Office there was no question that their basic legitimacy and desirability was accepted. In so far as change in Europe was to arise out of the war, it was to be achieved through and with these legitimate governments, not without them; and where changes were to be pressed for, they were mainly concerned with achieving a stabilisation of the existing social, economic, and political system, not its radical reformation. This commitment imposed limitations on the nature of SOE's task, and as Gubbins admitted, 'It was clear from the start that the maximum results could be obtained only by the maximum co-operation with those Governments. . . .'[18] Such co-operation was unlikely to be forthcoming, however, if SOE were to pursue objectives which clashed with those of the governments concerned; and, as has been pointed out, they were opposed to a strategy of violent direct action resistance. The views of the exiled governments on this issue became particularly clear following the entry of the Soviet Union into the war and the consequent full-scale mobilisation of European communists into the ranks of European resistance. The communists adopted a direct action resistance strategy, one facet of which was the assassination of individual members of the German armed forces. In France it was marked by the famous Metro Barbès assassination of 21 August 1941, which precipitated a gruesome spiral of reprisal and counter-reprisal culminating in the execution of 48 hostages at Chateaubriant on 22 October. The next day de Gaulle denounced the policy of assassination over the BBC, which led to a discussion in the War Cabinet and the decision that 'individual acts by French patriots against their German oppressors should not be discouraged'. This ruling alarmed SOE, SIS and the Foreign Office, both as a threat to subversive and intelligence networks in France, and to relations with the Allied Governments.[19] To back up its objection, the Foreign Office sought an official statement of views from the exiled governments, and these were circulated early in the New Year. Not one favoured incitement to violence, although not all were prepared actually to discourage it.[20] That this caution was motivated in part by instincts of self-preservation was clear, for their long-term prospects were precarious enough. At the height of the controversy, Dalton himself argued that these governments 'may be found not to have too much following when the storm breaks in their home lands. New men,' he added, 'who have stayed and faced out the German occupation, and have bolder and more revolutionary ideas, may be preferred to those who have lived, not very dangerously, abroad.'[21] In the minds of the exiles, therefore, it was all the more important to be seen not to be encouraging others too easily to sacrifice their lives and to provoke savage German reprisals. Thus, the formal and legal commitments accepted by the British government to recognise the exiled groups in London as the legitimate governments of Europe—commitments which in the aftermath of Dunkirk it would have been unthinkable not to give—were incompatible with the revolutionary goals and methods of SOE as first conceived by Dalton and other left-wing enthusiasts. As one historian of resistance has put it, the fact that London became the haven of exiled governments meant both that '[their] nature and composition . . . inevitably and logically . . . set the pattern of British thinking in regard to encouraging resistance in occupied Europe', and that Britain's 'long-term obligations . . . were those of legitimist restoration rather than of political revolution'.[22] In the short term, the 'wait and see' or 'secret army' strategy articulated within SOE fulfilled both the requirements—and capacities—of British strategy, and the interests of the governments-in-exile. In the long term, as the war progressed and in parts of Europe the resistance struggle radicalised the civilian population and drove deeper divisions between it and the prewar governments, the coincidence of political objective and resistance strategy on the part of the British government and the governments-in-exile fractured. At that point, as we shall see in later chapters, SOE became the focal point of bitter disagreement.

In 1940, however, these problems could hardly, if at all, be foreseen, and the formulation of the 'secret army' concept proceeded untroubled by any intimations of future civil war within the occupied countries of Europe. This was the period when SOE was still in its preparatory phase, and the theorising took place against a background where neither SOE had the operational capacity, nor Europe the will or ability, to give reality to Churchill's command to 'set Europe ablaze'.

The changes and development in the internal organisation of SOE in the months following Dalton's appointment can be passed over relatively quickly.[23] Lawrence Grand, whose activities as head of Section D had alienated influential figures in the Foreign Office, War Office, and SIS, was quickly dismissed. His place was taken by Sir Frank Nelson, whose position was that of Executive Director of the operational (that is, sabotage and subversion) side of SOE, which was known as SO2. Nelson was a businessman, a former Conservative member of Parliament, and immediately prior to the war he had been HM Consul in Bâsle—traditionally an SIS position. He held his post as Executive Director of SO2 (known by the symbol 'CD') until May 1942 when he retired and was replaced by Sir Charles Hambro. The propaganda side of SOE activities, known as SO1, was placed under the control of Rex Leeper of the Foreign Office, and was eventually, in August 1941, separated altogether from SOE and became the Political Warfare Executive (PWE). Another subsection of SOE, known as SO3, enjoyed a brief life as the body responsible for planning, but eventually sank out of view under the weight of its own paper. Within SO2, which is our main concern here, energies were directed mainly to the building up of the central headquarters which after October 1940 were located in Baker Street. This meant the recruitment of personnel, the creation of an administrative machinery, and all the other complex tasks of creating a functioning government department; and it all had to be done in great secrecy. Sections were established for each country in Europe, and each had to build up a body of expertise capable of planning and controlling operations from beginning to end. In the provinces, training schools for agents had to be formed and staffed. Only when these tasks had been accomplished could SOE be called operational. It was a long and difficult process, requiring co-operation from all branches of government. Not surprisingly, this was not always forthcoming.

The problems to be faced by SOE in its relationship with other branches of government had already been apparent in Section D's brief appearance on the stage. As an offspring of SIS, Section D had fallen foul of its progenitors in Broadway, not the least because the interests of an intelligence organisation were often the exact opposite of those of one dedicated to sabotage and subversion. The main requirement of the former was to remain inconspicuous, that of the latter to make its activities felt. This was a genuine conflict of interest which could only be solved by close co-ordination and co-operation at the top level to establish priorities, and no such top-level co-ordination was ever achieved. Conflicts of interest could not be eliminated, for they were inherent in the situation. An example from the early SOE days is provided by the reaction of the SIS representative at a meeting in December 1940 to discuss raiding parties on the European coastline. He told the meeting that SIS was against such raids 'as they might interfere with their organisation for getting agents into enemy-occupied territory'.[24] This objection did, indeed, place most of the coastal areas of occupied France out of bounds to SOE operations. More generally, the conflict of interest made itself felt in SIS's objections to direct contacts between SOE and the secret services of the governments-in-exile on the grounds that it would disrupt the intelligence flow from these sources. This delayed co-operation in the early months, and subsequently produced some very muddied rivalries involving the secret services of Britain and her European allies. In addition to these genuine conflicts of interest were the prejudices and resentments caused first by Section D's unorthodox behaviour, and then by its independence, in the form of SOE, from SIS control. Gubbins later recalled that amongst the established organs of Government as a whole 'at the best SOE was looked upon as an organisation of harmless backroom lunatics which, it was hoped, would not develop into an active nuisance. At the worst, it was regarded as another confusing excrescence . . . as a whole it was left severely alone as a somewhat disreputable child.'[25] SIS was no exception. As the senior secret service, it tended to regard SOE as an upstart organisation run by amateurs. Moreover, Sir Stewart Menzies, its head (generally referred to as 'C') was, throughout the war, much closer to the levers of power than was CD or his minister, enjoying amongst other things frequent and easy direct access to the Prime Minister. This may have been quite justified in view of the tremendous importance of the sources and content of secret intelligence to the British war effort (such as 'Ultra'), but it did little to help SOE when it came into conflict with SIS. Circumstantial evidence—and this is about all one is ever likely to find in this area—suggests that alliances between 'C' and various Service Chiefs against SOE were not uncommon, and were on occasion motivated more by a professional and conservative dislike of SOE's activities in general than by a justified objection to any particular operation. In short, where bureaucratic in-fighting was concerned SOE was at a severe disadvantage. Moreover, SOE was at a positive disadvantage for the first two years of its existence as it was dependent on SIS for its personnel, technical assistance in matters such as the production of forged documents, and communications. So far as this last item was concerned, W/T sets were in short supply, and W/T traffic was controlled by SIS. Under an agreement reached between SOE and SIS in September 1940 all SOE's W/T traffic was to be handled through SIS which was given the right to accept or reject it. This dependence on SIS lasted until 1942 and gave rise to probably well-founded suspicions that SIS did not refrain from exerting its rights under the September agreement to obstruct SOE operations of which it disapproved. Those in charge of SIS communications were widely believed to bear particular animosity against SOE, and rivalry between the two organisations in the early period of the war focused on this issue. Furthermore, all intelligence collected by SOE was to be passed to SIS, without the promise of reciprocity, which meant that crucial intelligence, including information from 'Ultra', was not always made available to SOE. Relations were somewhat eased after SOE established its own communications network in May–June 1942, but rivalry continued and Churchill in 1944 took the resigned view that 'the warfare between SOE and SIS . . . is a lamentable but perhaps inevitable feature of our affairs'.[26]

The Foreign Office more often than not sided with SIS in its suspicion and dislike of SOE. Here, too, there were genuine conflicts of interest which could not easily be resolved, but they were exacerbated by the personal animosity between Eden and Dalton and by the professional jealousies of two quite dissimilar organisations. Professor Hugh Seton-Watson has described the mutual animosities perfectly:

> Nearly all the earlier recruits [to SOE] lacked the habit of subordination to a regular hierarchy; were disciplined by no mandarin ethos; and were impatient or even contemptuous of the bureaucratic conventions of the diplomatic service and its auxiliaries. To the diplomats they often appeared brash, ignorant of things which diplomats were trained to regard as important, and at times a positive menace.[27]

Under the SOE 'Charter' Dalton was obliged to consult with the Foreign Office where its interests might be affected, and in order to regulate disputes, meetings between representatives of the two organisations were held on a regular weekly basis, presided over by Sir Alexander Cadogan, the Permanent Under-Secretary at the Foreign Office.

Bickham Sweet-Escott, whose unenviable job it was for some time early in 1941 to represent SOE at these occasions, later recalled that at most of them he spent his time explaining to the Foreign Office 'what had gone wrong and why'.[28] Often the Foreign Office vetoed SOE proposals on the grounds that sabotage and/or subversion might undermine the efforts of diplomacy. It was one of the inherent ironies that both organisations often felt they could best use their resources and skills in the same countries—in neutral states such as the Balkans, where a struggle for influence between Germany and Britain was played out from 1939 to 1941. Section D had run into this problem in 1939–40, and SOE ran into it in 1940–41. The Foreign Office, for example, vetoed certain sabotage operations in Rumania late in 1940 on the grounds that this would negate the effects of British diplomacy, although later on, as recent research has shown, the Foreign Office and SOE agreed on a joint strategy towards the Rumanian régime.[29] It would be misleading to suggest that there was little but conflict between SOE and the Foreign Office, and they often worked in harmony. But it would be equally misleading to ignore the fact that the interests of diplomacy and subversion were different; and as the war progressed, and Foreign Office attention turned increasingly to the shape of the postwar world, the conflicts became worse. These problems will be discussed as they arise in later chapters, but one example from 1940 might now be noted.

On 17 November 1940 a meeting took place at Woburn Abbey—the wartime headquarters of SO1—to discuss propaganda policy towards France. As Dalton and Jebb were present the discussion ranged over the entire field of SOE activities in France. Jebb, clearly reflecting Dalton's views, put forward proposals for the recruitment of agents to work in France and suggested that the main effort should be directed to training agents suitable for working amongst industrial workers. For it was here, Jebb asserted, that the best chance lay of arousing resistance to Germany. This proposal was objected to by Leeper, the head of SO1, who pointed out that 'The policy of encouraging a Left Revolution would come into conflict with the declared intention of HMG to arrive at a *modus vivendi* with the Pétain Government.' It would, moreover, offend Weygand, 'with whom, particularly, HMG wished to make contact'. As the discussion developed, Dalton himself intervened to oppose the view that SOE agents should be instructed to steer clear of all internal politics and to concentrate wholly on anti-German activity. 'It was unrealistic,' he said, 'to rule out internal politics altogether. For example any agent we sent to the French workers must at least be able to promise that Trade Union liberties would be restored.'[30] This illustrated some of the

problems which SOE faced. Apart from the whole question of supporting left-wing elements in Europe and the problems associated with SOE
recruitment, the discussion showed how foreign policy towards Vichy
France cut right across the desire 'to set Europe ablaze'. The result in
fact was that until Germany occupied Vichy France in November 1942
SOE was forbidden to carry out any major acts of sabotage there. Here,
from an early stage, was a limitation on SOE's scope at which its Charter had only vaguely hinted, and whose dimensions only gradually
emerged.

The most fundamental limitation of all on SOE's activities was provided by its relationship to the Chiefs of Staff Committee. The SOE
Charter had laid down in only vague terms that the general plan for irregular offensive operations should be in step with the general strategic
conduct of the war, and Dalton had been instructed to keep the Chiefs
of Staff informed in general terms of his plans, while in their turn they
would convey to him the broad strategic picture. This implied a greater
degree of equality between SOE and the Chiefs of Staff than soon
emerged in practice. Dalton indeed, as we have seen, started off with the
claim that 'subversion should be clearly recognised by all three Fighting
Services as another and independent Service'. The Chiefs of Staff
quickly made two things apparent. First, they would provide SOE with
its broad directives, and second, there would be no recognition of any
claims by SOE to be a fourth service. Throughout the war SOE was
refused any permanent representation on the Chiefs of Staff Committee, although there was close liaison at the Joint Planning Staff level,
and SOE representatives were usually called to meetings where matters
closely involving SOE were under discussion. This subordination of
SOE to the Chiefs of Staff Committee was compounded by two further
factors: the lack of sympathy and imagination on the part of the professional military for SOE's irregular operations, and, more important,
COS control of resources. The two were linked. The Chiefs of Staff
found difficulty in coming to grips with resistance movements at all—
they had had no training to do so, for a start—and had little idea of what
they might achieve in this field. On the whole, their attitude when faced
with the reality of particular operations and requests from SOE was
cautious, and this meant that they favoured the demands of the regular
services (or SIS) when it came to a question of priorities for supplies.
This was, notoriously, the case over aircraft.

. The controversy over whether the Chiefs of Staff were right or wrong
to limit the number of aircraft available for SOE operations in Europe
need not occupy us at this point, and will be dealt with as the occasion

arises later. The main point to be noted here is that aircraft were in short supply, and that SOE's plans required large numbers of them. Yet in 1940–1 SOE had to share only one flight of aircraft with SIS, increased in March 1942 to two squadrons. The fact that the Chiefs of Staff never gave SOE as many aircraft as it wanted and the subsequent complaints about this tend to obscure the fact that when SOE was established the possibility that its activities might be affected one way or another by aircraft availability was hardly considered. As Bickham Sweet-Escott's account makes clear, it was first assumed that SOE agents would be infiltrated into Europe *by sea*, and it only became apparent with experience that this was not feasible. This had truly profound consequences. It meant that agents would have to be more highly trained and of a different calibre than at first appreciated (agents had to be both physically more fit, and trained to use parachutes), and that SOE was now in competition with Bomber Command for the necessary aircraft (only bombers were suitable for dropping operations). The first factor meant it would take longer for SOE to become operational, as training programmes would have to be longer and suitable agents would be harder to find, while the second meant that SOE's strategy could only be fulfilled at the expense of the strategic bombing offensive. As the value of this was an article of faith in the strategic litany, it meant that SOE more often than not was denied the aircraft it demanded. It is true that Dalton could appeal to the Defence Committee if he felt aggrieved at Chiefs of Staff decisions over matters affecting SOE's operational capacity, and he did so from time to time. But the Defence Committee itself met infrequently, was not in practice the powerful body it was in theory, and in any case was just as likely to support the Chiefs of Staff as to oppose them. Churchill, as mentioned above, did not reciprocate Dalton's desire for a closer relationship, and Dalton constantly complained, both in private and to Attlee, that he had insufficient access to the Prime Minister. At major crisis points in SOE's history, as will be seen, Churchill intervened on its side; but in between time he was content to let it fight, and often lose, its own battles. Here, as in so many other cases, Churchill's romantic vision had no room for the mundane realities with which he left his subordinates to deal. Only when his direct personal interest and imagination was involved, as in the case of Tito's partisans or the French *maquis*, did he intervene actively to support SOE.

The SOE 'Charter' and the Churchillian exhortation to set Europe ablaze had been grand gestures promising much but made with little awareness, perhaps inevitably, of the limitations outlined above which soon made themselves felt on SOE. And underlying all these, and far more important than any other single one, was the fact that unless the Europeans themselves were willing to act, SOE could achieve nothing. In the words of an SOE report of 1943, 'SOE's activities cannot be developed, at will, in areas where a spirit of resistance does not already exist no matter how desirable such activity may be on strategic grounds. . . .'[31] The basic truth of this observation is fundamental to any evaluation of the success or failure of SOE.

What was the situation in Europe, and what were the possibilities for resistance, in these opening months of SOE's existence? Early in September 1940, MI(R), which was about to be integrated with SOE, drew up a report for the Chiefs of Staff which reviewed the probable state of readiness and ability of certain countries to rise against the Nazi régime. This report (largely drafted by Gubbins) formed part of a much wider review of future British strategy, the first strategic *tour d'horizon* since the Dunkirk disaster, and since it was the first major re-examination of future offensive strategy since the May 27 paper, its conclusions were of great relevance for the future of SOE.[32] As the first considered British analysis of the situation in Europe as it affected the likelihood of popular resistance in the aftermath of the French collapse and the German occupation of most of Western Europe, it was important both as a statement of British perceptions in September 1940, and as a point of reference which helped to shape future expectations.

Not surprisingly, the review still advocated the steady undermining of Germany through economic warfare, bombing, and subversion, and predicted that the spring of 1942 would see a passing over to the offensive. 'Revolt in patriot areas' was seen as an important contributory part of any final offensive. Subversion, it declared, would be important in two ways. First, as part of the process of attrition forcing the Germans to increase their occupation forces and undermining German economic strength by the sabotage of key industrial plants and communications systems. Second, it would lead to 'a general uprising, coinciding with major operations by our forces' which might eventually help the defeat of Germany. The review emphasised, however, that this major uprising 'would almost certainly be dependent upon British assistance, and would have to be carefully controlled if it were to be militarily useful'. For successful revolts in occupied Europe, there would have to be adequate preparation, effective propaganda, and a clear policy as to the economic and political future of Europe. In particular it emphasised the need to exercise control over resistance movements, to subordinate them to British strategic planning, and to discourage spontaneous and premature uprisings; the review emphasised:

It will be important to ensure that subversive movements should not be allowed to break out spontaneously in areas that individually become ripe for revolt. No appreciable results can be expected in the early future and we should organise these activities on a large scale so that they are timed to mature in relation to regular operations undertaken as part of our general policy.

The general conclusion of the paper was that 'none of the countries at present under enemy domination with the possible exception of Poland and Czechoslovakia is likely from its own resources to be in a position to initiate risings on any considerable scale. Such risings are only likely to be brought about as an outcome of careful plans and detailed organisations controlled and assisted from this country.' The accompanying proof was a country-by-country analysis of the state of popular opinion, with the projected conditions of Europe in March 1941 as the basis for estimates of readiness to rise against the Nazi régime. The full text is given in Document One of the appendices, but a summary of its main points can briefly be given here. Significantly the analysis began with Germany itself, and here the conclusion was that 'in the absence of a serious military disaster, there is no likelihood of any serious risings in Germany against the Nazi régime by March 1941', although after that date and under the impact of bombing and the effects of British economic warfare disaffection within the Party and Army might arise. There was certainly no chance of a popular rising in Austria, as there was every evidence that Austria had accepted German domination. The countries most likely to be in a position to rise against Germany in the spring of 1941 were Poland and Czechoslovakia. The evidence for this was multiple. The historic hatred of these nations for Germany, their 'adaptability to revolution and subversive activities acquired by past experience in subjugation to Russian, Austrian, and German invaders', the existence of a very active organisation within Poland (no mention was made here of Czechoslovakia)[33] with 'revolution and guerrilla war as its primary aim', the presence of considerable arms and supplies hidden in the country, and the existence of a special department of the Polish General Staff for subversive work (again, no mention was made of the Czech equivalent) were amongst the factors adduced. However, although the Poles and Czechs were far advanced in comparison with other countries, any risings would be doomed to failure unless they were accompanied either by successful major operations against Germany by Britain, or a general rising in other parts of Europe. These conditions were, of course, prohibitive: there was no foreseeable chance, as the rest of the review itself made clear, of either of these conditions being met. The rest of Europe offered bleak prospects. In Italy there was evidence of 'considerable anti-Fascist movement . . . particularly in the industrial areas of the North', but a successful uprising would require a considerable prior weakening of the Fascist régime induced by bombing and naval blockade. As for France, MI(R) cautiously refused to forecast what conditions might be in spring 1941, as much would depend on German policy and propaganda. It could only recommend increased British propaganda directed at France, although 'in North Africa the Arabs provide useful material upon which subversive organisations can be built'. In Belgium, German propaganda had apparently been successful, although with their tradition of resistance the Belgians might well eventually provide fruitful ground for subversion. In Holland, the Dutch were 'beginning to revive', but direct contact had not yet been established with groups inside the country. Further north, while Denmark offered no hope Norway was a seedbed of patriotic fervour, but conditions demanded considerable outside support and supply, and the best to be hoped for was local co-operation in coastal raids carried out from Britain. In southern Europe, communication had been made with dissident elements, but a successful revolt would require the concurrence and probably support of the Greeks and Yugoslavs (about whom nothing was said). Finally, the report concluded with remarks on Spain which are interesting in the light of later events. If the Germans were to occupy Spain, it said, there would be various sections of the population to provide a nucleus of revolt, including the remnants of the anti-Franco Republican forces. But to support such groups before a German invasion would be unwise, as it would prejudice the government's policy of 'supporting the powerful forces in the Spanish Government who are opposed to Spanish intervention in the War'. Thus, the report specifically recommended against involvement with anti-Franco *émigré* elements, a policy which was in fact to be very closely adhered to by the British government, despite the protests both of elements within SOE and of Labour members of the Coalition.

   The MI(R) report can be summarised as one of short-term pessimism but long-term optimism. The situation everywhere would be more promising after the shortages and hardships of the coming winter had made themselves felt, so that by the spring of 1941 Europe would be in a state receptive to the organisation of resistance movements supplied and encouraged from outside. The unstated implication was that by 1942, when the British at that time were envisaging their major offensive operations in Europe as taking place, there was a strong possibility that secret armies on the Polish and Czech model would be in existence. The problem, however, was that so much of this was mere guesswork based upon projections from history, extrapolation from the present, and stereotyped observations about national character. It is clear that much of the assessment of the current state of Europe MI(R) had little or no direct empirical evidence and was dependent upon sources within the governments-in-exile who had understandable reasons of their own for wishing to colour the picture. Direct contact with occupied Europe scarcely existed. The hopeful phrases about supplying arms and *matériel* from Britain begged many questions and the answers in the end often proved negative.

The highly speculative nature of the entire Chiefs of Staff report, including MI(R)'s analysis, was reflected in its treatment by the Defence Committee. At a meeting on 15 October presided over by Churchill,[34] it was decided not to forward the review to the War Cabinet on the grounds that events were moving too rapidly for the paper to offer any firm basis for decisions. Although Beaverbrook expressed disagreement with 'the form, the subject matter, and the conclusions of the paper', the rest of the Committee, and Churchill in particular, clearly did not dissent from the very broad suggestions for the future the Chiefs of Staff had made. At a further meeting of the Committee two weeks later Churchill confidently told his gathered Commanders-in-Chief that the period since June 1940 'had shown our ability to continue the war indefinitely', and that by 1942 Britain would be able to pass over to a major offensive. In the meantime, the economic assistance of the United States would bring war production to a peak. But what shape would this final major offensive against Germany take? Churchill did not pretend to give a firm answer, and fell back upon the analogy of the First World War; he told his audience:

The question might be asked, 'How are we to win this war?' This question was frequently posed in the years 1914–18, but not even those at the centre of things could have possibly given a reply as late as August of the last year of the War. For the moment, all that we could do was to bank on the pressure of the blockade accompanied by the remorseless bombing of Germany and Italy. By 1941, however, we would be in a position to take a medium operation of an amphibious nature; and by 1942 we should be able to deliver very heavy overseas attacks.[35]

If Churchill had little but faith to offer, the same was true for practically everyone else. Hopes and promises of future action, with the main priority on mere survival, were, in September 1940, about all that could be expected.

SOE itself was in the process of struggling to its feet. We have briefly mentioned the major problems it faced at this time, but what about its actual operational capacity, in other words, how many agents did it actually have in Europe at that time? While it is difficult to be absolutely certain about this in the absence of official figures, the number in Western Europe appears in September 1940 to have been nil. This is not surprising given the destruction to networks and contacts wreaked by the German *blitzkrieg* of May–June. As Sweet-Escott later recalled, when Section D closed down in July 1940, 'we did not possess one single agent between the Balkans and the English Channel',[36] and it had not been possible subsequently to infiltrate any. Nor is it surprising that the area in which SOE was strongest was the Balkans, in countries such as Hungary, Rumania, Yugoslavia, and Greece, where Section D had long been active. In this area, there were perhaps thirty agents. It was no wonder that Nelson reported in September that he saw 'no possibility of any quick results of a major type'.[37] This was a masterpiece of understatement. And the areas where SOE was established were themselves to fall victim to German invasion within six months, and SOE networks to be practically destroyed here too.

This background of hopes for an increased broadening and intensification of European resistance which could be co-ordinated with British strategy, combined with an actual capacity to act only in the neutral countries of the Balkans rather than the occupied countries of Western Europe, formed the context for SOE's first strategic directive of 25 November 1940. This came only three days after senior officials within SOE had complained that the communications situation was so bad as 'to make CD's activities in many cases almost impossible'.[38] This directive, the first in a series given annually by the Chiefs of Staff to SOE, was broad and ambitious. It bore little relation to the extremely limited resources available to SOE, but its existence was probably a useful and necessary lever with which at least to attempt to pry support and material from other government agencies. Its contents provide little guide as to what SOE actually did, but they do reveal the areas in which the Chiefs of Staff hoped subversive activity might be helpful, and make clear some of their strategic assumptions. As the Directive was, according to Foot, the outcome of a previous discussion between the Chiefs of Staff and Nelson and Jebb on 12 November, it presumably also reflected the areas in which SOE itself felt that useful work could be accomplished and embodied many of their assumptions too.[39]

The directive (the full text of which is given in Document Two of the appendices) defined the overall aim of SOE as being 'to prepare the way for the final stage of the war when, by co-ordinated and organised revolts in the occupied countries and by popular rising against the Nazi party inside Germany, direct and decisive military operations against Germany herself may be possible'. It recognised that while the initiative on land remained with the Germans it was difficult to state with any great certainty the areas where subversive activities would most help British strategy, but that given 'the important and even decisive part which subversive activities may play in our strategy' the objective should be to lay the foundation for subversive operations wherever they might be needed so as to be able to exploit any favourable situation. The Chiefs of Staff therefore painted very bold strokes. Defining the elimination of Italy as being the first among British strategical aims, followed by the continuation of attrition warfare in 1941 through the blockade and the air offensive, they said that the creation of political discontent and economic disorganisation in Germany and Italy should be a constant aim, with particular emphasis on the lowering of Italian morale. Communications between Italy and Germany should be disrupted (SOE had, in fact, discussed sabotage against the Swiss railways in September, and the Chiefs of Staff placed special emphasis on coal traffic passing through the country), and subversive operations undertaken in preparation for offensive operations in Sicily, Sardinia, Southern Italy and Pantelleria. On a longer time-scale, preparations should begin for eventual British offensive operations against the Continent, in Brittany and the Cherbourg Peninsula, the South-West part of occupied France, in the Low Countries and Southern Norway. Here, the Chiefs of Staff warned strongly of the need to avoid premature uprisings, an article of dogma already strongly implanted. Outside the occupied countries, efforts should be directed towards disrupting the supply of resources to Germany. Particular mention was made of Rumanian oil and of the need to anticipate a German invasion of the Balkans by making post-occupational plans for future resistance there. Similarly, preparations should be made to hinder a German occupation of the Iberian peninsula—although in contrast to the MI(R) report of September, the Chiefs of Staff made no specific recommendation against involvement with anti-Franco Republicans. In the Middle East, Lawrentian echoes could be heard in the recommendation that efforts might be made 'to raising the tribes to revolt when we are in a position to take advantage strategically of such a situation'. Seeking to establish priorities, the Chiefs of Staff concluded that the interference with enemy communications and attacks on enemy morale were of great importance. Thus, of objects which could be said to have first priority, they singled out the attack on Italian morale, the interruption of coal transport to Italy from Germany through Switzerland, the dislocation of communications and supplies to enemy supplies in Northern France, and the Low Countries, the obstruction of oil supplies to Germany from Rumania, and the preparation for the destruction of communications in Yugoslavia, Bulgaria, Portugal and Spain. Relegated to second priority were preparations to assist possible Allied operations in southern Italy and the offshore Italian islands, and to a third priority, preparations to assist Allied operations against France and the Low Countries.

The focus of the Chiefs of Staff on enemy communications not only reflected a wider strategic emphasis current at the time on such targets, but also highlighted the importance they attached to sabotage as a main function of SOE. Hitherto, the emphasis they and SOE itself placed on 'secret armies' had been stressed, but this directive made it clear that while in the long run this remained the objective, in the short run sabotage was to be of greater importance and was more likely to be effective.[40] It had, moreover, the important objective not merely of damaging enemy targets, but of creating and fostering the spirit of European resistance. Thus, the broad concept of subversion which guided SOE policy contained within it potentially if not necessarily actually conflicting requirements, and it was not always easy to say how these could be resolved. On the one hand, sabotage, if pursued too forcefully, might draw the full vigour of German repression and prematurely destroy the organisation of the 'secret armies'. On the other hand, too little activity and the discouragement of indiscriminate sabotage might have its own damaging effects on the morale of the underground armies and hinder their growth. A delicate balance had to be struck if the two facets of the guiding concept were to be held together. Success in doing this depended on two major assumptions: first, that the European organisations would be willing to accept outside guidance or control; second, that they themselves could maintain sabotage and direct action resistance at a relatively low level. This second assumption might have held over a short time, had the Soviet Union after its entry into the war not called for the communist parties of Europe to begin vigorous resistance activity. But by 1943, as will be seen, both assumptions were looking decidedly threadbare, and SOE itself was forced to step up demands for sabotage in order to maintain resistance morale.

As it was, the November directive, for all its shortcomings, provided SOE with an official seal of approval and set its main target for the immediate future as the disruption of enemy communications. SOE operations and planning over the next few months, such as they can be discerned from existing accounts and from the sparse indications in the official documentation available, reflected this concern. That same month SOE work in the Balkans was put on a new footing with the despatch to Belgrade of Tom Masterson to head the SOE mission there, and the decision shortly after that to send George Taylor on a special mission to the Balkans to take charge of the overall subversive effort in the light of the Balkan campaign which could now be forecast, and to begin post-occupational planning.[41] This, as we have seen, was one of the tasks set out in the directive. Early in the New Year, too, SOE prepared plans for action in Spain in the event of a German invasion, sent out a representative to Gibraltar, and presented plans for a direct strike at German air force pilots in France. Efforts throughout this period were also made to organise subversion in Rumania and interfere with oil supplies to Germany.

Nonetheless, despite the growing size of SOE and any weight which the Directive might have given it in the higher reaches of the war machinery, actual progress was small. Bickham Sweet-Escott recalled how, at the weekly meetings with the heads of country sections at which a report of progress was drawn up, discussions 'were grim, and we always looked forward to Wednesdays with a sinking feeling'.[42] Although there was generally some progress to report from the Balkans, and occasionally from Norway, elsewhere progress was imperceptible. Morale in Baker Street was low by the end of 1940. Little had been achieved, and the obstacles to achieving anything were perhaps more apparent than before. As the SOE war diary itself put it, the situation at the end of 1940 was that 'in the belligerent, occupied and so-called neutral countries of Central and Western Europe, no field staff existed; SO2's problem is to get the horse in after the stable door has been shut; and first of all the horse must be found. . . .'[43]

3 A Lean Year

The summer and autumn of 1940 had witnessed grandiose theories about the role of European resistance in winning Britain's war against the Axis powers; 1941 was to make it plain that there was a considerable distance between the dream and the reality. SOE was not yet operational, and the slow and difficult process of creating the administrative and logistical framework necessary for carrying out its task was to consume most of its energies. It was only in May, for example, that its French section's first parachuted agent landed in France. As it built up its operational strength and began to flex its muscles, SOE increasingly collided with the interests of other government departments and services. They reacted by trying, in some cases successfully, to limit the nature and scope of its activities. It also became more fully clear in 1941 that if it was to mobilise the occupied nations of Europe, where apathy and confusion were still widespread, SOE would have to deal with the governments-in-exile in London, and that this imposed limits on its power which had not been apparent in 1940. More important in the long run was the fact that by the end of 1941 both the Americans and the Russians were active belligerents and allies. Grand strategy for winning the war was bound to change, and with it the place and role of SOE. Immediately prior to Hitler's invasion of the Soviet Union, the concept of a European uprising detonated by small British landings was put forward by a section of the British military planning staff as the only effective means of defeating Germany, clear testimony to the desperate position facing Britain in the first half of the year. In the months following Soviet entry into the war, however, and especially after American entry in December, there was a gradual erosion of the 'detonator concept', and secret armies in Europe were no longer seen as carrying the key to victory. In February 1942 Dalton, the man whom Churchill had exhorted to 'set Europe ablaze', and who had talked of subversion and

50

European revolution as the Fourth Arm of warfare, was replaced as Minister in charge of SOE activities by Lord Selborne, a Conservative establishment figure. It was, if nothing else, a move symbolic of the changing role allotted to SOE and European resistance in British strategic thinking.

I

One of the first requirements of SOE was to establish its credibility amidst widespread scepticism and even hostility from older departments or services. The opportunity was presented to it early in January 1941.

As we have seen, the belief that the German war economy was vulnerable to a few well-placed and decisive blows was widely held at most levels of the British war machinery. In December 1940 a high level committee singled out oil supplies as being an Achilles' Heel of the German war economy. As a large percentage of German oil imports came from Rumania, and were transported through the Balkans (either by road, rail or on the Danube), there was scope here for SOE to prove its worth. Here, in the neutral Balkan states, networks had remained largely undisturbed by the *débâcle* of June, and sabotage and subversion were within its capacity. Moreover, by this time it was overwhelmingly clear that the Balkans were now the key area. On 6 January 1941 Eden told Churchill that 'a mass of information has come to us over the last four days, . . . all of which tends to show that Germany is pressing forward her preparations in the Balkans with a view to an ultimate descent upon Greece'.[1] Dalton seized the opportunity. With Attlee's support he convinced the Defence Committee of the Cabinet on 13 January 1941 to agree to a plan by which SOE would disrupt oil supplies to Germany by (a) bringing about an internal upheaval in Rumania, (b) blocking the Danube at Kazan and the Iron Gates, regardless of the susceptibilities of the Yugoslavs, and (c) attacking transport ships at Varna and Constanza. (Document Three of the appendices.) This SOE plan went hand in hand with a new bombing campaign designed to destroy Germany's synthetic oil production. The schemes were approved, and although Churchill expressed some scepticism he told Dalton a week later that local action and passive resistance throughout occupied Europe might embarrass the enemy out of all proportion to the energy expended or the loss incurred. Dalton should not hesitate, the Prime Minister said, to seek his support if he found opposition to special schemes on which he held strong views.[2]

The focus on the Balkans was not purely fortuitous. It had already become clear that the Germans were threatening the area, and their troops had begun to infiltrate Rumania. Bulgaria was threatened, and the British government was at this time desperately attempting to shore up the Greeks and the Yugoslavs. The decision to send a mechanised force to Greece had provoked a retort from the Prince Regent of Yugoslavia that it was 'rash and mistaken'. The day after the SOE plan for Rumania had been approved, Churchill told the War Cabinet that, in the face of clear evidence of forthcoming German moves in the Balkans, 'Prince Paul's attitude looks like that of an unfortunate man in a cage with a tiger, hoping not to provoke him while steadily dinner time approaches'.[3] Here, too, there was scope for SOE activity. At best, the policy of the Yugoslav government could be influenced and changed by clandestine methods. At worst, the government could be overthrown by subversion. And at the very worst, if the Germans did occupy the Balkan states, preparations could be made for subsequent sabotage and resistance. This last possibility had, indeed, been included in the November directive and had been discussed between the Foreign Office and SOE early in December.

It was in this context that Dalton decided to send one of his most important officials, George Taylor, to the Balkans. His task was to co-ordinate and strengthen SOE efforts to prevent the Balkan states falling under German control, to begin post-occupational planning, and to ensure the disruption of Rumanian oil supplies. Taylor, described by Sweet-Escott as 'a brilliant but ruthless Australian with a mind of limpid clarity',[4] was a wealthy businessman who had previously worked in the oil industry. Recruited into Section D in 1939, he had been head of its Balkan Section, and after the formation of SOE had become chief of staff to Sir Frank Nelson with general responsibility for the organisation of country sections and operations. Along with Gubbins and others, Taylor had helped develop the concept of the secret armies, and was a leading figure within the organisation. Dalton's decision to despatch him to the Balkans was a measure of the urgency of the Balkan situation and of the opportunity it presented to SOE of making a major contribution to the war effort and thereby improving its standing in Whitehall. According to Taylor, the direct origin of his mission came in December 1940 when Churchill told Dalton personally that the Balkan situation 'was the acid test for SOE'. After a meeting between Dalton, Nelson, and Taylor, it was finally decided that the latter should go out immediately with full powers inside SOE and strong recommendations to the military commander in the Middle East (Wavell) and British Ministers in the area to help SOE. Before he left, he was briefed at a major meeting presided over by Anthony Eden and attended by Dalton, Jebb, the Vice-Chief of the General Staff and the directors of military intelligence for the three services. Arriving in the Middle East on 29 January 1941—the day Metaxas, the Greek dictator, died—he worked with Wavell on preparations to help the Greeks, then travelled to Ankara, Sofia, Athens, Belgrade and Budapest to bring SOE preparations to a peak of readiness.[5]

In the event, SOE's operations in the Balkan states in the spring of 1941 were severely limited by factors largely beyond its control. In Rumania, Antonescu quickly overcame an Iron Guard revolt in mid-January which SOE had hoped, and attempted, to exploit. Their sabotage plans, which relied totally upon the National Peasant Party and its leader Maniu, came to nothing because the RAF could not provide air cover and Maniu refused to act without it. Little was accomplished in either Bulgaria or Hungary.[6] Most success—and it was of dubious advantage—came in Yugoslavia, where, after signing the Tripartite Pact with Germany, Prince Paul's government was overthrown by a *coup d'état* on 27 March.

SOE played an active part in the overthrow of the Prince Regent's government. Throughout 1940 its predecessor organisation, Section D, has been actively cultivating and in some cases financing Serbian politicians. As early as July 1940 the British minister in Belgrade, Mr Ronald Campbell, had reported the existence of Serbian elements prepared to carry out a *coup d'état*, and although that alternative was temporarily ruled out by London, SOE continued to remain in contact with them. Throughout the spring of 1941, as Prince Paul edged towards signature of the Pact, SOE stepped up its efforts to encourage opponents of the régime through propaganda and direct and often daily contact with leading politicians. When it finally became clear that Prince Paul's government would definitely sign the Pact, SOE, on London's authority, encouraged the resignation of ministers in an attempt to force the government's downfall. When this failed, and when the Pact was signed on 25 March, it sought to promote a *coup d'état*. In conjunction with the service attachés, who were in direct touch with discontented Army and Air Force officers, SOE exhorted and encouraged politicians associated with the conspiracy, and on 27 March their efforts were rewarded. The government was overthrown, the Prince Regent abdicated in favour of the young King Peter, and General Simović, Chief of Staff of the Royal Yugoslav Air Force, formed a new government. It was widely expected—at least on the British side—that this would lead to a denunciation of the Pact, and a clear alignment of Yugoslavia with Britain. Churchill was jubilant, and declared that 'Yugoslavia had found its soul'. Dalton quickly sought to capitalise upon the event and eagerly accepted the showers of compliments which rained down on SOE for its part in the *coup*, although he was well aware the direct contacts with Mirković, the key figure amongst the conspirators, had not been through SOE, but through the office of the Air Attaché. Subsequent events in Belgrade, where the Simović government temporised over denouncing the Pact and openly aligning with the British until the Germans invaded the country on 6 April, failed to diminish the reflected glory from which SOE benefited. Even the relatively small damage done to Danube shipping traffic by the partial implementation of SOE's sabotage schemes did not shake this confidence. But it is likely that any criticism was blunted by other developments of a far greater magnitude. By the end of April both Yugoslavia and Greece had collapsed, British forces had been evacuated from Greece, and in May, British forces in Crete surrendered. The British now had no foothold at all in Europe, and, as far as SOE was concerned, some of its best networks on the Continent had been destroyed.[7]

The SOE Balkan operations had revealed the limits of what could be achieved even in favourable circumstances. Most SOE sabotage operations were dependent upon the co-operation of individuals and organisations in the countries concerned, and in the two major sabotage schemes—the plan to sabotage oil in Rumania, and the attempt to block the Danube—it had proved difficult to overcome understandable if hardly heroic scruples on the part of those whose co-operation was necessary. The Yugoslav General Staff had refused to take action on the Danube scheme prior to a German invasion, and the chaos created by the invasion had then disrupted its smooth operation. Maniu and the National Peasant Party had sheltered behind the inability of the RAF to provide air cover for the schemes of sabotage in Rumania itself. As far as subversion in Yugoslavia was concerned, it had proved more successful; but even here, there were limits to what SOE could accomplish beyond encouragement to a course already agreed upon, and the *coup d'état* was a largely Yugoslav affair. SOE and the British government could not move faster than the Europeans themselves, and could certainly not create resistance or sabotage if it was not there—unless, perhaps, it was prepared to launch a campaign of indiscriminate sabotage which would set in train a vicious spiral of massive reprisals, more resistance, greater reprisals, and so on. As we have seen, however, the

British were broadly opposed to such a policy, as were the governments-in-exile.

If the Balkan events of the spring of 1941 revealed the objective limits to British sabotage and subversive action, two other SOE proposals of this period may be used to illustrate the kinds of problems which could arise from within the British war machinery when apparently straightforward plans were put forward. The first was a proposal for 'preparatory measures in Spain', which, like the second, Operation Savannah, was presented to the Chiefs of Staff on 3 February 1941 by Jebb and Gubbins.[8] Spain, like the Balkans, was an area of particular concern at this time, with fears that Hitler might take possession of the Peninsula in order to block the Western Mediterranean. To prepare for this seemed only sensible, and an obvious way to do so was to plan for guerrilla warfare in the event of a German occupation. Historical memories of the Spanish guerrilla war against Napolean added to the attractiveness of the idea. In addition, with the Civil War in Spain barely over, there were plenty of trained men, especially on the defeated Republican side, who would be willing to take arms against Fascism. SOE was, therefore, anxious to take some first steps to prepare the way, and to carry out the instructions of the Chiefs of Staff in their November directive to make preparations in the Iberian Peninsula 'to delay an enemy advance from the Pyrenees towards Portugal and Gibraltar by destruction of communications, guerrilla warfare, and economic disorganisation'. Their proposal was threefold. First, to send an SOE officer to Gibraltar to take charge of any special operations in Spain, Portugal, or North West Africa. Second, to send out an officer to act as chief of irregular operations in the Peninsula. And third, to select forty army personnel for irregular warfare. The Chiefs of Staff were less than happy. While agreeing with the first item of this package, they baulked at the remaining two. Sir John Dill, the CIGS, said that the Army could not spare forty officers (although Gladwyn Jebb, SOE's Chief Executive Officer, replied that they could be men from the ranks), and the Committee as a whole 'stressed their opinion that it was undesirable that Spaniards of the wrong political type should be trained in this country for action in Spain'. This objection was at the nub of the problem. Behind it lay the fear that the too obvious use of Republicans might offend the Franco government and provoke it into unequivocal, rather than merely ambiguous, entry into the German camp. This was the fear of Sir Samuel Hoare, the British Ambassador in Madrid. The Foreign Office accepted Hoare's view and despite criticisms and misgivings of Labour members of the Coalition followed a policy of appeasement towards

Spain which severely curtailed SOE plans. Although a small group of men trained for action in Spain was eventually sent to Gibraltar, Hoare vetoed any preparatory action there at all, and following the German invasion of the Soviet Union the group was disbanded. Later, in 1942, when it was feared that the invasion of Spain might be one German response to Operation Torch (the Allied landings in North Africa), new plans for guerrilla warfare were drawn up, and another SOE team underwent training. This time, however, although the Chiefs of Staff approved the plan, the Embassy in Madrid was kept 'completely in the dark'.[9] There were, however, other reasons why SOE plans in Spain and Portugal were kept on a relatively small scale. Two other British secret services had interests there which were considered to have priority. MI9, responsible for organising escape routes across Europe, had valuable lines across the Pyrenees to Madrid and Lisbon, while SIS operated from both centres into France and North West Africa.[10] On balance the government considered it advantageous not to risk disrupting these important networks by permitting more than a minimum of 'low profile' SOE activities and risking Franco's displeasure. Significantly, it appears that in Madrid SOE interests were represented by the naval attaché, Alan Hillgarth, who worked closely with SIS, and was thus well-suited to keeping SOE under control. Thus, in the Spanish and Portuguese cases SOE quickly learned that it would have to yield to the interests and susceptibilities of the Foreign Office, MI9 and SIS.

In the case of Operation Savannah, they ran into other problems. This was a plan to send a small sabotage team into France to blow up the bus which regularly carried German pathfinder pilots to and from their base near Vannes in northern Brittany. In its search for suitable men to drop by parachute, SOE picked out some Frenchmen in Britain—and were immediately accused by de Gaulle and the Free French of encroaching upon their sphere of interest and activity.[11] When the scheme finally came before the Chiefs of Staff, yet another obstacle was encountered. Air Chief Marshall Portal, Chief of Staff of the Air Force, had already told Gladwyn Jebb that 'he thought that the dropping of men dressed in civilian clothes for the purpose of attempting to kill members of the opposing forces is not an operation with which the Royal Air Force should be associated. . . . I think you will agree', he continued, 'that there is a vast difference, in ethics, between the time honoured operation of the dropping of a spy from the air and this entirely new scheme for dropping what one can only call assassins'.[12] If this was more than merely a polite way of saying that the Royal Air Force could or would not spare a plane for a parachute drop, then one can only admire the nice distinction drawn by Portal. To condemn attacks on enemy military personnel by allied civilians (or men dressed as civilians), while approving and sharing responsibility for the Allied bombing of defenceless civilians, was tortuous ethics. Nonetheless, it illustrated what was in some cases a very genuine abhorrence on the part of professional soldiers at SOE-type operations, and reveals the distance which had to be travelled before sabotage and resistance could be regarded as serious strategies of war by the military establishment. In this case, the operation was eventually approved, but the delays caused by the objection from de Gaulle and the Chiefs of Staff contributed to its failure. By the time the saboteurs arrived, travel arrangements for the pilots had changed and the plan could not be carried out.

II

In the late spring of 1941 British fortunes of war reached their nadir. The Greek expedition had been a fiasco, and following the surrender in Crete Britain now had no foothold in Europe. Nor had she gained any new allies. Fears that Vichy France might join the German side as an active belligerent were current, especially in view of Darlan's agreement that the Germans could use their bases in Syria and Lebanon. It was becoming apparent moreover that strategic bombing, Britain's major offensive weapon, was not living up to its promise, and that it was too inaccurate to destroy the German economy. Losses in the Atlantic were so heavy that in April Churchill ordered the Ministry of Information to discontinue its weekly reports. In mid-June Wavell's offensive in North Africa was called off. At home, the German bombing attacks on English cities were having a more serious effect than the government had wished to admit. London suffered its worst raid on 10 May, and *Mass Observation* reported that morale was in a dangerous state.[13] How was Britain actually going to *win*, rather than merely avoid defeat? Raymond E. Lee, the American military attaché in London noted a general sense of gloom and 'a growing apprehension on the part of the leaders'.[14] In this climate of gloom and desperation, the British Chiefs of Staff and the war-planning machinery were particularly receptive to plans which could promise victory with the limited resources available to Britain and its Empire, which still, after eighteen months of war, 'stood alone'. This was the context for a serious and prolonged discussion at the Chiefs of Staff level in May and June of an SOE-inspired plan which requested the war leadership to provide SOE with the resources to fulfil the widest and most ambitious claims of the 'detonator concept'.

As early as March Churchill had given instructions to his planning staff to prepare for a major review of future British strategy. In doing so, he had made it clear that national resources and manpower requirements made 'it impossible for the Army, except in resisting invasion, to play a primary role in the defeat of the enemy'. That could only be achieved by the staying power of the Navy, and air predominance. The Army could only contribute overseas 'in operations of a secondary order'.[15] This was, of course, only to repeat what previous strategic surveys had said, and represented nothing new. But it makes it clear that this relatively minor role planned for the Army was more than a temporary aberration caused by the shock of the defeat in France, and that all strategic planning in 1941 was to proceed from this basic and crucial assumption.

As the planners worked on their review throughout the grim months of April and May, SOE prepared both a plan of its own for subversive operations in 1941, and on a longer-term plan spelling out the requirements for the arming of secret armies in Europe. The mastermind behind this second study was Gubbins, who, as we have seen in the previous chapter, was responsible in large part for the formulation of the secret army idea in the first place. Much of Gubbins' energy and time up to this point had been spent in organising the Auxiliary Units which were to form the nucleus of a British resistance movement in the event of a German invasion. Many SOE personnel had been tied up in these preparations, and it was only at the beginning of April 1941 that SOE was told that it no longer need give first priority to them. Gubbins and others could now give more attention to offensive planning.[16] Towards the end of May Gubbins produced an ambitious plan envisaging three phases in SOE planning: the organisation and equipment of (a) a sabotage system, and (b) of secret armies; and (c) the ultimate revolt of the captive peoples of Europe. Gubbins, evidently impressed by the recent German techniques in Crete, added a new variation to this final phase. The Allied contingents in Britain would be retrained as airborne troops and parachuted in to assist the revolt. The full plan, if it was to be accomplished by the spring of 1942, would require 8000 sorties by the RAF, and the full-time use of over 400 aircraft. If the target date was a year later, it would require half the number. The ambitious nature of this plan can be appreciated by noting the single fact that at the time Gubbins was writing, SOE disposed of only one flight of aircraft—shared with SIS—and Bomber Command itself had only eighty operational bombers. The plan was quite unrealistic. But in the battle for scarce resources, it was a bold if utopian attempt, by positing an alternative strategy to that of the bombing offensive, to increase SOE's logistical capabilities. Gubbins was, indeed, well aware of the reality. He knew that SOE was far from operational. In an overall view of SOE's situation written only a month later he stressed that SOE's prime task was organisation and communications; only when that was accomplished could they 'direct all our energies towards operations'.[17]

Gubbins and the SOE staff worked closely with the Future Operations Planning Section of (FOPS) of the Joint Planning Staff. Their ideas, even if much watered down, are clearly impressed on the final version of the new major review of future strategy which finally reached the Chiefs of Staff on 16 June 1941—less than a week before Hitler's attack on the Soviet Union.[18] The radically changed long-term strategic picture created by Operation Barbarossa was to render the assumptions underlying this review largely obsolete, as Churchill was quick to point out. It is, nonetheless, of considerable interest and significance. It was the fullest evaluation to date of Britain's strategic dilemma as she 'stood alone'. With manpower requirements stretched to the full and with the need to maintain certain minimum living standards at home in order to preserve morale, the fundamental problem still remained, as it had done a year previously following the defeat of the French Army. How was Britain going to win, rather than merely avoid defeat? What offensive strategy could she adopt? In seeking to answer this question, the planners elaborated on the familiar triad of blockade, bombing, and subversion, and in so doing gave lucid expression to 'the detonator concept'. This marked the high-water mark of its acceptance amongst British strategists. And it was an important milestone in the history of SOE.

The FOPS set out in stark detail and with unassailable logic the limitation on future British offensive strategy imposed by the relative weakness of her armed forces. The demands of the domestic war economy imposed severe restrictions on the future size of the armed forces. In particular, when the Army had reached its planned sixty divisions in autumn 1942 it could not be expanded further without damaging the economy or cutting into the needs of the other services. Against this, the Germans already had 250 divisions, 90 of which were available for operations anywhere. *Even with full American help* (which was considered essential for victory), the planners concluded 'we cannot hope to defeat the existing Germany Army in the field and so open the road to Germany and victory'. The only alternative was to undermine the German war economy and morale until the enemy armed forces could 'be speeded by military action down the road to inevitable collapse'. Provided economic warfare against Germany was maintained at the current level, a marked deterioration would occur in her economy in 1942, and by 1943 she would be forced to make drastic reductions in her armed forces to deal with it. The decisive factor in the demise of the German war economy would be the bombing offensive on economic targets, particularly oil, heavy industry in the Ruhr, and transportation. In addition, sabotage and subversion would be of increasing importance, and thus SOE, the planners recommended, should be in close and continuous touch at every level with those responsible for the direction of military strategy: 'Only now emerging from its infancy', said the planners, SOE 'should play an ever-increasing role in our offensive operations'. This was essential in any event, but would be particularly important in view of SOE's role in organising future 'risings of the subject races'. Here, from SOE's view-point, was the kernel of the report (see Document Four of the appendices).

The planners, in predicting the form of the final offensive against Germany, turned as before to subversion. The optimum moment would be August 1942. At that time patriot forces must rise up against the Germans and destroy their local strength, seizing such objectives as military headquarters, broadcasting stations, loading grounds, and centres of communications. At this point, organised armed forces from Britain would have to assist either by air or sea. Using to maximum advantage the free allied contingents in Britain, the British armed forces (of which ten armoured divisions would be available) assisted by air power, would have the task of isolating each area of operations from the Germans and assisting the patriot forces to capture important centres and destroy enemy forces. The basic concept of these operations would be 'attack from within', and, in words which had been used by Dalton a year previously, the planners predicted that it could produce overnight 'the anarchy of Ireland in 1920 or Palestine in 1936'. Rather than suggesting specific theatres of operations, the planners, merely pointed out that only in Norway, Czechoslovakia, and Poland was the civilian morale currently suitable for effective patriot uprisings. Here, there were nucleus patriot organisations which could easily be expanded. Elsewhere, time was needed. France and the Low Countries were 'spiritually unready for revolt', and required much preparation and propaganda; certain Balkan countries showed promise. All required considerable aid in the form of arms, stores and personnel from Britain, and communications were vital. Thus, the planners concluded their report, the time had come when the necessary long-term plans should be prepared and equipment ordered. SOE and PWE (the Political Warfare Executive which had assumed SO1's propaganda tasks) should be represented at all stages and on all levels during planning and preparation. The allied governments-in-exile would have to collaborate closely in planning the role of their own forces, and full preparations would have to be made for the formation of local governments to take control in the aftermath of the uprisings. And, ironically in view of the future, a special study should be inaugurated to examine the feasibility of supplying the secret armies of Czechoslovakia and Poland by air.

Although the planners had clearly not accepted Gubbins' ideas in their entirety, this final section of their report bore the clear impress of his thinking. The concept of 'the attack from within', the use of free allied contingents for close liaison with the resistance forces, the role of airborne troops, even the singling out for special mention the high patriotic morale and advanced organisation of the Polish, Czechoslovak and Norwegian resistance forces, are all identifiable as his. And like many of his ideas before, they proved on closer inspection to be totally irreconcilable with the interests, demands and plans of the three regular services.

In particular, the plan clashed head-on with the demands of Bomber Command. Gubbins' scheme of May, based upon the arming of an estimated 130,000 men in the secret armies of France, Poland and Czechoslovakia, had required 8000 sorties, at a time when Bomber Command was flying an average of 2000 sorties a month. The joint planners' scheme, which foresaw uprisings all over Europe, would have required 12,000 sorties, or six months' full-time effort by Bomber Command. There was thus, in the words of the official strategic history, 'a direct incompatibility between the existing bomber policy and subversion of the scale now proposed'.[19] This more than any other single factor determined its fate, for there was no chance that the Chiefs of Staff and Churchill were prepared to abandon the strategic bombing offensive, which, whatever else it did, gave daily evidence to the British people that the offensive was being carried into Germany. This was the single most important practical obstacle to the plan, but even had the aircraft been available, it would have required a major gamble on the part of the war leadership. As the post-war official historian noted, 'an uncertainty beyond the ordinary hazards of war would overhang the whole operation'.[20] There was no way in which the General Staff would be able to gauge the actual fighting strength of the secret armies before D-day itself, and they would thus be bound to ensure that the regular forces *alone* were sufficient to control the situation—otherwise the once and for all uprising-cum-invasion might be a complete disaster. Once that principle was accepted, however, it made the uprising a purely auxiliary operation to the landings of regular formations and the primary role of the secret armies disappeared. It was not surprising, therefore, that the war leadership preferred certainties. As Portal, Chief of the Air Staff, told an SOE official: 'Your work is a gamble which may give us a valuable dividend or may produce nothing. It is anybody's guess. My bombing offensive is not a gamble. Its dividend is certain; it is a gilt-edged investment. I cannot divert aircraft from a certainty to a gamble which may be a gold mine or may be completely worthless'.[21] What this overlooked, of course, was that it was at this very time that studies were revealing that Bomber Command was hitting virtually none of its targets, and that the 'gilt-edged investment' consisted mostly of large holes in German fields. But on the principle of the matter, Portal was right, at least as far as the question of secret armies was concerned.

The plan did not, it should be noted, call for guerrilla or partisan warfare. It foresaw, on the contrary, a once-and-for-all uprising throughout Europe, regardless of the terrain, the very antitheses of guerrilla warfare. Moreover, it was to be carefully timed to coincide with landings on the Continent, and this implied control in some considerable measure from outside. Here again was the belief that large secret armies could be kept loyal to exterior governments. In not even raising the possibility that problems of political allegiance might arise, the planners overlooked what was eventually to become one of the greatest problems SOE had to face; which political faction to support within each national resistance movement. True, this was before the Soviet Union's entry into the war, and thus before the European communist parties' official and overt participation in resistance had made such questions acute. True, the planners were not assuming that the final offensive against Germany would be delayed as long as it was, and therefore there might not be time for major divergences to appear between the internal and external forms of national resistance. True, for most of the Western and Central European countries at this time there was little indication that major problems of allegiance would arise, except in the special case of France, and in many countries these problems did *not* arise on a major scale. Yet the fact that problems of political allegiance had so troubled SOE relations with France already, to the point where it had set up two separate sections, one to work with de Gaulle, and one without him, should have been an indicator. The assumption which prevented this from happening—that the problem arose precisely because de Gaulle and the Free French were *not* a legal government-in-exile—was a narrow and legalistic one. Within six months it was becoming clear, for example, that neither in Greece nor Yugoslavia was domestic opinion likely to accept without question the legitimacy of their governments-in-exile, and by 1943 the problem had become a major headache. But it was in part a headache precisely because of the deep reluctance to face the political dimension of resistance.

The FOPS report stimulated SOE into producing a further study in which the practical implications could be fully worked out and a programme for the future laid down. This took the form of a memorandum from Dalton himself to Churchill on 21 July, in which he claimed that SOE could 'if so directed, set in motion large-scale and long-term schemes for revolution in Europe'.[22] This Daltonian rhetoric barely concealed the fact that SOE had already scaled down the scope of its ambitions quite considerably. The Chiefs of Staff had not been overly enthusiastic about the planners' ideas which on their own admission were entirely different from those which had governed previous operations. Portal had been predictably the most critical, remarking caustically that he did not think that 'a patriot "Home Guard" on a grand scale would prevent disaster if Europe were invaded in the manner suggested'.[23] Dalton's report was accordingly written on a more realistic scale. He accepted the planners' assumption that autumn 1942 was the earliest date for action, and laid out the SOE requirements for a three-fold programme: subversive propaganda, serious sabotage, and the building of secret armies. The number of aircraft sorties envisaged was now reduced to about 2000, involving fifty aircraft, a considerable reduction on the figures suggested by the earlier Gubbins report. Dalton had achieved this by a radical piece of surgery: the arming of the secret armies of Poland and Czechoslovakia—which Gubbins and the planners admitted would have to be almost exclusively by air—was abandoned. Instead, the lion's share of the SOE effort was to go to France, where an army of 24,000 was to be equipped by autumn 1942, using 1200 aircraft sorties. The other countries to be supplied were Belgium and Holland.[24]

The full content of Dalton's memorandum is still secret. But what can be discovered about it indicates that already the entry of the Soviet Union into the war had had its impact. There were sound logistical reasons why the secret armies of Poland and Czechoslovakia could not be supplied on any large scale by the British and these reasons existed independently of the position of the Soviet Union. Its active participation, however, may well have been decisive in leading SOE to conclude that

British responsibility for arming them was both unnecessary, and undesirable for larger political reasons, perhaps on the grounds that they would inevitably enter a Soviet sphere of influence. That such long-term political calculations affected some SOE decisions at this time is clear. Julian Amery has recounted how, immediately following the outbreak of the German–Soviet war, a meeting took place in Cairo where it was agreed that while taking the lead in creating Balkan resistance movements Britain should seek to associate the Soviet Union with such work because 'it should prove easier to commit Moscow to support our friends while the Soviets were still fighting for their lives, than it might become later . . .'.[25] Whether similar arguments were advanced in the case of Poland and Czechoslovakia by Dalton cannot, in the absence of the evidence, be proved. What can be shown is that from this moment on the idea of arming the Polish or Czechoslovak resistance for 'secret army' purposes was abandoned. Agents, arms, and other supplies were infiltrated there over the next three-and-a-half years, although on a relatively small scale. But these were to aid subversion and sabotage, not to encourage and equip armed national uprisings. This decision contained a double irony and the seeds of future tragedy. It had originally been the existence of well-organised secret armies in these two central European nations that had inspired SOE's theory of secret armies in the first place. Without these two, there was nowhere, with the single possible exception of Norway, which in SOE's view was anywhere near ready at that time for a national uprising; France, the Low Countries, the Balkans, and Italy required substantial organisation and preparatory action. Secondly, although SOE now abandoned the idea of arming the Polish secret army, preparations for and the launching of a national uprising remained the guiding and paramount concern of the Polish resistance itself. That Britain could not support such plans was never properly appreciated by the Poles, and indeed ambiguities between SOE and the Poles seem to have existed on this score and may have led the Poles to expect more British support for the 1944 Warsaw uprising than was available (see below, Chapter 6).

The Joint Planning Staff was quick to seize on the radical implications this had for the entire SOE concept of 'the rising from within'. They told the Chiefs of Staff that in view of the requirement, admitted by all, of regular troop support for national uprisings, planning should be restricted to those areas where a British offensive was possible. This could only be across the Channel for reasons of fighter support and shipping. This meant not only the elimination of Czechoslovakia and Poland from the scheme, but also of Norway—the final member of

Gubbins' trio of existing secret armies. Priority should therefore be given to the reorganisation of secret armies in Northern France, Belgium, and Holland, in that order. As their organisation was still rudimentary, however, it would be premature to start supplying them with arms on the scale suggested by Dalton. The target date of autumn 1942 was, in their view, unrealistic, and it would only be in the light of progress over the following winter that a more realistic target date could be decided upon. As far as Norway was concerned, it would not be totally abandoned, as it was the most suitable area for subsidiary operations; the arming of its secret army could proceed over the coming winter, provided that this could be done by sea and did not affect the arming of British forces[26] (Document Five of the appendices).

This was all devastating enough to the original SOE conception, but more was to come. As the planners pointed out, 'secret armies can never operate until bombing has first created suitable conditions', an assumption which had been built into the earlier June report. In a situation where resources were stretched to their limit, and where aircraft for SOE purposes could only be supplied by Bomber Command, the conclusion was inevitable: 'It would be unsound', the planners recommended, 'to sacrifice the effectiveness of our bombing effort to these activities'. This was not all. It was also essential, they concluded, 'that provision of sorties for SO2 should not be allowed to interfere with the requirements of SIS'. In order to ensure the greatest economy in air effort, therefore, SOE and the Air Ministry should investigate together the availability of aircraft. These recommendations, contained in two short paragraphs, were the death blow to the entire SOE scheme. Bomber Command and SIS were, in effect, given priority over SOE. The former was reluctant at most times to provide any aircraft at all; and when they did, SIS claimed—and was granted—priority for its activities in Northern France and Belgium. In the 1943 directive to SOE for example, SIS was specifically given priority over SOE in these areas.

The planners were not totally unsympathetic to SOE needs. They accepted that subversive propaganda and sabotage could play an important part in the war, and agreed that SOE demands for additional W/T sets should be met in order to provide the communication network necessary for any wide-scale action. While the provision of arms for secret army purposes over the forthcoming winter should be only twenty-five per cent of that demanded by Dalton, the full requirements to support subversive activities and propaganda should be met. The special flight set aside for SOE and SIS purposes should be increased to a squadron, which, they said, 'would be enough to enable SO2 to make

an effective beginning both in subversive activities and in the organisation of secret armies'. Progress should be carefully monitored over the
winter of 1941–42, and further recommendations could then be made.

The outcome of this critique of Dalton's paper was that the Chiefs of
Staff at two successive meetings on 14 and 15 August 1941 agreed to
meet only a minimum of SOE's demands.[27] They accepted the need to
encourage subversion and sabotage, but expressed great scepticism
about secret armies and agreed to consider the provision of arms for
them only after the War Office had looked into their availability. They
approved the Air Ministry's decision to provide a full squadron of aircraft, but echoed the planners' concern that in view of 'the paramount
importance of good intelligence' SOE sorties should not interfere with
the requirements of SIS. Subsequently, in the autumn of 1941, 138
Squadron was formed, based at Newmarket, to service both SOE and
SIS special requirements. By November, nine Whitleys and three Halifaxes were at SOE's disposal, and Gubbins, SOE's Director of Operations, told Dalton on 3 November that 'these were more than sufficient
for all his prospective operations'.[28] They took no action to improve
SOE liaison with the Chiefs of Staff (indeed, the first *formal* liaison was
established only in January 1942) and no action appears to have been
taken on the recommendations for improved contact with the Allied
governments-in-exile. Secret armies in Poland and Czechoslovakia
were not even discussed and the Chiefs of Staff implicitly accepted that
Britain should not seek to provide them with arms for national uprisings. Even where the possibility of creating and supplying secret
armies in Northern France, Belgium and Holland was admitted, they
expressed grave doubts about their feasibility in the face of Nazi repression. Sabotage and subversion were to be supported, but the 'detonator concept', with the secret armies as its keystone, was abandoned.
They did not formally reject the concept, but by postponing it until the
distant future, and by subordinating it to the requirements of the bombing offensive, they placed it on the back burner and henceforward permitted it to die a slow death. It made occasional reappearances in
Churchill's speeches up to the summer of 1942, and in confidential brie-
fings on British strategy to the Americans before Pearl Harbour, but
these were simply the last flickerings of a concept which had been ex-
tinguished by its own internal contradictions, the scarcity of resources,
and the rapidly approaching promise of the intervention of large
Russian and American armies in the field.

Running parallel with this debate, and equally damaging to the original conception underlying SOE's formation, was a serious dispute

about the control of propaganda. From the outset, the position had been somewhat anomalous. SOE, in the shape of its subsection SO1, had been placed in charge of covert propaganda, but overt propaganda remained in the hands of the Ministry of Information and the BBC. This caused problems of co-ordination and control of policy when both overt and covert propaganda to a particular country had to be decided upon. It meant, from SOE's viewpoint, that it did not fully control subversive propaganda and was in constant dispute with other government departments. The 'V for Victory' campaign launched by the BBC in January 1941 had been a case in point, for it was conducted without reference to SOE who became concerned that it might incite Europeans to violence and sabotage to no purpose, and possibly to the detriment of SOE's own operations. After Brendan Bracken became Minister of Information in July 1941, an already bad situation became intolerable by the injection of the vitriol which characterised his and Dalton's personal exchanges. Eventually, after endless discussion, covert propaganda was taken over by a new organisation, the Political Warfare Executive (PWE), supervised jointly by the Foreign Office, the Ministry of Information, and the Ministry of Economic Warfare. A Cabinet decision in August 1941 finalised the arrangements, and SO1 was abolished. This decision, however necessary for internal purposes, further corroded the ideal of a combined subversive propaganda and resistance strategy under the direction of a single Ministry, although it is unlikely that it caused serious damage to British propaganda in Europe. It was, however, one more nail in the coffin of Dalton's concept of the Fourth Arm, and it provoked a torrent of bitter complaints by Dalton to Attlee in September when he declared that not since he joined the government had he felt so deeply dissatisfied both with the conduct of affairs and his own personal position. He was faced with Foreign Office 'appeasement' by way of blockade concessions in the occupied territories, and with a combination of two Conservative ministers and three officials in the newly formed PWE where, he suspected, 'the game is first to reduce to a minimum my influence . . . and then to endeavour to edge me out still further by gradually aggrandizing PWE at the expense of SOE'. He believed, moreover, that this was part of a general plan in certain political and official quarters to reduce the role of Labour ministers. Most difficult of all to accept, he told Attlee, was his exclusion from major decisions regarding strategy. Although responsible for subversive action in Europe he was neither a member of the Defence Committee nor had he been invited to it since the discussions nine months previously on Rumanian oil. Even more extraordinary and bitter was the fact that throughout the entire debate in June and July over the place of resistance in British strategy he had received 'not a word, either orally or in writing, from the Prime Minister',[29] Such an admission was eloquent testimony to the low priority subversion and sabotage now played in the long term plans of British strategy, and to SOE's relationship to the war leadership and the Prime Minister who only a year earlier had been responsible for creating SOE.

III

In the long run, the entry of the Soviet Union into the war was to have major consequences for Britain's relations with European resistance movements. As we have seen, it was British policy to avoid premature uprisings in Europe and to discourage resistance activity which would lead to massive reprisals against the civilian population, a view shared by the Allied governments-in-exile. Russian policy was quite different. Within a few hours of the German invasion, Stalin expressed a totally contrary conception of the function of internal resistance:

The struggle against Germany must not be looked upon as an ordinary war . . . It is not merely a fight between two armies . . . in order to engage the enemy there must be bands of partisans and saboteurs working underground everywhere, blowing the bridges, destroying roads, telephones and telegraphs, and setting fire to depots and forests. In territories occupied by the enemy, conditions must be made so impossible that he cannot hold out; those helping him will be punished and executed. Sabotage all enemy organisations.[30]

This instruction was not confined to the Russian people but was extended via the Comintern to the whole of occupied Europe, and communist parties throughout the Continent sought to put it into practice. The conception suited Russian strategic requirements—any action in the rear of the German lines, however desperate, was worth attempting to slow down the advance of the German armies. The British had been accused of wanting to fight to the last Frenchman. The Russians were prepared to die to the last European. But it was more than that. Communist dogma taught that imperialist wars should be transformed into struggles of the proletariat against the bourgeoisie. True, this was not an imperialist war in the sense that the Soviet Union was now a protagonist, and this meant that first priority should be given to the defence and survival of the Soviet Union. But provided that overriding priority was met, the active and formal participation of European communist parties in the war pursuing an activist strategy of partisan warfare would strengthen the proletariat, and the proletarian forces should seek to accomplish this. Thus, resistance in Europe became a potential arena for a civil war, and London and Moscow the 'two opposite symbolic capitals of European resistance'.

This was all, however, in the future. Britain's immediate response was to offer aid to Russia, and, so far as SOE was concerned, to enter into an agreement with its opposite number in Moscow for co-operation in subversive matters. There is evidence to suggest that even in 1940 the Soviet Union had been interested in some co-operation with SOE on sabotage in the Balkans, for Amery recounts how in the autumn of that year indications were given to the Soviet Union, in response to an indirect request, of German communications networks which the Russians were in a better position to attack than SOE.[31] But these contacts were broken off and it was not until immediately after the German invasion that a formal initiative was made by Moscow for worldwide co-operation with SOE on subversive action directed against the Axis powers. SOE responded by suggesting that such co-operation could take place on the basis that neither side would be expected to give details of any secret organisation (names of agents, exact methods of work, etc.). Discussion in the early stages should be confined to the strategic level, that is, SOE would reveal where they were acting effectively, and where they hoped to act in future, and on the basis of what the Russians revealed in their turn a common policy could be worked out. Subversive propaganda to the European working class might also be covered. Finally, SOE was prepared to send out Sir Charles Hambro to discuss the details in Moscow. It is not clear whether this visit ever took place, but it is clear that at the end of September SOE came to some sort of agreement with the OGPU (NKVD) involving an exchange of missions. The head of the SOE mission in Moscow for most of the war was to be George Hill, a former British secret agent in Russia, and a friend of the notorious Sidney Reilly. Like SOE's chief in the United States he also doubled as the chief SIS representative. Dalton enthusiastically told Churchill in late September that the Russians had shown 'extreme willingness to co-operate with us on subversive matters', and that the discussions in Moscow were likely to be 'very important indeed'. He added, rather unnecessarily, that it was vital that no wind of SOE–NKVD conversations should get out in Britain. At a time when Churchill and the government were attempting to balance praise and support for Russian resistance against the need to contain the spread of communism at home and elsewhere, the instruction was hardly necessary. Churchill would have found it rather difficult to explain why, if the BBC could not play the Internationale every night before the national news, it was acceptable for SOE (which did not officially exist) to enter into a working relationship with the NKVD, the very symbol of Stalinist dictatorship. In any case, leaving aside the ironies, it is doubtful whether in practical terms SOE–NKVD co-operation came to much in the long run. It is true that Dalton further told Churchill that SOE missions in the Balkans were conducted in strict agreement with the Russians, but this was in September 1941, which were early days. It is unlikely, once the Soviet Union was in a position to field its own agents, and distinctive communist movements had developed, that they were so co-operative. On the strategic level, they very soon began to attack Mihailović and the Chetniks in Yugoslavia (even if their support for Tito was less than it might have been); while on the tactical level there was little apparent reciprocity. Between 1942 and 1944 Allied planes dropped twenty-five Soviet agents into Western Europe for penetration into Holland, Germany, France, Belgium and Austria, and a small section in Baker Street was established for that purpose. But this was little more than a gesture and the operations took place on the least important level. The USSR did not reciprocate, and the British never allowed their assistance to become extensive.[32]

IV

SOE's operational capacity had been increased by the decisions of the Chiefs of Staff in August and September. But what, in the year since SOE had been established, had been achieved in terms of building up relations with Europe? The picture presented by Dalton to Churchill in September 1941[33] was hardly impressive—although it represented a considerable amount of work by SOE—and was considerably out of proportion with the bold strokes and the huge canvas so dashingly painted by SOE and Gubbins only three months previously. In France, twenty-one agents and organisers had been sent, and thirteen organisers and suborganisers recruited locally. In addition, SOE had assisted with the despatch of eight Free French and two Polish organisers. Communications remained the weak spot, for only two W/T sets were working. In Belgium, efforts had been 'dogged by bad luck', as Dalton disarmingly put it; an agent dropped in May had landed without his W/T set, and 'the pilot dropped him in a prisoner of war camp in *Germany*, and . . . he had great difficulty getting in to Belgium at all!' Two agents were now promising action, provided materials could be sent to them, and, Dalton said reassuringly, 'I think you may take it that something pretty big will happen in Belgium soon after that'. What, he left unclear. Even less reassuring was his assertion that, at present at least, SOE did not consider the messages received from Belgium to be bogus. In Holland, two couriers had been infiltrated by air, but reports had not yet been received. Considering the decision of the Chiefs of Staff only the month previously that, if secret armies had any role to play in the framework of British strategy, it was in these three countries, it was a poor prospect.

Elsewhere, the picture was not much brighter. Apart from Norway, where useful sabotage was being carried out and a coherent secret army existed, achievements were small. The German successes in the Balkans had practically wiped out the SOE networks. SOE's principal agent in Rumania had fallen into German hands, and the one W/T set captured. In Yugoslavia, however, agents were about to be landed by submarine on the Adriatic coast, and other agents had been sent via Istanbul; none, however, were established as Dalton wrote. Italy remained a black spot. Despite many attempts, Dalton reported, 'we have not so far been able (with one exception) to find Italians willing to risk going back home as our agents'. Overall, the picture was bleak, and just over a month later Gubbins confessed to Dalton that the arms made available by the War Office to SOE could not be distributed as fast as they were given 'through insufficiency of agents abroad'.[34]

Between the time of Dalton's writing to Churchill and the beginning of 1942, SOE succeeded in infiltrating a further 66 agents into Europe. France received the largest number (twenty-seven), followed by Poland (fifteen), Belgium and Czechoslovakia (eight each), Holland (four), and Norway and Denmark (two each). For a four-month period this was a considerable achievement, but however impressive it meant nothing unless within these countries there were individuals and organisations prepared to take action against the Germans. In this respect, the autumn of 1941 saw two decisive developments for the entire future of SOE operations in Europe. This was the emergence of nationally organised resistance movements in France and Yugoslavia.

The story of French and Yugoslav resistance movements is well-enough known not to require much recounting here. From SOE's viewpoint, the main facts were these. France was dealt with by four sections within SOE: sections EU/P, DF, F, and RF. The first concentrated upon Polish workers in France, mainly in north-eastern France, while the second concentrated upon escape routes, and neither is particularly important here; F section and RF section differed only in that the latter worked exclusively through the Gaullist Free French movement, while the former was kept quite independent—in the early stages of the war it was not at all clear that it was wise to rely totally on de Gaulle. Both sections, however, worked to construct relations with resistance in France for subversive and sabotage purposes, although it is of interest to note that until the autumn of 1941 de Gaulle himself appears to have attached little worth to active resistance, believing that the most important task for his organisation in France was the collection of intelligence. Until that time, the prospects from the SOE viewpoint were poor, for the resistance picture in France itself was less than inspiring. Agents had been infiltrated, but there was little for them to contact in the way of organised resistance. In September 1941, however, Jean Moulin came out of France as the accredited representative of three organised resistance movements in France, carrying with him the important message that for the first time since the German invasion the French will to resist had reached the point where arms and supplies could usefully be sent. Each of the three movements, Moulin reported, wished to establish liaison with Britain and the Free French in order to receive supplies and direction. Their objective was to arm 'French patriots with a view to eventual action in co-operation with the Allies on French soil'. Unless de Gaulle took the initiative, Moulin argued, the communists would reap the harvest of this renaissance of French national feeling. Not the least factor in this renaissance was communist resistance strategy. By supporting direct attacks on German occupation forces, they had provoked savage reprisals from the Germans. On 22 October 1941, forty-eight French hostages were shot at Chateaubriant; for many Frenchmen this marked the beginning of a national resistance to the occupation.[35]

Moulin's arrival in London in October 1941 represented a turning point for the future of the Free French and de Gaulle, who had the previous month formed the Free French National Committee as a further step in his claim to be the legitimate representative of France and of Free Frenchmen 'wherever they may be'. It also marked an important step in Britain's relations with French resistance. Moulin received de Gaulle's orders to return to France as his personal representative and create the nucleus of a secret army, and was parachuted back on 1 January 1942, the first step towards the creation of the *Conseil National de la Résistance* which owed its loyalty to de Gaulle. De Gaulle himself, inspired by Moulin's reports, raised directly with Churchill on 27 October the question of establishing in France an organisation to 'organise the French people for a nation-wide uprising at the appointed time, whose activity should be co-ordinated with future military plans and considered in relation to similar action in other European countries'. The British pledged their full support to the idea of creating a nationwide organisation 'with the object of securing unity in resisting the common enemy and ultimately achieving the liberation of France from the invader'. They simultaneously made it clear, however, that SOE was the responsible agency on the British side, and that it should have the right to contact organisers in France regardless of their political persuasion. Nonetheless, despite this refusal to accept the exclusivity of de Gaulle's National Committee in relationship to resistance in France, the British response indicated the extent to which SOE would now increasingly work through and with organised and active resistance across the Channel.[36]

In Yugoslavia, likewise, the autumn of 1941 saw the emergence of national resistance. Whereas the complications of the French situation inhibited unequivocal British support for de Gaulle, this was not the case in Yugoslavia. Initially at least the British seized upon Mihailović and his Chetnik movement as the sole representative of Yugoslav national resistance. At the same time, they chose to promote Mihailović as the main symbol of European resistance to Nazism.[37] As early as July 1941 there had been reports of guerrilla fighting in the Yugoslav mountains. On 23 August the Director of Military Intelligence commented on reports of such activity by recommending that 'our policy should be to damp down activity, keep things simmering but not allow them to boil over', and on 28 August Churchill asked Dalton about SOE contacts with the resistance fighters; a few days later he suggested to the War Cabinet that encouraging references about Yugoslavia should be made in the Press and that Britain should do everything possible to re-equip Yugoslav forces fighting against the Germans. On 20 September SOE landed a small group of men headed by Captain Hudson on the Dalmatian coast to make contact with the guerrillas, and within a short while Hudson was established, with a W/T set, at Mihailović's headquarters. By mid-October SOE was reporting to the Chiefs of Staff that Colonel Mihailović was the principal guerrilla leader, and that already couriers had provided him with five million dinar (about £20,000). Churchill was enthusiastic about the guerrilla activity because it appealed to his romantic nature; Eden was enthusiastic because, as he told the Defence Committee on 31 October, not only could it become a serious threat to the Germans, but because 'it will also enable us to assure the Soviet Government that we are doing everything possible to create a second front in the Balkans which they desire'. He also argued that support was important because 'other enemy-occupied countries would tend to regard it as a 'test case'.[38] Dalton, as we have seen, claimed that Anglo-Russian relations were being strengthened by the application in Yugoslavia of an agreed policy. He told Churchill that the Yugoslav revolt should be seen as an extension of the Libyan front and that it was 'not a mere 'side-show', but rather the first instance where underground work has resulted in open rebellion which, from our point of view, it is essential to keep going, both for its own sake and as an example to the rest of Europe and particularly to Greece'.[39]

Elsewhere in Europe, it was British policy to damp down premature revolt. In Yugoslavia, they were faced with what they believed to be widespread revolt, and they hoped that the guerrillas could be supported and encouraged to cause the maximum trouble from the beginning. In accordance with policy elsewhere, and with their limited capacity to lend assistance, they did, however, oppose the idea of a nationwide revolt which would involve urban guerrillas, thus initiating ruthless German repression. Consequently, they authorised the Commander-in-Chief in the Middle East (in whose area of command this fell) to support the guerrillas in the mountains with all possible means. By mid-November the Political Warfare Executive was instructing the BBC to describe Mihailović as the leader of the Yugoslav patriot forces, and within a short while Mihailović's name was known throught the Western world as a great resistance leader. For the next year SOE was to hold fast to this myth of Mihailović.

That it was a myth, and that within SOE and other branches of the British Government it was soon known or suspected to be a myth, is clear. Recent detailed research[40] has shown that a great deal of the fighting attributed to the Chetniks was in fact being done by the communists under Tito's leadership; that Mihailović was attacking the communists, and that by mid-November this was known to London; that on the strength of the mistaken belief that this fighting was over, the British agreed to send Mihailović further supplies; and that, despite their awareness of communist partisan resistance at this time they sought to back Mihailović as the leader of a united patriotic front in Yugoslavia; and that they asked Moscow to assist in this task. In short, the Yugoslav situation was far from simple, and as early as November 1941 the British were aware of the factors which were ultimately to destroy Mihailović and his movement and cause British policy-makers themselves endless headaches. But at a time when Hitler's forces were approaching the gates of Moscow, few were anxious to draw attention to the clay feet of the hero of Balkan resistance or to alienate the Yugoslav exile government.

Since June 1941, therefore, there had been three major developments with profound consequences for SOE: the invasion of the Soviet Union and the consequent mobilisation of the European communist parties into European resistance; the beginnings of a national resistance movement in France and the establishment of the first links between it and de Gaulle in London; and the development of guerrilla fighting in Yugoslavia with Mihailović as its perceived leader and hero. The attack on Pearl Harbour on 7 December 1941 added a fourth development to the list. Active American intervention in the war not only guaranteed ultimate victory, but it made redundant for once and for all the key role of the European secret armies which still lingered in British strategic thinking. It was ironic that this should have occurred just as SOE was entering its operational phase, and when the possibility of a secret army developing in France could, for the first time, clearly be seen. The practical consequences for SOE were not as great as they might have been, for the decisions of the Chiefs of Staff in August and September had already assigned SOE to a lesser role in grand strategy than propounded by its theorists. But with American entry into the war, and with the emergence of an Anglo-American strategy, a distinct phase in SOE's history came to a close, and a new one began.

Signs that SOE was entering a new phase were indicated when an internal crisis occurred in November with the threatened resignation of Sir Frank Nelson. The crisis blew over, and Nelson withdrew his resignation, but in the inquest which followed, conducted in person by Dalton, it emerged that internal strains on individuals and the organisational structure were being caused by three main factors.[41] First, the fact that SOE was now becoming operational—that is, it now had agents stationed in Europe capable of carrying out specific tasks—meant that it required a more disciplined and Service-like character. This required a clearer distinction between policy and purely operational matters, with ministerial intervention confined exclusively to the former. This led directly to the second and third factors. 'The Foreign Office was interfering too much in detail', Dalton was told by George Taylor. Sir Charles Hambro complained that 'the Foreign Office was a great danger to the efficient working of such an institution as SOE'. The complaint of too close a relationship with the Foreign Office—at least at the operational level—was counterbalanced by the third factor—the complaint of too little contact with the Chiefs of Staff and its planning machinery. Instead of the *ad hoc* presentation of SOE schemes to the

Defence Committee or Chiefs of Staff there should be direct and permament liaison at a lower level with the secretariat of the Chiefs of Staff
and the Planners. This was essential now that SOE was becoming
increasingly involved in operations of a military kind.

These criticisms reflected SOE's growing pains as it became operational. Steps towards the solution of each were taken over the next few
months. Permament liaison with the Chiefs of Staff secretariat was established in January 1942, and the new CIGS, Sir Alan Brooke, appears
to have been more sympathetic to SOE's proposals than his predecessor, Dill. In fact, on 6 January 1942, Dalton and Brooke had a
mutually satisfactory lunchtime meeting after which Brooke clearly
indicated that he thought more could be done to equip local resistance
movements. Similarly, three days later, Dalton met Mountbatten and
they agreed to put SOE–CCO relations on a stronger footing.[42] 'Ministerial interference' within SOE lessened when Dalton was replaced by
Lord Selborne in the government reshuffle of February 1942, and when
Gladwyn Jebb, Dalton's Chief Executive Officer, returned to the
Foreign Office and was not replaced. Foreign Office intervention was a
far more difficult question. As SOE–Foreign Office relations reached a
critical phase at this time, something more should be said about them.

The Foreign Office had not initially objected to the creation of SOE
under its own minister, but within a short while it became apparent that
their interests were bound to conflict. Dalton had urged in June 1940
that it was 'surely high time to cease being gentlemen, to become professionals, and to do a little body-line bowling at the Hun',[43] but when
this involved matches on neutral grounds the Foreign Office invariably
cried 'no-ball'. Difficulties had occurred over operations in the neutral
Balkan states in the early part of 1941, and over plans for Spain, Portugal, Switzerland, Turkey and other neutral states throughout the year.
There was a virtual embargo on sabotage action in Vichy France, and
the SOE–NKVD agreement had been closely vetted by the Foreign
Office. Part of the problem was that although SOE was in theory a
purely executive body, it had its own Minister with distinct views on
policy, and its operations were by their very nature bound to raise
foreign policy issues. Added to this was a personal rivalry between Eden
and Dalton which seriously affected SOE–Foreign Office relations
throughout 1941 and was only solved in February 1942 with Dalton's
removal to the Board of Trade. Profound mutual antipathy had led to a
virtual severence of relations in mid-1941, when Eden had successfully
combined with Brendan Bracken to wrest control of subversive propaganda away from Dalton and place it in the hands of the newly-formed

Political Warfare Executive, and this played a major part in Dalton's bitter complaints to Attlee in September. If he was concerned that Eden and Bracken would seek to enlarge PWE at SOE's expense, he must have been very seriously worried when Desmond Morton hinted to him on 19 December that in view of the creation of PWE it might be necessary to change the SOE Charter, and that he (Morton) should attempt to draw up the first draft of a new one.[44] Morton was too close to Churchill, to SIS, and to the levers of power within the government for this to be a mere idle suggestion. Dalton would have been right to be worried. According to Sir Alexander Cadogan's Diary, Churchill was thinking in February of dividing SOE's work between the Chiefs of Staff and the Foreign Office,[45] and even though this came to nothing, a new 'Charter' for SOE was under discussion with the Foreign Office at that time. Judging by the entries in the diaries of both Dalton and Cadogan, these discussions were acrimonious. Dalton referred to a memorandum by Cadogan on the subject as 'graceless and clodhopping', and a few days later Eden confessed that had he and not Halifax been Foreign Secretary in 1940 he would have kept subversive activities strictly under Foreign Office control. Discussions dragged on through March and April, by which time Dalton had been replaced by Selborne, and even as late as 22 April Cadogan was referring to the possibility of having 'to crash SOE altogether'. In May 1942, however, some sort of *modus vivendi* between the two was agreed upon with the signature of an SOE–Foreign Office 'Treaty'. Under the terms of this agreement SOE was to be responsible for obtaining Foreign Office approval for any operations which might affect Foreign Office interests in enemy or enemy-occupied countries, and the Foreign Office was to be kept informed of all developments of political significance. In all neutral countries the concerns of foreign policy were to be paramount, and no SOE action was to be taken without the consent either of Eden or of the head of the local diplomatic mission. Any peace feelers received were to be referred directly to the Foreign Office, and to ensure liaison on all questions there were to be regular fortnightly meetings between SOE and the Foreign Office, to which SIS representatives would be invited. This agreement meant amongst other things that—in Gubbins' words—'we were still under the crippling Foreign Office ban not to undertake violent sabotage in unoccupied France' (a prohibition which continued until Vichy was occupied in November), and that in the case of countries such as Sweden, where SOE action would be taken in the event of a German invasion, little effective preparatory action could be taken despite SOE's wishes.[46] As for improvements in the general tone of

SOE–Foreign Office relations, their subsequent development indicates that it solved little, if anything at all. In enemy and enemy-occupied countries, particularly in the Balkans, Foreign Office interests were involved at practically every move of the game, and 'consultation' more often than not took the form of conflict, disagreement, and mutual suspicion. The only improvement that did take place was that personal relations between Selborne and Eden were better than those between Dalton and Eden, but this was the result of the quite independent government reshuffle in February.

Dalton's departure from SOE marked the end of the first phase of SOE's life. He was succeeded by Lord Selborne, a personal friend and diehard Tory supporter of the Prime Minister who pursued a more conciliatory policy towards both Eden and Bracken. The change was symbolic. The grandiose theories of the detonator concept, of the secret armies in Europe, of left-wing revolution, of a combined programme of subversive propaganda and action, had all dissolved. There remained the more limited (but no less problematic or controversial) tasks of persuading resistance movements to co-ordinate with, but be subordinated to, Allied strategy, and of carrying out specific tasks of sabotage. Immediately following Pearl Harbour Churchill initiated strategic discussions with the Americans in Washington, and by early 1942 planning had begun for the Second Front in Europe. In this context, SOE increasingly became a weapon of war in the hands of the Chiefs of Staff. The independent 'fourth arm' of warfare was dead.

4 Survival and Consolidation

The new year began with Anglo-American strategic discussions in Washington, and much talk, expectation and hope of a Second Front in Europe in 1942. Now that strategic planning was more firmly focused on the offensive, and it became clearer than ever that SOE's work would be subordinated to the general strategic directives of the Chiefs of Staff, its independent existence came under close scrutiny. Attempts were made to restrict the scope of its activities, or even to abolish it. The Foreign Office, as the previous chapter has shown, were concerned at its encroachment on foreign policy matters and sought greater control or influence over SOE policy. The Allied governments-in-exile wished both to exert stronger control over SOE operations in occupied Europe, and to be more closely and directly associated with the Chiefs of Staff in the planning of a Second Front, thus bypassing SOE. The Secret Intelligence Service (SIS) claimed its own priorities in areas of Europe clearly earmarked for future invasion, and SOE–SIS relations became particularly problematic. These various claims and interests converged to create a major crisis for SOE in the late winter and early spring. This was surmounted, and SOE received its second directive from the Chiefs of Staff in May. The rest of the year saw the slow development of networks and an increasing number of agents infiltrated into Europe. Evidence began to emerge that Mihailović might be collaborating with the occupying forces, and SOE Cairo began to urge a change of policy towards him. In Greece, an SOE party successfully carried out the Gorgopotamos operation in November, and combined with successful Allied landings in North Africa and the victory at El-Alamein in the same month, this pointed towards the growing significance of guerrilla operations in the Balkans as a new focus for SOE activity in 1943. Throughout Europe, German reverses in the Mediterranean and on the Russian Front produced a mounting tide of European resistance which created an increasingly favourable climate for SOE operations.

I

The entry of the Americans into the war fundamentally changed strategic planning for the final offensive against Germany. In August 1941, British strategic plans were discussed with the Americans during the Roosevelt–Churchill meeting off Newfoundland which resulted in the Atlantic Charter. The British discussion paper, based upon the Joint Planning Staff Review of Future Strategy of June 1941, put forward the familiar triad of blockade, bombing and subversion,[1] but the Americans expressed disappointment at the lack of reference to a major land campaign in Europe beyond the operations in support of a general European uprising. When they finally commented officially on the Review in September 1941, they were critical of the optimistic faith in the bombing offensive and suggested that 'it should be recognised as an almost invariable rule that wars cannot finally be won without the use of land armies. Such land armies would have to be as large as the enemy's.'[2] This was an implicit condemnation of the concept of small landings to support popular risings in Europe. Indeed, on the section of the British paper dealing with subversion, the Americans declined to comment on the grounds that it was insufficiently clear to form the basis of practical campaign plans.

After December, there was clearly no need for the British military planners to insist on their views about this, for the prospect of large American land armies made it unnecessary. There was, of course, considerable disagreement about where and when the final offensive operations should be mounted, but their nature was clear. The possibility of landing forces to equal the Germans', and thus the ability to dispense with the need to depend upon local uprisings, now became so obvious that it hardly needed stating. The idea that the Europeans would liberate themselves aided only by small-scale landings at diverse points withered away slowly after American entry, although it was never formally put to rest. An important step in the process occurred at the Anglo-American staff discussions in Washington in December 1941. The agreed paper outlining the broad features of future strategy omitted a British reference to 'simultaneous landings in several occupied countries of North-Western Europe' as a feature of the final land offensive expected to take place in 1943. Instead, it referred more simply to 'landings in Western Europe'. This minor change in wording concealed a major shift in conceptions and assumptions about the final offensive, for the phrase omitted had long been an integral part of British verbal equipment when talking of the role of secret armies in the final assault on Germany.[3] Churchill himself, indeed, had still been thinking in these terms when he accompanied the Chiefs of Staff to Washington. In a personal paper prepared *en route* he envisaged simultaneous or successive landings of British and American armoured and mechanised forces in three or four European countries. Forces should be strong enough to enable the conquered peoples to revolt, but, he said, 'It need not be assumed that great numbers of men are required. If the incursion of the armoured formation is successful, the uprisings of the local population, for whom weapons must be brought, will supply the corpus of the liberating offensive.'[4] The outcome of the Washington discussions, however, meant that such ideas would not form any part of Anglo-American strategic planning. The invasion of Europe, wherever and whenever it did come, would not be determined in time or space by European revolt. The secret armies might well have an important role to play in assisting landings, but they would not form the 'corpus of the liberating offensive', and if necessary, landings could take place without them. From now on, secret armies were regarded as a bonus, rather than as an essential prerequisite for Allied landing in Europe.

In practical terms, what did all this mean for SOE? In one sense, very little. The Chiefs of Staff had already determined that supplies to equip secret armies in Western Europe should be on a smaller scale than requested by SOE and had suspended judgement on their potential usefulness. The Polish and Czechoslovak armies had been eliminated from consideration. Sabotage as a task for SOE remained unchanged. On the other hand, the Anglo-American decisions in which the envisaged role of the secret armies became peripheral rather than central to liberation, affected SOE's bargaining position, such as it was, for aircraft and supplies, and made it easier for SIS to claim priority over SOE in areas designated for possible invasion. SOE's position might not, in this respect, have been helped by a decision in March that it was safe for it to abandon its 'Claribel' schemes which had been prepared on the instructions of the Chiefs of Staff to cover action to be taken by SOE agents in Norway, Denmark, Holland, Belgium and France in the event of a German invasion of Britain. This meant that SOE planning for these countries was now purely of an offensive nature and on a time scale which was sufficiently long-term for it to have a lower priority than the interests of SIS.[5] In addition, the Anglo-American decisions on a timetable for operations and the beginning of planning for a Second Front prompted some of the Allied governments-in-exile to demand a greater voice in Allied planning at the expense of SOE, and, in some quarters, led to suggestions that its functions should be taken over completely by the Foreign Office and Chiefs of Staff.

The Washington Conference had agreed that the main priority in 1942 should be the protection of the main areas of Allied war industry, *viz.* the USA, the United Kingdom, and the Soviet Union, and the defence of the communications links between them. Offensive operations would consist of 'wearing down and undermining German resistance by air bombardment, blockade, subversive activities and propaganda'. The possibility of any large-scale land offensives against Germany in 1942, except on the eastern front, was considered as remote, but in 1943 'the way may be clear for a return to the Continent, across the Mediterranean, from Turkey into the Balkans, or by landings in Western Europe'. Greater precision was given to this strategy in April, when Marshall and Hopkins visited London and presented the arguments for planning a concentrated invasion of France in 1943—'the only place where the vital air superiority over the hostile land areas . . . can be staged by the United Powers', and permitting the massive concentration of an invasion force in the United Kingdom itself. The Chiefs of Staff accepted the principle of working towards a 1943 invasion, named 'Operation Roundup', and the War Cabinet endorsed this on 29 April 1942.[6] Two weeks later, SOE received its second general directive (see Document Six of the Appendices).

For some while, it had appeared doubtful whether SOE would survive to receive such a directive, for it was in the period January to April that its very existence was being challenged in certain quarters. The Foreign Office discussions and their outcome have been discussed in the previous chapter, but problems also arose from two other quarters. In April, General Sikorski visited Washington, and he returned to London enthused by the prospect of the Second Front which he and Roosevelt had discussed. On 13 April 1942 he suggested to Churchill the immediate formation of a common Allied General Staff to plan and direct operations which he envisaged might take place that year. Sikorski, like the Allied military planners, foresaw the need to intervene in Europe in 1942 in the event of two quite different developments: either the imminent collapse of the Soviet Union, or the defeat of German forces on the eastern front: 'One armoured division thrown on the Continent in 1942', he told Churchill, 'would prove more effective than five such divisions in 1943'. But regardless of the timing, Sikorski said, his proposal held good. A common staff of all the occupied countries should be established 'to prepare plans for the future insurrections of the conquered countries, in co-ordination with the general war plan, and particularly with the plans connected with landings on the continent'. This staff would also be responsible for the preparation of plans for external assistance to the uprisings, for the development of liaison with the occupied countries, for the issuing of directives to the secret armies, for the unification of sabotage and intelligence behind the German lines, and for the supply of arms and equipment.[7]

Behind Sikorski's proposal, which in effect meant that SOE should be abolished and its functions taken over by the proposed general staff, lay considerable Polish resentment against SOE. The Poles were in fact privileged amongst the Allied governments-in-exile in London, in that they were allowed to conduct their own communications with Poland using their own ciphers, and in the more general sense that both politically and militarily they enjoyed considerable prestige. Nonetheless, they were dissatisfied. The decisions of August 1941, by which the Chiefs of Staff had refused equipment for the Polish (and Czech) secret army, had led Sikorski to place the blame on SOE. The Polish general staff felt that it was being denied necessary aircraft, and in particular were annoyed that a request for an independent flight of aircraft exclusively for supplies to Poland had been refused. It is conceivable, too, that the Poles were annoyed at SOE's independent attempts at this time to establish liaison with Polish workers in Northern France.[8]

It is also likely that Sikorski's dissatisfaction was shared by other governments-in-exile and that they too were unhappy with SOE's control over operations into their countries, although they were also suspicious that Sikorski might dominate any such allied staff. Since Dakar, where it was believed (erroneously) that Free French indiscretions in the UK had been responsible for the fiasco, the British had been reluctant to tell *any* government-in-exile details of forthcoming operations. This naturally caused ill-feeling and mistrust. De Gaulle had never accepted the existence of the independent French section of SOE, and had even gone so far as to suggest to Eden in December 1941 that SOE should be dispensed with at least as far as French affairs went. The Norwegian government was also unhappy. Fears of a security nature led SOE throughout 1941 to conduct operations avoiding contact both with the indigenous resistance movement and with the Norwegian government itself. Various commando raids on Norway, leading up to the Second Lofoten Expedition of December 1941, in which SOE took a major part, resulted in heavy German reprisals on the civilian population, and in bitter recriminations in London. In April 1942, while Sikorski's suggestion was still being considered, the German discovery of an SOE sabotage operation at Televag led the Germans to destroy the village completely and deport the adult male population to Germany. The bitter resentment caused by previous SOE operations had already led, in January 1942, to the setting up of an Anglo-Norwegian collaborative committee consisting of SOE and Norwegian High Command representatives which met for the first time in February 1942 and in the long term produced a great improvement in relations; but the events at Televag can only have fed mistrust of SOE.[9] Similarly, relations between SOE and the Belgian government were far from harmonious, in large part because of factional fighting within the latter in which SOE became involved. This had created endless recrimination throughout 1941, and in February 1942 had led to a meeting between M. Pierlot, the Belgian Prime Minister, and senior SOE officials in an attempt to sort things out. This attempt failed. The Belgians, too, therefore were less than happy with SOE at this time.[10] As for the Poles' central European colleagues, Czech relations with SOE appear never to have been very close, and the logistical problems of supplying Czechoslovak resistance may possibly have caused the same resentment as felt by the Poles. On the other hand, it may have been the limited *success* of those SOE operations which did take place that caused the problem, for the Czechoslovak government and military attached little importance to organised sabotage and even tended to discourage it. They saw Czechoslovakia's main task as the provision of intelligence to the Allies, and were largely out of sympathy with SOE's purpose. The dramatic assassination of Heydrich in the following month by agents sent from London, and on the direct order of President Benes himself, was, paradoxically, a confirmation rather than a denial of this. Embarrassed by adverse comments in London about the lack of active Czech resistance and anxious to prove to the Allies that there *was* one and that the government-in-exile was still a force to be reckoned with, Benes sought political capital from the assassination. Lidice was the price the Czechs had to pay.[11]

These examples indicate the kinds of resentments and disagreements which SOE's preparatory operations in 1940–1 had provoked in the minds of the governments-in-exile in London by this time, and of which Sikorski's initiative was only the most extreme example. That they had at the very least expressed some similar discontent, or that similar discontent was perceived by the British government, is indicated by the response to Sikorski's suggestion. Churchill referred it to the Chiefs of

Staff for comment and reply and on 6 May they authorised Sir Alan Brooke, the CIGS, to inform Sikorski that the proposal had been rejected. Brooke subsequently pointed out to Sikorski that the specific functions suggested for the common allied staff were covered by SOE, that SOE co-operation with the military planners permitted activities in occupied Europe to be co-ordinated with the whole war plan, and that the general staffs of the occupied countries should refer all matters in connection with sabotage, secret armies, and the future action of occupied countries to SOE. Brooke, moreover, reiterated the basic decision of August 1941, that 'the physical problem of transporting materials for secret armies in Eastern Europe is insuperable'. Nor, he added, was an airborne invasion of Poland (or Czechoslovakia) from the United Kingdom a practicable possibility in the near future, although in the winter months a limited number of men and supplies could be dropped for 'diversionary activities'.[12]

This reply indicated firmly to Sikorski both that policy towards the Polish resistance remained unchanged, and that SOE would remain in being. As far as the first was concerned, the joint planners, in preparing Brooke's reply, had pointed out that not only was it difficult to supply Poland from the United Kingdom, but also that 'much as the Poles fear Russian intervention, it is Russia who must eventually be the controlling influence directing the tactical action of such armies' (that is, the secret armies in Poland and Czechoslovakia). As far as the second was concerned, the planners had opposed the proposal for a common allied staff on three main grounds. These were (a) that the Poles would probably dominate such an organisation, and that 'agreement within such a heterogeneous body would be extremely difficult to obtain', (b) that security would be impossible, and (c) that 'should agreement be reached within this common allied staff, very heavy pressure would inevitably be brought on the British Government which might well lead to unjustifiable dispersion of effort and the adoption of plans ill-designed to further the course of the war from the broadest point of view'. Instead, therefore, the planners recommended a strengthening of SOE.[13]

These thoughts, penned on 1 May 1942, came immediately after the strategic discussions and agreements relating to Operation Roundup of April, and less than two weeks before SOE's new general directive. Considering that for most of the period since the New Year SOE had been the object of suggestions that it be weakened or even destroyed, the planners' remarks suggested a considerable improvement in its state of health. It would not be unfair to suggest that it was in large part the result of the realisation by SOE's critics that, if it was abolished, its job would have to be done by someone else. As much of this job consisted of dealing with the governments-in-exile (at least in operational matters), who were often from the British viewpoint awkward, infuriating, and time-consuming, no-one, when it came to the breaking point, wished to take it on. For all that SOE appeared to the Foreign Office and Chiefs of Staff as an unruly sixth-form schoolboy unable to keep his grubby fingers off the tablecloth while constantly demanding second helpings when there were none, they were forced to recognise that he was indispensable in keeping the smaller boys in order. The Foreign Office recognised this in signing its 'treaty' with SOE in May; and the Chiefs of Staff recognised it in replying to Sikorski and in giving SOE their own directive on 12 May. Shortly afterwards, on 2 June 1942, they agreed that the substance of Brooke's reply to Sikorski should be sent to all the governments-in-exile, and to the Free French; and in addition it was sent to all commanders-in-chief abroad. This represented a considerable victory for SOE, and its survival was assured for at least another eighteen months, when yet another attempt took place to curtail or abolish it (see below, Chapter 5). It was in May 1942, too, that a major enquiry into the organisation and functioning of SOE conducted by a high Treasury official concluded that while its relations with other Government departments left a good deal to be desired, SOE was 'quite as much sinned against as sinning'. It thereby cleared SOE of some of the most serious allegations which had been made against it by critics who saw Dalton's disappearance as an opportunity to rid themselves of the organisation.[14]

The interests of intelligence collection and of sabotage and subversion were often incompatible. SOE, representing the latter, and as an organisation without a past or a future, had often come into conflict with its senior and well-established parent, the Secret Intelligence Service. Concurrent with the resolution of SOE's relations with the Chiefs of Staff, Foreign Office, and governments-in-exile, and related to them, arose the problem of SOE–SIS relations. With a Second Front now on the active agenda the relative priority of SOE and SIS operations in any given area was of more importance than ever, and close co-operation and consultation was required. On 1 May 1942—the day that the planners had recommended that SOE should be strengthened—the Chiefs of Staff discussed a report by the Joint Intelligence Committee (JIC) on SOE–SIS co-ordination in view of possible forthcoming operations on the Continent. This report recommended closer co-ordination between SOE, SIS and CCO (Combined Operations), but highlighted one of the

major problems in pointing out that since their interests often conflicted
it was difficult for these organisations themselves to come to agreement.
The JIC therefore recommended that until machinery could be set up to
do this the Chiefs of Staff should appoint an arbitrator to decide such
issues. More important from SOE's point of view, however, was the observation that

> The activities of SOE increase the alertness of the local authorities
> and greatly hamper the work of our intelligence. It is necessary that
> such activities should be avoided in areas where this adverse effect
> outweighs the results which these activities may be expected to pro-
> duce. This applies especially to areas where larger operations are
> likely to take place.

In short, the JIC was recommending that in the potential invasion areas
SIS interests should predominate.[15]

The Chiefs of Staff called for suggestions for an arbitration machinery and a conciliator to mediate SOE–SIS disputes to be appointed. But
it collapsed almost immediately, an indication of the depth of mutual
hostility. SIS furthermore was given priority over SOE in most of Western Europe. Already in April the priority granted to intelligence over
sabotage had led to a slowdown in sabotage in Denmark, and the fact
that for the whole period of the war more SIS than SOE agents were
infiltrated into Belgium is suggestive.[16] Indeed, the next year's directive
from the Chiefs of Staff, issued in May 1943, specifically stated that
'The requirements of SIS should in general be accorded priority over
your own operations in Norway, Sweden, France and the Low Countries, and . . . on the mainland of Italy and in Sicily'. This rule also applied for 1942. It was slightly ironic, perhaps, that it was in this same
month that SOE finally became independent of SIS for its communications.

The 1942 directive was issued to SOE on 12 May. Entitled 'SOE Collaboration in Operations on the Continent' it outlined the strategic
decisions for 1942 and 1943 approved by the War Cabinet and directed
SOE to 'endeavour to build up and equip para-military organisations in
the area of projected operations', while simultaneously taking particular care to avoid premature large-scale risings of patriots. The actions of
the resistance movements were envisaged in terms of two stages, co-
operation during the initial assault, and tasks after landing. The second
stage was later discarded, but in the first, the tasks would be (a) to prevent the arrival of enemy reinforcements by the interruption of road,

rail, and air transport, (b) to interrupt signal communications in and behind the battle area generally, (c) to prevent enemy demolitions, (d) to carry out attacks on enemy aircraft and air personnel, and (e) to disorganise enemy movements and support services by the spreading of rumours.[17]

If any further proof were needed this 1942 directive indicated the extent to which SOE operations in Western Europe had become integrated with military strategy as laid down by the Chiefs of Staff, and had ceased to be part—if they ever had been—of an independent 'fourth arm' strategy. From now on SOE operations in Western Europe were to be directed primarily to assisting the Allied invasion, which at this time was being envisaged for 1943, in other words, within a year. The injunction to avoid premature uprisings merely spelled out formally what had been *de facto* policy since SOE was established. But its reaffirmation was significant, for it reflected the concern of many of the Allied governments-in-exile. It enabled SOE's new ministerial head, Lord Selborne, for example, to tell Dr Gerbrandy, the Dutch Prime Minister, and Prince Bernhard, only three days after the issuing of the directive, that 'the purpose of SOE was to build up a disciplined force in Holland. We did not seek purposeless explosions: in fact they were the last thing we wanted, except for any special reason. Our hope would be to build up the force as quietly as possible to function when the balloon went up'.[18]

One final additional directive needs to be noted before passing on to look at SOE operations for the remainder of 1942. This was the directive on subversion in North Africa, approved by the Chiefs of Staff simultaneously with that on operations on the Continent. As this intimately concerned policy towards France and the Vichy régime it deserves consideration, especially in view of the subsequent North African landings in November 1942 which led to the German occupation of Vichy France and the development of the 'Mediterranean Strategy' in 1943. The background to the directive was Churchill's plan for operations against French North Africa, which he had been pursuing since late 1941. This 'Operation Gymnast' has been placed on the back shelf by the agreements made during the Marshall–Hopkins visit, but Churchill himself kept it very much in mind. When it finally became clear in the summer of 1942 that no action could take place in Europe to satisfy either the Russian demand for a Second Front or Roosevelt's political requirements for the use in 1942 of American ground troops, Churchill and Roosevelt managed to force its resurrection and reincarnation as Operation Torch. In May 1942, however, Gymnast–Torch was not any part of agreed Allied strategy, and it is therefore all the more interesting that the Chiefs of Staff should have issued SOE with a directive clearly designed to aid such an operation. It was long and detailed, but in essence consisted of four main objectives.[19] These were:

1. To prepare the ground for a negotiated agreement with French authorities of sufficient standing to ensure the entry and favourable reception of Allied forces in French North Africa. In pursuit of this agreement, SOE was authorised to inform the French authorities 'that, in the event of a secret agreement being reached they will be under no obligation to serve under General de Gaulle or the Free French National Committee'.
2. To ensure resistance by the French in the event of an Axis attack on French North Africa.
3. To stiffen French resistance in the meantime to Axis penetration.
4. To guard against premature action by patriots.

Additional sections of the directive instructed SOE to avoid any promises of postwar independence to the 'Moorish population', and 'to maintain the closest touch with SIS at all times to ensure that your respective activities do not clash'. This latter recommendation echoed Eden's concern that because accurate information about French intentions was vital, no action which might disturb SIS contacts should be undertaken. Here, too, SOE interest had to yield place to those of SIS.[20] The directive did not initiate British secret operations in French North Africa, for SOE was already in touch with dissident elements through its bases in Gibralter and Tangiers, and SIS had been stepping beyond the bounds of normal intelligence gathering to indulge in active operations of its own. In April 1942, indeed, SOE in North Africa had been approached by the French group already in touch with the American Office of Strategic Services (OSS) with a view to opening negotiations for an agreement with the British.[21] But it now tied SOE operations in with broader strategic directives and once more made it clear that SOE was to be subordinated to the needs of the Foreign Office and of SIS. It also indicated the extent to which SOE French operations were still being planned independently of the Gaullists, and may well in this case have reflected the profound antipathy to de Gaulle within the OSS. By the time that operation Gymnast–Torch became official Allied strategy, indeed, it had been agreed that OSS should take the lead in subversive operations in this area, the result of a wider SOE–OSS agreement reached in June 1942 and negotiated in

London. The agreement specified worldwide 'spheres of influence' for subversive operations, and under its terms, OSS took primary responsibility for subversion in North Africa, China, Korea, the South Pacific and Finland, while SOE was to take India, West Africa, the Balkans, and the Middle East. Responsibility for Western Europe was to be shared equally. This marked the formal inauguration of a relationship which reflected wider political tensions between the two Allies. There was close co-operation and integration in preparation for the Normandy landings, but elsewhere there was much mutual distrust over operations in Africa, Latin America, the Middle East and the Far East. Liaison on technical matters produced useful results, but operationally the two organisations tended to go their own way. Sweet-Escott, who spent several months in Washington in 1942–43 liaising with the OSS, found the experience demoralising. In general SOE–OSS relations were a microcosm of 'the sense of historic antagonism (which) continued to exist along with the spirit of co-operation generated by the war' so amply demonstrated in Anglo-American discussions about the future role of the British Empire in world affairs.[22]

By the end of June 1942, therefore, SOE had survived six months of turbulence including attempts to abolish it, and a major ministerial change. Anglo-American strategy had been under vigorous discussion, but it had been agreed in April that major offensive operations against Europe would not take place until 1943. In July, Roosevelt and Churchill agreed on Operation Torch—the landings in North Africa. With the strategic framework set at least for the short-term, SOE operations could be focused more firmly on aiding Allied objectives.

II

Both Operation Roundup and Operation Torch directed Allied attention towards France. What were British views towards the French situation, and how did this affect SOE French policy?

British policy towards France throughout 1941 had consisted of the threefold aim of hoping for and working towards a change in Vichy policy, of supporting all forms of resistance in France, whether Gaullist or not, and of supporting de Gaulle's Free French movement (renamed 'Fighting France' in the summer of 1942) as the symbol of resistance. The return to office in April 1942 of Pierre Laval, the very symbol of Vichy–German collaboration, led to a reassessment of this policy. Eden and the Foreign Office were by now quite sceptical of any change on the part of Vichy in the direction favourable to the Allies. Churchill, however, was more optimistic and less condemnatory of the Vichy leaders. He argued in June 1942 that, despite Laval's return to office, the slow but steady change in French opinion against the Germans, combined with American intervention and the certainty of Allied victory, might well lead to a sudden and decisive change in Vichy policy in favour of the Allies. In any case, Churchill said, only Vichy could deliver what the British and the Americans wanted, which was 'an invitation for British and American troops to enter French North Africa'.[23]

British policy towards Vichy, de Gaulle, and resistance in France in 1942 must be seen against the background of this objective. In telling Eden that 'There is much more in British policy towards France than abusing Pétain and backing de Gaulle . . .', Churchill had in mind the consideration of *realpolitik* dictated by Anglo-American strategic plans for landings in North Africa. Already, in April 1942, the Joint Planning Staff had concluded that the 'establishment' in French North Africa would remain loyal to Vichy, and, as we have seen, SOE's May directive on North Africa was based on the assumption that it was with them that an agreement would be made permitting the entry of Allied troops. In this context, SOE's relations with de Gaulle and with French resistance groups remained complex and troubled. De Gaulle was resentful of the existence of the 'independent' F section of SOE, and refused to acknowledge its existence. He had tried in December 1941 to bypass SOE altogether, and he made another try in July 1942. On 25 July he formally requested that the Free French should be associated in preparations for future offensive operations. In essence, this was a revival of the 'Sikorski plan' of April. The Chiefs of Staff were opposed to this, and on 20 August the War Cabinet supported them. They did, however, suggest that SOE could collaborate more closely with de Gaulle in regard to organising secret preparatory action in France, although they were adamant that control should not be handed over to him. As a result, a new co-ordinating committee was set up to link SOE and Free French activities.[24]

On SOE's side, attitudes towards de Gaulle remained ambivalent. On the one hand, initial mistrust had given way to a more positive attitude. Dalton, for example, had initially viewed de Gaulle with the same dislike that the French left (or most of it) had had for generals in politics since the days of General Boulanger in the nineteenth century, while Attlee had described de Gaulle and his entourage in July 1940 as practically fascist. Gradually this had changed, and by the beginning of 1942 there was considerable respect within SOE for de Gaulle as a symbol of

French resistance. The crucial point, however, was that he was regarded *only* as a symbol. No-one believed that it was through exclusive support of de Gaulle alone that the resistance in France could be mobilised. Sir Stewart Menzies, the head of SIS, told Sir Frank Nelson early in January 1942 that 'de Gaulle had not a great following but only a symbolic value', and this view was shared by firmer friends of de Gaulle than Menzies within SOE. Gubbins, who was eventually to succeed to Nelson's post as 'CD,' or Executive Director of SOE, and who since 1941 had, in Foot's words 'become a firm gaullist,' expressed the view only two weeks after Menzies' comment that 'it is clear that we cannot build up a proper secret army in France under the *aegis* or flag of de Gaulle; that we must do so through our independent French section until such time as a combination is practical politics'. To Gubbins, the whole point of SOE activity in France was that 'when the invasion came we would have men there to attack and cut communications and generally hinder German action. This would be of real benefit at the critical moment, even if the Germans were only held up for forty-eight hours'.[25] It is likely that in some part these views reflected the crisis in Anglo–Free French relations provoked in December 1941 by the occupation of St Pierre and Miquelon, but as 1942 unfolded the view found striking confirmation in SOE's eyes when the agents of F section began to report the existence of a major resistance network in unoccupied France which enjoyed close links with elements in the Armistice Army. This was the *Carte* network.

According to Foot, *Carte*'s existence exercised a dominating influence over F section's work throughout 1942. *Carte* was the code name for André Girard, a painter who lived in Antibes. He claimed to have established widespread contacts within the Armistice Army, and argued that with adequate preparation the *Carte* network in unoccupied France could muster a private army of 300,000 men that would at the right moment join with the Armistice Army and help liberate France. Most of Girard's claims were imaginary, and the security of the network was appalling. In November 1942 the names of 200 of its most important members fell into the hands of the Abwehr when a courier fell asleep on a train and a German agent walked off with his briefcase, and it was only a short while before the organisation was broken up. Nevertheless, throughout the preceding months the prospect of mobilising *Carte* as a readymade French secret army mesmerised SOE. Its attraction was obvious, for it fitted in perfectly both with Britain's strategic requirements, and with the view that in some way or another only Vichy-related elements could deliver the goods. On the very day of the Chiefs of Staff directives to SOE on collaboration with operations on the Continent and subversive activities in North Africa—12 May 1942—Sir Alan Brooke recorded the view that 'I do not . . . consider that General de Gaulle is in a position to bring in the French army in unoccupied France on our side. On the contrary, I consider that any attempt to link up the Free French with action by the French General Staff . . . would be disastrous'.[26] In SOE's view, *Carte* could do what de Gaulle could not. In August two top SOE agents were sent to France to bring back full details of the organisation, and they reported on it enthusiastically in the second half of September. Shortly afterwards, on 16 October 1942, the whole matter was discussed by the Chiefs of Staff.[27] Although little could be done to increase supplies the Chiefs of Staff were enthusiastic, and they agreed that two broadcasters designated by Girard could broadcast to France using a PWE short-wave transmitter. In the event, it very quickly became clear that the advantages of dealing with *Carte* were imaginary. On 8 November Anglo-American forces landed in French North Africa, the Germans retaliated by occupying the Vichy zone of metropolitan France, and the Armistice Army did nothing. Shortly afterwards, *Carte* itself was broken up and all of F section's high hopes dissolved. The episode is, however, of significance. *Carte* had appealed to so many people both within SOE and amongst the professional military staff because of its quasi-military character. It was believed to be disciplined, hierarchical, and in close contact with professional French soldiers. It claimed to be apolitical, and could easily be co-ordinated with Allied military strategy. In short, it was apparently every professional soldier's dream of what a secret army should be.

If SOE's direct contacts with France in 1942 came to little, much the same is true for their contacts with Belgium and the Netherlands. Here, indeed, was a story of disasters all around. SOE's problems with the Belgian government-in-exile have already been mentioned. Following the unsuccessful meeting of February 1942 between Pierlot and senior SOE officials, SOE–Belgian relations worsened. The main problem was that there were two bodies within the government-in-exile claiming authority over resistance matters, the *Sureté de l'Etat*, which reported directly to Pierlot, the Prime Minister, and the *Deuxième Section* of the Belgian Army, under the Minister of Defence. Complicating that were conflicting attitudes and loyalties to the Belgian king, Leopold, who had remained in Belgium, and the perennial conflict over resistance strategy. As Sweet-Escott later recalled, 'the Belgian problem consisted of reconciling the wishes of the Belgian authorities in London, who wanted to keep any organisation there was in Belgium intact till D-day, with the need of SOE to justify itself in the eyes of the British authorities who provided the facilities and naturally wanted quick dividends'.[28] On 4 June 1942 a top-level meeting between Eden and Spaak, the Belgian Foreign Minister, failed to solve the issues, as did a meeting a month later between Selborne and Spaak. A month after that, indeed, Spaak broke off all relations with SOE. The crisis was taken to the Chiefs of Staff in October 1942, and eventually some sort of *modus vivendi* was established. But these problems of liaison at the top level had an inevitable effect on operations in 1942. It was difficult enough to operate in Belgium (as in the Netherlands) because of the closely guarded coastline, the density of German air defence and security surveillance, and the thickly populated countryside. The political disputes and rivalries made things worse. Early in 1942 there was a rash of arrests, W/T sets were captured by the Germans, and these were successfully played back to Britain, with the result that for most of 1942 the SOE Belgian networks were completely penetrated by the enemy. Improvements came only in 1943.[29]

The Netherlands, however, presented the worst—and the most notorious—case of German penetration of SOE networks. SOE agents had been dropped into the Netherlands in 1941 for specific sabotage tasks, but it was not until the spring of 1942 that there existed an agreed framework for secret army operations. This was the 'Plan for Holland' of April 1942, drawn up by SOE and approved by the government-in-exile in the context of the spring strategic decisions. The plan was 'to build up an armed resistance organisation of over one thousand men who would lie low until the hour of invasion had struck'. This organisation would work closely with the *Orde Dienst*, one of the first organised Dutch resistance movements, and open sabotage was to be discouraged. The first agents to be dropped to carry out this plan left in June 1942, but, unknown to SOE, the Germans had already penetrated the existing networks and 'turned around' a W/T set and its operator. The results are too well known to need recapitulation, except to say that until the British realised what was happening, in the autumn of 1943, the so-called *Englandspiel* led to forty-three of the fifty-six despatched agents falling into German hands, of whom thirty-six were executed; all supplies dropped into German hands.[30] Allegations since the war have suggested that this whole operation was part of a cold-blooded deception campaign by the British to convince the Germans that an invasion on the Continent was imminent. There *were* deception campaigns in 1942, but there is no evidence to suggest that this was part of one. It was, instead, the result of carelessness within SOE, and, when discovered, severely damaged SOE's standing and credibility within the British war machinery; indeed, the episode almost led to SOE's abolition, as will be seen in Chapter 5. For the moment, however, SOE's disasters in the Netherlands in 1942 can be seen alongside failures in Belgium and France as evidence of the paucity of achievement—not always through its own fault—in Western Europe. The inability of the Allies to mount a Second Front in Europe in 1942 was matched by the inability of all concerned to create the accompanying secret armies which were still seen by the official strategists as having a role to play in liberation.

III

If 1942 was the year in which SOE ran networks in Belgium and Holland which were in fact mostly in German control, and built their hopes on an organisation in France whose potential turned out to be totally illusory (*Carte*), it was also the year in which it gradually became clear that the hero of Balkan resistance, General Mihailović, was also an illusion.[31]

Mihailović had been warmly embraced by the British government and other allies as the heroic symbol of European resistance to Nazism, and SOE had established a direct link with him in September 1941. Since then, however, it had been difficult for SOE to find out exactly *what* Mihailović's resistance activities entailed. Appointed Minister of War by the Yugoslav government-in-exile in November 1941, Mihailović, through his government, made expansive claims for his resistance activities. Unfortunately, however, SOE had lost contact with Hudson and could make no independent verification of these claims. Rumours grew, however, that far from leading active resistance against the Axis powers Mihailović was collaborating with the Italians in order to turn his main attention against his domestic opponents, the Partisans. On 7 August 1942 Maisky, the Soviet Ambassador in London, communicated an official Soviet note denouncing Mihailović's collaboration with the Italians.[32] This began a controversy which has continued to this day and over which historians have spilled much ink. There is now little doubt that Mihailović's forces were reaching agreements with the Italians in order to focus on anti-Partisan activity, and that they were carrying out very little sabotage or active resistance activity. The main question which has exercised British historians has been that of discovering why, once evidence of this collaboration came to light, SOE continued to back Mihailović for so long, and why, conversely, it took them so long to contact Tito and his Partisans who were fighting the Axis. It was not until May 1943, indeed, that a mission was dropped to Tito, and not until 1944 that all support for Mihailović was dropped. It has been suggested that the British were primarily motivated by political concerns, and even that there was a deliberate suppression of information about the effectiveness of partisan (that is communist) resistance activity. A clear case, it is argued, of anti-communism within the reactionary or conservative war leadership and amongst the military professionals. How true is this?

The original decision of the autumn of 1941 to throw support behind Mihailović has been made on the assumption that *all* Yugoslav patriots would unite behind him, including the communists, and that he could be persuaded to carry out suggestions for action made by the British through SOE headquarters in the Middle East (SOE Cairo). The Soviet note of August 1942 was hardly sufficient ground to reverse this policy because, if the report of Chetnik–Partisan conflict were true, denunciations of Mihailović by the communists could be expected as ritual propaganda and therefore not to be trusted without independent verification. It was decided to find out more from Major Hudson—with whom SOE Cairo was now in contact again—in order to verify or contradict the Soviet allegations. If they were true, however, this would not necessarily lead to immediate abandonment of Mihailović; instead efforts would be made to change his mind and bring about a reconciliation with the partisans. Hudson's reports were confused, however, and anyway after his long silence it was not completely certain that they were geniune. The decision was made in October 1942, therefore to send out another officer to Mihailović's headquarters to find out exactly what was happening. This was Colonel Bailey, who was finally dropped by parachute to Mihailović's headquarters on Christmas Day 1942. In the period between the decision to send him to Yugoslavia, and his first reports early in 1943, attempts had been made from a distance to persuade Mihailović to change his alleged policy. In September, General Alexander sent a direct message asking Chetnik forces to attack Axis lines of communication (to help Allied operations in North Africa), and in October the BBC was authorised to mention favourably partisan action in Yugoslavia—with the hope that this would provoke Mihailović into doing something himself. Neither of these approaches worked, and in mid-November an SOE appreciation reported that '. . . so far no telegrams have been received . . . reporting any sabotage undertaken by General Mihailović, nor have we received any reports of fighting against the Axis troops'.[33] It was exactly one year since SOE had presented him as the resistance hero of Europe.

It is clear that for long-term political reasons the Foreign Office supported Mihailović—the representative of the Yugoslav government-in-exile—from the moment he emerged in the autumn of 1941. They did so because they saw him as a barrier against a future communist Yugoslavia. Eden told Churchill on 17 December 1942 that on a long-term view he believed 'that we should be wise to go on supporting Mihailović in order to prevent anarchy and Communist chaos after the war', and early in January Foreign Office officials were expressing their concern to the Americans in London about partisan activities and the future communisation of Yugoslavia.[34] This political view coincided with the Chiefs of Staff's views of Mihailović's resistance strategy, which had a logic and justification of their own. Whatever Mihailović's views against sabotage, he had always maintained that when the time came and Yugoslavia was liberated he would rise up against the Germans. As early as June 1941 he had said that his strategy was 'to organise, not to fight, and when the Germans begin to withdraw, then to move in and seize power', a resistance strategy which one SOE officer dropped to the Chetniks described as rooted in a 'Salonika front fixation'—the belief that the Allies would land in the Balkans in force, as they had done in the First World War. Hudson reported Mihailović's view on 15 November 1942: 'When the General is satisfied that victory is certain, blood will not be spared.'[35] Until then, however, he would not be responsible for an activist policy resulting in massive reprisals against the civilian population (a German High Command directive of 1941 decreed that 50 to 100 hostages should be shot for every German soldier killed—and the Germans showed no hesitation in carrying out the order). This 'secret army' concept reflected Chiefs of Staff directives, and on 2 June 1942 Brooke, the CIGS, forwarded a memorandum to Churchill in which partisan action was deplored because

> they drive the more moderate opponents of the Axis into co-operation with any power that can restore a semblance of law and order. Although the activity of these wilder elements in the country will always necessitate considerable Axis garrisons, the policy of Mihailović to curb their activities in order to conserve his potential forces and to wait until his time is right.[36]

Whatever political prejudices and fears may or may not have lain behind Brooke's position, it reflected the military fact that in 1942 resistance in Yugoslavia was, from the British viewpoint, a secondary sideshow which could be supported only minimally. As long as Yugoslavia was of peripheral strategic importance, there was no advantage to be gained from abandoning Mihailović who was pursuing a 'quietist' resistance strategy which was in tune with general British policy throughout Europe. There was, therefore, a sound military reason for taking this line independent of longer-term views of Yugoslavia's political fate. From this perspective SOE in Cairo was not opposed to letting Mihailović reach local accommodation with the Italians in Montenegro as a means of obtaining Italian supplies which could, on Allied instructions from outside the country, be turned against the Axis. Contact with the Italians was not in itself grounds for condemning Mihailović unless it could be proven that it was done for purposes of attacking the partisans. Even when a clearer picture emerged, however, this in itself was not sufficient to change British policy. What became crucial then was that the Foreign Office and Chiefs of Staff interests moved in a direction which pointed to the need for a change in policy; the Foreign Office found exclusive support for Mihailović an embarrassment in Anglo-Soviet relations, and the Chiefs of Staff radically changed their views on their strategic requirements in the Balkans, a decision which in turn reflected wider strategic developments which will be examined in the next chapter. Information about partisan activity available through intercepts of enemy wireless traffic was not widely available, and SOE seems not to have received it until 1943. But that this was explicable by purely political motives, and that it would have made any difference, seems unlikely.

If results in Yugoslavia by the end of 1942 were meagre, neighbouring Greece appeared to be more promising. It was here in November 1942 that SOE scored its greatest success in an otherwise bleak year. As in Yugoslavia, SOE networks and contacts had been broken by the Balkan *débâcle* of April–May 1941, but with one important exception. SOE remained in wireless contact with a group of republican officers, and by the end of 1941 were also in touch with communists. SOE hoped to create a united front in Greece against the Germans (as in Yugoslavia) and very soon came to the conclusion that if this was to succeed, the Greek king, who had accompanied the government into exile, must be persuaded to promise that after the war Greece would return to a constitutional monarchy. Otherwise, SOE feared, the Greek monarchy would become a cause of division rather than unity. The cause of this fear was that the king was far too closely identified with the prewar Metaxas dictatorship and régime (Metaxas had died only in January 1941) in which the Venizelists (followers of the former pro-Allied Prime

Minister of Greece in the First World War) had been excluded from office. Indeed, SOE policy in Greece even before the German invasion had been to seek the return to Greece of exiled politicans and 'to bring people of Venizelist sympathies in line with the . . . régime'.[37]

The problem was that the Greek king and his government refused to go along with this and the Foreign Office was not prepared to force him to change his mind. Throughout 1942, therefore, the seeds were sown of a bitter political conflict which was to come to a head in 1943. The king would not yield, the Foreign Office pleaded in vain, and SOE became the object of both of their suspicions. Meanwhile, in Greece itself, the grounds for civil war were being prepared. By the summer of 1942 there were two major resistance movements in Greece carrying out guerrilla activity, both formed in September 1941. These were EAM, the National Liberation Front, founded by the communists, and EDES, the National Republic Greek League, which, as its title indicated, was opposed to the return of the monarchy. Its leader in Greece, Colonel Zervas, took to the hills in July 1942 to begin guerrilla warfare, and both he and EAM were receiving British financial and other aid. SOE's general objective in Greece up to this point had been laid down by the Chiefs of Staff. This was, while carrying out small-scale sabotage wherever possible, to work for the preparation and supply of a national revolt when, but only when 'the time was ripe'. In other words, SOE policy in Greece in 1941–42 was similar to that elsewhere in Europe. Paradoxically, however, the first SOE mission to go to mainland Greece was despatched for more spectacular purposes. On 30 September 1942 a twelve-man SOE mission was parachuted into Greece to carry out 'Operation Harling'. This had been requested by Middle East Command, and its target was the Gorgopotamos viaduct which carried the only railway line from southern Greece into the rest of Europe—a vital German supply line, which, if broken, could severely affect German supplies across the Mediterranean to North Africa. The operation was specifically conceived in the context of the Torch landings, and it was dramatically successful. Working with groups belonging to both ELAS (the military wing of EAM), and EDES, the mission destroyed the viaduct on 25 November 1942, putting the railway out of action for thirty-nine days.

The success of Operation Harling had profound effects. In the later words of the then Major Woodhouse, who took part in the operation, 'in the military context, it showed for the first time in occupied Europe that guerrillas, with the support of Allied officers, could carry out a major tactical operation co-ordinated with Allied strategic plans. It stimulated ambitious plans for developing Resistance, primarily in Greece, but also elsewhere'.[38] The possibilities of guerrilla action placed at the service of Allied strategy were indeed to exercise a fascination for Britain's military leaders in the following months, and as a result SOE activities in the Balkans assumed great significance in 1943. With guerrilla warfare came civil war, however, and both in Greece and Yugoslavia short-term strategic requirements were to come in ever-increasing conflict with Britain's postwar political aims.

IV

Two of the main keynotes of SOE policy towards European resistance in 1942 had been the avoidance of premature uprisings and the minimisation of the risk of civilian reprisals, and the close co-ordination of operations with strategic objectives. One further example of each may be given here before concluding this review of developments in 1942.

Early in the summer of 1942 Churchill's enthusiasm was fired by a reading of John Steinbeck's novel *The Moon is Down*, the story of resistance to the Germans in a Norwegian village. Could this be repeated all over Europe, Churchill wondered, if small arms and sabotage material were dropped on a massive scale to the civilian population? He addressed a direct memorandum to Lord Selborne requesting SOE to study the matter. Dalton had complained in October 1941 that Churchill did not 'focus well' on SOE affairs. Selborne would have been justified in taking the same view, for it should have been obvious to Churchill had he been focusing at all on the question that SOE policy had been to discourage isolated and undirected civilian direct action resistance for fear of provoking German reprisals. Selborne's reply to the Prime Minister was in accordance with this policy, and he recommended against it to the Chiefs of Staff when they considered it in August. Such a programme should only be embarked on, Selborne said, on the eve of Allied landings in Europe when it could help in railway sabotage and when the arrival of Allied forces would protect civilians against reprisals.[39] But part of Churchill's scheme *was* accepted, and that was the dropping of incendiary devices into Germany and Italy in the hope that they could be used by anti-Nazis and foreign workers against Axis factories. Such a scheme had in fact been proposed a year before, when Cherwell conceived it as part of a desperate remedy to sabotage the German war economy after it had become apparent that strategic bombing was not working. The Chiefs of Staff approved this part of Churchill's plan on 20 September, although the air staff effectively obstructed it until at least as late as the spring of 1943.[40]

If the SOE reaction to Churchill's enthusiasm reveals their caution in the matter of provoking reprisals against civilians and focusing attention on operations at the hour of liberation, two plans submitted by them to the Chiefs of Staff in late September/early October, illustrate how SOE operations were designed and timed to assist regular military operations. On 23 September 1942 SOE representatives laid before the Chiefs of Staff a plan for sabotage against the Belgian railways to help delay German troop movements into unoccupied France should the Germans retaliate in this way—as they did—against the North African landings. Alternatively, SOE suggested, a less comprehensive but similar plan might act as part of a deception campaign to aid the landings. Similarly, on 21 October, SOE presented a plan for railway sabotage in both zones in France, also in connection with Operation Torch, the object being to hamper rail movement to the French and Spanish Mediterranean coasts.[41] The Belgian plan was accepted, but that for attacks on communication into Spain was deferred until the threat of a German advance into Spain appeared more imminent.

It has been seen earlier how in June 1942 OSS and SOE came to an agreement on operational spheres of influence, and how it was agreed that Western Europe should be shared equally. In September a more important step was taken. The West European sections of OSS and SOE in London were fused, under the formal title of SOE–SO, though in practice it remained predominantly British, and for convenience's sake it will still be referred to here as SOE. American officers were now introduced into SOE sections, with some predictable results in terms of human relations. It meant, however, that so far as Western Europe was concerned there was on the whole a joint Anglo-American effort in the field of subversive warfare. SOE–SO became known as Special Force Headquarters (SFHQ) as from 1 May 1944.

On this note of Anglo-American co-ordination for Western Europe on the eve of the Torch landings in North Africa, it is convenient to finish this survey of SOE affairs in Europe for 1942. The verdict must be mixed. SOE was growing rapidly in size—by July it had a United Kingdom staff of over 2000 and a Middle East staff of over 600—it now controlled its own communications, and it had survived various onslaughts on its position in the early part of the year. Like the British war effort as a whole, however, most of the year was unspectacular, and it was not until November that an unequivocal success could be pointed to— Operation Harling, the destruction of the Gorgopotamos viaduct in

Greece. This, coinciding so closely as it did with the success at El-Alamein and the North African landings, pointed forward to a more positive achievement in 1943 when the strategic initiative passed to the Allies. With the achievement of close co-ordination of SOE activities with the requirements of military operations, SOE entered the second main phase of its existence.

5 A Year of Troubles

The Anglo-American landings in North Africa in November 1942 meant that there would be no cross-Channel invasion in 1943 and that the focus of the Allied offensive for that year would be in the Mediterranean. In this framework, allied strategists seized upon resistance in the Balkans, in particular in Greece and Yugoslavia, as a powerful auxiliary to regular military operations. Here, guerrilla warfare was intensifying in response to both internal and external factors, and its support by SOE as a means both of wearing down Axis strength, and of creating confusion about Allied intentions, assumed major significance. The increasing scale of European resistance in 1943 and SOE's growing involvement with it caused, however, profound difficulties. The strategy of preventing premature uprisings and concentrating on the build-up of secret armies, combined with the long delay before Allied landings took place, produced morale problems in the resistance and helped the Germans to make some spectacular gains against them. The guerrilla campaigns in the Balkans encompassed a struggle for postwar political influence between communists and non-communists, so that strategic objectives on the British side became inextricably linked with longer-term political objectives. The demand for increased material support to resistance brought the dispute over the allocation of aircraft to SOE to a head, while the political complexities led to major clashes between SOE and the Foreign Office in the early autumn. To cap it all, the revelation of German penetration of SOE networks in parts of Western Europe provided the ever-jealous SIS and Foreign Office mandarins with yet another stick with which to beat SOE. This led, in late 1943, to another massive attack on SOE's existence, which was only successfully overcome by Churchill's direct intervention on its behalf. From January 1944 onwards, however, SOE was safe from further onslaught, and could concentrate on what had

103

been its original prime objective—assistance in the liberation of Europe.

I

Between the decision to launch Operation Torch and the meeting of Roosevelt and Churchill at Casablanca in January 1943, intensive discussions about the shape of future allied strategy had taken place. These discussions, out of which emerged the so-called 'Mediterranean strategy', need not concern us in great detail, but some of their salient features need to be noted as they provide points of reference for SOE operations in 1943 and furnish the background for its 1943 directive.

As early as 30 October 1942, the joint planners had provided the Chiefs of Staff with a report on future American–British strategy for 1943 which omitted any reference to a cross-Channel invasion. Instead, the planners stressed the need to support Russian land operations by an intensification of the bombing offensive, and by a general tightening of the ring around Germany. On the possibilities of subversive action, they struck a sober note. Stressing the problems created by the fear of German reprisals, and the once-and-for-all nature of resistance uprisings, they concluded that there was 'no prospect of setting alight the patriot organisations in Western Europe on a big scale, in the absence of an Allied invasion'. Instead, a steadily increasing programme of sabotage should be entered upon in this area. They did, however, suggest a more concentrated programme of sabotage in Poland and the Balkans to coincide with the opening of a fresh German campaign in Russia in April or May 1943. The significance of Balkan resistance was pinpointed in a separate report on Mediterranean strategy. This concluded that there was 'great scope for guerrilla activities and the intensification of sabotage; both might affect Axis oil supplies from Rumania and Axis land and sea communications with their new sources of supply in Russia'. This was in the context of a renewed focus on Italy, with recommendations that either Sardinia or Sicily should become invasion objectives after the clearing of the North African coastline. The effect that increased Balkan resistance would have on the Italians as well as on the Germans was not to be underestimated, and in December the joint planners specifically drew attention to subversive activities in the Balkans as one of several methods by which an Italian collapse could be hastened.[1]

These ideas, many of which were embodied in the official memoranda on future strategy taken by the Chiefs of Staff to Casablanca, indicated the increasing importance in British eyes of the resistance movements in Yugoslavia, Greece, and Albania. 'We must,' the Chiefs of Staff told the Americans, 'give increased assistance to the insurgents in Yugoslavia and stimulate sabotage in Greece, since in both countries the garrisons are largely Italian.' They argued that the encouragement of intensified action would, in combination with other activities, help to produce an Italian collapse; at that point the Germans would be forced to garrison both Italy and the Balkans, with devastating effects on the Russian front. And as an Allied cross-Channel attack, or Second Front, was to be ruled out for 1943, such indirect support to the Russians was vital. With the adoption at Casablanca of the main features of the British strategic concept, and the agreement to aim for an occupation of Sicily in July 1943, resistance movements in the Balkans now became of prime importance for the first time. Not only was resistance to be encouraged as a way of tying down Axis forces and preventing their use elsewhere, but its support could be used as cover for deception purposes, leading the enemy to believe that the Eastern Mediterranean was to be the target of Allied landings.² This role for resistance was new. It was a question neither of secret armies, nor of simple sabotage. Instead, guerrilla activity—constant open warfare—was to be supported, for the purpose pure and simple of holding down enemy forces, regardless of whether the Allies were eventually going to land there or not. The strategic objectives might have been simple, but the consequences were highly complex. On purely theoretical grounds, the Chiefs of Staff might have thought twice about becoming involved in the support of guerrilla forces, for history had shown that guerilla war was always highly political and could not be reduced to a 'purely' military dimension at the dictate of outside forces.³ On more pragmatic grounds, however, the possible military advantage appeared to outweigh any other complications. The success of Operation Harling in Greece seemed to indicate that communists and non-communists could co-operate, and where Yugoslavia was concerned it was assumed that as British supplies began to flow to Mihailović he could be persuaded or forced to co-operate with the communists against the Axis forces in a joint strategy closely guided by the British. Such were two of the hopes or illusions with which SOE began the post-Alamein and post-Stalingrad year of 1943.

The priority accorded to resistance in the Balkans was clearly shown in the directive given to SOE on 20 March 1943 (see Document Seven of the appendices). This stressed that SOE operations should focus on current activities rather than on long-term preparations, which meant more simply that they should be focused on sabotage and guerrilla warfare rather than on preparations for future secret army uprisings.[4] A general order of priority for SOE operations saw the Balkans coming in second place behind the Italian islands, Corsica and Crete, but ahead of France, Poland and Czechoslovakia, Norway and the Low Countries, and the Far East. The Chiefs of Staff, moreover, directed that 'the requirements of SIS should in general be accorded priority over your own operations in Norway, Sweden, France and the Low Countries, and, if the appropriate Commanders-in-Chief agree, on the mainland of Italy and in Sicily'. This meant in effect that it was only in the Balkans that SOE could feel free to carry out operations relatively untramelled by the need to take into account the needs and sensitivities of SIS. The directive foresaw in the Balkans 'an intensified campaign of sabotage and guerrilla activities . . . during the spring and summer', which would be of the first strategic importance in impeding the concentration and consolidation of German forces on the Eastern front. In Greece, guerrilla activities should take precedence over sabotage, and in Yugoslavia and Albania there should be 'the fullest exploitation of guerrilla warfare from now onwards'. Finally the directive instructed SOE to prepare an appreciation analysing its capacity to fulfil the objectives, and at the end of the year to submit a report showing how far the directive had been carried out.[5]

The invitation to SOE to comment on the relationship between what it was being asked to do and the means it was provided with to do it resulted, predictably and legitimately, in complaints about lack of aircraft. These were given added weight by the conclusions in late March of an *ad hoc* committee on equipment for patriot forces, which had been set up by the Chiefs of Staff in December 1942, and consisted of representatives of the three services, the Foreign Office and SOE.[6] Its terms of reference included equipment both for resistance groups, and for patriot forces, which were defined as 'any forces which may be embodied in areas liberated by our armies'. The Committee reported that 'sabotage material and weapons in the hands of Resistance Groups within the enemy lines are likely to pay a relatively big dividend and could make a large contribution to the enemy's defeat', but at the same time emphasised strongly that 'unless present delivery facilities are considerably increased, full value will not be obtained from Resistance Groups at the crucial moment'. This, indeed, was its first recommendation, and when the Chiefs of Staff Committee considered it on 12 April they requested a supplementary report dealing more fully with the delivery problem. It remained for SOE itself, however, to highlight the detailed needs, and this it did in the appreciation of its activities for 1943 called for by the Chiefs of Staff.

Sir Charles Hambro (Nelson's successor as CD) told George Taylor on 2 April that he saw this as an opportunity to strengthen SOE's position: 'I am wording [the appreciation] in such a way', he told Taylor, 'that once it is approved [a] new charter will follow as a matter of course, and we shall finally be free from interdepartmental grab [?] and deliberate mis-interpretations.'[7] This turned out to be a vain hope, but the appreciation did perhaps in the long run contribute to the increased number of aircraft eventually allotted to SOE in the summer of 1943. Overall, SOE estimated that demands for aircraft exceeded supply by about 200 per cent, and placed on record that, 'owing to the inadequacy of air transport, resistance in the occupied territories cannot be further increased'. It was even open to doubt, it claimed, whether with existing resources resistance could be maintained at its present level throughout the coming autumn and winter. Analysing Europe regionally in the order of priorities suggested by the March directive, SOE was pessimistic of much being achieved in Italy, the Italian islands, and Crete, but saw Corsica as promising ground. The picture was brighter in the Balkans. In Greece, there were seven main resistance groups totalling 10,000 men, to five of which were attached British officers. It was anticipated that by August 1943 'preparations can be completed for participations in military operations on a serious scale of almost a national revolt', and to this end SOE claimed it was using its influence to range all resistance behind the king. In contrast to Greece, however, there was great difficulty in exercising similar directing influence over General Mihailović in Yugoslavia, due to SOE's inability to furnish material support through lack of aircraft. Such control was essential, SOE stressed, if Mihailović's attention was to be directed from internal issues to the fight against the enemy. But even with the ten additional Halifax aircraft which had already been found since January 1943 for the use of SOE Cairo, SOE estimated that this would be insufficient to give the British a directing influence, and it was probable that 'only fifty per cent of SOE's essential commitments in the Balkans can be met with existing air resources'. With the exception of Albania and Bulgaria, where the key was also aircraft availability, it was doubtful whether internal conditions would permit SOE to carry out the tasks demanded of it; neither Rumania nor Hungary was likely to offer promising ground without further deterioration in the Axis position.

In France, next in order of priority, SOE reported that the tide of resistance was mounting steadily, and that SOE agents were in contact with groups who were preparing for action when the Allies landed. Here, however, in contrast to Yugoslavia and Greece, guerrilla activity was to be dampened down, and in so far as it could be controlled, was to be reserved until the last moment when the Allies were close at hand. Once again, the appreciation stressed the shortage of aircraft, and claimed that for April alone not more than forty per cent of possible operations could be carried out. In Central Europe, resistance in Poland was strong and a source of constant apprehension to the Germans, but in Czechoslovakia 'the spirit of open resistance has been broken'. In Norway, Denmark and the Low Countries, the prospects were only moderate, with activity in Norway limited by inherent transport problems, and operations in Belgium still being affected by problematic relations with the government-in-exile. So far as Holland was concerned, there was no hint of suspicion of German penetration, and the appreciation reported that 'an organisation of some 1,500 men has been very carefully built up on a definite plan of action for the day of invasion'. Broadly speaking, SOE concluded, the areas where SOE could make a really effective contribution were (a) Corsica, (b) Greece and Yugoslavia, (c) France, (d) Poland, (e) Norway and Holland. With available resources, however, only forty per cent of demands could be met from the first three areas alone.

In their discussion of the SOE appreciation on 24 April,[8] the Chiefs of Staff were clearly reluctant to accept SOE's estimates without further analysis, and the appreciation was referred to the joint planning staff for examination. This in turn was delayed until after the further stages of allied grand strategy had been agreed upon, which meant until after the 'Trident' Conference in Washington in May. By the time this had produced an agreed Anglo-American strategy to be pursued following the invasion of Sicily (it was agreed to aim for a target date of 1 May 1944 for landings in France, and that this should have priority over Mediterranean demands),[9] several other important developments had occurred.

Only two days after the SOE appreciation, on 26 April 1943, the Soviet Union had broken off relations with the Polish government-in-exile following Polish allegations over the Katyn Forest massacres. They were not to be resumed, and from now on the USSR was to lend its support to pro-communist groups in Poland as the nucleus of the postwar Polish government. Although as early as August 1941 it had been made clear to the Poles that SOE could not support Polish plans for a secret army uprising, this break in relations added a further complicating factor. Relations with the resistance in Poland owing allegiance to the 'London' Poles—which were indirect anyway and conducted through the Polish government itself—were now directly affected by the requirements of Anglo-Soviet relations. Up to this point, Poland had been considered as falling within the British sphere of strategic responsibility; increasingly, the British now tended to argue that it was within the Soviet sphere—thus providing a convenient way of explaining to the Poles why more support could not be given.[10] Secondly, British relations with de Gaulle and the Fighting French underwent a serious crisis, precipitated by Churchill's too-eager desire to bring British policy as close as possible to that of Roosevelt. In Washington for the 'Trident' Conference, Churchill suggested on 21 May[11] that the War Cabinet should consider a definite break with de Gaulle, who was, in Churchill's (and more importantly in Roosevelt's) view, obstructing the policy of reconciliation between himself and General Giraud, agreed upon at Casablanca. The War Cabinet refused. Both Eden and Attlee told Churchill that agreement between the two generals was close, and that to drop de Gaulle would have very serious consequences. Not only would it lead to accusations of British meddling in French internal affairs, it would mean there was virtually no chance that any of the members of the newly formed *Conseil National de la Résistance* (CNR) would continue to function. The Joint Planning Staff, in fact, reported to the Chiefs of Staff on 25 May that the withdrawal of Fighting French support from the Allies would remove 50,000 men from resistance groups in France, and that 'the loss of this potential strength would greatly affect the chances of a successful invasion'. Nonetheless, despite this, and despite the de Gaulle–Giraud agreement reached in Churchill's presence at Algiers on 2 June, Churchill continued to express dissatisfaction at de Gaulle, noting on 13 July 1943 that de Gaulle's 'arrival at the summit of French affairs would be contrary to the interests of Great Britain'.[12] So determined did Churchill temporarily become to destroy de Gaulle, that he intervened directly in SOE policy in France to instruct Selborne to withhold any further payments to the French National Committee in London. On 19 June, two days after he had received a copy of a telegram from Roosevelt to Eisenhower in which the President clearly indicated he was finished with de Gaulle, Churchill told Selborne, in words obligingly provided by Desmond Morton, that 'we must be careful that the direction of the French resistance movement does not fall into the control of de Gaulle and his satellites here'. But as Selborne replied to this characteristically brusque and ill-informed interjection, French resistance was already 'almost solid in favour of de Gaulle', and it was to ask for its disintegration if de Gaulle were to be removed. It would, moreover, be immoral to abandon support for the evaders of labour conscription, who were being supplied with essential ration cards through the French Committee in London. 'They have,' Selborne told his erstwhile fellow defender of Britain's imperial interests in India, 'gone hunting a very big tiger with us, and we cannot leave them in the lurch.'[13] The formation of the CNR and the de Gaulle–Giraud agreement strengthened de Gaulle's influence over the French resistance; but British influence with de Gaulle, and thus with the resistance, could only suffer from attitudes such as Churchill's. The third major development was that relations with Mihailović had also taken a sharp turn for the worse. British relations with resistance in Yugoslavia are dealt with in more detail later in this chapter, but here we may note that in February Mihailović had made some strong anti-British statements, and that on 1 May SOE had prepared a directive to Mihailović ordering him to stop all collaboration with the enemy, to cease fighting the partisans, and to work with the Commander-in-Chief in the Middle East through Colonel Bailey, the British liaison officer who had arrived at Mihailović's headquarters in December 1942.[14] On 29 May 1943 Colonel Deakin was dropped to the partisans. British policy towards Mihailović had reached a crucial turning point. The fourth and final new factor we need to note before examining the response of the joint planners to SOE's own appreciation, was the supplementary report of the *ad hoc* committee on supplies for patriot forces. This was discussed by the Chiefs of Staff Committee on 25 May. It recommended that arms and equipment should be provided for 300,000 resistance fighters (in addition to those already supplied), and said that if delivery was to be made entirely by air and to be completed by 30 June 1944, SOE would require ninety-three aircraft based in the United Kingdom and forty-eight based in the Middle East. This represented a 480 per cent increase in aircraft availability in the United Kingdom, and a 240 per cent increase in Middle East. The response of the air staff to this was predictably cool, and all the Vice-Chief of the Air Staff could tell the Chiefs of Staff Committee was that while 'he saw no chance of our being able to deliver by air the full quantities of material in all theatres . . . it should be possible, by the transference of aircraft at the appropriate times, to boost deliveries in the critical areas'.[15] What these critical areas were, and what SOE policy in them should be, was a matter on which the joint planners were now, after 'Trident', in a position to advise.

The joint planners' report of 10 June in fact added little to the SOE appreciation of April in so far as its analysis of European resistance was concerned, and in suggesting priorities for SOE activities it virtually repeated SOE in listing them in the following order: (a) Corsica (where SOE eventually played an important role in the liberation of the island in September), (b) Balkans, (c) France, (d) Poland.[16] The main noticeable change was in reference to Mihailović's continuing failure to cooperate, his declining strength, and the direct contact which had by then been established with the partisans. The importance of the report lay in its recommendations to the Chiefs of Staff. These were to ask the Air Ministry and the Admiralty to report back within ten days on ways in which SOE's demands for increased transport facilities could be met, with a view to meeting supply requirements in the Balkans before the end of September 1943, and elsewhere before the beginning of April 1944. Whatever long-term decisions were made, moreover, the Air Ministry should meet SOE's existent request for an initial increase of eighteen aircraft. The supply of aircraft should not, however, be at the expense of SIS, and should be balanced against the major claims of the bomber offensive and the transport requirement for airborne forces.

This last proviso meant that a direct confrontation between the claims of SOE and Bomber Command was now inevitable. The war leadership would have to face seriously the issue which it had attempted to avoid by makeshift and *ad hoc* decisions in the past—what value was to be placed on SOE operations in relation to the rest of the war effort, and how far they were prepared to go to keep SOE in being? The crisis occasioned by the posing of this question took over six months to answer, and passed through two distinct phases. In the first, from July to September 1943, the issue was mainly restricted to the question of aircraft supplies and liaison with the regular services, although the Foreign Office became involved and fundamental questions were raised about SOE Cairo. Nonetheless, the dispute was kept in relatively low key. The second phase of the crisis, lasting from December 1943 to January 1944, was more bitter. Issues were raised which reflected fundamentally on SOE's effectiveness, and they called into serious question its very right to continue in existence. SOE, in fact, came within a stone's throw of being abolished. This first phase of the crisis will be dealt with immediately below; the second phase will be left until the concluding part of this chapter.

The conflict of priorities was starkly underlined when the full implications of the joint planners' report were quantified in terms of aircraft. The Chiefs of Staff had recommended on 17 June that the Air Ministry and SOE should jointly examine ways in which to increase aircraft deliveries in order to meet the required targets, and a further dimension was added on 23 June when Churchill, now thoroughly enthused by the Yugoslav partisans, laid down that supplies to the Balkans should be stepped up to 500 tons a month. This directive was made with typically Churchillian disregard for the severe industrial manpower crisis and consequent shortfall in bomber production which he himself was to take to the War Cabinet on 9 July. His request delayed matters until 24 July, when the Joint Air Ministry/SOE Report was laid before the Chiefs of Staff.[17] This stated that in order to meet the joint planners' requirements in full, SOE would require a total of 102 heavy bomber aircraft (thirty-eight for the Balkans, sixty-four for Western Europe). Set against SOE's existing establishment of forty seven aircraft (three squadrons) this meant an increase of fifty-five (three-and-a-half squadrons). To meet the additional requirements then laid down by Churchill on 23 June would mean another fifteen aircraft, or one squadron, producing a total figure of 117 aircraft, or seven-and-a-half squadrons (fifty-three for the Balkans, sixty-four for Western Europe). As the then operational strength of Bomber Command was forty squadrons, it was clear that, in the understated words of the report, the 'full SOE requirement . . . will therefore represent a substantial diversion from the bomber offensive, which could not be accepted except on very strong grounds'. The report also pointed out two important limiting factors on fulfilment of the full programme: first, it would mean a considerable increase in demand above the planned production of parachutes, and second, because reception arrangements in Western Europe were such that the SOE networks 'would not at present be able to deal with deliveries on the scale contemplated', this meant that a prohibitively large allocation would have to be made later. It was clear in any case, the report concluded, that the whole matter involved a decision on priorities between the requirements of SOE and the RAF.

It was on this last point, indeed, that Portal seized when he submitted the report to the Chiefs of Staff. In a note of 25 July he put the issue in the following terms:

Desirable as it may be to maintain and foster SOE activities, we must bring the problem into focus with the whole strategic picture.

The issue is a plain one. As we cannot provide aircraft for the transport of arms and materials to Resistance Groups except at the direct cost of the bomber offensive, what is the exact price which we are prepared to pay? I suggest that the answer should turn not on a C.O.S. directive issued in general terms in March last, but on an impartial consideration of the present strategical situation.

We are unquestionably obtaining great and immediate value from the bomber offensive. For all that, the weight of our attack falls far short of what it should be. At the end of June we were still 3 Heavy Bomber Squadrons below the target of 58, and in spite of every effort it has only been possible to increase the number of effective Medium and Heavy Bomber Squadrons in Bomber Command by 2½ in the last 3 months.

I have no doubt about the value of what is being done by SOE in the Balkans, or about the need to do as much more there as is possible. These activities accord with our general strategic plan, they exploit our present successes and should give us good and immediate results.

The same, however, cannot be said about the rest of Europe, where the efforts of Resistance Groups cannot be really profitable until next year. The real value which we shall obtain from these Groups will be an uprising. If such an uprising is to be successful—and it can only succeed once—it will demand conditions in which German resistance in the West is reaching the point of disintegration. We are not in a position to begin to apply the necessary pressure for another nine or twelve months unless the German war machine cracks seriously in the meantime. The most likely cause of this accelerated collapse is the bomber offensive which must not be handicapped by diversions to an operation whose value is obviously secondary.

Thus on strategic grounds, while I feel that there is a very good case for providing aircraft to back SOE activities in the Balkans, even at the cost, as it must be, of some small detraction from the direct attack on Germany, I feel that it would be a serious mistake to divert any more aircraft to supply Resistance Groups in Western Europe, which will only be of *potential* value next year, when these aircraft could be of *immediate and actual* value in accelerating the defeat of Germany by direct attack.[18]

In practical terms, therefore, Portal was prepared to offer SOE a total increase before January 1944 of only fourteen heavy bomber aircraft, all of which would be based in the Mediterranean, bringing the total there up to thirty-six. These would be primarily for Balkan operations. In Western Europe, however, there would be no increase above the twenty-two already available, but this should be capable of 'sustaining Resistance Groups in lively and vigorous condition until we can concentrate in turn on their ultimate exploitation'.

It was precisely this latter point, however, that Hambro contested on behalf of SOE.[19] He pointed out that if Portal's recommendations were accepted, only forty per cent of the requirement laid down by the Chiefs of Staff for the arming of patriot forces in Western Europe could be met.

Moreover, there would be an actual decrease in activity, because extra effort was needed to repair damage done to organisations in Western Europe through increased enemy counterattack. 'The maintenance of our organisations at their present strength and day to day activity,' Hambro said, 'requires an increase in our present effort.' In addition, he argued, the only way of countering a deterioration in morale which would almost cerainly occur when it became clear after the autumn that an allied invasion was not to take place in 1943, was to provide 'a steady flow of greatly increased deliveries of arms and other essentials'. Moreover, the growing *maquis* needed support, and it could not be assumed, as Portal had, that air supplies could all be dropped at the last moment—'the process of equipping resistance groups must be a gradual one spread out over a period'. Any decision which seriously affected Western European resistance groups should therefore be looked at closely for the effects on SOE–COSSAC plans for resistance action in connection with eventual Allied landings. Hambro showed less concern about the Balkans because, as he admitted, Portal's proposals would produce 'a considerable volume of delivery', although they would not in fact be on the scale demanded by Churchill, unless bases in Italy became available. And unless US aircraft were made available, he pointed out, the demands of OSS missions would also have to be met out of the proposal allocation (which was smaller than it seemed, for the equivalent of seven of the aircraft would be set aside for SIS and PWE purposes). Hambro's conclusion was not, however, to challenge Portal's figures so much as to suggest that an attempt be made to acquire American aircraft based in the Mediterranean for SOE's Balkan operations, thus freeing British aircraft for SOE work in Western Europe.

Hambro's arguments about Western Europe were not without force. But his reluctance to challenge Portal with a further demand for more *British* aircraft, combined with the fact that Balkan needs had been very substantially met, meant that the Chiefs of Staff decided on 27 July without much argument (and in the absence, it might be noted, of any SOE representative) that Portal's arguments and recommendation should be accepted. They agreed that 'we should support SOE activities in the Balkans as far as possible and at the expense, if necessary, of supply to the resistance groups in Western Europe'. No mention was made of any approach to the Americans for help, as Hambro suggested. Portal had won his case. At this point, however, he almost overstepped the mark by attempting actively to discredit SOE operations in Western Europe. As the meeting was closing, he produced an SIS report on German penetration of resistance networks in France which had almost certainly not yet been seen by SOE. Its conclusion was damning, and produced at this opportune moment it more than supported Portal's case. 'At the present moment', the report said, 'resistance groups [in France] are at their lowest ebb and cannot be counted on as a serious factor unless and until they are re-built on a smaller and sounder basis'. In the light of this information the Chiefs of Staff affirmed their earlier decision and agreed that the report should be sent to the JIC for comment.[20] In the meantime, however, Selborne had demanded that the entire question of aircraft supply be discussed by the Defence Committee of the Cabinet at its meeting on 2 August, and on learning this the Chiefs of Staff urgently reuested the JIC to have ready before then its analysis and comments on the SIS report. Clearly, if the report showed that SOE resistance groups had been penetrated or destroyed, the decision the Chiefs of Staff had made at the expense of supplies for SOE in Western Europe would be in large part justified.

However, the Joint Intelligence Sub-Committee which examined the question considered the SIS report to be exaggerated.[21] As SOE when consulted by the JIC had pointed out, the groups considered were exclusively 'RF' groups, that is, those associated with the Free French. These represented only forty per cent of the resistance groups in France with which SOE was in contact, and the remaining 60 per cent could provide employment for 'all, and more than all, the aircraft allotted for SOE purposes in France'. The report, therefore, failed to confirm Portal's gloomiest fears (or hopes). But in the course of exploring the question further, the Committee was led to some important conclusions about the relationship of SOE to both SIS and the Chiefs of Staff, and in doing so came by an indirect route to lend support to Portal's position. Critical of the fact that SOE had received previous reports from SIS along these lines but had not informed the Chiefs of Staff, the Committee recommended that some reorganisation be considered 'to bring SIS and SOE more closely together and in direct relationship with the principal organisation for the conduct of operations and intelligence' [i.e. the Chiefs of Staff under the Minister of Defence]. It is clear from this that the earlier attempt, in May 1942, to create machinery for the adjudication of SOE–SIS conflicts of interest, had failed. The Committee then found an additional reason for this closer co-ordination in SOE's constant need for aircraft, for which there were many conflicting demands. These, they argued, could only be adjudicated on a continuous basis by the higher military authorities, who would be in close touch with SOE affairs. Finally, the Committee returned once again to the question of intelligence. By reaffirming, in essence, the premises of

SOE's 1943 directive, that in France SIS activities should have priority over SOE, it came to the same conclusions as the Chiefs of Staff had already reached in response to Portal's arguments. Indeed, their argument echoed Portal's closely:

> As regards their work in organising the resistance movements . . . SOE activities in Western Europe have primarily a future and hardly an immediate value. In that theatre the resistance groups will only be able to come out into the open when Germany is on the verge of collapse. In the SIS sphere, however, intelligence from France, especially regarding the moves of German formations, is of the highest immediate importance as both regards quantity and speed of transmission. We therefore suggest that Intelligence needs should for the present have priority in France . . . It is for consideration, therefore, whether a temporary transfer of aircraft for SOE purposes from this country to the Middle East, at the expense of France, might not have sufficient immediate value to justify it . . . .

This report, supporting as it did the Chiefs of Staff position, was circulated in advance of the Defence Committee meeting.

The minutes of the Defence Committee meeting at 10.30 pm on 2 August 1943—a meeting which Sir Alexander Cadogan characteristically found 'tiresome'—are still withheld. But from Foot's account and from subsequent minutes, the main points are clear.[22] Portal persisted in the view that there could be no increase in aircraft available for SOE purposes in Western Europe, despite Selborne's arguments that far more were needed in order to keep existing movements continuously supplied with arms and ammunition. Although Churchill gave his support to Selborne—emphasising the immense value to the war effort of stimulating resistance among the people of Europe and declaring grandiloquently that 'the blood of the martyrs was the seed of the Church'—the final decisions of the Committee represented a triumph for Bomber Command. First, the number of UK-based aircraft available for special duties remained at the then establishment of twenty-two, but Middle East aircraft were increased to thirty-six—no more than Portal had offered anyway. Second, measures were to be taken in accordance with the JIC recommendations to improve COS–SOE coordination. This led in October to a number of arrangements by which SOE and the Chiefs of Staff were kept in closer touch. The most important of these was that all SOE activities in North-West Europe were brought under the operational control of COSSAC, which assumed general direction of planning and became responsible for instructions as to target priorities. In addition, CD was now sent the agenda of all future meetings of the Chiefs of Staff so that SOE could declare an interest in future operations and plans: 'At last', Gubbins later recalled, 'we had moved into smoother waters . . . .'[23] Thirdly, steps were taken to facilitate the use of Bomber Command aircraft for SOE (and SIS) purposes to supplement the squadrons specifically allotted to that task. This decision resulted in the issuing of a directive to Bomber Command by the Chiefs of Staff on 27 August, under which it took over operational control from the Air Ministry of all SIS and SOE-related flights. In practice, this produced little immediate change. Under the terms of the directive, the supplementary effort to be provided by Bomber Command was restricted to the dropping of equipment only over France, and it was for Harris to decide whether such efforts were feasible.[24] This escape clause was seized upon by Harris, and he 'fended off for several months more any extensive participation by his squadrons in SOE's work'; his only concession was occasionally to release Stirlings to help the special squadrons.[25] He could, however, find some support for his lukewarm response from a further report by the *ad hoc* committee on equipment for patriot forces, which on 4 September reported that its previous estimate of necessary aircraft had been rendered invalid by the discovery that aircraft were completing more successful sorties and carrying greater amounts of equipment than originally predicted.[26] These figures did not invalidate SOE's complaints that it was being discriminated against in Western Europe and France, but they made it easier for Bomber Command to justify their reluctance to furnish more support.

The debate over aircraft availability had scarcely died down when SOE's relationship to the war leadership was again raised in more severe form. This time the origin of the crisis lay in the Middle East. The background was SOE's handling of the Greek (and to a lesser extent the Yugoslav) resistance, and conflicts this had provoked with the Foreign Office. This is discussed in more detail in the following section of this chapter, and it is enough to note here that events in Cairo had led the Middle East Defence Committee early in September to propose changes to London which would, in effect, have abolished SOE in the Middle East. The proposal inevitably fuelled the fires of those who thought SOE London might also be abolished, and once again, on 30 September, Churchill found himself chairing a special meeting of ministers to consider SOE's future. Although no account of this meeting is available, we know the outcome.[27] The Chiefs of Staff recommended against any fundamental reorganisation of SOE on the grounds that 'any dramatic change . . . at this eleventh hour would militate against its efficiency at the very time when it is required to play a prominent part'. They did, however, argue for closer military control, and said that while SOE should preserve its integrity under the Minister of Economic Warfare, it would be required to work more closely with the Foreign Office, and its main policy would be settled in London between the Foreign Secretary and the Minister of Economic Warfare. In Cairo, a political guidance committee would be set up to advise the C-in-C Middle East, who would have sole responsibility for the execution of SOE policy towards Greece, Yugoslavia, and Albania. Finally, the right of the Chiefs of Staff to express their views to Churchill on any SOE matters was explicitly acknowledged.

The decisions of this meeting on 30 September, combined with the agreements shortly thereafter whereby COSSAC assumed operational control of SOE activities throughout north-west Europe, did much to satisfy all parties concerned. SOE was now, temporarily at least, out of the woods. The Middle East crisis had also produced personnel changes at the highest level which helped. Sir Charles Hambro 'resigned' as CD, and was replaced by Sir Colin Gubbins, who held the position until the end of the war; as a no-nonsense professional soldier, his appointment as CD at the moment when SOE was becoming in some respects more than ever an adjunct of the Chiefs of Staff and the area Commanders-in-Chief was an asset to SOE in its dealings with the regular forces. In Cairo, Lord Glenconner resigned and Keble was replaced, changes which after the bitterness of the August crisis helped to promote smoother relations with the C-in-C and Foreign Office representatives. In all areas, indeed, 'the decentralisation of considerable political authority to the various theatres and the recognition in those theatres of the contribution that resistance was making'[28] considerably eased SOE's work. Top-level strategic decisions indicated the importance now attached to resistance activities in the Balkans. The Québec Conference of August 1943, in confirming the decision to aim for Anglo-American landings in France in May 1944, had ruled out the possibility of Allied landings in the Balkans, declaring instead that 'operations in the Balkans area will be limited to the supply of Balkan guerrillas by air and sea transport, to minor commando forces, and to the bombing of strategic objectives'. The fact that this was to represent the only form of Allied engagement served to enhance the importance of such operations, and the surrender of the Italians in September further increased the potential and strategic significance of the Balkan resistance.

On 12 October, therefore, the Chiefs of Staff requested SOE to report 'what further efforts could be made to nourish the activities of the guerrillas in the Balkans'. SOE's report two days later showed that 200,000 partisans were operating in Greece, Albania, and Yugoslavia, and that there were eighty missions there in W/T contact with SOE Cairo. SOE recommended increased sea and airborne supplies, and expressed the hope that Eisenhower might make captured Italian equipment available for the guerrilla forces. Churchill was informed of SOE's views, and on 19 October the Combined Chiefs of Staff instructed Eisenhower to give 'the maximum possible assistance to the guerrillas in the Balkans'. Steps were subsequently taken to revise the command structure for the Balkans and eastern Mediterranean, and in that same month an advanced SOE base was established at Bari, in southern Italy. The support of guerrillas in the Balkans was now clearly of major strategic significance.[29] The question now became—which guerrillas?

II

In Yugoslavia, British policy throughout 1942 had been to support Mihailović and the Chetniks, despite knowledge that they were on occasion collaborating with the Italians. The support was, however, extremely limited. Only twenty-five sorties had gone to Mihailović through the whole year, and only four Liberators were available in January 1943 for SOE work in Yugoslavia, Greece and Crete. In the spring it was estimated that there were ten missions in Greece, twelve in Yugoslavia (all with Mihailović), and five in Albania. This total of twenty-seven missions was to increase rapidly in the first half of the year, rising to above seventy by August. But in January, when Churchill passed through Cairo, the position was grim, and SOE had nowhere near enough aircraft even to begin seriously the stepped-up programme of operations in the Balkans demanded by the strategic discussions and decisions of the preceding weeks. Largely as a result of Churchill's prompting, six Halifaxes were immediately provided for SOE from within the Middle East, and on 4 March the Chiefs of Staff agreed to provide four more, thus bringing the total number available for Balkan operations to fourteen. But even then only the Liberators had the necessary range to reach Yugoslavia from Cairo, and between April and June 1943 a mere thirty tons of supplies were dropped into Yugoslavia.

This made it difficult to exert any leverage over Mihailović, with whom relations were becoming increasingly problematic. As Jozo

Tomasevich has pointed out, so long as the Mediterranean was not an area of major operations, 'what went on in Yugoslavia did not matter much, and the Chetniks' collaboration with the Axis was allowed to pass'.[30] The Casablanca decisions changed all that, and guerrilla warfare as an important facet of Allied strategy forced the British to look very hard at SOE policy in Yugoslavia.

As early as January 1943 SOE Cairo had become converted to the view, on the basis of intercepted German communications, that the partisans were doing more effective fighting than the Chetniks against the Germans. When Churchill passed through Cairo in January, Colonel Keble, Chief of Staff of SOE (Cairo), presented him with a report stressing the importance of giving support to partisan groups in Croatia and Slovenia, proposing that British officers be sent to both sides, and asking for more aircraft for SOE work in the Balkans. Churchill told Selborne that he agreed with the report, and shortly afterwards Foreign Office officials were telling the Americans in London that they favoured contacting the partisans. SOE London was less convinced, and Selborne personally remained commited to Mihailović. When the issue was put to the Chiefs of Staff they at first rejected it, on the grounds that SOE had sufficient resources to support one side only, and that 'under the partisans chaos would probably ensue when the Axis forces were defeated'.[31] But after further discussion, and in pursuit of a more active guerrilla campaign in the Balkans, they asked SOE in April to make direct contact with the partisans, and at the end of May Colonel Deakin was dropped to Tito's headquarters. Almost simultaneously, Churchill was busily expounding his personal views on the future in the Balkans to Generals Marshall and Eisenhower in Algiers. Arguing for an invasion of the Italian mainland, he told them that such a move would open up the Balkans to tremendous but indirect Allied pressure. Discounting any hopes of sending regular forces, he painted a picture of revolt in Yugoslavia, Greece, and Albania formented by outside aid; a reversion almost to the detonator concept of 1940–41.[32] With Churchill's enthusiasm behind them, the Chiefs of Staff on 17 June 1943 informed the Foreign Office that Britain should begin supplying the Croatian guerrillas and partisans with war *matériel* and they instructed Cairo in that sense on 27 June. As Winant, the American Ambassador in London, reported to the State Department three days later, this represented an important modification in British policy to Yugoslavia, and from now on the partisans would be provided with material aid on a fairly substantial scale.[33]

Although Selborne remained a vigorous defender of Mihailović, he was sufficiently quick to seize upon the Chiefs of Staff decision to place an immediate request for more aircraft in the Middle East. On 18 June he complained directly to the Prime Minister about the lack of suitable aircraft for supplies to Yugoslavia, indicating that a continuation of the situation would not only deny the guerrillas necessary supplies, but would also disadvantageously restrict British influence over events. This argument clearly won Churchill, for on 22 June he forwarded Selborne's request to the Chiefs of Staff, saying that 'All this is of the highest importance . . . this demand has priority even over the bombing of Germany.' Thus the gauntlet was thrown down to Bomber Command, the results of which we have seen in greater detail above. The upshot was an increase of Middle East aircraft available to SOE to thirty-six,[34] and from June onwards military supplies began to be sent to the partisans. In the last three months of 1943 they received about 2000 tons.

Churchill's interest was also reflected in his decision in July to send a personal representative to Tito and the partisans in the shape of Fitzroy Maclean. While this was a testimony to Churchill's enthusiasm for Tito, it betokened less esteem for SOE, of which Maclean was not a member, and for which he rapidly gained much mistrust and dislike. According to Maclean, in fact, SOE actively opposed his mission.[35] As SOE was to learn, Churchill's interest in European resistance, intermittent and erratic as it was, was never to be taken automatically as support for SOE.

From June 1943, therefore, the British were supporting both Mihailović and Tito. But the steady accumulation of evidence that Mihailović was still refusing to attack the Germans, combined with Maclean's own report to Churchill on Tito and the partisans in November, strengthened the hand of those who argued that support for Mihailović should be withdrawn entirely, and that Tito should be given exclusive backing. This case was put by SOE Cairo on 19 November 1943 (it was SOE Cairo which early in 1943 had taken the initiative to urge the earlier shift in policy), and recommended by the Joint Intelligence Committee on the 25th. A few days later, at the Teheran Conference, Churchill, Stalin and Roosevelt authorised a military directive that the partisans should be given supplies and equipment to the greatest possible extent; they made no mention of Mihailović.[36] Material aid to the Chetniks was now stopped. Anxious to salvage what they could, Eden and Churchill urged the Royal Yugoslav government and King Peter to dismiss Mihailović, in the hope that somehow Tito—who had just formed a National Committee in Yugoslavia through the so-called Jajce resolutions—could be induced to co-operate with the king. They still hoped for some unified anti-German resistance, and to avoid a communist Yugoslavia. In pursuit of this policy, the Foreign Office opposed any final break with Mihailović *until* Tito had indicated he would be willing to meet King Peter; whereas SOE Cairo wanted an immediate break, without conditions, in order to safeguard the position of the British liaison officers with Mihailovicć's forces, and to induce Tito to work more closely with the British. Again, as in the spring, it was intervention by the military which proved decisive. In February 1944 the Commander-in-Chief Mediterranean recommended immediate withdrawal of the liaison officers with Mihailović, and on 17 February the Chiefs of Staff ordered Cairo to carry this out. Support for Mihailović was, at last, over, although there were still hopes in the Foreign Office that Chetnik elements could be encouraged to co-operate with, and act as a leavening of, the partisans.

In Greece, events took a different course. The first British liaison officers had arrived for Operation Harling in November 1942, but then stayed on in a permanent role in order to fulfil a directive from the Chiefs of Staff 'to give all-out support to guerrilla warfare [in Greece] even to the extent of prejudicing the activities of secret groups [presumably SIS]'. EAM-ELAS and EDES, the two main antagonistic forces in Greek resistance, had co-operated with the British to carry out the Gorgopotamos viaduct operation, but shortly afterwards fighting broke out between the two groups and by the early spring of 1943 there was civil war within the Greek resistance. SOE, however, sought the co-operation of EAM-ELAS and EDES through the creation of national bands. The purpose underlying this project was the encouragement of unified guerrilla warfare throughout Greece, under British control, in accordance with the strategic objectives laid down by the Chiefs of Staff in November and confirmed at Casablanca. As the March directive to SOE put it, 'an important part of your activities is . . . to create a diversion to co-ordinate with our attack in the Central Mediterranean'. The strategic importance of Greek resistance, therefore, lay in no small measure in the part it would play in strategic deception. Five days after the decisions of the 'Trident' Conference in Washington, Myers in Greece received instructions from Cairo to finalise preparations for widespread demolitions in late June and early July to coincide with the Allied invasion of Sicily. This campaign, known as 'Operation Animals', was highly successful and reached a climax when on 20 June the Athens–Salonika railway line was broken in six places. Hitler believed—even after the landings in Sicily—that Allied landings would take place in Greece, and German forces which might have been deployed elsewhere were diverted to safeguard the Balkan coastline.[37].

Following the successful completion of 'Operation Animals', Myers was then instructed by SOE Cairo to dampen down resistance activity and to limit sabotage to the minimum necessary to maintain morale and help in recruiting. This decision laid open the way for a diversion of resistance energies away from fighting the enemy to the troubled question of postwar political ambitions, and raised in acute form Britain's political interests in the Greek resistance.

In the course of preparing for Operation Animals, SOE had already run up against the major problem which was to confront all its Greek operations. This was the question of whether Britain's long-term interests in Greece, which were perceived by Churchill and the Foreign Office as lying with the monarchy, could be reconciled with the short-term necessity, as perceived by SOE; of working with EAM-ELAS, as well as with EDES. 'Animals' had demanded such collaboration, but the Foreign Office was extremely unhappy about it, as was Churchill. The Foreign Office, indeed, was profoundly unhappy about most of SOE's Greek operations, on the grounds that SOE plans to co-ordinate the guerrilla bands in Greece had both been decided upon and began without their knowledge, and that SOE had lent support to elements in Greece hostile to the monarchy. This was quite true, although SOE Cairo theoretically acted in liaison with the Greek government in Cairo, through an Anglo-Greek Co-ordinating Committee. But the Committee was in practice, in George Taylor's words, 'a complete farce, because in order not to provoke tremendous trouble . . . the Committee only discussed plans in Greece which were acceptable to the Greek Government . . . the real operations of SOE . . . were never mentioned at all'.[38] This was less irresponsible than it might appear, for it was an attempt to circumvent the hopeless contradictions in policy towards Greek resistance as represented in instructions sent personally by Churchill to the Minister of State in Cairo on 18 March, and obstinately pursued for the next few months. On the one hand, Churchill defined British policy as one of support for the king and the existing Greek government, and indeed strengthening it, so that 'there should be a strong Administration in Greece as soon as liberation takes place or our operational needs demand'. It was an essential feature of British policy, therefore, that the exiled government's position in Greece itself should be strengthened, and here, said Churchill, 'the fundamental Anglophilism of the Greek people should predispose the various factions to follow a strong and clear lead from HMG'. On the other hand, Churchill continued:

In view of the operational importance attached to subversive activities in Greece, there can be no question of SOE refusing to have dealings with a given group merely on the grounds that political sentiments of the group are opposed to the King and Government, but subject to special operational necessity SOE should always veer in the direction of groups willing to support the King and Government and furthermore impress on such other groups as may be anti-[?monarchy] the fact that the King and Government enjoy the fullest support of HMG. In general nothing should be neglected which might help to promote unity among the resistance groups in Greece and between the latter and the King and Government.

SOE agents need not carry on propaganda on behalf of the King and Government nor should they indulge in political discussions but they must not on the other hand allow their silence on political issue to be misinterpreted by leaders with whom they cooperate as meaning that HMG are indifferent to the future of the King and Government and are prepared to acquiesce in a change of régime. Wherever it is necessary for SOE agents to give support or money to leaders of doubtful loyalty it will be convenient that they should stress the fact that this support and money is being given at the instance and in the interests of the King and Government. It may be that certain of [?our own] groups are unwilling to take immediate part in resistance operations. This fact should not prevent our maintaining contact with them and giving them encouragement on the understanding that they will be of use to us as the moment of liberation approaches.

Instructions in the sense of the preceding paragraphs in which SOE London concur should be issued forthwith through Anglo-Greek Committee to SOE officers in Greece.[39]

This was a counsel of perfection, if not fatuity, and reflected both Churchill's own naivety about the motives of those resisting in Greece, and the various attempts being made in March and April by the Foreign Office in London to gain firmer control over SOE Greek policy. It was repeated again in April,[40] and instructions along these lines were sent to Myers in Greece, where he did his best to carry them out by giving support to both Zervas and ELAS, and by achieving an agreement in July whereby the various factions agreed to co-operate under the command of Middle East headquarters in Cairo. But such an agreement could not last, and the Foreign Office remained so suspicious of SOE that Eden despatched his own emissary to Greece to report personally to him on the situation.

Mutual distrust between SOE and the Foreign Office came to a head in August 1943 with the visit to Cairo of a delegation from the Greek resistance groups, including representatives of EAM-ELAS. The main issue was the demand on the part of the Greek resistance representatives that the king should not return to Greece before a plebiscite had been held on the future of the monarchy. SOE Cairo supported this view, knowing as it did the depth of republican feeling in Greece. But the Foreign Office supported the king in his refusal to accept such an arrangement, and it was aided by yet another pro-monarchist intervention by Lord Selborne, who told Sir Orme Sargent on 19 August 1943 that the Greek guerrillas 'have no claim to speak for the whole of the people in Greece on matters of this sort'. Churchill added his voice, by telling Eden from Québec (where the 'Quadrant' Conference was taking place) that the Greek king must be firmly supported, and that 'strict control should be kept over SOE'.[41] For Churchill, indeed, support for the king was a deeply rooted dogma, and his adamant interest in the question was sufficient to prevent any waverings on Eden's part. In the bitter discussions which took place in Cairo in August, all the old accusations from the Foreign Office that SOE was pursuing an independent policy were raised, and after the Greek delegation had returned to Greece empty-handed SOE stood accused of having meddled impardonably in foreign policy matters. It was out of this situation and as a result of SOE Cairo's attempts to obstruct Maclean's mission to Yugoslavia, that early in September the Middle East Defence Committee proposed the virtual abolition of SOE Cairo. As we have seen, this culminated in the ministerial meeting of 30 September, chaired personally by Churchill, at which any fundamental reorganisation of SOE was rejected. Ironically, only two days later Churchill told Myers—who had left Greece with the resistance delegation, and was then prevented from returning despite the urging of Wilson—that SOE had been meddling in the work of the Foreign Office, 'and if it had not been for me they would have gone under'.[42] Had it not been for Churchill's dogmatic adherence to the obstinacy of the Greek king, however, the crisis might never have occurred in the first place.

Following the breakdown of the Cairo talks in August, there was a quick deterioration of the situation within the Greek resistance. Fighting between the rival groups broke out and was ended—temporarily only—with an armistice, known as the Plaka Agreement, signed on the last day of February 1944. In the months preceding the armistice, there had been continued disagreement on the British side over which group to support. Both the military in the Middle East and SOE wanted the

British government to support EAM-ELAS as 'the only party in Greece', in General Wilson's words, 'which can give us effective aid in killing Germans'. The Chiefs of Staff in London supported this view, describing EAM-ELAS as 'the most effective resistance movement in Greece'.[43] Sir Orme Sargent of the Foreign Office expressed a totally contrary belief in a bitter and characteristic comment on SOE in January 1944: 'The truth of course is,' he said, 'that the whole guerrilla movement in Greece has been largely fiction created by SOE in order to justify a vast expenditure of money and raw material in that country. . . .'[44] Churchill, who had previously described EAM-ELAS as bandits, now, in February 1944, described them as 'base and treacherous, a mere scourge on the population'. This Manichean view of Greek politics on Churchill's part was to involve Britain even more deeply in Greek affairs in 1944.

In both Yugoslavia and Greece considerations of short-term strategic necessity had come into conflict with considerations of postwar politics. SOE, as the 'executor' of Chiefs of Staff *and* Foreign Office decisions concerning resistance in occupied Europe, fell foul of both. Where there was broad agreement at the higher reaches of Government, there was little problem for SOE; where there was disagreement, SOE became the scapegoat. In the delicate balance to be struck between long-term and short-term considerations, the former was deemed to be more important in Greece than the latter. In both countries the British desired non-communist postwar governments, but Greece had higher priority, as a hostile Greece would threaten British postwar interests in the Eastern Mediterranean. Moreover, and this was a factor of equal importance, the wartime strategic significance of Greek resistance was not as great as that of the partisans in Yugoslavia, and thus from a British viewpoint it was more expendable. This is true at least after the invasion of Sicily, when the deception campaign in Greece was of immense importance. After Operation Animals, however, the anticipated role for the Greek resistance was to lie low and wait for an allied invasion. The problems that this dormant policy posed for Greek resistance indeed was one of the reasons which prompted Myers to bring out the delegation to Cairo. And this dormant policy lost its *raison d'être* with the 'Quadrant' decisions, in August, which ruled out any possible invasion of Greece. Thus, after August 1943, the contributions of the relatively small Greek resistance movement to Allied strategy could only be regarded as minimal. This, considered against the long-term political objectives, and combined with Churchill's own profound sense of commitment to the Greek king, led to an antipathy to the EAM-ELAS forces which contrasted sharply with attitudes and policy towards Tito's partisans. In Yugoslavia, conditions were quite different. The very size of the partisan forces meant, first, that they were a far more important factor than the Greeks, and second, that whatever the British might wish, it could not be seriously assumed that the partisans could be 'controlled' by them. In Greece, the British liaison officers 'gave orders' to the resistance. There was no question of that in Yugoslavia. The partisan resistance movement was thus larger, more powerful, and more independent than its counterparts in Greece.[45] British hopes for a postwar relationship with Yugoslavia were thus transferred from Mihailović to Tito, and it was hoped that the short-term strategic gain might also carry longer-term political dividends. On an optimistic view, therefore, there need be little conflict between short-term strategic and longer-term political requirements.

III

As we have seen, the Chiefs of Staff considered that the intelligence needs of SIS should have overall priority over SOE operations in Western Europe and Scandinavia in 1943. Within that overall framework, SOE continued to work towards the long-term objective of building up organisations to co-ordinate resistance action with Allied strategy at the moment of liberation, and in the short term to carry out specific acts of sabotage. Premature uprisings continued to be discouraged, and SOE made it clear that guerrilla activities outside the Balkans would and could receive little support. In October 1943, operational control of SOE activities throughout this area was formally handed over to COSSAC, and the Chiefs of Staff were to issue no further directives of their own on operational matters. By the beginning of 1944, therefore, SOE resistance activities and plans in Western Europe had become an integral part of overall Allied strategy.

SOE affairs in France developed unevenly in 1943. On the one hand, acts of sabotage increased, the spirit of resistance grew stronger, the *maquis* emerged in response to labour conscription, and the first detailed plans were drawn up for co-ordinating resistance activity with the Allied invasion of 1944. On the other, the struggle between de Gaulle and Giraud adversely affected co-operation between segments of French resistance, and between the British and the Gaullists; the Germans launched a major offensive against resistance circuits and succeeded in destroying or penetrating many; and the *Conseil National de la Résistance* (CNR), formed after months of patient effort by Jean Moulin to unify French resistance behind de Gaulle, was broken up by the Germans almost as soon as it was formed. By the end of the year, however, the worst was over, and attention became focused on Operations Neptune and Overlord.

The 1943 directive to SOE made it clear that its efforts in France were to be primarily devoted to preparations for the 1944 landings. For 1943 itself, SOE should continue sabotage activities, and here the Chiefs of Staff attached the greatest importance to action in pursuit of the anti-U-boat campaign. They made no mention, however, of guerrilla activities in France. Preparations for a nationwide resistance campaign closely co-ordinated with Allied landings, and sabotage against military objectives were, therefore, the two main tasks of SOE. In theory, the ground was suitable. The Germans had occupied the southern zone in November 1942, thus creating the conditions and climate for a national resistance, and incidentally relieving SOE of the requirement imposed by the Foreign Office since 1940 of not offending Vichy by carrying out sabotage. The German *relève*, or labour conscription, increasingly forced young men into hiding and into the *maquis*. Resistance sentiment veered steadily in the direction of rallying to de Gaulle as its leader rather than merely its symbol. In practice, however, each of these factors carried countervailing disadvantages.

The Germans launched a massive counterattack on French resistance groups in 1943. The illusions in which SOE had indulged in 1942 over the *Carte* network had already been punctured by its failure to produce results, as it had promised, when the Germans occupied the southern zone in November 1942. They finally disappeared when the organisation was smashed by the Germans in the spring of 1943.[46] Throughout the year, the German attack on F section's circuits continued, leaving its principal field organisations leaderless. The 'Prosper' circuit, which replaced *Carte* as F section's leading circuit, was broken up by the Germans in late June–early July, in circumstances which have led to much postwar controversy over claims that it was deliberately betrayed by the British themselves in an elaborate game of strategic deception with the Germans. It has been suggested in particular that SOE was used as part of the 1943 deception plan, whereby the Germans were to be deceived into thinking that a cross-Channel invasion was to take place in 1943, and that SOE agents in France were manipulated and betrayed in order to lend authenticity to the exercise. Although SOE *was* involved in 'Starkey', no satisfactory or convincing evidence has ever been produced to substantiate such charges, and given the enormous risks such a policy would have involved for the 1944 landings it seems a far-fetched and highly improbable notion.[47] Other F section circuits were also broken up and/or penetrated, while its special sabotage parties for 1943 were unimpressive. Moreover, SOE's impact on the anti-U-boat campaign was slight, as the U-boat bases were too heavily guarded to be effectively penetrated, and the reports of successful anti-U-boat sabotage which appeared in various SOE papers throughout 1943 were misleading.[48] A certain amount of sabotage by regular circuits was, however, accomplished.

The misfortunes of F section activities were shared by RF, which worked with the Gaullist resistance. It was primarily through RF's work that SOE hoped to co-ordinate the national resistance effort to co-incide with the Allied landings in 1944. But the Gaullist resistance was hampered by the de Gaulle–Giraud dispute which occupied most of 1943, and, more importantly, by German counterattack. The first months of the year were promising. Moulin succeeded with Dewavrin and Brossolette in persuading the resistance movements to agree to the formation of the *Conseil National de la Résistance* (CNR) in May as an instrument to co-ordinate policies in France, and to rally support behind de Gaulle. This patient work was undone in June, when the Germans arrested Delestraint, the leader of the Gaullist secret army, and a dozen leading Gaullists including Moulin himself. The effort to rebuild the structure took time, and it was not easy to replace Moulin, who was tortured and killed. The *débâcle* also produced recriminations between SOE and the Gaullists which delayed matters. SOE insisted that the Gaullist secret organisation in France must decentralise to prevent or contain German counterattack, and that the general direction of the movement should be kept out of France altogether. This SOE mistrust of Gaullist security following hard upon Churchill's attempt in July to dispense altogether with de Gaulle and his control over French resistance held up attempts to rebuild networks for some time, and at the end of the year the 'whole system for articulating a national uprising of the French people'[49] was still in a state of disruption.

What of the *maquis*? On 10 March 1943 de Gaulle wrote to Churchill informing him of the presence in France of 50,000 men of 'high fighting quality' who were evading labour conscription. What could Britain do to help and support these men and what role could they play? Churchill's reply, after consultation with the Chiefs of Staff and SOE, was that only limited help could be given, and that because no direct help in the shape of an Allied invasion could be expected, the numbers of men gathering in the *maquis* should be kept to a minimum, and at all costs a premature uprising should be avoided: 'The British SOE,' Churchill told de Gaulle, 'have warned those people in France with whom they are in contact to do everything in their power to prevent the present wave of resistance from spreading.' Newspapers in the United Kingdom were to be advised to dampen down publicity about guerrilla activities in France.[50] The relative discouragement of guerrilla activity and the desire to keep groups of *maquis* as small as possible, was clearly reflected in the SOE appreciation of April. To act otherwise would have been inconsistent with SOE's 1943 directive and with its supply capabilities, and it was not until 1944 that the *maquis* came to play a more important role in SOE and French affairs.

Elsewhere in western and north-western Europe there was a similarly mixed picture as in France. Resistance grew steadily, but the Germans counterattacked with some success, and because SOE's main concern was now to build up organisations for action not in 1943, but in 1944, the achievements of this year must of necessity seem rather pedestrian. The year began well for SOE in Scandinavia, with the successful destruction in February of the heavy-water plant at Rjukan in southern Norway. This followed unsuccessful attacks by the Royal Air Force and Combined Operations, and was a feather in the cap for the advocates of the superiority of sabotage by resistance groups. It helped SOE's position and credibility as a whole considerably.[51] The success of the Rjukan attack was symbolic of the improved relations between SOE and the indigenous Norwegian resistance which enabled them to co-co-ordinate planning with the COSSAC framework for action in 1944. As we have seen, relations between SOE and Milorg had been strained in the earlier stages of the war, as SOE had attempted to work independently. The creation of the Anglo-Norwegian Co-ordinating Committee in February 1942 had been a first step to improving matters, and in September 1942 relations were placed on a firm footing with the definition by SOE of a long-term policy for Norway which specifically committed SOE to working through and with Milorg.[52] From then on, SOE and Milorg worked together, and 1943 saw the first fruits of this collaboration. Industrial sabotage was the main focus for that year, although it was somewhat limited by the overall SIS policy which put a ban on much activity on the west coast.

Sabotage was the main focus in Denmark, too, but here it had a political rather than a purely military or industrial purpose. Denmark's anomalous status had had for SOE a paradoxical effect. As an independent, neutral, but occupied, country with its own government, Denmark offered SOE certain opportunities in the early years of the war. Because there was no government-in-exile, and because what little resistance which existed was completely 'unofficial', SOE worked directly with resistance groups untroubled by intermediate bodies. This gave it considerable control over Danish resistance, whose main task in 1941–2 was to provide intelligence. SOE appears here to have acted as an 'agent' for SIS, as it was SOE which had established and maintained links with the so-called 'Princes' in the Danish General Staff, who provided much useful military intelligence. By the beginning of 1943, however, it was decided that Danish resistance should expand considerably, and the advantages of tying up German forces and disrupting their communications with Norway at the time of Allied landings in the West began to weigh more heavily on the minds of those responsible for planning resistance action in 1944. But SOE could not work in a vacuum. Resistance in Denmark had been limited in scale because the German occupation had been light-handed and because resistance was seen by many Danes as disloyal to the existing Danish government. The best way to create a growing and nationwide resistance movement was to provoke the Germans into repressive action and force them to take over executive power. To this objective SOE applied itself in the early months of 1943, with total success. From March onwards weapons and sabotage material were dropped to Denmark in increasing quantities, and SOE agents instructed to launch a more active sabotage campaign. Although SOE could not claim the whole credit for the rising tide of resistance sentiment and activity which characterised Denmark in the first six months of 1943, the imposition of direct rule by the German army and the resignation of the Danish government on 28 August 1943 was an outcome for which SOE had assiduously worked. On the resistance side it led to the formation of a Freedom Council, representing various resistance groups, of which Flemming Muus, SOE's chief representative in Denmark, was a member. It was through this Freedom Council that Danish resistance action in 1944 was to be successfully co-ordinated with allied strategy.[53]

Developments in the Low Countries were, from SOE's viewpoint, in dismal contrast to those in Norway and Denmark. In Belgium SOE activities continued on their unsatisfactory course, with only some marginal improvement. The main problem remained that of relations with different and rival agencies of the government-in-exile. At first, SOE had attempted to work through the *Sûreté de l'État*, a section of the Belgian Ministry of Justice, with which SIS contacts were close. But in 1942 an attempt had been made to increase contact with the Belgian Military authorities, with catastrophic results. Spaak, the Belgian Foreign Minister, had broken off all Belgian contacts with SOE in August 1942 and although by the beginning of 1943 they had been re-established they were still unsatisfactory, and hampered operations. Nonetheless, the first steps towards planning co-ordinated action in conjunction with the 1944 landings took place within the COSSAC framework. But in December the commander of the Belgian secret army was arrested, and SOE suspended contact with its field force because of doubts about the security of certain resistance groups. In Holland, the disaster was complete. For eighteen months, SOE supplied and dropped agents to its organisation in Holland unaware that it had been penetrated by, and was under the control of, the Germans. Suspicions about the organisation finally led to the suspension of air drops to Holland in June 1943, but confirmation of the worst fears did not come until November. At this point, all flights to Holland were halted and not resumed until March 1944. The whole structure had to be rebuilt from scratch, and the co-ordination of Dutch resistance with allied strategy was seriously affected. Of far greater consequence to SOE as a whole, however, was the threat that revelation of the *Englandspiel* posed to SOE's continued existence. It provided its many domestic enemies with the perfect opportunity to launch yet another attack on its independence, and 1943 came to an end with Selborne fighting to preserve SOE's existence. Before passing on to examine this crisis, however, something should be said about SOE's relations with Polish resistance.

IV

The example of the Polish secret army had exercised a crucial influence on SOE in its formative stages, for it was largely by extrapolation from the Polish resistance that the concept of the secret armies acting as a crucial fifth column within German-occupied Europe had arisen. The Poles were highly regarded in London, and enjoyed a privileged position amongst the European exiled governments. The Polish government-in-exile maintained its own wireless stations, and enjoyed independence of communications with Poland. Moreover, so far as its relations with SOE were concerned, the Polish government had the sole right to decide what missions to send and who the agents would be, so that SOE in effect became merely a supply agency. In the years 1940–2, Poland had occupied a large amount of SOE time, money and effort, and in 1943 the Polish resistance was described by the Joint Planning

Staff as being 'the strongest, best organised and most determined under-ground movement in Europe'.[54] Yet the Poles were profoundly discon-tented. This discontent sprang from two sources. The first was the role assigned to Polish resistance by Allied strategy, and the second, arising from it, the relative paucity of Allied supplies arriving in Poland. Whereas the Poles saw the climax of their effort as being a national uprising on the eve of the German collapse—the coming into the open of the secret army[55]—the British had decided as early as August 1941 that support for such an uprising was impossible. They had therefore told the Poles that their support through SOE would have to be limited to supplies for sabotage purposes. While this decision may already have been influenced by an awareness that the Soviet Union would object to British support for an uprising on the Russian frontier, good reasons could be found for it in the logistical problems associated with supply to Poland. The Poles nonetheless found it difficult to accept the British view, and Sikorski sought to change the position by seeking to bypass SOE—as in 1942—and by appealing directly to the Americans on sev-eral occasions. Neither campaign met with success.

Developments in 1943 moved steadily against the Polish government. In April diplomatic relations with the USSR were broken off, and the Poles became an increasing embarrassment to the Western Allies in their relations with Stalin. The tide of war had changed, and in the summer the Red Army began to push its way steadily westward towards the disputed Russo-Polish frontier. In June General Rowecki, Com-mander of the Secret Army in Poland, was captured by the Gestapo, and almost immediately afterwards General Sikorski was killed in a plane crash. This adversely effected the quality of Polish leadership at a crucial time, when the Poles were becoming more keen than ever that Allied support should be provided for the secret army in order to be in firm possession of the country before the Russians arrived.[56]

In late June 1943 the Polish government-in-exile made an official ap-proach to the Combined Chiefs of Staff in Washington requesting an in-creased supply of equipment for the Polish Secret Army, while General Sosnkowski, the new Polish Commander-in-Chief, told Sir Alan Brooke that 'six hundred trips by air until April 1944 will be necessary for the most indispensable needs of the Secret Army in Poland'.[57] The basic conception underlying the proposal was that the Secret Army would seize control of central Poland and then be reinforced by the transfer to Poland of the Polish Air Force and the Polish Parachute Brigade. In general the uprising would be co-ordinated with and form part of the Allied offensive in Europe, so that Allied forces could link up with the secret army after no more than three weeks. Moreover, a strengthening of the secret army would improve the Poles' leverage with the Soviet Union and might persuade Stalin to reopen relations. The political significance of the Polish resistance was obvious. While the new Prime Minister, Mikolajczyk, hoped it would pave the way for more supplies, the British and the Americans were only too aware of the dangers, especially in view of the forthcoming Foreign Ministers' meeting in Moscow. Two months after the Polish request and after consultation with SOE and the Chiefs of Staff in London the Combined Chiefs replied officially on 23 September that because the secret army could not take part against the Axis until direct land or sea communications were immediately in prospect, and because of a lack of suitable aircraft, they were unable to fulfil the Polish request, although supplies for purely sabotage purposes would be increased. But certainly the most important reason remained unstated—the hostile reaction likely to be produced in Russia if the West *did* supply the equipment.[58] The Combined Intelligence Committee had advised the Chiefs in Washington that 'In present circumstances, the Russian reaction to any attempt to equip fully the secret army in Poland would be violently hostile', and as the Joint Staff Mission told London, the negative recommendation was based on the idea that otherwise there would be friction amongst the Allies, since the Soviet Union might consider support for the secret army as being designed to oppose a Russian advance beyond the 1939 frontier. The Combined Chiefs of Staff reply enabled Brooke to inform Sosnkowski on 7 October that the British could provide no more aircraft either, and to insist once again that on all operational matters the Poles should deal with SOE. This, understandably, displeased the Poles, and Sosnkowski protested directly to Selborne. Pointing out that only 65 tons of equipment had been dropped to Poland between February 1941 and October 1943, he requested that two squadrons of long-range aircraft be made available immediately for flights to Poland, and that a southern base for such flights be established in Italy.[59] In forwarding Sosnkowski's views to Churchill, Selborne, while saying he would postpone a request for an increase in aircraft allocations to Poland until January 1944, nonetheless evinced sympathy for the Poles. 'I confess to great sympathy with the Polish standpoint', he told Churchill on 21 October,

> They braved Hitler in 1939 on Britain's guaranteed support. They have been crucified. They have not winced. Alone among our occupied Allies they have no Quisling. They have incurred considerable

casualties in very successfully attacking German communications to Russia at our request. They have an organised army of 250,000 in Poland which only needs equipment. To be told that Britain cannot afford them more than 6 aircraft is a bit hard.

But expediency, too, Selborne argued, might dictate a more positive response. While the increased aid he visualised would not be of much strategic significance and would be unlikely therefore to excite adverse reaction from Russia, it might on the other hand facilitate 'the very difficult role we may later have to play with them (the Poles) in regard to the Eastern Frontier'.[60] Eden and the Foreign Office also favoured increased aid within very closely defined limits, but for slightly different reasons. By the beginning of October Eden had come to the belated conclusion that Polish–Soviet relations could only be improved if the frontier question were openly confronted at the forthcoming meeting of Foreign Ministers at Moscow. His view was that the Poles should be persuaded to accept territorial losses in the East to Russia, roughly up to the so-called 'Curzon line', in exchange for gains in the West at the expense of Germany. The Polish underground would be an important factor in negotiations. On the one hand, it should be sufficiently strong and active to help the Poles in their negotiations with the Russians; on the other, it should not behave in such a way, as for example by launching a premature uprising or by resisting the entry of the Russians into the disputed territories, as to alienate the Russians or give them the opportunity of destroying the underground, 'thus facilitating any designs they may have of running Poland in their own way'. The War Cabinet agreed with Eden's views,[61] and he proceeded to Moscow prepared to discuss both the frontier question and the Polish underground with the Russians. In the event, the frontier issue was not raised, but Molotov told Eden that the Soviet Union would only welcome the despatch of arms to Poland if they were destined for 'safe hands'. But who, he wondered aloud, had 'safe hands' in Poland?

Molotov's view simply confirmed that Western support for the Polish secret army would alienate the Russians. But support for sabotage activities was another matter. As Eden told the Chiefs of Staff on 30 December, an important factor in Russo–Polish relations would be 'the ability of the Polish Government to convince the Russians that the Polish Government means business . . . on political grounds therefore we are in favour of giving maximum practicable support to the Polish underground movement's sabotage activities'. On the other hand, Eden added, the large-scale arming of the Polish secret army was an entirely different matter, and 'one about which we should have to be very cautious in view of Russian susceptibilities'. The practical limits imposed upon SOE's ability to help the Poles therefore coincided with the view of the Foreign Office, which was perhaps fortunate, for as a Chiefs of Staff report expressed it in January 1944, 'special operations in Poland are bound up with political considerations to a greater extent than in any other country'. Thus no conflict comparable to those over Greece and Yugoslavia developed between SOE and the Foreign Office where Poland was concerned, although as the next chapter indicates the Poles may have misread Allied intentions as transmitted to them by SOE. The Poles had failed to heed SOE's clear indications in the past that they should not count on support for the secret army, and they failed to heed this advice too. As the Joint Staff Mission told London, the Poles 'appear to be living in a world of make-believe'.[62]

Poland was only one—if the most important—of the three European countries for which the Chiefs of Staff in London still held operational responsibility. The others were Hungary and Czechoslovakia. A directive for all three was issued to SOE on 20 October 1943. This provided guidance on strategic objectives and suggested how the aircraft available for operations into Europe as a whole should be allocated in reference to the three countries. In all three, the Chiefs of Staff looked to continuing and increased sabotage against German military and industrial objectives, and requested that preparations be made, in consultation with COSSAC, for intensified sabotage campaigns to coincide with Overlord (or Rankin, the code name for operations in the event of a sudden German collapse). Poland's importance was reflected in the allocation of aircraft. Of the aircraft available then or in the future for Europe outside the Balkans, twenty per cent of air effort was to be set aside for Poland, with Hungary and Czechoslovakia receiving five per cent each.[63]

Early in November, SOE submitted the report on its 1943 activities which the Chiefs of Staff had requested in issuing the March directive. This raised the question of whether a new directive for 1944 should be issued. On the grounds that operational control of most SOE activities was now in the hands of the area Commanders-in-Chief (with the exception of central Europe), the Chiefs of Staff decided against a new directive. On the other hand, they decided that they should still have the right to suggest relative priorities for subversive operations, and on 26 November they amended the list so that the Balkans came first, followed by enemy-occupied Italy. Third came France, followed by the Aegean Islands and Crete, then Poland, Hungary, and Czechoslovakia together. Norway and the Low Countries came sixth, and finally—as in the past—the Far East. The list is a useful indicator of the changing character of SOE-supported activities, for the Balkans and Northern Italy were the scene for guerrilla and partisan warfare on a scale which in its early years SOE had not foreseen, and indeed had foresworn. Even in France, the third on the list, open fighting by resistance groups against the Germans prior to the liberation was to assume significance and to receive support from SOE in 1944.[64] But before SOE could achieve anything in 1944, it had first to surmount the challenge to its very existence posed by the reverberations of the *Englandspiel*.

V

On 1 December 1943 a bombshell was dropped on SOE affairs when the Vice-Air Chief of Staff, Air Marshall Bottomley, announced that the Commander-in-Chief of Bomber Command had suspended all flights in connection with SOE operations in Europe. The reason, Bottomley told his colleagues on the Chiefs of Staff Committee, was the discovery by the Air Ministry that the entire Dutch SOE network had been penetrated and controlled by the Germans since 1942; the general ban on flights reflected a fear that the Dutch situation was duplicated elsewhere in Europe and that the safety of air crews might be in jeopardy. He suggested an immediate enquiry by the Joint Intelligence Committee.[65] Thus began the final phase of the crisis which had begun in the summer over SOE's effectiveness and usefulness as an independent agency within the government. It was a crisis which it barely survived intact.

Churchill and the Chiefs of Staff were in Teheran when the news of the *Englandspiel* broke, and the Vice-Chiefs of Staff therefore reported their concern to Attlee, the Deputy Prime Minister. He immediately summoned a special ministerial meeting on the following day, to which were summoned the Secretary of State for Air, and Lord Selborne and Sporborg of SOE. Having heard Air Marshal Bottomley explain the background, including his claim that SIS had issued warnings to SOE about the situation in Holland which had been ignored, Selborne said he would welcome a full enquiry; but he claimed that earlier SOE and SIS enquiries caused by previous suspicions about the Dutch situation had proved negative, and that German penetration in Holland was unlikely to have had effects elsewhere. The Secretary of State for Air then voiced suspicions about the SOE organisation in Denmark and Poland, and the meeting accordingly instructed the Joint Intelligence

Committee to investigate the situation in Holland, to make an immediate report on Denmark and Poland, and, should the allegations about German penetration prove to be true, to undertake a general investigation of SOE networks throughout Europe. In the meantime, Bomber Command should suspend all SOE operations to Holland, Denmark and Poland.[66] On the following day, the JIC cleared the SOE Danish organisation, and flights to Denmark were resumed;[67] but the general enquiry by the JIC went ahead. Its report was ready for discussion by the Chiefs of Staff on 3 January 1944, prior to a full discussion in the Defence Committee on 14 January.

This report on the German penetration of SOE in Europe was extended by the JIC from an examination of SOE's security in Europe, into a general review of SOE's work in Europe as well as its higher direction and organisation.[68] Its overall tone was damning of SOE, and it represented the most severe criticism the organisation had received from an official investigative body. The report was in two main sections. The first dealt with SOE operations and security in Europe, the second with its organisation and higher direction. The Committee looked closely at SOE European networks (but excluding the Balkans), and concluded that while SOE in Holland had been penetrated for several months there was no evidence of a similar situation elsewhere. Where, as in Belgium, there was evidence that the security of certain groups was suspect, the JIC reported that 'the precautions taken by SOE appear to be satisfactory'. This did not mean that the Committee was very happy, however. It was concerned that in Norway security might in future be compromised by the secret army, and it considered the independence of the Polish resistance to be highly dangerous. Moreover, it said, 'credits transmitted by SOE to the Poles are used in a manner which if the Russians knew would have a disastrous effect on Anglo-Russian relations'. In France, it expressed disapproval at the overcentralisation of groups under the control of the French National Committee,[69] and, returning to the Dutch fiasco, it charged that SOE should have operated on the assumption of German penetration from at least August 1943. Passing on to observations about SOE's operations in Europe, the Committee damned it with faint praise. It failed to make any reference to the achievements of the Polish secret army, it completely omitted the Balkans, referred somewhat scathingly to 'some degree of small-scale sabotage in France', and pointed out that 'there is no resistance movement in Germany with which SOE are in contact'. The overall effect was to ridicule SOE operations, and the impression that the report sought to condemn SOE was reinforced by the conclusions dealing with its higher direction and organisation. These demanded radical change. They called for much closer outside control of SOE (although it is not clear exactly by whom or what), demanded closer co-ordination with the Chiefs of Staff, suggested the separation of subversive from para-military or guerrilla operations, control by theatre commanders, and 'co-ordination with SIS, the necessity for unification of intelligence and subversive activities and the institution of a single system of clandestine communications'. This last suggestion alone was tantamount to the abolition of SOE, for its origins in 1940 lay precisely in the separation of subversion from intelligence, and SOE had fought for two years for the right to have its own communications system. The JIC now sought to reverse that, and it is difficult to resist the conclusion that this repre-sented the wishes of SIS and the culmination of their intermittent but persistent attempts to regain control over their wayward offspring.

Selborne clearly saw that if the report went unanswered there was little future for SOE. He therefore prepared a detailed defence and refu-tation of the charges and also sought to ensure that no decisions about SOE itself should be taken before the return of the Prime Minister, who, having fallen seriously ill with pneumonia after the Teheran Confer-ence, was recuperating in Marrakesh and did not in fact return to Eng-land until 17 January.

Selborne's memorandum on SOE operations in Europe, with its annexes, was over thirty pages long, and contained an enormous weight of evidence designed to counter the JIC charges.[70] As an opening gen-eral remark, the Minister pointed out that German penetration was inherent in the work of any secret organisation (and, he parenthetically and caustically remarked, SIS were well aware of that). War was a risky business, and enemy counterattacks were to be expected. On the specific question of the security of SOE in Europe, he complained that the JIC report was tendentious. The independence of the Polish secret organisa-tion was not the responsibility of SOE, but had been decided upon by higher authority in 1940; and precisely because of it, SOE could hardly be held responsible for Polish policy decisions. In France, the over-centralisation of the Gaullist resistance was another area where guilt by association was unjust. SOE itself had strongly discouraged this overcentralisation, and had been careful to maintain its own indepen-dent F section separate from the Gaullists. As for the fiasco in Holland, Selborne made no attempt to deny it, but he was anxious to clear SOE of the charge that it should have halted operations in August 1943. The fact was, he said, that suspicions had led to a complete suspension of op-erations into Holland at the end of June, but that following three months of investigation—including work by SIS—it was concluded that one or two groups had escaped German penetration. With the Air Ministry's consent, and with their knowledge of the risks, two trial sorties were made. They failed, and from mid-November SOE had admitted that their organisation in Holland was completely under German control. The JIC charges on this point were, therefore, misleading.

The Minister was equally adamant in defending SOE's record in Europe. Losses and casualties were not out of proportion to what had been achieved. In 1943, in the area covered by the JIC report, losses in aircraft had been 2.8 per cent, and for all SOE theatres, 1.56 per cent. These were low figures, Selborne pointed out, when considering the highly dangerous nature of SOE missions. Casualties in agents were not excessive either; they amounted to 14 per cent of agents despatched in 1943, of whom a third had been Gaullist French. He went on to highlight SOE's achievements in the liberation of Corsica ('primarily an SOE operation'), in the implementation of a widespread sabotage campaign in Denmark since August, and in stimulating resistance in the Balkans, as evidence of SOE's effectiveness overlooked by the JIC. (To strengthen his argument he might well have pointed out that SOE's 1943 directive had placed Corsica and the Balkans as high priorities, whereas areas such as France, the Low Countries and Scandinavia were given a relatively low priority.) He also appended a detailed list of sabotage acts carried out in 1943 by organisations under the control of SOE. In addition, he claimed, 100,000 tons of shipping had been sunk or damaged by SOE agents in 1943, and several ships had been captured. Since July 1942, SOE had been the sole suppliers of scarce foreign currency (mostly in small denominations) for use by SIS and various service departments—especially the Air Ministry, who required it to assist evading air crews making their way back to the United Kingdom. This work had been highly successful.

Selborne reserved his greatest criticism and scorn, however, for the JIC recommendations about SOE's higher direction and organisation. He caustically suggested that had the JIC troubled to consult the Joint Planning Staff, and even SOE itself, many errors and misunderstandings could have been avoided. As it was, the recommendations and suggestions were largely unhelpful. For example, he pointed out, the proposal that subversive and paramilitary operations should be separated and placed under different authorities had been inherent in the reform of SOE suggested by the Middle East Defence Committee in September, and had been rejected at the meeting chaired by the Prime Minister on 30 September. The entire question of SOE–COS liaison had also been examined at that time, and the recommendations made and accepted had produced no subsequent complaints from the Chiefs of Staff. Was it really necessary, he asked, to review again decisions which had been reached after much debate only three months previously? Turning to the very top level of command, Selborne defended the decision of the War Cabinet in 1940 to separate SOE from SIS. In his opinion, indeed, the desirability of this separation was greater now than ever before, as SOE work increasingly came into the limelight. Even if it was decided that control of SOE should be removed from the Minister of Economic Warfare and placed under the Minister of Defence, moreover, he felt strongly that a ministerial subordinate would be essential. Finally, Selborne said, SOE should be given its due and its chance. It was a service which had had

to learn and devise the techniques of subversion, sabotage and secret warfare without any nucleus of experienced professionals to guide them, as in other Services and Government Departments. This Service is accordingly continually growing in efficiency, and daily developing the art of warfare in a new sphere. Notable special operations already stand to its credit, and all that it asks is that it should be given the confidence which it deserves and be freed from the feeling that any setback which the fortunes of war may bring is going to be made the occasion by other Departments for immediately demanding its dismemberment.

This spirited defence of SOE was considered by the Defence Committee on 14 January 1944, with Attlee, in Churchill's continued absence, in the chair. The Chiefs of Staff had already forwarded their own independent conclusions on the JIC report to him, and these were hardly favourable to SOE's continued existence. In agreeing with the general conclusions of the JIC report, they considered that the best remedy from a military point of view 'was to be found in placing SIS and SOE under the Minister of Defence'; but should that prove impossible, then the need for closer integration of the two organisations was so great 'that SOE should now be placed under the control of the Secretary of State for Foreign Affairs'.[71]

These various proposals for radically altering the control of special operations were not, however, discussed, as Attlee ruled that such basic questions should be set aside until the return of the Prime Minister. No-one seemed inclined to challenge this view, although Eden was very anxious to make it plain that he was opposed to any amalgamation of SIS and SOE. The latter, he said, 'was an organisation rapidly established to meet immediate wartime needs, whereas SIS were a long established service playing a completely different type of role'. Much of the meeting was taken up instead with the details of the report, until Selborne intervened to say that there were two urgent matters which needed decisions. The first was the resumption of flights to Holland, to rebuild the SOE organisation; and the second was a decision on the allocation of aircraft to SOE for 1944, a request which had been with the Chiefs of Staff for the past month. The Committee approved the resumption of operations to Holland, and asked the Chiefs of Staff to give urgent attention to SOE's request for aircraft. In addition, it asked SOE and the Chiefs to make recommendations about the future operational control over SOE activities in Poland and Czechoslovakia, and called for greater involvement of RAF officers in planning SOE air operations as a means of closer surveillance over SOE reception arrangements.

This was the extent of the Defence Committee's intervention. SOE was now able to resume normal working, but with two major questions unresolved: its higher direction and future as an independent agency under the Minister of Economic Warfare, and the future control of operations in Poland and Czechoslovakia (all others in Europe by now being under the operational control of COSSAC or the Allied Commander-in-Chief Mediterranean). The first and outstanding question was reserved for Churchill's decision. Although no written record of this can be found, it is clear that he favoured SOE's continued existence as then constituted, and ruled to that effect shortly after his return to London. Indeed, within ten days of his return he was actively involving himself with SOE in discussions about support to the French *maquis*. No further attempts to alter the SOE structure were made before it was finally disbanded at the end of the war. In thus deciding, Churchill therefore overruled the Joint Intelligence Committee, SIS, and the Chiefs of Staff. On the eve of the Allied invasion of Europe, in which patriot organisations were designed to play an important supporting role against the German forces, it meant that SOE could concentrate singlemindedly on its task, without the distractions of attacks from its enemies at home.

Before finally leaving the events of 1943, however, it should be noted that German penetration of SOE was not the only worry expressed about its security. As concerns about the postwar world and future relations with the Soviet Union increasingly dominated the minds of those responsible for strategic, diplomatic, and intelligence matters, fears arose about communist penetration of SOE. Shortly before the

Englandspiel crisis broke, in fact, an indication that there had been some such penetration was given when a Captain B. L. Uren, 'an army officer on special duty', was sentenced to seven years' imprisonment on a charge of having passed secret information to a high-ranking member of the British communist party, Douglas Springhall. Uren worked for SOE, and Springhall, who had long recruited in Britain for the Soviet Union's espionage services, had already been imprisoned in July for obtaining secrets from an Air Ministry employee.[72] While evidence is lacking as to Uren's offence, it is possible that he had passed on to Springhall information about peace feelers received by SOE from Hungary. But whatever it was, the fact of communist interest in the inner workings of SOE served to fuel the flames of SIS and Foreign Office anxiety and contributed to the intensity of the attack against SOE in December. It also foreshadowed the growing importance which concerns over Soviet and communist objectives in Europe were to play in SOE operations during and after liberation, and presaged the purge of all known communists from Britain's secret organisations.

6 Invasion, Liberation, and Order

As the Soviet military advances of 1943 and 1944 underlined the extent to which the Soviet Union would be a major factor in the affairs of postwar Europe, the British war leadership began to define more clearly Britain's own interests in Europe and what these implied for future relations with Moscow. The lessons of the 1930s and the exhaustion of Britain's financial power in the course of the war itself indicated that Europe would be more important than ever before. Not only did Britain's political and commercial interests demand the quickest possible restoration of order and security in Europe, and the maintenance there of politically sympathetic régimes, but there were vital security interests involved. In 1944 the Foreign Office defined these as being, first, 'the security of the United Kingdom against long-distance air attack and, still more, against the domination of Europe by a single Great Power' (a traditional British foreign policy objective), and second, 'the security of our vital sea and air communications in the Mediterranean and elsewhere'. But if the future of Europe was crucial to British interests, and the Soviet Union was to emerge from the war as the predominant power in Europe, it meant that an Anglo-Soviet alliance would have to be the foundation stone of British policy in Europe. Friendly relations with the Soviet Union would guarantee the possibility of at least some British influence in east and south-east Europe which the course of the war would bring under Soviet occupation, while in western Europe (including Italy), Scandinavia, and the eastern Mediterranean (including Greece and Turkey), British influence would be exercised more directly and with little likelihood of Soviet interference or objection. This appreciation was not based upon any illusions about Soviet benevolence towards the West, but on a pragmatic reading of Soviet interests. These, it was believed, would require an immense programme of postwar reconstruction and rehabilitation which would

144

focus Soviet energies away from territorial expansion and communisation abroad, towards internal recovery and international collaboration with her wartime allies. This priority would be reinforced by the fear of future German recovery, so that the Soviet Union would count heavily on the co-operation of her allies in imposing stringent and effective measures for preventing a revival of Germany as a menace to Russia. Thus, self-interest would dictate a continuation of the wartime alliance into peacetime. On the basis of these assumptions, the British government by 1944 had an increasingly clear view of relative priorities in Europe. Within the framework of the over-arching Soviet alliance, Britain would consolidate her influence in France, the Low Countries, Spain, Portugal, Scandinavia, Turkey, Greece, and eventually Italy. In central, east, and south-east Europe, Soviet security interests would be recognised and respected, and there should be no direct challenge to predominant Russian influence in Yugoslavia, Albania, Rumania, Bulgaria, Poland, Hungary or Czechoslovakia. Although in these countries there was room for some British influence to be exerted, it was clear that overall British interests in European security would, if necessary, mean the sacrifice of specific interests in any one of these countries.[1]

From Teheran onwards, the British government began to move gradually (and not always without considerable hesitation) towards a series of more explicit agreements with the Soviet Union along these lines, with the impressive victories of the Red Army in Europe often forcing the pace (in January the Red Army reached the Polish eastern frontier of 1939, and by mid-April had reoccupied practically all Soviet territory). That relations with the Soviet Union were a crucial consideration in Britain's policies towards resistance movements was indicated clearly on 3 January 1944 when Eden reported to the War Cabinet on events in Greece, Yugoslavia, and Poland. He told the Cabinet that in Greece the Soviet Union was now prepared to support British efforts to achieve a reconciliation between the rival resistance movements, while in Yugoslavia SOE was preparing the necessary evidence to justify the imminent final breach with Mihailović. Lastly, Eden reported, the Foreign Office and SOE were preparing to enter discussions with the Russians about the Polish resistance movement, and it was proposed that the right of the Poles in London to communicate with their resistance forces in Poland without SOE being aware of the content of their messages should be removed.[2] Simultaneously with this evident concern for the preservation of satisfactory Anglo-Soviet relations, the government was also beginning to focus more closely on the longer-term implications of the Soviet alliance for British security interests. Already, in

October 1943, these interests had been explicitly recognised as an essential component of any military advice the Chiefs of Staff should give to the government on matters concerning the Soviet Union, and in discussions in the following months over the dismemberment of Gemany the Chiefs of Staff recognised the pre-eminence of concerns about a potential Soviet threat to British security. However much expressed in language concerned exclusively with the war against Germany, military advice and decisions were now formulated with a keen eye on the shape of the postwar world.[3]

I

This background provided an increasingly important framework for decisions about SOE operations in 1944, the year in which SOE reached the peak of its fighting effectiveness. It would be too simple to say that there was a shift from 'short-term military' concerns about the war against Germany to 'long-term diplomatic' concerns about Britain's postwar political interests, because this suggests a false dichotomy between strategy and diplomacy. Strategic decisions about the war against Germany were no more made in a political vacuum than were diplomatic activities in a strategic vacuum; and the Chiefs of Staff military advice to the government now specifically took into account not only German threats to British security, but also possible Soviet threats to Britain's long-term interests in Europe. It was true, however, that the essential precondition for *any* British future in Europe lay with the liberation of western Europe by Anglo-American forces, and thus the immediate priority for SOE in the first half of 1944 was playing its part in the success of Operation Overlord, and its companion in strategic deception, Operation Bodyguard. These two operations overshadowed most allied thinking during the first six months of 1944.

At Teheran agreement had been reached by Churchill, Stalin, and Roosevelt on the strategic plan for 1944 involving the Anglo-American landings in France (Operation Overlord). As an important supplement to Overlord, agreement was also reached in principle on the major strategic deception campaign, Operation Bodyguard. This plan's two main components were Operations Fortitude and Zeppelin. Fortitude was designed to point to the Pas-de-Calais as the invasion area, and here resistance groups in north-west France and the Low Countries were well-placed to assist such deception by, for example, increasing sabotage in the area to indicate imminent landings. How far this led to the deception and deliberate sacrifice of SOE agents and supported groups remains open to conjecture, but speculation should be tempered by the appreciation of one fundamental point. However tempting the prospect of using resistance groups may have been, the possible benefits had to be weighed against the very serious strategic and political risks involved. Action to support deception was counterproductive if it destroyed the ability of resistance networks to take action during the *real* operation—Overlord—or, if by cynically sacrificing *résistants* the political objective of securing good relations with Britain's west European neighbours was damaged. In short, and in the absence of any conclusive evidence, it seems most likely that SOE's role in Bodyguard in Western Europe probably assisted deception only if this did not damage the contribution it would make to Overlord; and this was its main *raison d'être* by 1944. Plan Zeppelin, the other half of Bodyguard, was designed to keep German troops tied down in the Balkans by simultaneously suggesting that an Anglo-American invasion could be expected there, and by stimulating resistance in the satellite countries through subversion and bombing. This would keep the Germans preoccupied, and help to divert attention away from the crucial Overlord area. The details of this highly complex strategic deception plan were worked out by the London Controlling Section, and Colonel Bevan, its head, eventually signed a protocol with the Russians in Moscow on 3 March 1944 for Anglo-Soviet co-operation on Bodyguard. The need to protect Bodyguard itself, as well as the demands of Overlord, were to influence decisions about SOE activity during the first half of 1944.[4]

II

Western Europe

So long as the future of SOE and its operations in Europe had been in doubt, several major and pressing issues had been deferred. The clearing of SOE of the main charges against it, combined with Churchill's return to London in mid-January, at last produced decisions. Instructed by the Defence Committee, where Eden supported Selborne in his insitence that it was during the next six months that the work of the resistance movements against Germany would prove vital, the Chiefs of Staff finally turned to these issues on 19 January.[5]

A basic and pressing question was that of the allocation of aircraft. At the beginning of 1944 the total allotment of aircraft to SOE was 58 (the figure laid down by the Chiefs of Staff in July 1943), the majority of which were based in the Mediterranean and designated for work in the Balkans. In addition, two squadrons of US heavy aircraft had been set aside for support of the Polish resistance, but these were not yet operational. These aircraft had a combined calculated lift of 532 tons per month. Since July 1943, however, SOE had been given a number of new commitments and existing ones had grown. The Cairo Conference of November had given high priority to arming the Yugoslav partisans, and in that some month the Chiefs of Staff had placed the supply of arms to the Italian partisans second on SOE's priority list. In addition, AFHQ were now calling for increased supplies to the French *maquis* in southern France in connection with the projected Anvil landings. Elsewhere, the run-up to D-Day meant that the next five months were vital. COSSAC's plans for the French resistance alone required a minimum delivery of 350 tons per month, while in Central Europe increased support to the Polish resistance might involve fifty more sorties per month. These new and increased commitments amounted to a total of 1400 tons of supplies per month for the European resistance, or 300 aircraft. This would represent a substantial increase in SOE's need for aircraft, and, conversely, a considerable diversion of aircraft from other tasks. In SOE's view, it was time both to increase the total number of aircraft to align its resources with its commitments, and to redress the imbalance between Western Europe and the Balkans created by the July 1943 decision to throw the weight of SOE's effort to the Balkans. SOE had therefore officially requested in December 1943 an increase in the number of UK based aircraft, an increase of aircraft reserves in the Balkans to maintain a constant first-line strength, an approach to the Americans for fifty additional aircraft for SOE–OSS work, and a supplementary effort to ensure that COSSAC's minimum targets in the invasion areas be reached.[6] Despite the obviously growing significance of resistance forces, and despite, too, Churchill's own evident enthusiasm for considerably increased support to the French and the Poles in particular, in which he was backed by Eden, the regular military leadership continued to display both its suspicions of SOE and its preference for the strategic bombing offensive which had characterised its views since 1940. When they considered the matter on 19 January the Chiefs of Staff were no more willing than they had been in the past to accept all of SOE's requests, their traditional conservatism reinforced by the recent *Englandspiel* experience. But they did, reluctantly, accept that more would have to be done. Consequently, they agreed to an increase of 60 sorties per month and to an approach to the Americans, while arguing at the same time that many of SOE's problems of supply to the Balkans would be relieved by the transfer of the main base for operations to southern Italy (Bari). Their response did not meet SOE's full requirements, but Sporborg, Gubbin's deputy, said that it 'could be regarded as satisfactory'.[7] This was a fair response. The evidence available suggests that with some exceptions the supply of aircraft was no major problem after that, but this was late in the day for an organisation which the Chiefs of Staff had described as of the very highest importance in July 1940, and it did not prevent the need for disruptive diversions from one area to another over the next few months.

That Bomber Command still remained grudging in its attitude towards SOE, and was committed to its strategic bombing offensive to the point where by prevarication and other tactics it attempted to avoid implementation of the orders given to it, became apparent in its response to the attempt to arm the French *maquis* in the following crucial months prior to the Anvil landings in southern France. As far back as the Québec meeting between Roosevelt and Churchill in August 1943, it had been agreed that the possibilities of supplying bands of guerrillas by air in the south of France should be explored, and Churchill's enthusiasm for this plan had been rekindled by Emmanuel d'Astier de la Vigerie during the Prime Minister's enforced stay in North Africa. D'Astier, the Commissioner for the Interior in the French Committee of National Liberation, insisted that more should be done for supplies to the French resistance. In doing so, he was reflecting deep sentiment expressed in debates in the French Consultative Assembly in Algiers early in January. Here, several speakers had unanimously emphasised that the French resistance was starved of supplies, complained that the Allied staffs had ignored it, and accused the Americans and British of witholding support for political reasons. The question had therefore assumed an important political dimension by the time d'Astier met Churchill again personally in London on 27 January, and by that time the Foreign Office had thrown its weight behind the French request on the grounds that 'we shall immensely aggravate our difficulties unless we ensure that when D-Day comes the Resistance Groups (and the French Committee, which increasingly follows their lead) have confidence in the Allied High Command and are willing to co-operate with it'. This in turn reflected increasing Foreign Office concern in 1944 that postwar Anglo-French relations not be jeopardised.[8] Churchill's personal enthusiasm was fired by d'Astier and by meetings with agents directly involved in SOE's activities in France, and by his then obsession with the Anzio landings and the Italian campaign, where he envisaged valuable diversionary support being given by *maquis* activity in southeast France. In addition, his romantic temperament led him to draw extravagant analogies between the *maquis* and the Yugoslav partisans. He told Lord Selborne and other high officials on 27 January:

> He wished and believed [that it was possible] to bring about a situation in the whole area between the Rhône and the Italian frontier and between the Lake of Geneva and the Mediterranean comparable to the situation in Yugoslavia. Brave and desperate men could cause the most acute embarrassment to the enemy and it was right that we should do all in our power to foster and stimulate so valuable an aid to Allied strategy.[9]

It was made immediately clear, however, that if there was to be any embarrassment it was to be at home, for Portal, on behalf of the RAF, lost no time in insisting that no decision should be taken which would result in the diversion of any part of the major bombing offensive over Germany. It would be 'deplorable if anything were done at this stage to upset our bombing effort and thus affect the spirit of those taking part in it'. Coming as it did within a week of the Chiefs of Staff reluctant decision to yield to pressures from the Defence Committee for increased support to SOE, and followed as it was by a refusal a week later to provide more aircraft for flights to Poland,[10] Portal's comments indicated how little had really changed. The subsequent intervention by Sir Archibald Sinclair, the Minister for Air, repeated a tactic by now firmly established whenever prospects of increased aircraft support for SOE were discussed. Not only did he support Portal's demand, but expressed the view that if supplies to the *maquis* were given higher priority, they should not be allowed to interfere with the essential requirements of SIS. RAF solicitude for SIS interests was not new, invariably coincided with issues related to SOE, and was sufficiently frequent for it to have become an informal working alliance. In this case, the Air Force could be certain that Menzies and SIS would leap into the fray against the prospect of increased activity in France, and predictably enough within a few days SIS was circulating a report that fewer than 2000 French guerrillas could be expected to work together in conjunction with an invasion. It was clear that although SOE had survived the German penetration enquiry, its domestic opponents remained no less hostile than in the past.[11]

Between Churchill's enthusiasm for the French *maquis*, backed by the Foreign Office, on the one hand, and the overt opposition of the RAF combined with covert opposition from SIS on the other, a compromise formula was agreed upon whereby while neither the bomber offensive nor SIS needs would be interfered with, supplies for the French *maquis* would receive first priority over other SOE operations. This was the first time since 1940 that resistance in France had received top priority, and the results showed in considerably increased numbers of sorties to France in the following six months and a new concentration by SOE on the support of guerrilla activity in the south. But this temporary enthusiasm on Churchill's part for the *maquis* (as distinct from the rest of the French resistance) threw much careful planning into disarray, and illustrated once again the problems which could occur when Churchill intervened too closely in matters with which he was not familiar. In response to the decisions of the 27 January meeting, Selborne had submitted a plan aimed at providing arms for 16,000 *maquis* during February, to which the Prime Minister responded by demanding a doubling of that figure in March. At the same time, however, he was not prepared to see aircraft diverted from supplies to the Yugoslav partisans, despite the fact that air drops to the *maquis* could only be carried out by the aircraft already allotted to SOE in the Mediterranean for Yugoslav and other Balkan supplies. Nor was he prepared to force a showdown with the RAF and insist on more aircraft being made available. The result, not surprisingly, was confusion. SOE Cairo blew up in exasperation, informing London on 9 February that 'the recent sweeping demands for the diversion of air sorties to France . . . have reduced the Balkan programme to something near chaos' while the OSS reported that British Army authorities were exasperated by Churchill's 'projection of his authority into the strategic picture for diplomatic ends'. Eisenhower and SHAEF headquarters were not much more pleased than the authorities in Cairo, for they had not been originally consulted and, as Walter Bedell Smith, Eisenhower's Chief of Staff, told Churchill on 3 March, it was not in accordance with Overlord planning to give such high priority to arming the *maquis* at the expense of the resistance elsewhere in France. Under pressure from these presentations, and with subterranean sniping from within his own entourage, particularly from Desmond Morton, who was deputed to deal with the matter and whose SIS contacts led him to draw attention to every possible failing in the SOE effort to the *maquis*, Churchill slightly relented. Although he uttered a characteristically defiant remark to the effect that 'the mountain peoples have had little enough', he agreed in March that greater priority should be given to supplies for the resistance in north-west France, and in May, of the 446 successful sorties to France, only 148 went to the *maquis*. But once the D-Day landings had been successfully accomplished with the assistance of the resistance in the north and north-west, he returned to the charge. On 20 June he urged Selborne to support the *maquis* in open guerrilla warfare: 'Every effort must be made to supply the *maquis* at once with rifles, Bren guns, Piat guns, mortars and Bazookas with ammunition . . . Pray tell me if I can help you to accelerate action'. Selborne was receptive, if only in part to demonstrate that SHAEF and the sceptics had been proven wrong by the events surrounding the Overlord operation in underestimating the contribution SOE could make through the French resistance. That this contribution had indeed been larger than expected was indicated by Desmond Morton's reluctant admission to Churchill on 17 June that 'the Resistance has so far done a better job than I expected they would'. Selborne capitalised on the atmosphere to circulate a report on the SOE contribution to Overlord to his Cabinet colleagues, and to suggest to Churchill that SHAEF planning left something to be desired. It also inspired him to make the unfortunate suggestion that Brigadier Myers, 'of Greek guerrilla fame', might be appointed as a 'super liaison officer' to General Koenig on *maquis* matters, where his experience in the Greek mountains might be quite valuable in the Haute Savoie. Selborne should have known that suggesting Myers' name to Churchill was like waving a red flag at a bull, as Myers had been withdrawn from Greece in 1943 at Foreign Office request for showing too much sympathy to EAM-ELAS, and Churchill's irrational hostility to the latter was no secret. Predictably, Churchill refused the suggestion about Myers, and Selborne's other proposal for increased support to the *maquis* beyond the framework of SHAEF plans was quashed by the Chiefs of Staff and by SHAEF itself on the grounds that it would involve a dispersal of effort which would have no operational value. And at a Chiefs of Staff meeting on 24 June Gubbins, who offered criticisms of supply arrangements to resistance in north-eastern France, was firmly put in his place by the CIGS, Sir Alan Brooke, who said forcibly that he had no doubt SHAEF knew what they were doing, and that in any case SOE should confine discussion of such problems to within SHAEF. Although SOE still had a role to play in France, it was clear that the successful completion of Overlord meant that its affairs in that country were now of subsidiary interest to the war leadership, and that they were content to delegate matters to Eisenhower.[12]

What in fact had SOE accomplished to assist Overlord? This, after all, represented the litmus test of SOE's strategic value, for ever since 1940 its main, although by no means sole, justification lay in the contribution it would make to the Allied return to the European continent. It was this factor which had saved it from disintegration and break-up in January during the German penetration scare, and was to save it again in April when it was once more ran afoul of the Foreign Office over affairs in Rumania. As has been seen, the strategic contribution that European resistance might make to eventual allied victory had steadily diminished in the minds of the military planners and the war leadership since 1941. In COSSAC planning, and in the plans approved at the Québec Conference in August 1943 ('Quadrant'), this process had reached the point where no firm military reliance at all was placed on the contribution resistance might make during the Overlord operation. In the words of the official historian of the campaign in the West, the resistance movement's 'heterogeneous composition, paucity of equipment and lack of military experience, and the impossibility of calculating the size and efficiency of resistance groups, prevented [it] playing an integral part in military operations which depended on exact and secret plans. From the Allies' point of view its achievement was to be regarded as a bonus.'[13] This COSSAC view was shared by Eisenhower's staff after the creation of SHAEF and during the months leading up to D-Day. It meant that support to the European resistance in the Overlord area of north and north-west Europe was strictly limited by the prior requirements of the regular armed forces, but that within those limits priority was given to France in an effort to extract the maximum 'bonus'.

SOE's role in the D-Day landings had been sketched out as early as August 1943, and in September SOE (and OSS) sections dealing with north and north-western Europe had been placed under the operational command of COSSAC. In January 1944 these sections were combined to form a combined headquarters, which on 1 May then became known as Special Forces Headquarters (SFHQ), operating within the framework of SHAEF directives. SOE's assistance to Overlord and Neptune (the actual landings) was designed to cover two stages, the first prior to the landings, and the second on and after D-Day itself.[14]

In the first stage, SOE directed sabotage in accordance with COSSAC and SHAEF requirements throughout western Europe. The main targets were railroads and locomotives, and, in northern France and Belgium, canal networks. Factories producing strategic goods were also targets, and here SOE assisted in blackmail campaigns to persuade factory owners to co-operate in the sabotage of their own enterprises (they were successful in the Peugeot case, but not in that of the Michelins). Power supplies—electricity, petrol, and oil—were also prime targets, as was shipping, especially in Scandinavia. All these attacks were designed to create the maximum interference with German war production and to damage the communications networks leading to the landing areas which the Germans would need for bringing up reinforcements.

SOE also had an important role to play in Bodyguard, the campaign of strategic deception, and, in Selborne's words, 'the dispersal of enemy troops and their concentration in areas removed from the bridgehead became one of the most important tasks demanded of SOE'.[15] Deliveries to the Pas-de-Calais area were increased before D-Day, and after the landings false action messages were broadcast to the area, thus assisting the successful deception accomplished by Bodyguard. As indicated previously, however, it is difficult to say much about this and its consequences for resistance groups, while so much material about SOE and Bodyguard itself remains classified. Further afield, the Germans were encouraged by an increased tempo of sabotage and other resistance activities to maintain garrisons which might otherwise have been used to strengthen their forces in the invasion area. It was this strategic imperative which lay behind the government's urgent attempts in the spring of 1944 to produce a joint Allied declaration recognising Denmark as a partner in the fight against Nazism, with a view to further increasing the level of Danish resistance in the country. Even in the absence of this declaration, in March 1944 there were eight divisions of German troops in Denmark as opposed to only four in the preceding August.

In the second phase of SOE activity connected with Overlord, the main objective as defined by SHAEF was to obstruct German reinforcements pouring into the Allied bridgehead, and in selected areas to encourage guerrilla activity so as to further divert their energies from the Normandy beaches (such as, for example in the south of France). In other parts of Europe, however, resistance forces were to lie low, except when called upon to carry out specific sabotage operations. There was little point in calling resistance in the open in Belgium, Norway and Denmark so long as they remained far distant from liberation, and a low-profile policy, with the implicit threat of eventual uprisings, might just as effectively tie down German troops—although it might, and did in some cases, equally cause severe problems of morale in the resistance movements concerned.

On D-Day itself and in the immediately following crucial period of consolidation, extensive sabotage plans were put into effect by SOE to disrupt railway communications and thus slow down or prevent German reinforcements reaching the invasion area. Assisted by massive Allied air force attacks, the resistance created severe congestion, with

3000 confirmed rail cuts between 6 and 27 June. SHAEF later estimated that the normal delay imposed upon enemy reinforcements by these operations, and by the accompanying harrassing operations, was between forty-eight and seventy-two hours, with some noteworthy and oft-quoted exceptions such as that of the 2nd SS Panzer Division, delayed twelve days in its move to Normandy from south-west France. The French resistance forced even more serious delays on German divisions moved from the Mediterranean area, and both main railway lines up the Rhône valley were closed for most of the crucial post-D-Day period. There was also a considerable degree of success in the sabotage of tele-communications networks, which amongst other things had the advantage of forcing the Germans to resort to wireless communications where valuable tactical intelligence could be intercepted. In general, exceptionally good liaison between allied staffs and resistance groups was further assisted by the infiltration of 93 Jedburgh teams, consisting of SOE, OSS, and French officers, who were dropped in uniform and were highly trained in guerrilla tactics and sabotage techniques.

The results achieved by SOE and the resistance were substantially better than predicted by the cynics. Outside the beachhead area, local risings took place, which SOE did its best to control, not always success-fully. In Holland, the effects of the *Englandspiel* had been to prevent the co-ordination of SHAEF plans with those of the Dutch resistance, but in Belgium, where COSSAC operational plans were issued in November 1943, resistance activities, initiated on 8 June, were if any-thing more successful than in France, with major attacks on communi-cations, transport, and power supplies. Once the Allied forces had crossed the Seine, however, railway sabotage hindered the Allies rather than helped them, and sabotage operations ceased, to be replaced by greater emphasis on countersabotage—the protection of major ports, public utilities, and important industrial plants against destruction by the retreating Germans. One of the most successful and strategically useful achievements of the Belgian resistance was in this field of coun-tersabotage, where important port facilities in Antwerp were saved. In accordance with the changing emphasis on helping the Allies rather than hindering the Germans, the Belgian secret army was mobilised on 31 August to receive allied forces and help in mopping-up and law and order tasks, although there was also some small-scale guerrilla activity in the Ardennes. On the same day that the Belgian secret army was mobilised, a SHAEF order set up the Dutch forces of the interior, and the dropping of arms to the Dutch began in earnest, to be followed shortly thereafter, and in connection with the Arnhem landings, by a railway strike initiated on 17 September which lasted until the end of the war. However, severe German reprisals forced SOE subsequently to suspend air operations, and to call for the suspension on the part of the Dutch population of violent action. SOE agents were instructed to lie low until the eve of liberation. Once allied forces crossed the Rhine early in March 1945 these restraints were lifted, and orders for attacks on communication networks issued. As in the case of Norway and Denmark, the greatest priority in SOE planning at this stage was countersabotage, which meant here the protection of ports, canals, and flood control systems; and, as also in the case of Norway and Denmark, these countersabotage plans proved unnecessary, and the main job of the Dutch Forces of the Interior became the assumption of responsibility for law and order during the liberation period.

The larger problem which SOE had faced throughout its existence, that of maintaining morale in resistance groups where immediate action was not called for, was well illustrated in the Norwegian case. The June 1944 SHAEF directive for Norway specifically prohibited any overt action by the Norwegian resistance, as no military operations were planned there and because calling resistance into the open could lead to its decimation by the Germans without hope of assistance by regular allied forces. Instead, instructions were given for the preparation of action when German troops were withdrawn or surrendered, or when German power collapsed. The primary task as defined by SHAEF was countersabotage, and SOE was instructed to ensure the protection of power stations, communications, public utilities, and the preservation of law and order. In the interim, Milorg was to be strengthened by the despatch of as many trained SOE personnel as possible, and certain specified and limited sabotage was to proceed. This essentially largely passive and waiting role for the Norwegian resistance at a time when Allied armies were advancing across France and Belgium and liberation was in the air caused a severe crisis of morale, and in December 1944 SHAEF was forced to lift the restraints it had imposed in June. On 5 December a new SHAEF directive ordered a large-scale campaign of sabotage against the Norwegian railways designed to hamper German withdrawal from the country, or alternatively to force German troop transport on to the open seas where it could be more easily attacked by air action. This campaign, whose beginning roughly coincided with but was independent of the panic produced by the Ardennes counteroffensive, successfully reduced the rate of German withdrawal from Scandinavia and helped to restore the bruised morale of the Norwegian resistance; and in the event, the elaborate countersabotage plans drawn up in June turned out to be redundant when the Germans surrendered on 8 May 1945.[16] The desire to prevent German troop withdrawals from Scandinavia to western and central Europe also affected SOE operations in Denmark. A general strike was called by the Freedom Council on D-Day, and helped delay German troop movements during the early stages of Overlord, but it was not until later that resistance was mobilised on a large scale. A SHAEF mission for Denmark was formed in September 1944, and early in 1945 sabotage was intensified. In one instance in February there were over one hundred successful sabotage attacks on transport being used to carry German troops to the western front, and, combined with Norwegian action, considerable delays were caused to German reinforcement and regrouping attempts. Here, too, elaborate countersabotage plans proved to be largely redundant.

Military historians have not yet produced the closely detailed analyses which would allow definitive conclusions to be drawn about the value of SOE's tactical and strategic contribution to Overlord, and the claims and counterclaims of interested parties lead into dangerous waters. SOE was never very popular with the regular military establishment, and, as Gubbins put it, was often looked upon as 'an organisation of harmless backroom lunatics'.[17] Hence, the regular military tended to be sceptical of SOE's achievements, and by the same token SOE tended to inflate them. Assessments about SOE's strategic contribution are, therefore, particularly difficult, and much of the basic information still remains classified. What is clear from the small amount of contemporary evidence available is that sceptics were agreeably surprised at the size of the 'bonus' delivered by SOE efforts during Overlord, and that at least where SHAEF and AFHQ were concerned the benefits gained from SOE efforts were considered to have well outweighed the costs. Early in 1945 a special committee was set up in London to evaluate the usefulness of SOE operations *vis-à-vis* the plans of the Allied Commanders in the field, and two days after the German surrender the Chiefs of Staff approved a proposal from Gubbins that SHAEF and AFHQ be approached for information to compile such reports. SHAEF produced its assessment in July, and AFHQ in November. Both were complimentary to SOE, and although drawn up in collaboration with SOE, appear to represent as objective an opinion as could be reached in the circumstances. SHAEF went so far as to say that 'without the organisation, communications, material, training and leadership SOE supplied . . . resistance would have been of no military value', and that 'SOE operations made a substantial contribution to the victory of the Allied Expeditionary Force'. This, combined with the

AFHQ conclusion that in southern France the *maquis* efforts to disrupt the movements of enemy reserves and reinforcements was 'amazingly successful', clearly indicated that whatever the value of the specific tactical and strategical judgments, the 'mere bonus' expected of SOE had been larger than anticipated and of considerable (but still not fully defined) strategical value. Ironically, one of the areas of SOE activity singled out by both SHAEF and AFHQ as having been of special value was the provision of military intelligence. Intelligence collection had not been one of the specified tasks set out by the War Cabinet in the SOE Charter of 1940, its agents were not permitted to be trained in intelligence duties, the higher echelons of the Secret Intelligence Service had consistently regarded SOE with hostility, and SOE had been obliged to pass on to SIS all intelligence which came its way without any promise of reciprocity. Yet SHAEF reported that Montgomery considered that the provision by resistance of information had been invaluable (thereby adding another item to the list of complaints about Montgomery's failure to acknowledge in public his indebtedness to good intelligence). AFHQ, in like manner, reported that during the final offensive in Italy SOE reports of enemy troop movements 'were of particular value to intelligence'. Here, therefore, was a clear and unanticipated benefit of SOE activities which must be added to the balance sheet.[18]

Of equal if not greater importance was the assistance SOE gave to British political objectives in Western Europe. Here the emerging concept of a West European postwar *bloc* closely linked to Britain played its part in shaping SOE activities. By 1944 Eden and the Foreign Office had concluded that Britain's postwar role would hinge upon Britain's relations with a western European grouping within the wider framework of an Anglo-Soviet understanding. As the Foreign Office put it in August 1944, 'politically and commercially we require the speediest possible restoration of order and security in Europe . . . we might consolidate our position in the countries of western Europe and Scandinavia, in Turkey, Greece, and eventually Italy . . .'.[19] Shortly afterwards, just prior to Eden's departure for the Moscow Conference, where Stalin and Churchill set the seal on the spheres of influence agreement in the Balkans, the Chiefs of Staff expressed anxieties about future Russian military hostility and the consequent need to consolidate British control over north-western Germany, and the Foreign Office officially approached the Americans with a plan whereby Britain would help to rearm the western Europeans.[20] In this scheme for western Europe France was the crucial link. Given that the majority of the French resistance was behind de Gaulle, Eden and the Foreign Office throughout the months preceding D-Day worked hard to improve and cement Anglo-French relations. This was not easy given Roosevelt's deep dislike for de Gaulle and Churchill's receptivity to the President's views, nor given the demands of Eisenhower and SHAEF who wished to launch heavy bombing attacks on western Europe in order to soften up the Germans prior to D-Day. As Eden told the War Cabinet on 30 March 1944, in successfully persuading it to pursue only a restricted programme of bombing, such attacks might do considerable political damage to future Anglo-French (and Anglo-Belgian) relations, as they would involve heavy civilian casualties.[21] This concern for the preservation of good relations with de Gaulle and the French National Committee was eloquently shown in Foreign Office support for increased supplies to the French *maquis* early in 1944, at a time when the question had clearly become of major importance in the minds of the French National Committee in Algiers. Hitherto the Foreign Office had not shown much interest other than a largely hostile one in SOE's affairs, and the change of tune was significant. Combined with the fact that by 1944 F section of SOE, which had originally been founded to work independently of Gaullist forces, was now to all intents and purposes working with de Gaulle and the French resistance, meant that British support to French resistance could only help the consolidation of de Gaulle's power in postwar France, and the re-emergence of France as a victor power and the lynchpin of a western European *bloc*.

Where the smaller countries of western Europe were concerned—Holland, Belgium, Norway and Denmark—close postwar relationships with their governments were seen as vital to British interests. This political concern set the broader framework for SOE activities, where a general pattern of increased concern with countersabotage and the maintenance of law and order could be discerned once the success of the Normandy landings was assured. As Gubbins himself said, it now 'became highly important to prevent wholesale destruction by the Germans of economic assets that would delay the recovery of the liberated countries, and so create unemployment, distress, famine and political unrest'.[22] SOE operations and plans had largely depended upon the cooperation of the governments-in-exile, and where SOE strategy contradicted their wishes considerable difficulties had arisen and invariably been resolved by compromise solutions reached in the interests of larger political harmony.

In Holland, most operations were carried out with the approval of the Dutch government, and after the fiasco of the *Englandspiel* in 1942-43 particular care was taken to achieve closer co-operation. After the setting up of the Dutch forces of the interior (NBS) under the command of Prince Bernhard (who worked directly to orders from Eisenhower), SOE (and SIS) worked closely with departments of the Dutch Government as advisors to Bernhard. The main function of the NBS in 1945 was to help the advancing Allies and assume responsibility for order in the interim period between the German surrender and the return of the government from London.[23] SOE–Dutch relations were helped by the relative harmony within and between the resistance and the government-in-exile, while the absence of guerrilla warfare with its inevitable radical political implications further smoothed matters.

Things were not so easy in the Belgian case. The government-in-exile was weak, divided between civilian and military elements, and riven by disagreements over the questions of the monarchy. SOE's need to work closely with the Belgians meant that it became to some extent involved in these disputes. SOE's 1940–41 policy of the sharing of agents and the joint planning of missions had eventually come to grief when it became entangled with intraBelgian rivalries, and in 1942 the problem assumed such dimensions that Eden intervened to smooth matters over. At one point Spaak, the Belgian Foreign Minister, broke off all Belgian relations with SOE. But the technical and political requirements of Anglo-Belgian co-operation eventually led to a reorganisation in London and to some improvement in 1943 and 1944. Greatest emphasis was placed on support to the secret army. The *Front de l'Indépendence*, a national front organisation of left-wing leanings with which the Belgian government reluctantly co-operated, received fewer supplies and arms than the secret army, and when the Allies entered Brussels their first priority was to disarm the resistance. The first SOE mission to reach Brussels had as its priority task arrangements for the flying in of arms shipments for the *gendarmarie*. The political climate remained disturbed until the end of the year. The Belgian government resigned shortly after its return to the capital, and a new government including communists and FIL members were formed. Troubles within this government and demands for the surrender of arms by the resistance led to riots in November which were quelled by British troops. Shortly thereafter the resistance was disarmed, and the panic produced by the German counteroffensive in the Ardennes in December led to the moderation of internal political conflicts. Although British intervention had been, and indeed was, justified in military terms, the political need for a friendly Belgium had clearly influenced events.[24]

In Norway, also defined by the Foreign Office as lying within the Western *bloc*, SOE policy, after an initial attempt at independence, worked closely with the Norwegian government-in-exile after the creation of an Anglo-Norwegian Committee early in 1942 and the decision to work closely with Milorg in September of that year. The Anglo-Norwegian Committee, consisting of representatives of SOE and the Norwegian High Command, met on a monthly basis right up to the conclusion of the war, thereby keeping British and Norwegian policy in step and contributing to particularly good Anglo-Norwegian relations in 1944–5. In the concluding stages of the war SOE directives stressed the maintenance of order when the Germans surrendered—'law and order, for several weeks before the Allied forces were deployed, was entirely exercised by units of the Resistance Movement . . .'.[25] Milorg, assisted by only small numbers of British troops flown in after the German surrender on 8 May, successfully rounded up and disarmed the more than 400,000 German troops still in the country. This was not, in any event, a particularly difficult task, as Norwegian resistance was well united, there were few of the political divisions within the resistance or between the resistance and the government-in-exile which characterised many of the other European resistance movements, and the few communist groups were subordinated to Milorg. Restoration of the prewar order and future participation of Norway in a western *bloc* were assured.

Denmark was a case apart.[26] There never was a government-in-exile, and SOE strategy in 1943 had deliberately sought to provoke direct German rule in the hope of stimulating greater resistance. The formation of the Freedom Council in September 1943, which amongst other things defined the political goal of the resistance as being the restoration of the prewar democratic order, made possible closer links and greater co-ordination between Britain and the Danish resistance, and SOE had a representative (Flemming Muus) on the Council. Through this Freedom Council, which acted as a *de facto* Danish government, resistance activites were co-ordinated with Allied strategy and SHAEF directives, and SOE, with no *de jure* government-in-exile to work with, was in a particularly strong position *vis-à-vis* the resistance. Nonetheless, the overall political situation remained delicate. The Danes wished to obtain recognition as an Allied nation. The British were willing to agree, anxious to gain a friendly postwar Denmark, and, as the end of the war approached, alarmed at the prospect of a Russian occupation of Denmark or of postwar Soviet claims against her. On the other hand, these concerns had to be balanced against the desire for good relations with the Soviet Union, which in May 1944 had refused to consent to a three-power declaration granting Denmark *de facto* Allied status—instead the USSR recognised only a 'Fighting Denmark', represented by the Freedom Council. For this reason, SOE plans drawn up in the spring of 1944 for the creation of a paramilitary force to assist invasion plans bypassed the Danish General Staff, elements of which were suspected of planning a civil war against the Danish communists, whose activities were otherwise contained by the Freedom Council. The importance of the Council increased with agreements it reached with Danish politicians in the summer of 1944 on the composition of the postwar government, and as the chances of severe internal political divisions lessened, SOE and SHAEF increased the level of their support, and now became willing to co-operate with elements of the Danish armed forces. Here, too, therefore, SOE policy was closely tailored to the political need to ensure a politically united and harmonious Denmark for the postwar Western European *bloc*.

III

The Balkans
If SOE relations with the resistance in western Europe proceeded relatively smoothly from the viewpoint of British strategic and political interests, this was not the case in the Balkans, and 1944 saw several major issues reach their climax. The programme of increased airborne assistance to the French *maquis* had caused dismay in Cairo, and early in February complaints had reached London that the programme of supplies to the Balkans had been severely disrupted. To this operational confusion was added the chaos of Balkan politics, and the often conflicting views of different levels and departments within the British government itself.

Conflicts between SOE and the Foreign Office over policy towards the Greek resistance had almost led, as has been seen in the previous chapter, to the demise of SOE Cairo in September 1943. Since then, the situation had scarcely improved, and Foreign Office suspicion of SOE activities in Greece had reached new depths on 23 January with Sir Orme Sargent's allegations. The conflict this time was over the strategic role designed for Greek resistance for the next few months, and paradoxically the Foreign Office temporarily emerged as the champions of more active guerrilla activity. SOE, in conjunction with the military authorities in Cairo, had prepared a strategic plan for Greek resistance known as Operation Noah's Ark, the object of which was, on the liberation of Greece, so to harass German withdrawal that enemy units could not be transferred to other fronts without considerable reorganisation, retraining, and reequipping. As part of the preparatory phase of Noah's Ark, SOE Cairo suggested that the guerrilla movement, which as a result of the civil war was 'almost played out and requires a rest', should lie low and recoup its strength, at least until March.[27] This proposal met with immediate objections from the Foreign Office on the grounds that British policy in Greece had to carry the Russians with it and that Moscow would be unlikely to accept such a passive role for the resistance. Moreover, it argued, unless the guerrillas were instructed to fight the Germans vigorously, they would merely continue the civil war—and this would undermine the Foreign Office desire to achieve the reconciliation between the two main groups which Eden had mentioned to the War Cabinet on 3 January as Britain's main objective. SOE's plan, therefore, was open to serious political objection.[28] It was also open to strategic objections on the part of the Chiefs of Staff. Not only did Sir Alan Brooke consider that 'it was bad psychology to adopt a plan which had as its avowed object a policy of waiting until the enemy began to withdraw before hitting him', with any consequent damage to resistance morale, but of far greater weight was the fact that the Noah's Ark proposal was out of tune with the demands of Bodyguard. As he told the Chiefs of Staff on 7 February, 'the criterion of our policy in Greece should be the number of German divisions pinned down there'. For this reason he favoured a more active programme of resistance in Greece, and argued that this could best be achieved by resuming full support to EAM-ELAS. To this end he supported a proposal from Cairo for the return of Myers to Greece.[29]

The Foreign Office was predictably dismayed by this proposal, and both Eden and Churchill, who had strong feelings about EAM-ELAS, now intervened again personally. Eden described EAM-ELAS as 'a thoroughly unscrupulous gang of communist fanatics', while Churchill expressed his feelings on 14 February by saying that giving weapons to EAM-ELAS would not increase their effort against the Germans, 'but only secure the domination of these base and treacherous people after the war'. Both the Prime Minister and the Foreign Secretary were opposed to Myers' return to Greece, and on the 25th Churchill declared that 'The return of General [sic] Myers cannot be allowed, as he is the chief man who reared by hand this cockatrice brute of EAM-ELAS. There is no comparison between them and the bands of Marshal Tito. They are a mere scourge on the population, and are feared by the Greek villagers even more than the Germans.'[30] Both the Foreign Secretary and the Prime Minister appeared oblivious or indifferent to the implications of all this for Bodyguard, and when the Vice-Chiefs of Staff and SOE and Foreign Office representatives met to discuss Greek policy again on 29 February it was agreed that Churchill's attention should be drawn to the issue. It was also agreed that a possible solution to the differences within the Greek resistance might be to appoint a British commander—although Gubbins, who represented SOE at these discussions, was extremely doubtful about this proposal. On 2 March the Vice-Chiefs of Staff once again reiterated, this time directly to Eden, that in the interests of Bodyguard, matters with EAM-ELAS should not be pushed to a breaking point.[31]

The issue in the event did not have to be faced. On 28 February Woodhouse had managed to achieve an armistice between ELAS and EDES which satisfied all parties concerned, and with its secret clause committing the resistance forces to facilitate the entry of allied forces into Greece before the end of the occupation, which had been leaked to the Germans within three days, kept open the threat of Allied landings in the Balkans. The armistice, indeed, led Eden to adopt a somewhat cavalier position towards the concerns of the Vice-Chiefs on the Bodyguard question, for he then pointed out that Woodhouse had successfully used the threat of denunciation of ELAS without producing undesirable effects. This was not an argument which the Vice-Chiefs would accept, and they insisted once again on 16 March that because any break with EAM-ELAS would seriously jeopardise deception plans they should be fully informed of any such intentions. Nor did SOE support the Foreign Office proposal for a British commander to be appointed to control all guerrilla forces in Greece. As Sporborg pointed out, the risk was that such a commander would become isolated from both the guerrillas and the Greek population, and thus lose all authority. As Wilson supported the SOE viewpoint on this issue, no further action was taken for the time being.[32]

As a result of the armistice SOE supplies to EAM-ELAS were resumed, and the Greek resistance temporarily assumed a back seat to more urgent considerations affecting SOE operations, such as the Rumanian question, which erupted in April (see below p. 177). But the situation was far from stable. In March the communists established a proto-government of national unity in the Greek mountains, and it became more clear than ever that EAM-ELAS were in control of most of Greece. The desire to reverse this trend, and the inevitable refocusing of attention on Greece in London, showed that the Greek and Rumanian questions were closely related. If Rumania was destined to be within the Soviet sphere of influence, then Britain should assure itself of predominance in Greece. This issue was raised as a matter of urgency in a personal telegram to Churchill from the Resident Minister in the Middle East, Lord Moyne, on 8 May. Moyne put his concern bluntly to the Prime Minister:

> What worries me is the fear that, unless the Russian pursuit of the Germans out of the Balkans is parallelled by simultaneous action on our part to chase them out of Greece, the Russians will arrive on the Greek frontier to find the German mobile troops withdrawn, only a few scattered German fortress battalions holding out, and EAM in control.

Moyne suggested the swift appearance of British forces in Greece (up to two divisions) as essential, and urged Churchill to throw his weight behind immediate action.[33]

Churchill was more than ready to respond to this appeal. The idea of despatching a British force to Greece upon a German withdrawal had been discussed as early as September 1943 and the pace of the Russian advance in the spring of 1944 was such that the question of Britain's future influence in the Balkans was now urgent. A division into spheres of influence was emerging as the best that Britain could hope for, and on 18 May Eden informed the War Cabinet that he had recently told the Russians 'that if they wished us to allow them to take the lead in Rumania they should be prepared to reciprocate by allowing HMG to do likewise in Greece'.[34] Consequently, Eden had no hesitation in pressing for the despatch of a British force to Athens at the moment of German withdrawal. Such a move would be a wise precaution, he said, even if EAM-ELAS did enter a representative Greek government and even if guerrilla forces were reorganised into a national army; and to lend support to his argument he circulated to the War Cabinet the summary of a report by a former British liaison officer in Greece which described ELAS as 'a well-organised gang of terrorists' and called upon British troops to clear up Greek matters when the Germans withdrew.[35]

Within a month of this renewed denunciation of EAM-ELAS by Eden, events both in Western Europe and Greece itself had altered the dimensions of the problem. The success of Overlord meant that the requirements of strategic deception need no longer be a factor in policy towards Greece, while in late June EAM-ELAS made it clear that it was not going to enter a new Greek coalition government as had been indicated by the so-called Lebanon Charter of 20 May. Eden seized upon this opportunity to propose that EAM-ELAS be publicly denounced, and that British liaison officers to it be withdrawn, in other words that all support and relations with the left-wing Greek resistance be stopped. Neither SOE nor the Chiefs of Staff were now opposed to measures to reduce EAM-ELAS influence in Greece, and the opposition they expressed to Eden's proposal was aimed at the means, not the objective. Selborne, who was already about to become involved in a major fight with Eden over the forced repatriation of Soviet citizens to Russia,[36] vehemently objected that Eden's plan would be self-defeating. He told Churchill on 14 July:

> It would mean abandoning Greece to EAM. To do so would be a gross betrayal of the Greek people [and] . . . would leave EAM a clear field . . . It has been part of our policy for some time to keep the Russians out of Greece. We cannot claim Greece as a sphere in which our influence should be predominant if we evacuate the country and leave it to civil war and anarchy.

Moreover, he pointed out, it would endanger the lives of many Greeks who had co-operated with the Allies. The wisest thing in the circumstances would be to persist in the course already set and avoid a break with EAM-ELAS.[37] These arguments, in combination with a Joint Planning Staff report on the military implications of a break with EAM-ELAS which specifically pointed out that it was in Britain's long-term *military* interest that 'the government in Greece should be friendly to us and should not be dominated by Russia', led the Chiefs of Staff to join with SOE in opposing Eden's proposal in its entirety. On 19 July they advised Churchill that denunciation would strengthen the EAM leadership, and thereby 'render their overthrow more difficult when the time arrived for our re-entry into Greece'. Action against EAM should be limited instead to cutting off supplies. (This in essence represented no change, however, for as SOE London pointed out to its representatives in New York, ELAS had received no military stores for several months.[38]) The force of the SOE–Chiefs of Staff argument was apparently increased when news arrived in London in late July of the arrival of a Soviet military mission in Greece. The War Cabinet thereupon authorised an increase in the number of personnel under Woodhouse's control in Greece, and agreed to despatch a force of 10,000 troops and two or three Air Force squadrons to Greece when the Germans withdrew. The Soviet Union was not to be informed immediately of the decision, although the Americans were.[39]

With the War Cabinet decision to commit regular British forces to Greece, and the actual despatch of those forces in October, SOE's role in Greece diminished rapidly in significance. The defeat of EAM-ELAS by the British intervention in Athens in December 1944 ensured that Greece would not go communist and that Britain's long-term political and military interests in the eastern Mediterranean would be preserved. Whatever the subsequent criticisms and controversies over SOE's role in Greece, SOE's quarrels with the Foreign Office in 1944 had been over methods rather than over this basic shared objective. Few would have disagreed with Halifax's opinion of January 1939 that 'a weak and defenceless Greece would operate to the detriment of our security in the Mediterranean',[40] and SOE's involvement in Greece at least ensured that some moderating force would be applied against the left-wing forces of EAM-ELAS. There is no evidence to substantiate the wilder claims of the Foreign Office that SOE had 'created' EAM-ELAS, and most of the confusion in policy towards the Greek resistance was caused not by SOE but by the failure of the war leadership to give it consistent and comprehensive directives.

The divergence between British policy in Greece and Yugoslavia which had begun to take shape during 1943 culminated in Yugoslavia early in 1944 in the final abandonment of Milhailović and the decision to give exclusive support to Tito and the partisans. Implicit in this shift of policy was the belief that nothing could be gained politically or militarily from continued support for Mihailović, and that British support for Tito and the partisans would in the long run exert a moderating political influence, and best serve British postwar interests. These were, in any case, considered to be less of a priority than in Greece. Ever since Fitzroy Maclean had arrived in Yugoslavia in September 1943 as Churchill's personal representative to Tito, the Prime Minister had been pressing for the full British effort to be thrown behind the partisans and had himself become deeply involved in the whole Yugoslav question. On the eve of the Cairo Conference which preceded the Big Three summit meeting at Teheran, Churchill had noted that 'we have failed to give any real measure of support to the partisans and patriots of Yugoslavia and Albania. These guerrilla forces are containing as many [German] divisions as are the British and American armies put together. Hitherto they have been nourished only by droppings from the air . . . [and] . . . no ships with supplies have entered the ports taken by the partisans . . .'. Although Churchill was incorrect both in his estimate of how many German divisions were being tied down by the partisans, and in his belief that the partisan forces had received no supplies by sea (650 tons of supplies reached Tito by sea in October, and 1950 tons in Nobember), he continued to press the case at Teheran with both Stalin and Roosevelt. The result was that the Big Three agreed in their final communiqué that 'the partisans in Yugoslavia should be supported by supplies and equipment to the greatest possible extent, and also by Commando operations', a decision subsequently transmitted in operational orders to Eisenhower.[41] Simultaneously with this move to increase support to the partisans, the British now moved decisively—if belatedly—towards the final break with Mihailović. On 19 November 1943 SOE Cairo formally recommended that all aid to Mihailović be stopped and that the British liaison officers with the Chetniks be withdrawn. The Joint Intelligence Committee in London agreed with this recommendation on 25 November.[42] These decisions predated Churchill's own conversion to that position which occurred when he passed through Cairo early in December on return from Teheran. In conversations with both Maclean and Deakin, who had come to Cairo from partisan territory, Churchill was presented with full details of Chetnik collaboration with the enemy and as a result he urged King Peter to remove the Mihailović government. From now on, Churchill was to regard Mihailović as 'a millstone around the King's neck', and he pressed strongly for his repudiation and denunciation. He also told Tito personally on 8 January that he had decided no further military support should be given to Mihailović, and orders to that effect were sent to Cairo shortly thereafter. They made little practical difference, as in the previous two months Mihailović had only received the grand total of eight tons of supplies, compared with over 1500 tons for Tito, and no more were now sent. In his plea for a denunciation of Mihailović, Churchill was supported by both SOE and the military, but there was some disagreement about this with the Foreign Office. Eden, as he had explained to the War Cabinet on 3 January, hoped to see some sort of compromise agreement between King Peter and Tito based upon the unification of all resistance forces in Yugoslavia, and thought he could obtain Soviet support for such a policy. He therefore hoped to strike a bargain with Tito whereby the latter would indicate his willingness to work with the King in exchange for a British break with Mihailović, and for that reason, too, the Foreign Office resisted the immediate withdrawal of liaison officers.[43] In the face of the partisan denunciation of the Royal Yugoslav government in the Jajce resolutions of November, their undisputed control over practically the whole country except Serbia, and the fully documented evidence which reached London in mid-January 1944 proving the extent of Chetnik collaboration, the Foreign Office position proved untenable, and on 17 February Eden dropped his demands. Thereupon orders were sent to Cairo for the withdrawal of British liaison officers from Mihailović, and the last of them, including the Head of the Mission, Brigadier Armstrong, left Mihailović at the end of May, just a week before the Allied landings in Normandy.

During the period between the decision to withdraw the British Mission to Mihailović in mid-February and its departure at the end of May, there was considerable discussion in London about the position of the Chetniks. It was recognised that they controlled most of Serbia, and it was hoped that if they could be removed from Mihailović's control they could play a more active and useful role than in the past. It was this hope—that the Chetniks were not totally beyond redemption and that (without Mihailović) they could be persuaded to co-operate operationally with the partisans—which led the War Cabinet on 15 March to agree that King Peter should officially be urged to dismiss his government, including Mihailović as War Minister, and appoint a new government which would create the possibility of some unity among the resistance forces in the country.[44] This decision was not uninfluenced by the views of Colonel Bailey, who since September 1943 had been political adviser to Armstrong. Bailey arrived in London on 3 March, and in discussions with Eden and Churchill had urged upon them both the importance and potential of the Chetnik forces in Serbia, and the need to dispose of Mihailović. This was the first time that Churchill had received first-hand information about non-partisan resistance in Yugoslavia, as hitherto he had dealt exclusively with Maclean, who believed that British support for the partisans was the best way of preventing Tito and Yugoslavia from falling totally under Soviet domination.[45] The hope that some Chetnik–partisan co-operation could be achieved reflected the hope that political advantage for Britain could still be extracted from the Yugoslav situation, and the Foreign Office thought the non-communist Serbians could be kept in play. Hence, Eden supported a recommendation in May by Lieutenant-Colonel Hudson, SOE's first agent in occupied Yugoslavia, to the effect that the Serbs could still be persuaded to fight with the partisans against the Germans, and that supplies to them be renewed. This idea was shot down by both SOE and AFHQ, who pointed out that partisan groups were already operating in Serbia, and with the final consent of King Peter to dismiss his government, including Mihailović, and with the empty 'compromise' agreement between Subašić, the new Yugoslav Prime Minister, and Tito on 16 June, further discussion along these lines ceased.[46]

These decisions, coinciding with Overlord, can be taken as a suitable termination date for a consideration of the SOE role in Yugoslavia. Ever since Maclean had arrived in Yugoslavia in September 1943 SOE's role had been diminishing, a consequence which SOE Cairo clearly foresaw and which had led them in the first place to oppose his appointment and then subsequently to be less than co-operative with him. Subsequent changes in command arrangements in the Mediterranean and Balkan areas had further diminished SOE's role to the benefit of the regular military and AFHQ, and with the creation of the Balkan Air Force on 1 June, charged not only with all air operations in the Balkans but also with the co-ordination of planning and execution of all special operations across the Adriatic, SOE HQ in Bari (transferred from Cairo earlier in the year and known as 'Force 266') now became firmly surbordinated to the regular military and confined itself exclusively to technical assistance and advice. SOE, in fact, now no longer bore any responsibility for operational policy governing supplies to the partisans, although SOE channels continued to be used for this purpose.[47] For the next few months British support to the Yugoslav partisans continued in an amiable climate, but after Tito's unannounced visit to Moscow in September relations began to deteriorate. There was increasing friction over Tito's territorial claims in the Trieste area and by the end of 1944 this was generating British fears about communism crossing the frontiers of Yugoslavia into Austria and north-east Italy. This in turn became a factor affecting the shape of SOE operations in these countries, as will be seen below.

Just as 1944 saw the loosening of British ties with the non-communist resistance forces in Yugoslavia, so too in Albania links were severed with non-communist factions. In mid-1942 SOE Istanbul had established links with Albania, where a few months previously partisan activity had begun under the sponsorship of the Albanian communist party. In September of the same year the communist party of Albania formed a National Liberation Movement (LNC) on the classic communist model. In February 1943 SOE Cairo had instructed Myers in Greece to link up with groups in Albania, and this was followed by the despatch of an SOE mission specifically to work in Albania in April 1943; by August 1943 SOE had nine officers, fifteen other ranks, and eight separate W/T links in Albania. It had first appeared that Albania might escape the internecine conflicts which characterised the resistance in both Yugoslavia and Greece, and that unlike its neighbours Albania might produce a unified resistance movement. But this proved to be a vain hope. The Italian surrender in September 1943 produced a scramble for postwar power only too familiar, and open conflict between the LNC and the Balli Kombetar (BK), a conservative nationalist movement, soon broke out, with the BK resembling the Chetniks in its willingness to give priority to struggle against the communists rather than against the Germans who began moving troops into the country after the Italian surrender. There was, in addition to the LNC and BK, a third resistance force in the north of the country, headed by Major Abas Kupi, an ex-army officer who had broken away from the LCN.[48]

Following the larger pattern of their increased interest in Balkan resistance as a strategic weapon in 1943, the Chiefs of Staff first became interested in Albanian resistance in the autumn of 1943, and in October were informed by SOE that there were 4000 to 5000 active guerrillas in the country, and the potential for 30,000. At about the same time Brigadier E. F. ('Trotsky') Davies was parachuted into the country with orders to back any group that would fight the enemy. In December he recommended that the LNC should be given exclusive backing, and that Britain should break all links with the BK. Such a recommendation was unwelcome in London on both political and strategic grounds. As in the case of Yugoslavia, the Foreign Office, while aware of communist strength amongst the guerrillas, was unwilling to concede everything to the LNC without extracting some advantage and at least ensuring the survival at the end of the war of forces other than purely communist ones. Strategically, Albania played a part in the 1944 deception campaign designed to keep alive the German fear of an Allied Balkan invasion, and for these two reasons it was decided early in 1944 to give some support to the third resistance group, that of Abas Kupi in the north, as a counterweight to the LNC. In April 1944, therefore, an SOE party was dropped to Kupi to urge him to take more positive action against the Germans. The policy was a failure. In May it was reported that the LNC was still the only movement in Albania actively resisting the enemy, and on the day after the Normandy landings, when the question of sending arms to Kupi was raised, SOE recommended against it on the grounds that it would provide no military advantage, that it would encourage civil war, and that it would alienate Tito who had contacts with the LNC.[49] The Chiefs of Staff confirmed that at this stage there was no military advantage in providing Kupi with arms, and subsequently they and AFHQ succeeded in ensuring that practically all British military aid (which was minimal in any case relative to that being provided for Yugoslavia) should go to the LNC. A Balkan Air Force directive of 28 June noted that the LNC was the only element in Albania actively resisting the enemy, although this did not prevent a temporary embargo on British supplies in order to force the LNC to moderate its attacks on Kupi's movement. Nonetheless, the British soon threw their support behind the LNC and took the line that 'as we are entering a new phase, the prevention of civil war overrides [the] policy of aiding anyone who will fight the Germans'. This meant refusing to supply Kupi with arms, which, in the Foreign Office view, would inevitably be turned against the LNC and produce civil war. Here, as elsewhere, longer-term political interests now dictated the nature of SOE operations. The decision to throw exclusive support behind the LNC represented both a recognition of the LNC's power, and the hope that by supporting it Britain would retain some degree of postwar influence, and, in particular, thereby prevent the emergence of a *bloc* of Balkan states sympathetic only to the Soviet Union. And in the longer run, some even more optimistic Foreign Office officials hoped that the LNC might alienate popular sympathies, fail to establish an acceptable government, and open the way for a return of King Zog. On 24 August 1944 an agreement was signed between the British and the LNC, and Kupi's days were numbered.[50] In October he disbanded his movement and left the country, and within a year Enver Hoxha's communist government had been recognised by the British. Within three years, however, SOE personnel were mobilised by the Secret Intelligence Service to use Albanian emigré elements to create a resistance movement against the Hoxha régime as part of a wider attempt by Britain's postwar subversive agencies to foster new resistance movements in Europe—this time not in Nazi, but in communist, Europe (see below, p. 206).

IV

The Satellite States
In the satellite states of Bulgaria, Rumania, and Hungary, SOE's activities since 1941 had been on a much smaller scale than in Greece, Yugoslavia, and Albania, and they remained so in 1944. But they are not without interest, and indeed its relationships with groups inside these countries throw useful light on SOE's wider place within British wartime strategy and diplomacy. On the diplomatic front, Britain's interest in the satellite states was to explore whether they might be detached from the Axis by some modification of the unconditional surrender formula. However, Eden made it clear that in doing so it was also in Britain's interest not to damage Anglo-Soviet relations. It had become clear by the end of 1943 that in the case of Rumania Soviet interests were

to be respected, and in general that the allies were unable to agree to a common strategy to deal with the barrage of peace feelers from the satellite states which followed on the Italian surrender in September of that year. On the strategic front, however, some agreement was reached, and at Cairo the Chiefs of Staff had argued that everything possible should be done 'to promote a state of chaos and disruption in the satellite Balkan states'. This provided the framework for SOE activities in the first half of 1944.[51] As we have seen, the British had signed a protocol with the Russians in Moscow on 3 March 1944 for Anglo-Soviet co-operation on Bodyguard. A subgroup of plans dealing with southeastern Europe was known as Zeppelin, and part of this plan dealt with the role that Bulgaria would play. On the same day that Bevan signed the protocol in Moscow, Eden suggested to Churchill that greater priority be given to bombing and subversion in that country. The object should be either to bring about a *coup d'état* or to batter the Bulgarians into suing for peace, and either way thereby forcing the Germans to occupy the country and produce the necessary conditions for a really formidable guerrilla movement. 'I would not,' Eden added darkly, 'relish being a German if I were stationed in Macedonia.'[52]

The Chiefs of Staff had already approved a bombing programme against the satellites in January, with Bulgaria first on the list, followed by Hungary and then Rumania, but overall priority for targets in the satellite countries had remained low. The renewed interest in Bulgaria produced considerable discussion as to whether this low priority could be altered, and it was suggested that Britain might make a determined effort to detach all three satellite countries from the Axis by an intensified and co-ordinated programme of bombing and invasion threats. This superficially attractive idea encountered three main obstacles, two of which were political, and the third strategic. On the political side, the Americans, who would have to provide most of the bombers, would not agree to such a large diversion of effort to an area of Europe on which they suspected the British had long-range political designs. Secondly, neither were the Russians interested in formulating a joint policy with the British, and as the Foreign Office laid down that such co-operation was essential to overall Anglo-Soviet relations, this objection was crucial. Thirdly, the assumptions which underlay the plan itself were suspect. The belief that the satellites were willing to sign a separate peace and detach themselves from the Germans was based upon the evidence of peace feelers from these states. But these peace feelers were based on the assumption that *British* landings in the Balkans could be expected, and because the strategic needs of Bodyguard meant that they could not be disabused of this idea, the peace feelers were largely based on a false premise. The proposal for a co-ordinated and simultaneous programme against the satellite states (which had originated from Cairo), was therefore dropped, and as a result of a Joint Planning Staff report, drawn up in close consultation with SOE and SIS, it was decided to concentrate on Bulgaria alone. Here, it was argued, the effect of recent bombing attacks (Sofia was bombed in January) indicated that quick results might be expected, and Sofia offered a better target than either Bucharest or Budapest. Moreover, SOE and PWE activities could be coordinated with diplomatic activities by the Russians, because Bulgaria was not at war with the Soviet Union, because of traditional Russian influence there, and because of the recent Russian agreement to Bodyguard, which meant that 'there is good hope that they would support our action'. Moreover, if Bulgaria deserted the Germans, this would not only force the Germans to find ten divisions for its occupation, but would also lead to the removal of Bulgarian garrison divisions from Greece and Yugoslavia. The Chiefs of Staff accepted this plan, and as a result SOE was requested to consider what action they could undertake in Bulgaria in its support.[53]

SOE's original contacts in Bulgaria had been mainly with the left agrarians led by G. M. Dimitrov, and when Bulgaria signed the Tripartite Pact with Germany in March 1941 Dimitrov had been smuggled out of the country to Istanbul. Various unsuccessful attempts had been made with Dimitrov's help to establish contact with dissident elements in Bulgaria in 1941 and 1942. In mid-1942 the communist party of Bulgaria had formed a 'fatherland front' (OF) whose national committee comprised members of the communist, social democratic, and agrarian parties, and certain dissident army officers. SOE tried to establish contact with the OF *via* Bailey's mission with Mihailović, but were obstructed by the latter, and by June 1943 SOE Cairo was planning to send a special mission to work into Bulgaria from Yugoslavia. In October, two SOE agents with the Yugoslav partisans in Macedonia reported that the latter were willing to help SOE make contact with the Bulgarian partisans, who were reported to be 8000 in number, and well-organised but ill-equipped. As a result, Cairo immediately reinforced the British mission and requested sabotage attacks on a chrome mine and the Skopje–Djevdjelija railway line. Shortly afterwards General Wilson felt able to inform the Combined Chiefs of Staff at the first Cairo Conference that resistance in Bulgaria was growing, and in mid-December 1943 Major Mostyn Davies of SOE met the Bulgarian partisan leader in Macedonia.

The year 1944 began with optimistic SOE estimates about the possibilities of the partisan movement in Bulgaria. SOE Cairo informed London on 13 January that the partisans numbered several thousand, were causing the Bulgarian Government considerable anxiety, and could be usefully directed to attacking strategic targets such as the Sofia–Nish railway line.[54] In February Mostyn Davies reported that there were 12,000 partisans, with a much larger number of dissidents in the militia. By this time, Davies had been joined by another SOE agent, Frank Thompson (brother of the historian E. P. Thompson), and both were ready to move into Bulgaria itself, so that the potential for supplementing the British bombing attacks on the country with guided resistance activities seemed reasonably good, and was one factor in the choice of Bulgaria as the most vulnerable of the satellite states. As noted above, the Chiefs of Staff asked SOE as a result of that decision to provide a plan for intensifying activities in Bulgaria. SOE replied that there was great potential, but that much would be needed in the way of supplies, a reply which received a predictable response from the Chiefs of Staff. The diversion of aircraft from the Middle East to the Far East meant that supplying the Bulgarian partisans could only be done at the expense of other SOE operations, and the Chiefs of Staff were not prepared to cut down on supplies to Yugoslavia, Northern Italy, or southern France, especially as SOE's organisation in Bulgaria was in such an embryonic state.[55] And as it was clear by that time that Bulgaria was to be in the Soviet sphere of influence, expenditure of further resources in a losing cause was clearly useless. Tragically, however, it was worse than that. At about this time both Davies and Thompson, who had moved into Bulgaria, were captured and shot by the Bulgarian police,[56] and direct contact with the OF (fatherland front) was lost until August 1944, when a few British supplies were sent. By this time, however, Bulgaria was on the eve of being occupied by the Red Army, which entered the country on 7 September to the accompaniment of an uprising by the partisans. On 4 September the Foreign Office ruled that no more British secret agents should be sent to Bulgaria, and indeed opposed the inclusion of SOE experts in the Allied Control Commission to Bulgaria, as well as to Hungary and Rumania, for fear of alienating the Russians. At the end of the month the existing SOE missions in the country were expelled by the Russians.

If strategic, logistical, political, and diplomatic factors severely limited SOE's accomplishments in Bulgaria, this was even more true of its activities in the other two satellite states of Rumania and Hungary.[57]

The former had been the scene of much Section D activity in 1939–40, mainly because of the British interest in sabotaging oil supplies to Germany and Danube shipping. Their main contact before the German advance into the Balkans forced them out was with Maniu, leader of the National Peasant Party, with whom they left a W/T set. SOE's objective, much as before, was to stimulate an anti-Axis movement in the country under Maniu's leadership, and, much as before, the Rumanians demanded guarantees that SOE could not give; namely, that Rumania would not fall under Russian control once the German front collapsed. Opinion in Rumania was both anti-Soviet and anti-German, and ultimately SOE activities in Rumania were to be severely curtailed and finally terminated because of Foreign Office determination that Anglo-Soviet relations should not suffer as a result. Although in May 1942 Eden referred to 'the vital importance of any revolutionary movement . . . from the point of view of its probable effect on German oil supplies', SOE sent no missions into the country in 1942, and in March 1943 the Foreign Office indicated clearly that on Rumanian matters it would defer to the Russians, by ruling that all peace feelers from Rumania should be referred first to the Soviet Union. As officials in Washington put it early in 1944, the British were very ready 'to suggest that Rumanian affairs lie naturally and necessarily in Russian hands'.[58] In August 1943 SOE sent a mission in *via* Yugoslavia, which made contact with a representative of Maniu, but shortly thereafter its leader, Major David Russell, was killed, and after Rumanian peace feelers began to come thick and fast following the Italian surrender in September 1943 SOE was forbidden by the Foreign Office to make contact with Alexander Cretianu, the Rumanian minister in Ankara, who had had previous dealings with SOE. At the Moscow foreign ministers' meeting in October, Molotov made it clear that the Russians were opposed to contacts with Maniu. Eden appeared to accept this, but because it was not clear whether Molotov meant that he was opposed to *British*, rather than Russian, contacts with Maniu, the ground was prepared for a serious Anglo-Soviet misunderstanding which erupted in April 1944, and which led to yet another round of speculation about SOE's survival.

The background to this was that on 22 December 1943 SOE dropped a mission, codenamed 'Autonomous', into Rumania, under the leadership of D. A. G. de Chastelain, former sales manager of an oil company in Rumania, and Section D's man in Bucharest in 1939–40. Its task was to disrupt German communications, to organise a *coup d'état*, and to contact Maniu. Although the Foreign Office knew about the

'Autonomous' party, it had decided that the Russians would not be informed until after it had arrived in the country. The party fell into the hands of the Rumanian authorities almost immediately, and when the story threatened to leak out the Russians were then told. There was no reaction then, nor in fact for three months. In the meantime, SOE concentrated their efforts on the so-called Stirbey mission. Prince Stirbey, a Rumanian elder statesman, was brought out to Cairo as Maniu's emissary, and in mid-March 1944 met British, Soviet, and American representatives.[59] These talks took place immediately following the signing of the Bodyguard protocol in Moscow, and appear to have been designed primarily with the needs of strategic deception in mind. A note by Colonel Bevan, the Controlling Officer, to the Chiefs of Staff earlier in the year on the question of whether or not a Rumanian surrender offer should be rejected, stated that for deception purposes 'No suggestions should be made that we shall not be ready to take advantage of the Rumanian offer this spring', that is, the expectation (and threat) of Allied landings in the Balkans should be kept alive.

By this time the Red Army had reached Bessarabia, and this, combined with the German occupation of Hungary in the same month, led to hopes of a change of sides by the Rumanians. The Russians promised that Transylvania would be returned to Rumania, and in order to increase pressure Bucharest was bombed by an Anglo-American attack on 21 April. In the meantime, SOE was preparing to send joint SOE–OSS parties into the country, and on 26 April SOE in Moscow informed the Russians of these plans. The Foreign Office, in fact, had even gone so far as to suggest to SOE that the Russians might be included in the first party to be dropped, an indicator of their desire to maintain good relations with the Russians on Rumanian matters. This approach by SOE Moscow precipitated, unexpectedly and dramatically, a violent Soviet response. Not only was the suggestion turned down, but on 30 April Molotov, in a personal message to Churchill, now denounced the 'Autonomous' party in Bucharest (of whose existence the Russians had long since been informed) of having reached an Anglo-Rumanian agreement behind the Russians' backs. Molotov's reasons for choosing to react this way may be speculated on, but so far as SOE was concerned it had drastic, and almost fatal, consequences. Churchill, while simultaneously refuting Molotov's allegations as groundless and demanding an apology, vented his anger on SOE whom he accused of wrecking British diplomacy. He commented bitterly that 'it does seem to me that SOE barges in in an ignorant manner into all sorts of delicate situations . . . It is a very dangerous thing that the relations of two mighty forces like the British Empire and the USSR should be disturbed by obscure persons playing the fool far below the surface'. He felt so deeply about the matter that he even suggested, temporarily, that the proposal he had turned down only four months previously for the breakup of SOE and the division of its responsibilities between the Foreign Office and the military should be adopted, the only moment in the entire war when Churchill appears to have been ready to dismantle SOE. Ironically and perhaps typically it was over an issue where SOE was not to blame, and was another example of Churchill's failure to 'focus' on SOE. There was yet another acrimonious exchange of views between Selborne and Eden, the former accusing the latter—as he was to do again over the forced repatriation of Soviet citizens to Russia—of appeasement. A more important consequence operationally was that all further SOE operations to Rumania were banned (although SIS operations were not), and within a few days Eden began talks with the Russian Ambassador in London about spheres of influence in the Balkans, whereby Rumania would be traded off for Greece. These discussions culminated in a formal agreement to that effect later in the year at the Moscow Conference, but as it had been clear for some time that Rumania would be a Russian sphere of influence this merely set the *ex post facto* seal of approval on what had been for some time actual British policy. On 4 September 1944 the Foreign Office expressed the view that 'pending further instructions no member of any secret organisation should be sent either to Rumania or Bulgaria', and de Chastelain, who had left Bucharest after the King's *coup*, was not permitted to return. After 12 September, when an armistice had been signed, a British mission arrived in Bucharest, but its role was destined to be minimal as the result of Churchill's determination to keep to the agreement with the Russians as a means of keeping them out of Greece. Once again, the scale of the SOE effort in the Balkans had been very severely circumscribed not merely by logistical problems, but also by wider and more momentous political considerations and in the interests of postwar Anglo-Soviet relations.

A somewhat similar pattern was to be seen in Hungary, although here the hope that Britain might share influence on an equal basis with the Soviet Union, expressed in the fifty–fifty formula reached at Moscow in October 1944, ensured a somewhat more active, although still low profile policy. Intermittent SOE contacts with opposition groups in Hungary had existed throughout the war, and in March 1943 an SOE W/T link had been established between SOE in Istanbul and Laszlo Veres, who represented an important group within the Hungarian foreign ministry. In August, Veres moved to Istanbul to open serious talks with the British about the possibility of Hungarian surrender, and the British responded by asking the Hungarians to prove their goodwill by providing Veres with proper credentials, by denying transit facilities to the Germans, and by carrying out minor sabotage. Veres was sent back to Budapest with two W/T sets, and with the knowledge of Admiral Horthy he began to transmit information back to SOE Istanbul about Hungarian–German relations. In the following month—October 1943—SOE began to suggest that the Veres group should accept a small SOE party which would advise the Hungarians on how best to resist German demands through sabotage and other means (Hungary was as yet unoccupied), and already, in August, SOE had despatched an agent to Bosnia, Basil Davidson, with the mission of contacting Hungarian resistance elements.[60] The proposal to send an SOE mission to talk to the Hungarians was, however, quashed by the Foreign Office in December, on the grounds that such a mission was inimical to Anglo-Soviet relations (and may, incidentally, have lain behind the Uren–Springhall incident discussed in the previous chapter). It was only early in 1944, after Veres had made it clear to SOE that the Hungarian government had decided to make contact with the Russians to arrange the surrender of Hungarian forces still fighting on the Russian front, that Eden lifted his ban on the SOE party. The Chiefs of Staff approved the project on 15 March 1944, but it was cut short drastically by the invasion of Hungary by German forces and the consequent dispersal of the members of the Veres group. The German occupation did not, however, deter SOE. Their aim now was to make full use of Yugoslavia as a base from which to penetrate Hungary, and Tito agreed that Hungarian resistance forces could contact his forces in north-east Croatia.[61] In addition, between April and September at least six SOE groups were sent directly into the country; all were captured or forced to withdraw, and no more appear to have been sent. Here, too, the advance of the Red Army and the exigencies of the Anglo-Soviet alliance closely defined the limits of SOE activities.[62]

The most tragic consequence of the German occupation of Hungary in March 1944 was the end of the relative security which the 800,000 Jews in the country had enjoyed and the beginning of their deportation to the extermination camps. Against this sombre background, a long-standing issue which had involved SOE since the beginning of the war once again assumed topicality. This was the question of SOE's relations with organised Jewish groups. As far back as 1940 Section D and Moshe Sharrett of the Jewish Agency had reached an agreement over collaboration in underground activities, mainly in connection with sabotage operations in Rumania and the Balkans, where both sides had an urgent interest in creating as many obstacles in the way of the Germans as possible.[63] Plans were also drawn up to use Palestinian Jews to establish resistance and sabotage networks throughout the Middle East in order to disrupt German or pro-German activities, and as early as the summer of 1940 British instructors were training young Palestinian Jews in sabotage operations in Palestine itself. In 1941 SOE-trained saboteurs assisted in the invasion of Syria, and later in the same year SOE was training wireless operators for groups designated as stay-behind parties should Palestine be occupied by the Germans. So long as this threat remained real, SOE–Jewish collaboration remained relatively close, with the Palestinian Jews on their part also seeing co-operation with the British as strengthening the Zionist cause. In March 1942 SOE had drawn up a comprehensive post-occupational plan with the co-operation of the Palmach, the strategic reserve of the Haganah, and in the following month an SOE saboteur training course had been set up at Kibbutz Mishmar Haemek from which over a hundred Palmach members benefited. But the Germans did not arrive. After El-Alamein the programme was terminated, and in 1943 SOE–Palmach relations were broken off amidst growing British fears of a Jewish revolt in Palestine.[64] The long-term political conflict between British and Zionist interests in the Middle East now set the framework for subsequent SOE–Jewish contacts.

As early as October 1943 Professor Lewis Namier had expressed to the British government the Jewish Agency's fear of the likely consequences for the Jews in Hungary in the event of German occupation, and in February 1944 Sharrett had submitted a plan to the British for the stimulation of Jewish resistance in central and south-eastern Europe. The plan had insisted on the organisation of large and purely Jewish groups under Palestinian Jewish direction, and the British High Commissioner for Palestine had objected to it strenuously on the grounds that 'any avoidable extension of further opportunities to Palestinian Jews for training and organisation is strongly to be deprecated from the point of view of internal security of the country'. On these grounds, the plan was turned down by the Commander-in-Chief and the resident minister in Cairo in April.[65] The beginning of Jewish deportations from Hungary led to a renewed attempt in June and July to gain support for a joint SOE–Jewish plan. This time, Sharrett attempted the direct approach. He flew to London and on 2 June asked Randolph Churchill to pass on to the Prime Minister a plan for dropping 100

Jewish soldiers, or 'Palestinian civilians', into Transylvania and sub-Carpathian Russia to work into Hungary and disrupt the Germans by stimulating widespread resistance. According to Bauer, Churchill gave the scheme his full support, and 'all doors opened'. A Jewish Agency representative entered into detailed discussions with SOE in Bari, and operational planning began. Both the Balkan Air Force and AFHQ agreed in principle with the plan, although by this time it appears to have been proceeding on the basis that organised Jewish groups would not be involved, and the Jewish volunteers would be chosen from those already in the British armed forces, and closely subject to SOE control. A plan along these lines was approved by the Chiefs of Staff on 10 August. But shortly thereafter the plans were abandoned, and SOE Bari terminated its efforts. Although direct evidence is lacking, it seems clear that a combination of two factors had killed the scheme. First, general British reluctance to pursue SOE-related activity in what was now acknowledged to be a Soviet sphere of influence; and second, perhaps subsidiary in this instance, conflict between Britain's longer-term interests in the Middle East on the one hand, and any increased moral obligation and military expertise which might accrue to the Zionist cause as a result of such co-operation with the British government on the other. In the view of the British government, these considerations overrode any possible assistance which might be given to the doomed community of Jews in Hungary. And once again SOE activities were firmly controlled within the scope of wider British policy.

V

Poland and Czechoslovakia

SOE's links with resistance in Poland and Czechoslovakia, like those in the Balkans, were closely shaped by the evolution of Anglo-Soviet relations. Both countries had a unique relationship with SOE, which in effect acted merely as a supply agency, with agents coming under Polish or Czech control once they entered the field. SOE made no attempt to establish independent contacts, and in the case of Czechoslovakia neither the government-in-exile nor the resistance leaders favoured SOE's desire to promote campaigns of sabotage in the country. Their strategy, on the contrary, was to preserve a secret military organisation intact and wait for a national rising at the moment of liberation. Because of both countries' geographical situation, however, British supplies could not easily be provided (there were, for example, only about forty operational nights *per year* for Poland prior to the establishment of the SOE base at Bari),[66] and by the beginning of 1944 it was clear that both countries would be liberated by the Red Army. These factors contributed to a *dénouement* in Poland and Czechoslovakia remote from the minds of those in SOE who in 1940 had singled out the Polish and Czech secret armies as the models and exemplars for the resistance movements in occupied western Europe.

So far as Poland was concerned, Eden's report to the War Cabinet on 3 January indicated that the situation now demanded a change in SOE's relations with the Polish government-in-exile, Hitherto, the government-in-exile had sent messages to the Polish underground uncensored, but as the Foreign Office now wished to consult with the Russians about the Polish resistance (with the crossing of the Polish eastern frontier by the Red Army in January the behaviour of the Polish resistance had become a major political issue) this privilege, Eden said, should be removed.[67] The Joint Intelligence Committee subsequently agreed that the Poles should deposit copies of their cyphers with the British, but at the same time recommended that the Russians not be told this— otherwise they too would demand copies. Likewise, on 19 January, the Chiefs of Staff now asked the Air Ministry for closer supervision of supply packages sent to Poland.[68]

Although Churchill eventually vetoed the suggestion that the Poles reveal their cyphers he did so only on the understanding that *en clair* copies of all messages should be handed over,[69] and it was clear that the British were anxious to keep a close political eye on all matters pertaining to Polish resistance. While on political grounds the Foreign Office supported a proposal by SOE for maximum aid to the Polish underground for sabotage operations, it simultaneously reiterated the arguments against support for secret army activities and Eden expressed discontent that the government did not have as much control over Polish resistance as they did over that of their other European allies.[70] The Chiefs of Staff likewise turned down a proposal from SOE that operational control of SOE activities in Poland and Czechoslovakia should be placed under either Eisenhower or Wilson, and decided to retain it for themselves in London. This would enable the Prime Minister and the Foreign Office to keep the closest possible eye on developments, and had the additional advantage, as Sporborg of SOE recognised, of avoiding 'possible repercussions of American political influences on the very delicate Polish situation'.[71] The Defence Committee, under Churchill's chairmanship, supported this decision, while simultancously calling for increased supplies to the Poles.

The situation was indeed delicate, for the Polish problem threatened increasingly to upset all calculations of future Anglo-Soviet harmony. By now the Red Army had entered the disputed eastern territories of Poland, Stalin had threatened to attack and disarm any members of the Polish resistance who opposed the Russians, a communist-dominated 'national council of the homeland' had been set up to organise resistance in opposition to the home army, and fears grew in London that the Polish resistance might take action into its own hands. By March, Anglo-Soviet relations over Poland had deteriorated to the point where Stalin had 'relapsed into moody silence'.[72] Against this background, SOE came under strong pressure from Mikolajczyk, the Polish premier, to supply more arms for the resistance. Supplies had been minimal over the winter months partly because of flying conditions and partly because of the caution induced temporarily by the scare over German penetration of SOE, and as soon as Churchill returned personally to London in January Mikolajczyk extracted a promise from him that over the next three months the supply of arms to the home army would be trebled.[73] But this appears to have been another case of Churchill acting on his own in such matters, for neither the Foreign Office nor SOE were keen on providing the Poles with arms supplies. Their views prevailed, with the result that in April Mikolajczyk complained bitterly that there had only been two flights to Poland in the previous two months.

The Polish government-in-exile had consistently chosen to ignore the many signals made since 1941 that the British government could and would not support the Polish resistance in its ambitious plans for a national uprising or in its hardline stance on relations with the Soviet Union. It continued to do so, and on 25 April, after a meeting between Churchill, Selborne, and a delegation from the home army, Churchill observed gloomily and fatalistically that 'a decision to resist, regardless of the consequences, is the privilege of every nation, and it cannot be denied even to the weakest'. Three weeks later, the Joint Intelligence Committee, after consultation with SOE, concluded that responsibility for an uprising must be left to the Poles, and reaffirmed the conclusion reached the previous autumn that Polish resistance activities could not be of much use to Overlord. On the basis of this report, the Chiefs of Staff on 20 May once again made it clear that there could be no increase above the already agreed figures in supplies to Poland, and, shortly afterwards, declined a suggestion by SHAEF that they act as intermediaries between the Poles and the Russians in an attempt to co-ordinate Polish sabotage with Red Army requirements. These decisions should be left to the Poles. Despite this unpropitious atmosphere, however, there were in the period April–July 1944 174 successful sorties to Poland, and 114 men and 219 tons of supplies were dropped.[74]

SOE's role as intermediary between the Chiefs of Staff and the Polish Government was particularly difficult, and as events moved towards the tragedy of the Warsaw uprising it became even more agonising. The links between Gubbins and the Poles were strong, and SOE and the Polish General Staff had worked closely together from SOE's inception, although Sweet-Escott later recalled that the Poles and the Czechs refused to let copies of their messages to the resistance go much further than Gubbins personally. The latter was strongly sympathetic to the home army, and it is possible that his personal sympathies were misinterpreted by the Poles as an indication that at the moment of truth British supplies and arms for the home army would be provided. Certainly, when General 'Tabor', deputy Chief of Staff of the home army, informed Gubbins on 31 July of the imminence of the rising in Warsaw and asked for help, SOE's official response was to support the idea of transporting the Polish Parachute Brigade to Warsaw, and of sending in a British liaison mission. The former idea was one which had been discussed on several occasions between Gubbins and Sikorski, but both were opposed by the Foreign Office on strategic and political grounds, and the Chiefs of Staff vetoed them on 2 August. A similar proposal transmitted *via* SOE for the dropping of the Parachute Brigade was turned down a month later, while Polish sympathisers at SOE HQ at Bari, from which the few flights to Warsaw were made, on at least one occasion attempted to bypass the operational control of all SOE flights to Poland by Slessor, Commander-in-Chief of the Royal Air Force in the Mediterranean and Middle East.[75]

The failure of the Warsaw uprising and the crushing blow it delivered to the Polish underground did not quite mark the end of SOE's interest in the country, and Eden himself at a Cabinet meeting on 2 October proposed that further agents be dropped into Poland to obtain information about the state of the underground.[76] Throughout 1944 SOE had strongly supported Polish requests for a British military mission to be sent to Poland, and immediately prior to the uprising it had been decided to send a mission headed by Colonel D. T. Hudson, now returned from Yugoslavia. However, Stalin vetoed the idea, and in the interests of Anglo-Soviet harmony its despatch was postponed. It was only after further pressure from the Poles and SOE (from Gubbins in particular, who himself had been a member of the British military mission to

Poland in 1939) that the mission was eventually dropped in late December 1944. By this time, however, flights to Poland had been suspended following Mikolajczyk's resignation as Polish Prime Minister, in February 1945 the home army was disbanded, and shortly thereafter many leading members of the resistance were arrested by the Russians.[77] SOE retained a residual interest in Poland in 1945, as seen in the following chapter, but if any proof were needed the events of 1944 had shown that SOE's relations with the Polish resistance were strictly subordinated to the search for an Anglo-Soviet agreement.

SOE's 1943 directive had called for priority in Czechoslovakia to be given to sabotage operations to obstruct German communications, and thereby implicitly abandoned the 'secret army' concept which in 1940 and 1941 had provided much of the motivating force and rationale behind SOE's own existence and activities as an independent agency. This stress on sabotage also conflicted with the strategy of the Czech underground, which was to preserve as much as possible the remnants of the movement left in the drastic aftermath of Heydrich's assassination and work towards a national uprising at the moment of German departure. Hence, the call for intensified sabotage was rejected, and, as Lord Selborne informed the Defence Committee on 4 February 1944, 'SOE had made several attempts to encourage the reorganisation of resistance, but had met with no success and had received little support or encouragement from the Czechoslovak Government'. It was only after Benes returned to London from signing the Czech-Soviet Treaty in Moscow in December 1943 that a call for more active struggle against the Germans was issued.[78]

As in the case of Poland, however, the British were both faced with tremendous technical limitations on their ability to supply Czech resistance, and with the political and strategical fact that Czechoslovakia was within a sphere of predominant Soviet interest. That Britain recognised this was made clear in their refusal to enter a civil affairs agreement with the Czechoslovak government-in-exile in March 1944. Their reply to an appeal from the Czechoslovak government on 30 August 1944 for supply and bombing assistance to the Slovak uprising was therefore unequivocal. Eden made it clear that it was vital 'to keep in step with the Soviet government over this from the start and not to take any action with which the Soviet government are not in complete accord',[79] and the Chiefs of Staff agreed that the Russians should be consulted first. While this reply was being awaited, a further request from General Ingr, Commander-in-Chief of the Czechoslovak armed forces, this time for British assistance in promoting an uprising in Bohemia and Moravia, was likewise turned down. Ingr's approach, made late in September, did, however, raise the serious question (similar to that which had occurred in the Polish case) of how far the Czechs had been kept fully informed by SOE of the abandonment by the British of material support for their goal of a national secret army uprising. In turning down the Czechoslovak request the Chiefs of Staff pointed out that in a directive of 20 October 1943 SOE had been instructed to focus exclusively on sabotage activity in Czechoslovakia, but that Ingr's request and an accompanying comment by SOE indicated that the latter 'have considerably exceeded those instructions, and have in fact led resistance groups in Czechoslovakia to believe that they may expect British assistance for a large scale rising'. Gubbins' reply to this allegation was to point out that SOE had continued to work on the basis of the March 1943 directive, which, Gubbins claimed, had not been abrogated by the later one of October. The March directive, while giving priority to sabotage, had not ruled out supplies to the Czech secret army and indeed had stressed the political importance of military action when German strength was weakened. Thus, SOE had come into contact with the secret military organisation in Czechoslovakia and had supported Czech attempts to promote both sabotage and military action, although, Gubbins stressed, 'neither the Czechoslovak Authorities nor the Partisans have been given to understand that they might expect unilateral assistance in support of a large-scale rising, or indeed British assistance at all in arming and equipping a Secret Army as apart from Sabotage and Guerrilla Organizations'. And, he added, 'it has been anticipated that the Czech General Staff would make demands, but they have always been informed that supplies would not be forthcoming without the direct approval of the Chiefs of Staff'.[80] This carefully drafted reply left open the possibility that SOE had been somewhat ambiguous in its commitments to the Czechs, and it immediately led the Chiefs of Staff both to order a review and revision of all directives to SOE covering operations in countries where subversive operations were still taking place, and, secondly, to respond in a somewhat less negative tone to Ingr's appeal than they had in September over the Slovak uprising. Thus, while reiterating that any operations in support of a rising should, like the timing of the rising itself, be carried out and determined by the Russians, the Chiefs of Staff stressed to Ingr that SOE would continue to help as much as they could in the supply and assistance of sabotage operations. The concession also met the Foreign Office desire not 'to leave the Czechoslovak Government with the impression that we are no longer interested in Czechoslovakia and that we regard them as being entirely in the Soviet sphere of interest'.[81] It was this concern not to alienate Benes which only shortly thereafter led to a *volteface* in the Foreign Office position over supplies for the Slovak uprising, for on 25 October they urged that SOE be allowed to make small deliveries to the Slovak forces in order to compensate for the negative decision regarding Bohemia and Moravia which, the Foreign Office said, 'has been taken very badly by President Benes' (perhaps a further indication that the Czechs might have been encouraged in false hopes). Moreover, there was evidence that the Americans had dropped supplies to the Slovaks, the Russians welcomed the rising, and thus Britain was open to adverse criticism for standing aloof.[82] But the Chiefs of Staff were not keen to change course, especially as the Russians had as yet failed to respond to requests for information about their intentions and wishes, and in mid-November, when the uprising collapsed amidst Czechoslovak recriminations directed against the Russians, the question of SOE support to Slovakia died a natural death.[83] Decisions reached later in the year further reduced the scale of support to Bohemia and Moravia, although, as in the case of Poland, low-level SOE operations continued into 1945 in an attempt to retain some minimal political leverage and influence.

VI

Enemy and Ex-enemy States

One of the major paradoxes of SOE's activities was that although it had been established to mobilise a fifth column in a Nazi-dominated Europe, and action directed against Germany (and its ally, Italy) had inspired the creation of Section D in 1938, Germany itself remained low on SOE's priority list until after D-Day.[84] It was only in August 1944, in fact, that Germany became the first priority target for SOE activities. The reasons for this are not difficult to establish. SOE work throughout Europe depended on the support it received from, and the effectiveness of, the indigenous resistance movements, and the difficulties facing the anti-Nazi resistance in Germany would have presented SOE with tremendous problems in finding, infiltrating, and maintaining SOE missions in Germany. The overriding limitation, however, was imposed by the policy of unconditional surrender, and by deepgrained scepticism of the value of much German resistance activity. Ever since the

Venlo affair of 1939, when two senior SIS officers had been lured by the promise of contact with dissident German elements into the clutches of the Gestapo, such contacts had been regarded with deep distrust, and SOE had been ordered either to ignore any such approaches or to pass them on to the Foreign Office and SIS. This line had been reinforced by the Casablanca declaration on unconditional surrender, and even after the July bomb plot of 1944 SOE, in tune with other British agencies, remained sceptical about German resistance.

This was not to say, however, that SOE was totally idle with respect to Germany. A German section (section X) had been set up within SOE late in 1940, and it acted as the focus for the activity of a number of agents attached to missions in neutral countries such as Switzerland, Sweden and Turkey. In Switzerland, for example, the SOE mission established some useful but limited contacts with German socialist groups such as the *Internationaler Sozialistische Kampfbund* (ISK) and the International Federation of Transport Workers, through whom small-scale sabotage of German rolling stock in the Basle marshalling yards was accomplished. SOE toyed with more ambitious schemes for Germany, such as the subversion of the enormous armies of foreign labour in the Reich, but these schemes came to very little, if anything, because of the opposition of the governments-in-exile, reluctant to see their own citizens exposed to risk in this way, and concerned about the political consequences of such activities to their own survival.

When Germany did become SOE's first priority, it was too late for much to be accomplished, and the limited resources available could hardly be built up sufficiently quickly to be of much strategic use. In the remaining nine months of the war SOE and SIS together sent into Germany about nineteen agents, the first being sent in jointly with OSS on 1 September 1944. This agent was a member of the ISK, and he succeeded in providing a certain amount of information about other ISK groups in the country. But the overall results of this and other missions were meagre, and the main contribution of SOE personnel in Germany was to undertake denazification tasks after the surrender, and, during 1945, to keep a close eye on the activities of the German communists and to help in counterintelligence.[85] The growing importance of this latter activity is seen more closely if we look at the case of Austria, which formed part of the Reich until the end of the war and which, like Germany, was destined for four-power control.

Austria had been annexed to Hitler's Reich in 1938, and indeed the *Anschluss* had been the proximate cause of the setting up of Section D.

In 1940 Julius Hanau, who then headed Section D operations in Belgrade, arranged for sabotage against German railway communications in Austria, carried out by members of the Slovene minority, and in 1942 and 1943 a few Soviet special operations agents were dropped into the country by SOE. At least one SOE agent entered Austria from Yugoslavia in 1943, but 'its organiser never felt safe, felt he was doing no good, and soon came out again'.[86] But working inside Austria was as hard as working inside Germany, and, as in the German case, it was not until 1944 that SOE turned its attention there more seriously. When it did, the hope that partisan operations could be stimulated had to be offset against a transparent concern about communist influence in the country, whose postwar restoration of independence was considered to be in British interests. The main SOE mission was known as the 'Clowder Mission', working into the Austrian provinces of Carinthia and Styria from partisan territory in Yugoslavia, although G. E. R. Gedye, the well-known journalist who worked for SOE in Istanbul, had contacts in Vienna, and in June 1944 an SOE mission also began to work into the Tyrol from an Italian partisan base in the Alps. The Foreign Office kept a close eye on developments. On 9 June, three days after D-Day, a joint Foreign Office–SOE meeting decided that should contact be made in Austria with a national organisation, 'in which most of the leading political parties were alleged to be represented', SOE agents should refuse any suggestion of allied recognition. This organisation was the *Osterreichische Freiheitsfront* (OFF), which SOE described as bearing 'too close a resemblance to a normal communist layout to exclude the probability that it is at present a product of communist propaganda'.[87] At that time the only active resistance in Austria was identified by SOE as emanating from the Slovene minority where partisans were operating under the control of the Slovene Headquarters of the Yugoslav partisans. This fact also introduced a complicating political dimension, especially when Anglo-Yugoslav relations deteriorated towards the end of the year. On the whole not much hope was held out for profitable SOE operations, and one Foreign Office official echoed a widespread view when he observed that 'were it not for the importance of keeping Austria separate from Germany, we could let this flabby country stew'.[88] This remark complacently ignored the very severe security measures being taken by the Germans—one of their techniques at this time was to parachute in false agents in order to flush out and liquidate opponents of the régime, a campaign which met with some gruesome success.[89] Nonetheless, it made clear that SOE activities were closely linked to British political concerns, and by the end of 1944 distaste for the OFF had become much more explicit. By this time SOE in the field had, against the background of deteriorating relations with Tito, broken with the partisans, who, in the Foreign Office view, were controlled from Moscow, and in November the SOE officer concerned suggested that it might now be useful to give wholehearted support to the OFF. This idea was quashed at a joint SOE–Foreign Office meeting on 22 November, on the grounds that the OFF was a communist organisation controlled from Moscow, that British support might discourage elements who would otherwise be willing to oppose communism, and there was 'no reason why we should fight the communists' battle for them'. The hapless officer was instead left with the deskbound advice that 'you should steer a middle non-political course as a British officer'. Shortly thereafter he disappeared.[90] Almost simultaneously, AFHQ, which had taken control of special operations into Austria in October, clamped down firmly on Slovene partisan activity in Austria and forbade the support of partisans in Austria altogether.[91] That this was because of political fears about a general communist–partisan linkup from Slovenia across northern Italy and into Austria seems clear, and it coincided with the clampdown on Italian partisan activity (see below, page 195). The rejection of partisan action in Austria was confirmed when the Clowder Mission recommendation of February 1945 for the future of SOE operations in Austria was accepted. Rejecting support for the OFF on the grounds that 'it would probably develop into an Austrian EAM [and] the small military dividend which it could ever pay is disproportionate to the political dangers inherent in its support,' and anticipating little likelihood of much resistance activity by the Austrians, Clowder recommended that SOE efforts should be directed at sending in a number of *coup-de-main* parties, and in providing reconnaissance and liaison units when the Allies entered the country. That political factors were well to the fore in mapping out a role for SOE was further indicated in Clowder's claim that only it could provide the specialised assistance to overcome the efforts of communists to get control of Austria, the attempts of elements in the country to prevent its separation from Germany, and the attempts to continue the war subversively and by guerrilla action.[92] British anxieties for the future of Austria were well illustrated in their dislike for Karl Renner's government which assumed power at the end of the war. This predominantly social-democratic and communist coalition was strongly opposed by the British, who refused to recognise it. They were particularly concerned about the fact that the Ministry of the Interior—and hence the police—was under communist control, and it was not until elections in

November which gave the communists a mere five per cent of the vote and produced a more moderate government that anxieties lessened.[93] Nonetheless, fears for the future remained, and anti-communism was now replacing anti-Nazism. As a directive of November 1945 to SOE in Austria made clear, the Soviet Union was now the main threat against whom special operations should be aimed (see below, Chapter 7).

. . . there is no place, today, for stupid doctrinaire prejudices against 'Fascism' as such. If some Fascist toughs will murder M[ussolini] and a few more and then join with others, representing the Royal Family, the Army, Industry, the Italian workers and peasants, we must not reject them for the sake of some thin theory. What we want is that Italy shall stop fighting against us and, if possible, fight against Germans instead.

This entry in Dalton's diary for 20 December 1940, following meetings with Churchill and Lord Halifax, indicates the nature of SOE's early interest in Italy (as well as demonstrating a cavalier disregard for the ideological sensitivities of the labour movement and Dalton's own rhetorical appeals for a democratic crusade against fascism). Such hopes, and whatever action SOE may have taken to support them, came to nothing. No direct contact with internal Italian resistance elements was made before the end of 1941, there were sporadic and unimpressive attempts throughout 1942 and early 1943 to infiltrate propaganda and organise small-scale sabotage from Switzerland, and the first SOE mission was parachuted into Italy in December 1942, only to be captured shortly thereafter.[94] By this time the British were receiving numerous peace feelers from within Italy, and in March 1943 the War Cabinet was informed that SOE had been in contact with two senior retired generals (Badoglio and Caviglia) about a possible *coup* against Mussolini. But stung by criticism over the Darlan deal, and presented with the formula of unconditional surrender in January 1943, the British government was not prepared to become involved in such talks.[95] Although an SOE transmitter provided the crucial link between Badoglio and Eisenhower during the discussions over armistice terms in August–September 1943, SOE's role in Italian affairs did not assume much significance until 1944, when it came to centre around relations with the armed anti-fascist resistance in the German-occupied north of the country.

This armed resistance was strongly left-wing in character, and although by no means exclusively communist, the communists here, as elsewhere, played a prominent role. It quickly became apparent that SOE relations with the partisans would proceed within the framework of an allied strategy which, while seeking to utilise the northern partisans for the maximum military assistance they could give to the allies in their campaign to drive the Germans out of Italy, would also safeguard Italy from a future communist takeover. As early as February 1943, SOE itself had proposed an increased scale of activity in Italy on the grounds that 'unless the liberal elements are strengthened by moral aid, communism becomes the only alternative to fascism', and this motive, as well as anxiety not to be outbid by the Americans, underlay the future SOE Italian programme. The desire to prevent the emergence of a postwar communist Italy, or of an Italy under Soviet influence, was implicit in the exclusion of the Soviet Union from effective participation in the occupational control machinery set up after the armistice, and in Churchill's insistent support for the monarchy and Badoglio government; before normal political life was resumed in Italy, time was needed for liberal and moderate forces to strengthen themselves against the power of the Italian Communist Party. Churchill told Wilson in Cairo in November that whoever held Rome held the title deeds to Italy, and he reaffirmed its political importance in discussions with both Eisenhower and Wilson in Tunis the following month. Thus, when supplies for the partisans in northern Italy was placed second in SOE's overall European priority list in November 1943, support was limited to the encouragement of small groups of partisans carrying out specific and limited sabotage and intelligence operations, rather than for the creation and maintenance of partisan armies waging guerrilla warfare, which is what the partisans had in mind; and SOE in Italy was instructed on Christmas Eve 1943 to have no further direct dealings with the antifascist underground in Rome.[96] The British had no desire to see such partisans setting up liberationist 'governments' behind enemy lines and challenging the authority of the Italian government, although they did their best to express their opposition in purely military terms, and there were indeed some legitimate nonpolitical reasons why support of the nature and of the scope requested by the partisans were difficult to grant at that time.

The return to Italy of Palmiro Togliatti, the leader of the Italian Communist Party (PCI), in March 1944, followed shortly afterwards by Soviet diplomatic recognition of the Badoglio government, led to more explicit fears for the future of Italy. On 13 March Churchill told Roosevelt that he was alert to the dangers of a communist Italy, and two months later he asked Eden whether or not they were 'going to acquiesce to the communisation of the Balkans and perhaps of Italy'. Harold Macmillan, political adviser to General Wilson, Supreme Allied Commander in the Mediterranean, reflected to his American colleagues in March on the particular importance the British government attached to a stable Italy in the Mediterranean, and in mid-April complained to them about the growing strength of the communists and of the Soviet Union's 'striving for diplomatic Sovietization of Italy as a focal point in a wider European programme'. A simultaneous Allied Control Commission report noted with alarm the growing power of the communist party and called for more decisive action to deal with it.[97] On 11 May 1944, less than a month before D-Day and the liberation of Rome, the Foreign Office defined British objectives in Italy as being threefold. First and most important was the need to check communism. Second was the need to create a stable and prosperous Italy looking to Britain in the postwar world; and third was the mobilisation of Italian resources and manpower for the war against Germany. This last objective was the least important, as it was also the most impracticable.[98] This statement clearly subordinated military to political objectives, and implicitly made it clear that SOE operations in Italy would not be permitted to follow the pattern of Yugoslavia and Greece. Much of this concern was focused on the growth of the communist party in the south, that is, in liberated Italy, but it served to fuel anxieties about the situation and about partisan objectives in the north. If they became dominated by the communists, and if they gained control of territory, then postwar Italy would clearly be lost to the West. It was, therefore, after the liberation of Rome, when these political anxieties reached a new peak, that the question of how to deal with the partisans became a major problem for the military authorities and the Allied Control Commission. The partisans existed, they could make a useful military contribution, and there was no question of ignoring them. On the contrary, on 7 June General Alexander, commander of Allied armies in Italy, appealed to them to rise against the Germans and sabotage their communications, and much useful military assistance of this kind was provided by them over the summer months. These months, in fact, marked the high point of partisan–Allied relations, and, in the words of a postwar SACMED report, 'partisan forces in Italy were a considerable menace to the enemy from the fall of Rome until the end of the campaign', particularly on the Fifth (US) Army front.[99] Sixty-two SOE personnel and nineteen W/T sets were infiltrated into northern Italy in August alone, a higher figure than for any other Mediterranean country with the exception of Yugoslavia, and in October fifty new parties were ready to go either to reinforce or supplement the existing fifteen SOE missions. For the three months of July, August and September 1944, more supplies were sent to Italy than to any other country, again excepting Yugoslavia. Even in this period, however, political precautions remained to the fore. As the Allies advanced, disarmament of the partisans who welcomed them was the first priority of the Allied military government, while following a two-day visit to Rome by Churchill in August it was agreed that economic assistance should be injected into the country 'in order to prevent disturbances arising out of shortages of food'. So far as supplies to the partisans went, while there appears to have been no overall discrimination against communist groups, care was taken not to provide large-scale deliveries of rifles, small arms and ammunition, but to concentrate instead on clothing, sabotage equipment, and Sten guns.[100]

In October a new crisis in SOE–partisan relations arose. The end of the Allied advance in Italy and the diminished role this implied for the armed resistance, following upon a marked reduction in supplies in September partially caused by the diversion of aircraft to the beleaguered Polish resistance in Warsaw, produced bitter complaints of abandonment by the resistance and to pressure from SOE officers in the field which led Selborne to protest personally to Churchill on 24 October. Selborne was the last person to be motivated by left-wing sympathies, and indeed was to be found defending Franco's record against criticism by Attlee only three weeks later. In pressing for the continuation of the existing levels of supplies to the Italian resistance he was, however, protesting at the high priority still being given to Tito and the Yugoslav partisans (both countries being served out of the same aircraft pool), concerned about damaging British and SOE credibility in northern Italy to the advantage of the OSS and Americans, and worried that a cutback would so damage morale that the partisans would be useless when needed in the spring. Mixing his metaphors with abandon, he told Churchill that 'When you have called a *Maquis* out into open warfare it is not fair to let it drop like a hot potato. These men have burned their boats and have no retreat. If we fail them with ammunition, death by torture awaits them.' But his protest was to no avail, and the decision by AFHQ to restrict supplies to northern Italy 'to the minimum necessary for the maintenance of existing commitments' culminated three weeks later in General Alexander's notorious message to the resistance of 13 November 1944 ordering them to halt large-scale military operations, to save their munitions and material until further orders, and generally to 'lie low' for the winter.[101]

Alexander's proclamation has been seen by some Italian historians as a deliberate attempt to destroy or weaken the partisans for political motives, and it has also been suggested that Churchill had been given *carte blanche* by Stalin for such a move at the Moscow Conference of October 1944.[102] Allied policy was both more subtle and less cynical than this. In the first place, Alexander's proclamation was followed not by a reduction but by an increase in supplies to the partisans; in November and December, in fact, Allied supplies reached new levels, the December figure being twice that of November, hardly suggestive of a desire to destroy the partisans.[103] In the second place, there were far more effective ways of controlling them. By November political anxieties about the partisans had reached new heights, magnified by projections from events both in Greece and Yugoslavia. The Greek political situation was deteriorating and heading towards civil war, with EAM-ELAS refusing to surrender arms to British troops which had landed in October. Harold Macmillan, acting head of the Allied Commission in Italy, drew specific parallels with the Greek situation, considering that 'we had to get control over these movements right from the start . . . before they became, as in Greece, mere instruments of Communism'.[104] To these fears were added more direct concerns caused by the sudden deterioration of Anglo-Yugoslav relations and Tito's public claim in September for the annexation of Trieste, and, later, for the Austrian province of Carinthia. Although the territorial dispute was in the long run to divide rather than unite the Italian and Yugoslav partisans, this was not obvious in the autumn and winter of 1944, and indeed some Italian partisan groups in north-eastern Italy placed themselves under Tito's operational control.[105] This, combined with British disillusionment over Tito's behaviour in flying secretly to Moscow in September (on 20 November Churchill told Wilson that his confidence in Tito had been destroyed and in turn Wilson complained to Maclean about 'partisan misdemeanour in Italy'),[106] produced fears of a Communist takeover in north-eastern Italy, with links to the Yugoslav and also to communist (Slovene) partisans in southern Austria. It was no accident therefore that it was precisely at this time that AFHQ put a ban on all supplies to the Slovene partisans (see above, p. 190). As a consequence of all this, it was decided that greater control over the partisans was needed. In November, therefore, Major-General Stawell, who was in charge of all SOE activities in the Mediterranean, proposed new arrangements to link partisan activities more closely to the instructions of the Allied Command, to ensure that the Committee of Liberation of Northern Italy (CLNAI) did not emerge as a rival to the government of Italy, and to provide the partisans with necessary financial support. Arrangements along these lines were made at a secret meeting in Rome on 7 December between SACMED and representatives of the CLNAI. In exchange for a guarantee of continued financial support for resistance activities in the north, the CLNAI agreed to carry out allied military instructions, and in particular to carry out all measures 'which will safeguard the economic resources of the territory against scorching, demolitions and like depredations'. Furthermore, the CLNAI agreed to maintain law and order and to recognise the Allied military government upon German withdrawal. A subsequent agreement of 26 December between the CLNAI and the Italian government ensured that the former would not challenge the authority of the latter.[107]

These agreements, reached simultaneously with the climax of the Greek crisis and Churchill's personal visit to Athens, were of greater significance than Alexander's directive in confirming and furthering the British (and American) interest in preventing the emergence of a postwar communist Italy. They had the advantage of preserving and using the partisans for military objectives, while emasculating them politically. At the operational level, renewed emphasis was placed upon the immediate disarmament of the partisans in liberated territory and their reintegration into the civilian labour force. As Macmillan expressed it in January, 'Unless we are very careful, we shall get another EAM-ELAS situation in northern Italy. The operations of SOE in arming nearly 100,000 so-called patriots will produce the same revolutionary situation, unless we can devise a system for, immediately on the liberation of the territory, taking them into either our or the Italian army'.[108] In the occupied areas, supplies were increased to the partisans, but these were mainly designed to assist in sabotage, rather than in the creation of armed bands, and the greatest emphasis in Allied instructions to the armed resistance now became countersabotage, that is, the protection of industrial installations and public utilities from German destruction.[109] The logical extension of this policy came early in February 1945, when AFHQ ordered SOE to take particular care in the issuing of arms and to discourage the uncontrolled expansion of armed units. This and further measures taken in the three months prior to the liberation of Italy, discussed in the following chapter, confirmed that SOE's support for Italian resistance was to be circumscribed by the wider political goal of ensuring a stable non-communist Italy for a future western European *bloc*.

VII

The year 1944, which had begun with the greatest challenge to SOE's existence since its creation, became instead the year when it reached the greatest deployment of its resources. The peak of its activity was reached in September, when it was employing almost 10,000 British service personnel, and its operations had contributed both militarily and politically to Allied successes.[110] As postwar political objectives became more explicit and moved increasingly to the fore, it had also emerged more clearly than in the past that SOE operations were inextricably linked to perceptions of future British needs in Europe, which in turn focused around relations with the Soviet Union. The Moscow Conference of October had seen Churchill and Stalin give *ex post facto* validation to the division of Europe into spheres of postwar political influence, while strenuously denying that they were doing so. On the British side, while future co-operation with the Soviet Union was seen as possible and desirable, the Soviet Union was now also seen as the greatest political threat to their interests in Europe. In the same month the Chiefs of Staff explicitly expressed their fears about future Soviet hostility, and shortly afterwards, as we have seen, essentially political decisions were reached which directly affected SOE operations in both Austria and Italy in an attempt to reduce the chances of a communist takeover upon German collapse. Against this background, it is not therefore surprising that discussions should have begun in earnest about the future of SOE activities in peacetime.

On 9 November 1944 SOE received a new directive from the Chiefs of Staff which still remains classified because of its overtly political objectives,[111] and two weeks later the future of SOE itself was raised. With the planned dismantling of the Ministry of Economic Warfare once the war with Germany was over, the question arose of who in future would control SOE, and what its future relationships would be with the Foreign Office and SIS. On 23 November Eden made his bid for Foreign Office control. He told Churchill that there would be a peacetime need for a covert organisation to carry out special operations, that the wartime experience had proven the need for special operations and secret intelligence to be under the same controlling head, and that as SIS was already under Foreign Office control the logical solution would be to give SOE to the Foreign Office: 'Nothing but chaos', he asserted, 'can ensue if we try to have two secret organisations not under the same control working in foreign countries in peacetime'. Despite the reservations of Cadogan, who opposed proposals that the Foreign Office 'should take over all these fantastic things. We aren't a department store', Eden's ideas were accepted, although at the insistence of the Chiefs of Staff, who hoped that ultimately both SOE and SIS would come under the control of a Minister of Defence, the measure was adopted as an interim solution only. Moreover, SOE was to retain its own head (Gubbins), and not be subordinated to SIS. This continuing organisational separation of SOE and SIS was to continue until after the war with Japan was over. Until Selborne resigned as Minister of Economic Warfare on 31 May 1945, however, SOE remained formally under his control. But any idea that Special Operations were concerned exclusively with the war, and would end with the demise of SOE itself, were clearly illusory. There was still a need for some fifth column activity in Europe.[112]

7 Epilogue

The final year of the war began in a particularly sombre mood. The progress of the war had slowed down, political problems between the West and the Soviet Union, and between the British and the Americans themselves, were becoming more acute, and in Britain itself the end of the coalition government was in sight. The euphoria of September, when the Joint Intelligence Committee had predicted an early end to the war and when Anglo-American forces had crossed the German frontier, had dissipated to the point where Churchill described the military situation in early December 1944 as 'serious and disappointing'.[1] Earlier calculations about the end of the war had been sufficiently upset for SOE to have retained or recalled personnel due for release. In mid-December the German Ardennes offensive had substantially slowed down progress on the western front, and the positions lost were not regained until the end of January. Meanwhile, the renewed Red Army advances early in the year further strengthened the Soviet position in Eastern Europe. In Western Europe, the assertion of British political interests caused considerable controversy. In late November, Churchill intervened to prevent the appointment of Sforza as Foreign Minister in the Italian government, and on 29 November British troops were used to prevent radical and left-wing demonstrations against the Belgian government. On 6 December, fighting broke out in Athens between British troops and the armed Greek resistance. British actions produced a serious, if temporary, Anglo-American rift, and Churchill's coalition government came under strong criticism at home for seeking to destroy or weaken democratic forces in Europe. An impassioned debate took place in the House of Commons on 7 and 8 December, and although Churchill survived a motion of censure, criticism from the labour and liberal parties made it clear that the wartime political consensus was breaking down. It also threw into relief the conservative nature of British foreign policy,

199

and the determination to preserve Western Europe from communism. Likewise, fears of communism in Germany, whose political future under four-power zonal occupation remained indeterminate, were echoed in Churchill's resistance to Stalin's demand for heavy reparations at the Yalta Conference, in February. Severe terms, and dismemberment of Germany, Churchill feared, might produce revolutionary upheaval.[2]

Against this background, in which the contours of a divided Europe were becoming daily more clearly defined, renewed discussion about SOE's role in Czechoslovakia was the first SOE matter to occupy the attention of the Chiefs of Staff in the new year. While Czechoslovakia had long since been recognised as lying predominantly within the sphere of Soviet interests in Europe, and the Chiefs of Staff had made it clear in their discussions with SOE in the previous September that no encouragement was to be given to the Czechs to mount a large-scale national uprising on the Polish model, a future British role in Czechoslovakia had not been entirely discounted. There was still, the Chiefs of Staff had concluded in December, some political advantage to be gained from low-level support of the Czechs. They had therefore agreed to direct Wilson that ten successful sorties a month, in combination with ten American sorties, were all that were required 'to obtain our political objective of maintaining Czechoslovak goodwill and also to develop a measure of resistance'.[3] Wilson, however, considered that even this level would interfere with supplies to the Yugoslav partisans and the northern Italian resistance, and early in January he suggested halving the amount. Despite protests by Gubbins, who sought once again to ensure maximum support for the Czechs, the Chiefs of Staff laid down that 'all operations in Czechoslovakia are of a low priority and generally subject to the more important requirements of SACMED', although, for political reasons, they insisted there should be a minimum total number of ten sorties each month. As Czechoslovakia had received only three tons of supplies for the entire period June to December 1944 (excluding drops for the Slovak uprising), SOE operations were transparently now of a token nature only. So far as Poland was concerned, where the Chiefs of Staff had likewise retained operational control of SOE operations for political reasons, a decision in December to resume flights only to areas under German occupation meant that with the liberation of the country in January by the Red army, SOE supplies there came to a final halt.[4] So closed the final chapter in the story of SOE and the secret armies of these two countries.

The main concern in London over SOE operations remained, however, Italy. Although operational control had long since been transferred to the Mediterranean, London kept a close eye on the situation. The Foreign Office was unhappy about the December agreements with the CLNAI, and regarded the situation as potentially very dangerous because of the increased prestige that the CLNAI in the North now enjoyed. Sir Alexander Cadogan told the Chiefs of Staff on 9 January that Eden considered the situation ominously reminiscent of Greece, and feared a civil war. For this reason, the Foreign Office required that SACMED should keep the very closest eye on developments within the Italian resistance. The Chiefs of Staff, who were as anxious as Eden to head off a repetition of the Greek situation, agreed, and instructed Alexander, who had now replaced Wilson as Supreme Commander in the Mediterranean, on these lines. Shortly thereafter Alexander reiterated to SOE Italy that the northern partisans should be discouraged from the uncontrolled formation of armed contingents, and instructed them to take particular care in the distribution of arms. A number of new British liaison officers were dropped into the north to control resistance activities, and, as recommended by the Foreign Office, an officer was despatched to work with the CLNIA in Milan.[5] But these efforts could only partially influence the evolution of events. By the end of February partisan ranks had swollen to 100,000, and regional and local groups were planning uprisings to drive out the Germans. Political anxieties in London once again rose. Early in March, Churchill once more stressed to Eden the particular importance of saving Italy from communism, especially in view of the now open hostility of Tito's Yugoslavia, and later in the same month, before the renewed Allied offensive in Italy began, Macmillan expressed dismay that 'arms and ammunition were still being put into the hands of the resistance groups in considerable quantities'.[6] In fact, non-military components formed an increasingly large share of supplies to the Italian partisans in March, along with increasing emphasis on the protection of industrial installations and the 'maintenance of order'.[7] When the Allied offensive began on 15 April the partisans were actively discouraged from insurrectionary action, and, in the event, the worst fears of the Foreign Office about a repetition of the Greek situation failed to materialise. Concern over the political future of Italy, as well as over the future of the Trieste area, also played a part in the secret negotiations between the Americans and the British on the one hand, and the Germans in Italy on the other, which began early in March. But the extent to which this motivated policy must remain at present speculative, for it is not necessarily true, as has been argued, that an early surrender by the Germans in Italy would have benefited the Allies politically.[8] The demand on SOE personnel in Italy reached a peak at this time, with forty missions in the northern part of the country. They also reached their peak in other countries in Western Europe nearing liberation. On 25 March SOE reported to the Chiefs of Staff that 'resistance activities in [Norway, Denmark, Holland and Italy], both actual and preparatory, are running at a very high level and the calls upon manpower in respect of them will tend to increase'.[9] While the main part of this effort was dedicated to the final elimination of Nazi power in Europe, a substantial segment was also devoted to helping to ensure that the vacuum of power was filled in ways acceptable to British interests.

The treatment of resistance in the sphere of western influence contrasted sharply with that accorded to resistance in the area conceded to be in the Soviet sphere, and one final intervention by the Chiefs of Staff in SOE's relations with Czechoslovakia underlined this once more. Almost simultaneously with the beginning of the Allied offensive in Italy, SOE suggested that it might now be appropriate to transfer operational control of SOE activities from the Chiefs of Staff in London to SHAEF. Patton's forces had by this time entered western Czechoslovakia, and Czech resistance, Gubbins argued, might now be able to play a useful role to the west in sabotage and tactical intelligence. SOE personnel in Czechoslovakia had been shifted westward ahead of the Russian advance, were now concentrated in Bohemia and Moravia, and could assist Patton's army, provided operations were co-ordinated through SHAEF. This last attempt by Gubbins to provide the Czech resistance with a role in the strategy of the western powers came to nothing. The Chiefs of Staff rejected the proposal on 24 April, and the whole question of future SOE operations in Czechoslovakia was referred to the Foreign Office.[10]

Reference to the future of SOE operations pointed to the fact that, as the Chiefs of Staff themselves noted on 1 May, a week prior to the German surrender, 'SOE had no directive as to future tasks'.[11] Steps were now taken to remedy the omission. On 26 May, three days after the Joint Intelligence Committee had noted that there was no longer any need for Britain to be conciliatory at all costs with the Russians, and five days prior to his resignation as Minister for Economic Warfare and the transfer of temporary control of SOE to the Foreign Office as agreed in late 1944, Lord Selborne officially raised the question of SOE's long-term peacetime future with the Chiefs of Staff.[12] As a result, an *ad hoc* Committee on the Future of SOE was set up under the chairmanship of

Cavendish-Bentinck, chairman of the Joint Intelligence Committee, and its recommendations accepted by the Chiefs of Staff on 14 August, immediately prior to the end of the Japanese war. Under the terms of this report, SOE was to return to its old master, SIS. It was to be amalgamated with SIS under a common head ('C'), although there were to be separate Special Operations and Secret Intelligence branches of the Service. The larger and longer-term question of who was to control SIS, the Foreign Office or the Defence authorities, was deferred for the outcome of a major review of the entire British intelligence effort by Sir Findlater Stewart which was then taking place. The Defence Committee approved the Cavendish-Bentinck recommendations on 31 August, and as the result of subsequent arrangement between SOE and Menzies of SIS for the merging of the relevant sections of SOE with SIS in early 1945, SOE's existence as an independent agency, separate from SIS, which had begun in 1940, was at an end. On 30 June 1946, SOE officially ceased to exist.[13]

If SOE no longer existed, however, special operations continued. In the months following the German surrender the number of SOE personnel in Germany remained above the estimated levels because of directives given to SOE by the occupying authorities. These included not only short and medium-term tasks concerned with the elimination of Nazism, such as the interrogation of Nazi internees, but also 'longer-term tasks', which, while left unspecific, referred to clandestine activities and preparations in the event of a communist or Soviet threat to the British zone of Germany. Similar arrangements pertained in the British zone of Austria, where in September 1945 the Chiefs of Staff underlined the importance of retaining an SOE contingent.[14] The nature of Special Operations activities in peacetime was revealed more clearly in a directive on long-term objectives approved provisionally by the Chiefs of Staff on 4 October 1945. This defined the tasks of SOE (and of its successor, the Special Operations branch of the SIS) as, first, the creation of a skeleton network capable of rapid expansion in case of war, and, second, the servicing of the clandestine operational requirements of the British government abroad, subject, however, in every case to the express approval of the Foreign Office. Priority was given in carrying out these tasks to countries likely to be overrun in the earliest stages of any conflict with the Soviet Union, but not as yet under Soviet domination. This directive therefore ruled out for the time being clandestine operations (not, however, espionage) in Eastern Europe, and focused attention on countries such as Germany and Austria where the political future still remained open. On the basis of this directive, the Chiefs of

Staff provided a detailed directive in November for Special Operations in Austria (see Document Eight in the appendices). It also meant that certain Middle East countries were now an important arena for Special Operations activities, and Sir Alexander Cadogan informed the Chiefs of Staff on 27 October that it had been decided there should be a Special Operations branch in Persia, Iraq, and the Levant States; discussions to arrange this were already under way. There was considerable discussion about the Special Operations peacetime directive between the Foreign Office and the Chiefs of Staff, and a final version was not approved until February 1946, four months before SOE itself ceased to exist.[15] Subsequently, following the breakdown of the Anglo-Soviet alliance and the outbreak of the Cold War in Europe, the exclusion of communist Eastern Europe from the attention of the Special Operations branch of SIS was lifted, and the British became involved once again in the encouragement of subversion, sabotage, and resistance in 'occupied' Europe. According to Philby, the Special Operations branch became involved in subversive activities within the Soviet Union itself (particularly the Ukraine), as well as in planning for post-occupational resistance in Turkey. Other sources have provided circumstantial but undoubtedly largely accurate accounts of an SOE-type operation in Albania in the late 1940s. Mounted jointly by SIS and the CIA, successor to the OSS, this operation was designed to foster an anti-communist resistance movement against the communist régime of Enver Hoxha, which had belied Foreign Office hopes in 1944 of an early collapse.[16] Run in detail by ex-SOE personnel including Gubbins, but ultimately under the control of Philby, the operation was betrayed to the communists and culminated in disaster. Practically all the agents infiltrated into the country were immediately arrested and executed or imprisoned.[17] This represented a final ironic and tragic symmetry of sorts. The German penetration of SOE which had provided SIS with ammunition for its strongest offensive against SOE during the crisis of December 1943–January 1944, was in turn matched by the Soviet penetration of SIS; and in both cases it resulted in the destruction of networks and the deaths of agents involved in the attempt to foster resistance movements in Europe.

Conclusion

The creation of SOE in July 1940 was a desperate and hopeful expedient born out of the critical situation Britain faced following the collapse of France. It was given ambitious tasks with extremely limited resources, and its wartime performance fell short of expectations. But its performance cannot be judged in isolation from the wider context of Britain's war effort, and much the same conclusion might be reached about the performance of the regular services. Without the support of American and Soviet forces, those of Britain and her Empire could never alone have fulfilled the promises made by Churchill to cleanse the world of Hitler and Nazism. Criticisms of SOE's achievements, where these measure its performance against the claims made for it in 1940, turn out, on closer inspection, to involve criticisms of a wide range of assumptions, institutions, and performances going well beyond SOE itself. Neither Bomber Command nor SIS, for example, were sympathetic to SOE, and there are *prima facie* cases to be made for their occasional deliberate obstruction of SOE activities. On the other hand, not all of SOE's complaints about shortage of aircraft were justified, as in some cases a lack of operational officers and cipher staff were more important factors, while in the last analysis SOE could move no faster than the Europeans themselves. On the whole, much misunderstanding might have been avoided had the war leadership provided better co-ordination of special operations with the Chiefs of Staff machinery and had they treated SOE seriously rather than regarding it as a wayward child alternatively to be neglected and then chastised for going its own way. SOE–SIS relations at the top level were also extremely poor, and the failure to provide a clearly defined and understood co-ordination to decide on priorities was a sorry reflection on those who claimed to be running the war efficiently. SIS was sufficiently entrenched in power, its position consolidated by the prestige conferred upon it by Ultra, to enjoy the upper hand over SOE, and in the pursuit or protection of its own objectives actively sought to discredit it. Yet an organisation which harboured a Soviet agent as its possible future head was hardly in a good position to throw stones at others, and if SOE was on occasion careless or had networks penetrated by the Germans, SIS was probably no better. Lord Selborne's pointed defence of SOE against its critics within SIS during the German penetration scare over the winter of 1943–44 that 'the danger of penetration is inherent in the work of a secret organisation, as I think SIS will confirm',[1] was unwittingly close to the mark.

The task assigned to SOE by the war leadership, whose members subsequently suffered a collective attack of amnesia about the hopes pinned upon action within Europe as a means of winning the war, revealed the continuation into the Churchill administration of certain traditional assumptions about Britain and its relationship to European democratic and national sentiment, and of beliefs and hopes about the fundamentally fragile nature of the Nazi dictatorship and Britain's ability to destroy it through indirect means of warfare. Two major and quite disparate ingredients went into the making of SOE. First was Churchill's romanticism, which enlarged and fed upon his own memories of quasi-guerrilla fighting on the north-west frontier and in South Africa, and upon the legacy of T. E. Lawrence and the revolt in the desert. His imagination was seized by these images from the heroic days of imperialism, and his political beliefs were imbued with the Whig doctrine of England as the standard bearer and very personification of freedom. As A. J. P. Taylor has said, Churchill 'regarded the British cause as the cause of freedom and national independence all over the world . . . He supposed that this view was universally held and that in every country an indignant majority of eager patriots was held down by German agents. [He] was essentially led from this to exaggerate greatly both the extent of resistance to the Germans and its effectiveness.'[2] It was a noble but essentially innocent view, like many of those Churchill held about ordinary people, and views like it inspired many of those who became involved in SOE operations. One SOE agent found himself in the company of Serbian patriots looking down from the Serbian hills over to the Danube and he later recalled how 'rosy dreams of Lawrentian exploits right in the heart of Hitler's Europe swam through our minds. Anything seemed possible . . .'.[3] But such innocence and martial enthusiasm stood SOE in good stead, for Churchill's attraction to the idea of resistance certainly helped in 1944, when he returned from North Africa enthralled by the prospect of *maquis* uprisings in France and decreed that despite the *Englandspiel* tragedy SOE should continue in being. On the other hand, Dalton was right to complain that Churchill did not 'focus well' on SOE. His interventions on operational matters were sometimes ill-informed and disruptive; for long periods of time he took no interest in SOE's problems at all; he was resigned in the face of SOE–SIS rivalry; and he clearly sufficiently distrusted SOE to make Fitzroy Maclean his own personal and independent representative with Tito. Churchill's interest was not always a dependable asset. The other main ingredient which went into SOE was the idealism of those who thought of the war as being the opening stage in a European revolution or a 'People's War'. This was common currency on the left, and was best encapsulated in a left book publication of the summer of 1940 entitled *100,000,000 Allies if We Choose*, an argument for the mobilisation of the democratic forces in Europe now under German occupation, and one component in the broader attack during the post-Dunkirk period against the establishment and the 'guilty men' of Munich and for a more vigorous prosecution of the war. Dalton echoed these views in his own ideas about SOE, and here too there was a large dose of naïvety, which reflected the general failure of the English left to understand totalitarianism, a failure of imagination which led Orwell in 1941 to use the metaphor of the cardboard tank to convey the illusions of the left about Nazi military strength.[4] Innocent romanticism and naïve idealism might have been essential mobilising forces for SOE, but the harsh realities of the war quickly changed matters. Ironically, Dalton's socialist vision of a European revolution, when translated into effective operational terms, became an essentially conservative strategy. It proved impossible to work into occupied Europe without some minimal co-operation from the governments-in-exile to whose restoration Britain was committed, and this inevitably shaped SOE's policies. To a greater or lesser extent all these governments were threatened by the growth of resistance within Europe, and the more profound resistance became the greater the potential threat. Although SOE often resisted the tendency of these governments to refuse any intensification at all of resistance activities, especially where these involved more vigorous programmes of direct action resistance, in general the belief in passive resistance and the slow building up of underground armies coincided with the interests of British strategy, at least in the early part of the war. Thus in fact, if not necessarily in intent, SOE's strategy became a conservative instrument, for the rising tide of communist and left-wing resistance in Europe was eager for more activity, and largely uninterested in the restoration of prewar governments. To what extent leading figures within and around

SOE saw it more explicitly as an instrument against communism in these early stages is open to conjecture. Dalton himself, however, was talking as early as December 1941 of the need for Britain to provide Europe with an alternative to communism, at a time when Eden was in Moscow listening to Stalin tell him that he was 'prepared to support any special arrangements for securing bases etc. for the United Kingdom in Western European countries'.[5] One figure who throughout the war played an important but still shadowy role in British dealings with resistance, Major Desmond Morton, was certainly no friend of the left. Morton was a close and important adviser to Churchill, and it is apparent from glimpses afforded by the available documentation that he was the main channel for much of his information about resistance matters. In French affairs he played an important part as chairman of the Committee on Foreign (Allied) Resistance, which in practice dealt mainly with the Free French, and in 1940 he was appointed to act, in his own words, as 'father confessor' to the Allied governments-in-exile.[6] Like so many of them, he was deeply concerned with the spectre of postwar European communism,[7] and his advice undoubtedly reflected these views. He had, moreover, strong SIS links and residual loyalties, for he had worked for SIS in the interwar years, and he certainly aligned himself with Menzies in many of the SOE–SIS conflicts. Within SOE itself people such as Gladwyn Jebb, who acted as Chief Executive Officer of SOE during Dalton's term of office, showed little sympathy towards the left in general or the Soviet Union in particular. Jebb in fact had opposed the policy of collective security in 1938 on the grounds that it 'would provoke a war in which defeat would be disastrous and victory hardly less so, because either way it would place the whole of Europe at the mercy of Russia'. Even Gubbins, who later was frequently to claim that SOE had been given a purely military task, was quick to claim in private to Lord Selborne that but for SOE's wartime work many of the west European countries might have been lost for NATO in the early days of the Cold War.[8] As for Selborne himself, he was a deep-dyed conservative and monarchist, although this did not prevent him from acting on occasion as the loyal spokesman of his field officers when they felt they were being deprived of support, even though this might involve pleading for more support to the left-wing Italian partisans. But whatever their personal inclinations and prejudices, these men were in the last analysis forced by circumstances and by the Chiefs of Staff, the Foreign Office, and ultimately the War Cabinet, to operate in the direction they did, which was to work closely with the governments-in-exile and to build up secret armies whose uprising would eventually be detonated by Allied landings. This priority of a relatively quiescent and preparatory resistance strategy was reflected in SOE–SIS relations. The latter never fully accepted the SOE–SIS divorce of 1940, and its subsequent behaviour only too often resembled that of an embittered ex-spouse. Nonetheless, there were genuine conflicts of interest between the claims of special operations and of intelligence, and the fact that in Western Europe SIS was given priority over SOE until 1944 is an indicator of the priority given to intelligence needs by the war leadership.

Several developments led to a shift in emphasis in SOE strategy in 1943. The needs of the Mediterranean strategy and of strategic deception now that the Allies had shifted to the offensive, combined with morale problems amongst resistance groups instructed to follow a passive resistance policy, and the outbreak of large-scale guerrilla fighting in the Balkans, led SOE to give more encouragement to activist resistance and, for the first time, to support guerrilla activities. This shift in emphasis, however, fractured the broad coincidence of SOE strategy on the one hand and foreign policy interests on the other, and led, particularly in the Balkans, to conflict with the Foreign Office, culminating in the crisis of September 1943 when an attempt was made to abolish SOE Cairo altogether. It has been said that SOE did not make policy, but rather that it bumped into it.[9] If so, 1943 was the year of collisions. The muddle of conflicting authorities in Cairo, so well described by Woodhouse,[10] contributed to the problem and is a factor not to be underestimated; but it was a symptom rather than a cause, for at the heart of the matter was the fate of future British interests in Greece. It was not simply a question of strategic versus diplomatic interests, for the Chiefs of Staff were as aware as the Foreign Office of the importance of Greece for Britain in the post-war world, but rather a question of how these long-term strategic and diplomatic interests were to be reconciled with the need for some collaboration with EAM–ELAS, the left-wing resistance. Behind this lay the emerging *de facto* division of Europe into spheres of influence. Undue focus on the Greek and Yugoslav cases, where apparent contradictions in British policy can be explained by Britain's differing interests in the two countries and by the markedly different morphologies of their resistance forces, can obscure the fact that elsewhere in Europe the problems of aligning foreign policy objectives and the needs of strategy were much less severe. Here, SOE strategy was pursued within the framework of agreements over division of Europe into spheres of influence, and the ultimately abortive post-war Anglo–Soviet alliance so assiduously pursued by Eden since 1941. At

Québec in August 1943 Churchill and Roosevelt agreed in general that Britain and the United States should continue to support the various governments and régimes as then recognised by them throughout the rest of the war,[11] and in Western Europe, which Stalin in December 1941 had virtually agreed should be a British sphere of influence,[12] SOE operations and planning were not only designed to assist in the Normandy landings, but also to help ensure the preservation of order at liberation. While the preservation of order had a military rationale, and was also designed to counteract whatever retreating dirty tricks the Nazis might have devised—as Quintin Hogg claimed in the House of Commons in December 1944[13]—it was also designed to prevent seizures of power by the communists or by other left-wing groups. This was clearly seen in the case of Italy, but it was true elsewhere, and, although only a small part of SOE's total effort, it nonetheless meant that SOE's operations were not as exclusively military as sometimes suggested.

In central and eastern Europe SOE operations were likewise shaped by broader-range British interests, although in many cases genuine operational problems reflected underlying geopolitical realities, which in themselves helped shape these interests. The refusal to support the Polish and Czech secret armies, as distinct from purely sabotage operations, were cases in point. In those parts of the Balkans where it became clear that liberation would be achieved by the Red Army, SOE activities were limited by the Foreign Office desire to preserve good relations with the Soviet Union. This often meant supporting in some degree or another left-wing partisan movements, such as in Albania and Bulgaria, limited though support was. In areas where the Foreign Office hoped to maintain some influence in the postwar world, but conceded the greater interest to the Soviet Union, such as in Czechoslovakia, resistance support reflected this duality.

SOE was not a simple organisation dedicated exclusively to defeating the Nazis, although to some of its members it no doubt seemed like that. Those who later claimed to see in SOE the workings of 'perfidious Albion' were closer to the mark, although there was clearly much projection involved on their part. The counterpoint to romantic recollections by Englishmen of Lawrence of Arabia is Milovan Djilas's comment on the deep suspicion which greeted the arrival in September 1941 of the first SOE officer in Yugoslavia: '. . . we saw in Lawrence of Arabia', Djilas later wrote, 'not an idealist hero, but the perfidious, arrogant champion of an empire'.[14] It was certainly true that SOE operations embodied the pursuit of British interests as perceived by the war leadership, and thus were neither disinterested nor 'purely military' (whatever that may mean). If conclusive proof were needed of the degree to which political concerns beyond that of simply defeating Germany affected SOE operations, it would be found in the policies it pursued in Italy, Austria, and Germany itself in 1944 and 1945, and in the explicit directive of 1945 which made it clear that SOE's main enemy was communism and the Soviet Union. The emergence of this theme in SOE operations was, however, no sudden or unforeshadowed result of German defeat, but reflected the broader wartime process by which British interests in Europe were seen to be at first compatible with, and then threatened by, the Soviet Union and European communism.

DOCUMENTARY APPENDICES

Document 1

'Probable state of readiness and ability of certain countries to rise against the Nazi régime'. Report prepared by M1(R), forming appendix to the Chiefs of Staff Review of Future Strategy, 4 September 1940, COS (40) 683 in *CAB 80/17*.

GENERAL

The internal tendencies in enemy and subject territories may be an important contributory factor in the defeat of Germany. The position in each country is summarised below. For purposes of comparison the estimated conditions as at March 1941 have been selected.

GERMANY

2. At the moment the Germans are neither ready nor able to rise against the Nazi régime, and it is considered that the country is more firmly united behind Hitler than ever before. By next spring, the German morale will be weakened by monotony of diet, air bombardment and propaganda, but it is considered that it will be by no means broken. Should the shortage of food through blockade become severe, it is possible that local revolts might occur inside Germany, but this could only occur if the effective control of the authorities were very greatly reduced by disorganisation of communication and intercommunication facilities on a widespread scale. Even in the latter case, however, the existence of the records of the Gestapo are likely to have a severe limiting effect.
3. There are certain areas, however, which are believed to be

213

particularly fruitful to disaffection. These areas are, in order of importance:

(a) The Ruhr and the Rhineland.
(b) Hamburg, Bremen, Stettin and the North Coast ports.
(c) The Silesian industrial districts, especially the recently incorporated parts.
(d) The Sudetenland.

4. In the event of food shortage on a large scale ensuing in Europe during the coming winter, it is considered that Germany is likely to suffer less than the majority of other countries for two reasons. In the first place, the nation has for a number of years been systematically accustomed to a greatly reduced diet, which has undoubtedly increased its ability to withstand privations. Secondly, the Germans, in their position as masters of the land mass of Europe, and as possessors of the most efficient system of administration and transportation in Europe, should be able to ensure that reasonably adequate proportions of available European supplies are made available for the use of their own population.

5. It may be concluded, therefore, that, in the absence of a serious military disaster, there is no likelihood of any serious risings in Germany against the Nazi régime by March 1941. The situation beyond that date is conjectural, and will depend on the extent to which the internal conditions and morale in Germany are affected by increasing air bombardment and the effects of economic pressure. It is improbable that any large-scale rising will occur from below, but internal security will become a growing commitment, and disaffection within the Army and Party may arise.

AUSTRIA

6. There is every evidence that Austria has now accepted German domination. It is not considered that the Austrians are ready or able to rise against Germany.

POLAND AND CZECHOSLOVAKIA

7. Although it is not considered that the existing Polish and Czecho-Slovakian subversive organisations, amounts of arms and materials, and the possibilities of supply, will be far enough advanced by March 1941 to merit a general rising, yet it may be stated that these countries

are the most likely to be in a position to rise against Germany next Spring for the following reasons:

(a) The historic hatred existing between the Poles and the Czechs on the one hand and the Germans on the other.

(b) The adaptability of these nations to revolution and subversive activities acquired by past experience in subjugation to Russian, Austrian and German invaders.

(c) The present existence of a very active organisation inside Poland and with revolution and guerrilla warfare as its primary aim.

(d) Outside organisations actively at work in collaboration with us having the same end in view.

(e) The existence of considerable but insufficient quantities of arms and explosives hidden in the country.

(f) The existence of connecting links in surrounding Balkan countries with considerable supplies of materials at their disposal in Alexandria.

(g) The existence of a special department of the Polish General Staff for this work.

8. German reprisals against acts of sabotage and subversive activity have, however, been of such a brutal character, and the spread of German influence in the Balkans has been so marked, that Polish and Czech subversive activities supported by us have been seriously handicapped of late. Ways and means of overcoming these present difficulties are under consideration at the moment.

9. It is considered, however, that although the Poles and Czechs are far advanced in comparison with other countries, any rising is doomed to failure unless accompanied by successful major operations against Germany by Great Britain or a general rising in other parts of Europe.

10. It is probable that the prevention of premature and spontaneous risings in these countries will become increasingly difficult during the coming winter; undoubtedly famine and want will tend to drive certain groups to ill-timed activity. The effect of this on further subversive activities in these countries would be disastrous.

ITALY

11. There are indications of considerable anti-fascist movements throughout Italy, particularly in the industrial areas of the north. It is impossible, however, to state now to what extent the country will be

ready and able to rise against the fascist régime by the end of March 1941, since this will depend on what occurs in the interval. Italy's readiness to rise against the fascist régime will be in direct ratio to the degree of success which attends our arms between now and March 1941 and will also depend on the degree to which the war can be brought home to the Italian population in the Peninsula itself. If, for instance, we should be able to bomb objectives in Italy continuously throughout the winter and if during the same period we were to sink a large proportion of the Italian fleet, then Italy might well be ready to rise against the fascist régime by next spring.

12. Whether she would be *able* to do this, however, is another question, and would depend on the degree of control which Mussolini is able to exert through the fascist police and militia aided by the Germans. This in turn will be largely influenced by the extent to which the régime is weakened during the coming winter. In the last resort it would depend on the attitude of the army and this is impossible to assess at present.

Conditions in Italy, therefore, point to the importance of weakening the régime with all the means at our disposal, especially air bombardment, intensification of the blockade, offensive naval and land operations and propaganda.

13. Conditions in Italian East Africa justify special mention since this colony is isolated from Metropolitan Italy. The control of the Abyssinian interior already occupies the attention of a proportion of the Italian garrisons, and the necessary conditions for stimulating a rising of the tribes are already in being. So long as the present scale of our attack is not increased the Italians should be able to maintain control and to hold out perhaps till the summer of 1941. An increase in the scale of attack would, however, improve the prospects of bringing about a large-scale revolution throughout Italian East Africa. In any event it is necessary that everything possible should be done to create such internal conditions in Abyssinia as will not only occupy the attention of a large proportion of Italian troops, but will also compel them to resort to oppressive action on a wide scale, thus compelling them to expend their limited resources.

FRANCE

14. It is too early yet to be able to give any reliable forecast as to the likely position in France next Spring. Much will depend on the policy adopted by the Germans in the occupied areas, and the extent to which German propaganda on the one hand, and the irritating effect of a

hostile occupation on the other, will or will not succeed in setting the various sections in France against each other. German propaganda will aim to set the French against us. It is therefore important that British propaganda should bring home to the French the fact that their only salvation lies in the ultimate victory of Great Britain, and that Germany is responsible for their condition. In North Africa the Arabs provide useful material upon which subversive organisations can be built, but here, also, their economic difficulties may be exploited by Germany to our disadvantage.

BELGIUM

15. Such information as we have from Belgium at the moment suggests that German propaganda has been very successful there. However, with their tradition of resistance, it is to be hoped that when the hardships inseparable from the Nazi régime this coming winter have taken their toll the Belgian people will be fruitful ground for subversive activities.

HOLLAND

16. The Dutch are already, according to reports, beginning to revive, and obstruction is beginning to grow. There is, therefore, a possibility of creating a 'freedom party' in this area. A nucleus organisation to this end has been left behind, together with a certain amount of material, but so far attempts to get in touch with this organisation have failed.

DENMARK

17. The prospects of subversive activities in Denmark on any scale are very small indeed.

NORWAY

18. Reports indicate that the Norwegian people are becoming more and more dissatisfied with the German rule and would be prepared, at least in the west, to take part in disturbances against the Germans, provided that they can be organised, given supplies of explosives, arms and ammunition, and directed as to their employment. The Norwegian government are anxious to formulate plans for extensive operations of this sort with the British authorities. At the time of invasion steps were taken to initiate the formation of a 'freedom party': this party has been

created, and exists on a comparatively large scale.

19. While the long nights and snow in the winter should make the suppression of revolt somewhat difficult, yet it must be remembered that Norway is a country which can be effectively kept in hand by control of a few big centres. The present German garrison of 12 divisions also is more than adequate to keep the country in subjection.

20. It is not considered, therefore, that the Norwegians, unassisted from outside, will be in any position to carry out effective revolts by next Spring. The best that can be hoped for is some local co-operation with coastal raids and forays carried out from this country.

ALBANIA

21. Communication has been established with the dissident elements from and in Albania. There should be little difficulty in creating at least a considerable amount of unrest in this area, though it is doubtful whether this would be big enough to be described as a rebellion. To plan a successful revolt the concurrence, if not the assistance, of the Yugoslavs and Greeks would probably be necessary.

SPAIN AND PORTUGAL

22. If the enemy overruns these countries, there are various sections which provide a nucleus for revolt, including the large numbers of Spaniards who fought against Franco in the Civil War, but it would clearly prejudice our policy of supporting the powerful forces in the present Spanish government who are opposed to Spanish intervention in the war, if we now become involved in any intrigues with anti-Franco *émigrés*.

Document 2

'Subversive Activities in Relation to Strategy'. SOE's first general directive from the Chiefs of Staff, 25 November 1940, COS (40)27(0) in *CAB 80/56*.

MEMORANDUM

This paper has been prepared with a view to guiding the Special Operations Executive as to the direction in which subversive activities can best assist our strategy.

STRATEGICAL PLANNING OF SUBVERSIVE ACTIVITIES

It is essential that subversive activities should be planned with due regard to our strategical policy. Similarly our strategy and current plans should take account of the contribution which subversive activities should make towards the military and economic offensive.

To this end it is important that:

(a) The Joint Planning Staff and the Director of Combined Operations should consult the Special Operations Executive during the preparation of their plans and that any subversive activities required should be included as an integral part of these plans.
(b) The Air Staff should consult the Special Operations Executive in the day-to-day study of offensive operations against enemy and enemy-occupied territories.

The regular exchange of information and ideas between the Staff organisation and the Special Operations Executive is provided for by weekly meetings between representatives of the latter and the Strategical Section of the Joint Planning Staff. Similarly Special Operations Executive are in close touch with the Air Staff. In the succeeding paragraphs are defined the lines on which future strategy is likely to develop and those areas in which we think that subversive activities are most likely to be able to assist our military operations.

FUTURE OFFENSIVE STRATEGY

As our forces expand, our policy will be directed towards exploiting our amphibious power to the full, with the object of striking with land forces at outlying enemy positions. By such operations we shall aim at stretching our enemies, using up their resources, straining their communications, and gaining positions from which we can tighten the blockade, strike deeper at our enemies and generally support revolt against them.

In particular, the elimination of Italy comes first among our strategical aims, and would be a strategical success of the first order towards the defeat of Germany, which is our main object.

Apart from the aim of eliminating Italy, our major strategy in 1941 is likely to be a strategy of attrition. We shall maintain and wherever possible intensify blockade and the air offensive, and generally endeavour to wear down the resistance of our enemies by amphibious and other offensive operations within the limits of our resources.

It is not our intention to build up an army comparable in size with the German army. Our aim, while building up very powerful air and naval forces and maintaining our merchant shipping tonnage, is to create an army which, in addition to providing for our needs at home and overseas, will be capable of providing a striking force on the Continent when the morale of the enemy forces has been considerably weakened. The process of undermining the strength and spirit of the enemy armed forces, especially those in the occupied territories, should be the constant aim of our subversive organisation.

On a long view, it should be the particular aim of our subversive organisation to prepare the way for the final stage of the war when, by co-ordinated and organised revolts in the occupied countries and by a popular rising against the Nazi party inside Germany, direct and decisive military operations against Germany herself may he possible.

LOCALITIES IN WHICH SUBVERSIVE ACTIVITIES SHOULD BE ORGANISED

In the present stage of the war it is quite impracticable to state with any certainty or precision the localities where military operations will take place in the future. The most we can do is to define those areas where we think that subversive activities will be most likely to assist our strategy or interfere with that of the enemy. It must be emphasised that our major strategy must necessarily depend to some extent upon enemy action so long as our enemies still possess the initiative on land. For instance, our strategy in Spain will depend on whether Spain is attacked, and on Spanish reactions, neither of which can be foreseen at present. The same applies in the Balkans. Again, our attitude towards France and the French colonies will be influenced by our relations with the Vichy government and their own relations with our enemies.

We are, however, very conscious of the important and even decisive part which subversive activities may play in our strategy. In the circumstances to which we have referred in the preceding paragraph, we feel that if we are to exploit the use of subversive activities to the full, these activities must be planned on a very big and comprehensive scale. Our aim, in fact, should be to get subversive activities laid on and ready for execution in all areas where there is any chance that they may be needed, so that, wherever the fortune of war may require action, the ground will be prepared in advance.

At the same time, we appreciate that some indications of the relative importance of different areas and the type of subversive activities within them which are likely best to assist our strategy, would be helpful to the Special Operations Executive.

ENEMY COUNTRIES

In Germany and Italy our constant aim should be to create political disunity, discontent, economic disorganisation and dislocation of communications.

In particular, special attention should be paid to the lowering of Italian morale; interruption of communications, especially of coal, between Germany and Italy; and subversive activities in anticipation of our offensive operations in Sicily, Sardinia, Southern Italy and Pantellaria.

ENEMY-OCCUPIED COUNTRIES IN EUROPE

In the enemy-occupied countries we should also create economic disorganisation and dislocation of communications. While maintaining the national spirit and passive resistance to our enemies, our aim should be to undermine the morale of the enemy, to eliminate the influence of any pro-enemy elements and generally to keep alive pro-Ally feeling.

To meet the requirements of long-term plans the ground should be prepared for our own offensive operations in Brittany and the Cherbourg Peninsula, the South-West of occupied France, Holland and Belgium, and Southern Norway.

While preparing the ground for eventual revolt in the enemy and enemy-occupied countries, we should guard against any premature outbreak which must be avoided until our own selected time. Abortive attempts can lead only to the elimination of individuals and organisations which we may later wish to make use of as part of a larger plan.

FRENCH NORTH AND WEST AFRICA

In view of the uncertain political future of the French Colonial Empire it is not possible at present to lay down a definite strategical policy. We are of opinion that present activities should be confined to work of an exploratory nature, and to the fostering of pro-British feelings among the local population. Particular care should be taken not to precipitate native risings in Morocco.

The most likely area where we might eventually wish to base our forces is Tunisia, particularly in the neighbourhood of Tunis and Bizerta.

NEUTRAL COUNTRIES IN EUROPE

In any neutral countries from which the enemy draws supplies, our activities should be directed towards causing the maximum interference with such supplies. In particular, immediate destruction of communications by rail and road, especially of oil to Germany, in Roumania, would be of great assistance.

Preparations for destruction of communications between Germany and Italy and the south and east through Yugoslavia, Hungary and Bulgaria should also be made in case of further Axis moves to the southeast and arrangements subsequently to create economic disorganisation so as to hinder the enemy from exploiting the resources of the occupied areas.

In Spain and Portugal preparations should be made to delay an enemy advance from the Pyrenees towards Portugal and Gibraltar by destruction of communications, guerrilla warfare, and economic disorganisation. At the same time, preparations should be made for co-operation with our own offensive action in South-Western Spain, Tangier, Spanish Morocco, the Azores, Canary Islands, Madeira, the Cape Verdes and the Balearics.

In Switzerland we would lay special stress on the immediate interruption of trade—particularly coal trade—between Germany and Italy, so long as Swiss neutrality is not endangered by our action.

MIDDLE EAST

Subversive operations in the Middle East—including Italian East Africa, Turkey, Syria, Iraq, Iran, Libya and the Dodecanese—are under a Special Operations Executive representative who works in close touch with the Commander-in-Chief, Middle East.

In Italian East Africa and Libya efforts should be directed to the harrying of enemy communications and destruction of his supplies, particularly in the ports: and to raising the tribes to revolt when we are in a position to take advantage strategically of such a situation.

In the Dodecanese in particular the way should be paved for our own offensive operations.

FAR EAST

We feel that any subversive operations in the Far East designed to meet the situation of war with Japan should be carried out in close co-operation with the Commander-in-Chief, Far East, at Singapore, and we are not at present in a position to offer guidance.

PRIORITY

It should be the constant aim of all subversive operations to interfere with the enemy's communications and his supplies wherever and whenever opportunity offers, and to lower the morale of enemy troops in all enemy-occupied territory. In particular, while the enemy's numerical superiority in the air and the intensity of his submarine campaign continue to dominate our strategy, every effort should be made to reduce the enemy's ability to maintain these forms of attack.

Against this background, we consider that the following requirements are all of *first priority*:

(a) Attack on Italian morale.
(b) Interference with communications across the Italian northern frontiers, so long as this does not endanger Swiss neutrality.
(c) Interference with communications and supplies to enemy army and air forces in northern France, Belgium and Holland.
(d) Interference with communications by rail and river from Roumania to Germany and Italy, particularly of oil.
(e) In the Middle East, interference with enemy communications, and preparations for:

    (i) Co-operation with our own offensive operations.
    (ii) Sabotage, including destruction of oil supplies.

(f) Preparation for destruction of communications in Yugoslavia and Bulgaria.
(g) Preparations for destruction of communications in Spain and Portugal, particularly on the Franco-Spanish frontier and for guerrilla warfare in event of a German advance.
(h) Preparation of organisations for co-operation with our own forces should we require to operate in the Azores, Madeira, Cape Verdes, Tangier, the Balearics, Spanish Morocco and southern Spain.
(i) Action against enemy shipping in neutral ports.

Requirement of *second priority* we consider to be:
    Preparation of an organisation for co-operation with our own forces should we require to operate in Tunisia, Sicily, Sardinia and southern Italy.

Requirements of *third priority* are:
(a) Similar preparation in Southern Norway, Brittany and the Cherbourg Peninsula and the South-West of occupied France.
(b) Similar preparations in Holland and Belgium.

Many places have been mentioned in the preceding paragraphs where subversive activities in preparation for offensive operations are proposed. The greatest care should be taken that such activities do not disclose our precise intentions. The enemy must be led to expect attack on the widest possible front and not in any particular locality.

(signed) DUDLEY POUND
J. G. DILL
C. PORTAL

Document 3

'Interference with German Oil Supplies'. Memorandum by the Special Operations Executive, 8 January 1941, COS (41)3(0) in *CAB 80/56*.

I. This paper is based on the following assumptions regarding the assistance which would be given to SOE by other departments of HMG.

1. FOREIGN OFFICE

A. Removal of all diplomatic restrictions on our plans. This would mean that we would work on the assumption that the Foreign Office would not object to any particular scheme being put through for the sole reason that it would be likely to result in a rupture of diplomatic relations.
B. Positive help from diplomatic missions. Heads of missions would have to be instructed to give us every sort of assistance in restraining the governments to which they were accredited from taking action against our organisation and associates.
C. Passport facilities etc. Our people would have to be in a position to promise foreign nationals, who might be asked to help us, virtually anything they wanted in the way of British passports, travel documents, etc.

2. THE SERVICES

We would want the full co-operation of the Services particularly on the lines of:

A. Communications. We would probably require to move our people backwards and forwards at very short notice and we must be in a position to obtain the necessary facilities, e.g., seats on planes, simply by asking. We would also probably require at least one aeroplane permanently at our disposal to stand by to take off agents in an emergency.

3. We would require very large funds to be placed at our disposal.

4. At the same time it may be argued that if action is attempted on the large scale suggested below, it might, more especially in Roumania, result in a premature rupture of diplomatic relations before our plans for carrying on with the mission are completed.

5. It must also be recognised that H.M. Minister at Bucharest holds (from his own local angle) that major sabotage in Roumania should not be carried out at the present time since this might render his own position untenable. The chief representative of S.O. in the Balkans, also on the assumption that the maintenance of H.M. Mission at Bucharest for the next three months is highly desirable in order that he may perfect his plans to meet a German invasion of the Balkans, has echoed the views of Sir Reginald Hoare. This representative was of course unaware at the time of the views recently expressed by the Chiefs of Staff in General Ismay's letter of the 20th December to Mr Jebb and also of the importance now attached in London to making every effort without further delay, and overriding all other considerations to strike at German oil supplies from Roumania.

II. POSSIBLE LINES OF ATTACK

1. SUMMARY OF TARGETS

A. The oil supplies in question are those which go to Germany from the Roumanian oilfields and refineries plus the supplies coming from Russia across the Black Sea which are landed at the Balkan ports of Varna and Constanza.

B. The oil is transported substantially by two methods, river and rail. (We have just learnt that it is apparently proposed to send some supplies to Italy by road tank waggon but this would be a negligible quantity and would not affect the proposals under discussion). There is also the possibility that the Germans may build a pipeline from Ploesti to Bratislava or Vienna but, after careful investigation, experts in this country are of the opinion that this operation, which presents great difficulties, could not be completed in under six months in any case, and it therefore would have no bearing on this discussion. When the river Danube is navigable, approximately 130,000 tons per month are now (i.e. last months of 1940) being transported by this means and approximately 70,000 tons a month by rail. The river has, in fact, just begun to freeze over and, while there can be no certainty as to the period of freezing, we can probably assume that it will not be fit for traffic before the middle of March. Given complete German control of the Hungarian and Roumanian railways systems it has been estimated that under optimum conditions the carrying capacity of the railways for oil might be increased to 140,000 tons by April and 200,000 tons by June. When the Danube reopens for navigation it is possible that its capacity can be increased to 200,000 tons per month on the assumption that additional tugs and barges will be made available from Germany.

2. ATTACKS ON THE OIL AT SOURCE

A. Planned destruction of the oilfields, refineries and essential plant is now quite impossible. Such a project would require:

(i) The use of considerable numbers of expert personnel.
(ii) The use of quantities of demolition materials on the spot.
(iii) Uninterrupted access to the fields for at least 48 hours.

Unfortunately, owing to events and to a policy over which S.O.2 neither has nor had any control, none of these conditions now exists, nor can they now be recreated.

B. There is the possibility of causing fairly serious damage to the fields and refineries, particularly by fire, if a serious internal upheaval could be brought about in Roumania on the lines suggested below.

C. Direct attack by persistent bombing might do considerable damage to the fields by setting the wells on fire and could very likely destroy the refineries.

D. The traffic in Russian oil across the Black Sea can be attacked both by destroying the tankers carrying the oil and by destroying the depots at the ports of reception.

3. ATTACK ON RAIL TRANSPORT

A. Small-scale interference. This type of sabotage work is at the present time being steadily carried on in Roumania by S.O.2 agents on the lines of derailment of oil trains, occasional rail-cutting, insertion of acids into axleboxes of tank cars and engines, blowing up of pipelines, etc. Undoubtedly a certain hindrance of the oil traffic from Roumania to Germany is in consequence taking place, but it is negligible compared with what is required by the Chiefs of Staff.

B. Large-scale interference. This could take the form of planned large-scale sabotage, i.e. attacks on bridges, tunnels, permanent way at critical points, marshalling yards in Roumania, Yugoslavia and Hungary, the latter of which forms a sort of bottleneck for railway transport to Germany. To action on these lines there are several objections which in our view are overwhelming. First, as regards Hungary, it is impossible for us to operate there effectively on this scale. Secondly, this sort of large-scale planned sabotage is very difficult to arrange under present conditions with any frequency or continuity. It can be very quickly and easily repaired. It provokes an immediate reaction on the part of the local governments and would lead to the suppression of the various organisations concerned which, in turn, would prevent us from carrying out more important schemes. We consider it useless for the purpose in question. On the other hand, if a serious internal upheaval could be caused in Roumania a good deal of damage could be done to the railway system and transport services could be disorganised probably for a considerable time.

There is one bridge, plans for the destruction of which stand in a class by themselves. This is the Yalomitza Bridge between Ploesti and Bucharest over which must pass all oil supplies from the Roumanian fields destined for transport by the Danube and a small part of the supplies destined for transport by rail. If this bridge could be destroyed at the beginning of the period when the Danube again becomes navigable, this could prevent the resumption of river traffic for as long as was required to repair the bridge. This should be at least a week and, if the destruction was really successful, several weeks.

C. Air attack on marshalling yards and other vital railway points. We cannot judge how effective this would be, but at least it would have no harmful result on our local organisations.

4. ATTACK ON RIVER TRANSPORT

A. Small-scale attacks on tugs, barges, etc., by sabotage methods. This is what the old organisation were doing, principally in

Yugoslavian waters in the Autumn of 1939 and in the Spring and early Summer of 1940. In the light of our experience we are definitely of the opinion that it is quite useless. Only a negligible number of tugs and barges could be destroyed and the effect, like that of the railway sabotage, is simply to put the local authorities and the Germans on their guard.

B. Air attack on the great winter harbours on the Danube—Vienna, Regensburg, Passau, Degendorf, Linz, Kornenburg and Bratislava etc., which will be crammed tight with tugs and barges during the winter; also on locks such as that at Passau and on river port equipment. It seems to us that this is the simplest, most direct and one of the most effective means of paralysing transport of oil by the Danube. A successful concentrated attack, if practicable, would put the river virtually out of use during the vital months from April onwards.

C. In the past we have investigated three main schemes for blocking the Danube, one at Kazan, one at the Iron Gates and one just below Bratislava, in the region of Győr. Of these, the last-mentioned is now quite out of the question and the second, though useful, would be comparatively temporary in its effect. But the really vital blocking operations should be carried out at Kazan where there is a good chance that, by bringing the high cliff on the southern bank down into the river in a fairly narrow gorge, it could be blocked for as long as is needed for our purpose.

III. SUMMARY OF POSSIBLE SCHEMES

It seems to us that the useful lines of attack can be reduced to:

A. Air attack on fields and refineries. This is not within our sphere.

B. Air attack on marshalling yards and other railway targets. This is not within our sphere.

C. Air attack on winter harbours and port facilities, etc. This is not within our sphere.

D. Attempting to bring about an internal upheaval in Roumania, resulting in damage to fields by sabotage, and to refineries, plant, permanent way, rolling stock and in a general breakdown of services. This is our business and we believe there would be a chance of bringing it off—given the facilities set forth in Para. 1.—likewise the destruction of the Yalomitza Bridge.

E. Blocking the Danube at Kazan and possibly the Iron Gates as

well. This is our business. Detailed plans have been prepared by
S.O.2, but those for Kazan are in the hands of the Yugoslav General
Staff who will clearly not take action in advance of a German invasion of Yugoslavia. It would be the function of S.O.2 to secure the
final completion of the preparations and then, by a large and ju-
dicious expenditure to ensure that, irrespective of the wishes of the
Yugoslav government, the charges were fired at a moment suitable
to us.

F. Attack on the Italian tankers bringing Russian oil across the
Black Sea, on the depot ship at Varna, and on port facilities at Varna
and Constanza.

IV. CONCLUSION

S.O.E. are prepared, if so instructed, to do their best to carry out
schemes D, E and F.

Of these, D, might or might not come off, but the extent to which it
would reduce German oil supplies, if successful, would not be very material seeing that a Roumanian rising would be very quickly quelled by
additional German troops many of whom are already quartered in the
oilfields.

F, though useful, would not have very large effects.

Scheme E is the only one which, if successful, would be likely to deal
the Germans a really crippling blow. It is unfortunately, also likely to be
the hardest to bring off. We recommend, nevertheless, that no expense
or effort should be spared to achieve it, more especially since the preparations required would be less likely to cause a rupture of diplomatic relations than those required in connection with scheme D.

An appendix, giving further details of schemes D, E and F is attached.

APPENDIX
OUTLINE OF PLANS FOR D, E AND F ABOVE

I. ROUMANIAN UPHEAVAL

A. We have already certain lines prepared for this though our plans up
to the present have aimed at the raising of serious trouble in Roumania only in the event of a more complete German military occu-
tion. We have, however, the necessary connections with various

organisations in Roumania, such as the Peasant Party, the Communists and certain sections of the Iron Guard, which could be used to produce an upheaval as quickly as possible.

B. We would require for this purpose very large funds, which cannot be closely estimated.

C. We would also require the right to call upon His Majesty's Minister for appropriate action from time to time to fit in with our schemes.

D. We would need to be able to offer British nationality travel documents, etc., to the leaders of the various groups, who would be helping us and some to their supporters.

E. It would, of course, be desirable to cause the proposed interruption of rail traffic while the Danube was still frozen, so as virtually thus to cut off supplies of oil to Germany to the Balkans. The general upheaval at which we must aim, however, would need a good deal of preparation and we doubt if it would be possible to set our zero hour earlier than two months ahead at the best.

F. It is difficult to estimate the probable effect in terms of actual quantities of the proposed upheaval, but it should, at least, be possible to prevent any stepping-up of the present rate of rail-borne supplies.

II. BLOCKING THE DANUBE

A. Detailed plans for the blocking of the Danube at points in the Kazan defile have existed since September last year and were well on the way to completion by the middle of December 1939, when the Yugoslav government intervened, stopped the work and took over the mines which had already been laid. Approximately a month ago, our representative in Belgrade, who had been for a long time in negotiation with certain sections of the General Staff regarding the completion of the Kazan scheme by the Yugoslav authorities themselves, were able to report that the authorities concerned were now prepared to consider going on with the work and we handed over to them the plans in our possession.

B. What now has to be done can be divided into two phases:

   (i) Completion of the scheme by the Yugoslav authorities. There is no hope of getting the scheme completed, i.e. having the additional shaft sunk and charges made, except by the Yugoslav authorities themselves. With diplomatic pressure from the Minister, plus bribery by us, there is a fair chance that we can get the work proceeded with and finished before the river again becomes navigable. The argument, of course, to be used to the Yugoslav government and the only condition on which they would possibly agree to complete the work, is that it should be done as a precautionary measure of defence against the German invasion and that the charges would only be fired after Yugoslavia had been attacked.

(ii) The second phase is for us to try to arrange to fire the charges at the appropriate moment without the knowledge of the Yugoslav government. This would have to be done almost entirely by bribery.

C. The assistance required would be:

(i) Foreign Office decision and explicit instructions to the Minister to co-operate in our plans.

(ii) Finance for the bribing operations. We cannot give an estimate of how much would be required, as this would need a careful review of the personalities concerned, by our representatives in the field. We would, of course, have to spend a lot of money.

(iii) The same Foreign Office, Home Office and Colonial Office facilities in the way of passports, travelling documents and visas for our associates as in the case of Roumania.

(iv) Possibly the use of a civil plane to implement promises of evacuation which it may be necessary to make to parties involved.

D. Timing. There is no point in blocking the Danube until it is again navigable. This in turn is usually some time after the actual thaw, since the breaking up of the ice usually coincides with a violent current, which renders navigation impossible in certain reaches—let us say about the end of March.

E. It is virtually impossible to say exactly what the effect of blowing in one side of the Kazan defile would have on the course and navigability of the river, but our engineers, who examined the scheme in the latter part of 1939, were of the opinion that it would probably prevent all traffic at least for several months.

III. ATTACK ON BLACK SEA TANKERS AND PORTS

There are at present four Italian tankers plying between Batoum and Varna and Constanza. They are discharging approximately 17,000 tons of oil per month at Varna and 9000 tons at Constanza. There are no proper port facilities at Varna for the despatch and storage of oil and another tanker, moored in the harbour, is being used as a depot. We should hope to arrange by bribery for the destruction of the depot ship and one tanker in Varna harbour. This should result in the reduction of the quantity transported from Batoum.

We assume that the scheme discussed with Admiral Cunningham in June for sending a sabotage raider into the Black Sea, which might lead to the destruction of all four tankers, is still regarded as contrary to the foreign policy of His Majesty's government.

Document 4

'The Distant Future', extract from the Joint Planning Staff's Review of Future Strategy, 14 June 1941, JP(41)444 in *CAB 79/12*

OUR FINAL OFFENSIVES

255. By means which have been discussed in previous sections we hope in due course to lower the power of the German war machine. Conditions of economic collapse in territories under German control will by then have created widespread discontent among subject peoples. The morale of the Germans themselves will have been lowered, and their armed forces will have been reduced in efficiency and mobility. A sudden collapse, as in 1918, is, however, unlikely to occur.

256. While we look forward to such a process of deterioration in the powers of our enemies, it must be remembered that our own stamina is also limited. In order to avoid utter exhaustion ourselves, we must hasten the end. At some period in the future we must intervene with armed forces on the Continent (see para. 5). The effort involved in shipping modern armies with the ground staffs of Air Forces is so great that even with American help we can never hope to build up a very large force on the Continent. By this time, however, the threat of invasion of the United Kingdom will have been so reduced as to liberate some forces for a continental campaign, which would, in itself, reduce any threat to our islands still further. We must, therefore, devise a means of enabling a force of a few divisions to take advantage of the enemy's increasing difficulties and operate successfully in an offensive in German-occupied territory. The solution to the problem appears to us

to lie in the use of subversive action to make up for lack of normal military formations.

CAMPAIGNS OF LIBERATION

257. In areas where German power has become sufficiently weak, subjugated peoples must rise against their Nazi overlords. Such rebellions can only occur once. They must not happen until the stage is set, until all preparations are made, and until the situation is ripe. The armed forces at the patriots' disposal must be sufficient to destroy the local German forces. The reduction in German powers must be sufficient to prevent their reinforcing affected areas adequately.

258. By the time these conditions are obtained, we should have achieved such a degree of air superiority, combined with naval and military strength, as to warrant the despatch of certain armed forces from the U.K., whether invasion has been attempted or not. We might be able to operate some ten or more divisions (mostly armoured troops), with a considerable air force, particularly if our offensive operations were so directed as to clear the invasion ports area. Smaller forces might be sent from Middle East to the Balkans.

259. The German Army, even with its 250 divisions, is very spread out. They cannot be strong everywhere. With every fresh accession of territory they become further stretched. As their mobility is reduced, their difficulties of reinforcement of threatened areas increase. They become more and more vulnerable.

NATURE OF OPERATIONS

260. The object of our operations would be the liberation of the area concerned from Nazi rule with a view to enabling an alternative government of its own to assume control locally.

261. The attack from within will be the basic concept of such operations. The Germans have demonstrated the advantages of the attack in depth, their forward columns receiving help in advance from fifth columnists and air-borne troops. We must go one better. Their fifth columnists were traitors and comparatively few in number. Provided we give them the necessary training and the required preparations, we shall be able to draw on large numbers of patriots of high morale. We should be able overnight to produce the anarchy of Ireland in 1920 or Palestine

in 1936 throughout the chosen theatres of operations.

262. In a German invasion of England, vulnerable points, communications and possible air landing places are protected by the Home Guard who know every inch of their own areas. On the other hand, when our offensive is carried into German-occupied territories, the Home Guard will there be on the side of the invaders. Patriots will, beforehand, have been secretly organised and armed with personal weapons, such as Sten guns, bombs and explosives.

263. At the chosen moment in each area, these patriots will seize such objectives as headquarters, broadcasting stations, landing grounds and centres of communications. They will attack officers, sentries, guards and alarm posts and, where possible, barracks, camps and aerodromes. They will destroy German communications leading to the theatre of operations.

264. The patriots will, however, need the support of organised armed forces. For this purpose full use must be made of the 'free' Allied contingents now in our territories. In addition, in most cases, British armed forces will be required.

265. The roles of British armed forces will be to isolate the area from German intervention from outside, to assist the patriots in the capture of important centres and to destroy enemy formed bodies within the area. Powerful air forces will be used to interrupt the German communications and harass their troops. If we have access to the country by sea, armoured formations will be landed to strike swiftly and deep into the area. Sufficient infantry formations will be required to protect the bases and harbours on which these armoured troops depend.

266. There will be no methodical advance from one linear objective to another. The only line to be secured is the boundary of the theatre of operations which enemy reinforcements must be prevented from crossing. Within the theatre chosen, we must establish a number of protected areas where our forward aerodromes, dumps and maintenance arrangements will be located. These protected areas will be captured in succession by armoured formations and used as advanced bases for further operations directed to the complete destruction of enemy forces within the theatre of operations.

267. The roles of the 'free' Allied contingents will be to supply the rebels with specialists using equipment which cannot be put into the country clandestinely beforehand. In this category are, for example, signals, engineers, anti-tank and anti-aircraft artillery. In addition, small, well-armed mobile columns may be required to work in close cooperation with the patriots.

268. In allocating 'free' national troops or British forces to tasks the principle to be observed will be that 'free' national troops will be used wherever very close co-operation with patriots is required. British troops will be used for larger operations and, on completion of their tasks, will hand over to local forces.

THEATRES OF OPERATIONS

269. It is clearly essential that the inhabitants should be of sound morale and willing to act wholeheartedly against the Germans. Such conditions obtain now in Norway, Poland and Czecho-Slovakia. Moreover, in these countries, nucleus patriot organisations exist and could easily be expanded.

In France and the Low Countries there is a potential patriot mass, but it requires organisation and much propaganda preparation. These countries are, as yet, spiritually unready for revolt.

Certain Balkan countries show promise of future rebellion. Even in Italy there is some hope.

270. An essential prerequisite for operations of this nature is the introduction of considerable quantities of arms, stores and personnel into the country. This process is nowhere easy, even in the case of France and Norway. For Poland and Czechoslovakia, despatch by air over vast distances is the only possible method and would involve a great expenditure of effort for comparatively small loads.

271. Another important prerequisite is adequate means of communication with patriot 'cells'. Once again, this is easier when we have sea access than when we are dependent on aircraft or wireless.

272. Finally, the method of invading with armed forces must vary greatly. Given sufficient landing craft of the types we have already developed, we could land quite large forces reasonably quickly across the Channel into northern France or Belgium. We could also send adequate forces to Norway. For the Balkans, forces could be sent from the Middle East by sea. But the provision of armed forces to support risings in Poland and Czechoslovakia is clearly far more difficult and must depend on air transport. In any event, we cannot hope to introduce into Poland or Czechoslovakia armed forces at all comparable with those which could be transported by sea. Fortunately, in the case of these two countries, the potential value of the patriot forces, given the necessary arms, is very high.

PREVIOUS PREPARATIONS

273. All such operations will require careful planning and lengthy preparation. While we are still far from the stage when any general uprising in any occupied country—even if it were possible—would assist our cause, the time has now come when the necessary long-term plans should be prepared and equipment ordered.

In particular, the air implications of preparing and supporting a rebellion in Poland or Czechoslovakia require careful study.

274. It must always be remembered that the basis of these operations is the attack from within. Subversive action and propaganda are essential features and must form an integral part of plans and preparations. It follows that the authorities responsible for subversive action and propaganda must be represented at all stages and on all levels during planning and preparation.

275. At least a portion of the 'free' allied contingents now in our territories will have to be specially organised and trained for their allotted roles. Not all of these soldiers are required for the defence of Great Britain or the Middle East. Many will, however, not be suitable for the special tasks they would have to carry out in campaigns of liberation. But those who are suitable should be formed into special units for this purpose.

It is realised that such reorganisations, and indeed all these plans for rebellions, would require the active collaboration of the 'free' governments concerned.

276. Finally, full preparations will be required for the formation of a local government in order to take charge of the masses of armed patriots which will have risen and to restore, as soon as opportunity offers, the basic necessities of economic life.

CONCLUSION ON THE DISTANT FUTURE

277. In the distant future, offensive operations are likely to take the form of campaigns of liberation in occupied territories. The general nature of such operations would be armed rebellions by the local population, supported by small organised units of 'free' national forces and, as far as possible, by our armed forces.

278. The whole nature of warfare of this type is very different from campaigns which we have so far conducted. It corresponds more closely

to those campaigns conducted against us in Ireland or Palestine. The attack from within is the basic conception. Subversive action and propaganda will be at least as important as the operations of our normal armed forces.

279. The planning and preparation for such distant future offensive operations should be begun now. In making all these plans and preparations, the authorities responsible for subversive action and propaganda must be represented at all stages and on all levels.

280. Certain reorganisations in the 'free' allied forces will be necessary and the co-operation of 'free' governments will have to be assured.

FOPS
12 June 1941

Document 5

'Special Operations Executive'. Report by the Joint Planning Staff, 9 August 1941, JP(41)649 in *CAB 79/13*.

In anticipation of the instructions of the Chiefs of Staff we have reviewed the proposals put forward by the Minister of Economic Warfare in C.O.S.(41) 147(0). Our comments are as follows:

2. The plan falls into two distinct parts:
    (a) Organisation of subversive propaganda and other subversive activities including sabotage.
    (b) Organisation of secret armies.

SUBVERSIVE PROPAGANDA AND OTHER SUBVERSIVE ACTIVITIES

3. We believe that these can play a most important part in our offensive against German economic life and morale. Sabotage may be a most valuable complement to the bombing efforts of the R.A.F., particularly in attacking targets where there is no secondary objective, such as very small targets and targets in occupied areas. Sabotage should therefore be directed chiefly in accordance with the bombing policy aim.

4. In Poland and Czechoslovakia a highly organised sabotage force already exists and supplies sent there could be used at once. In the other countries concerned it will however be necessary first to build up the organisation to a state when supplies could be utilised. We think therefore that an overestimate has been made of the arms and equipment to

be delivered during the first six months to countries other than Poland and Czechoslovakia.

SECRET ARMIES

5. If the British Army is to return to the Continent in the final stages of the war, the assistance of local patriot forces will be essential at some period of the operations. Our expeditionary force would be enormously assisted if part of these local patriot forces were previously secretly organised and armed, so that they could be employed effectively in interrupting communications, attacking aerodromes, and other diversionary operations from the commencement of our attacks on the Continent. We agree that secret armies can only operate effectively if supported by fully equipped forces; their organisation therefore should be limited to those areas where our offensive is possible.

6. For reasons of fighter support and shipping, our main Continental offensive can only be launched across the Channel. Norway appears at present to be the most suitable area for any subsidiary operations which may be desirable. Priority in the organisation of secret armies should therefore be given to Northern France, Belgium and Holland, in that order.

7. It appears, however, that in these countries no attempt has yet been made to organise patriot forces as secret armies. Until some progress has first been made in the organisation there must be considerable doubt regarding the practicability of this part of the scheme.

8. The aim of the programme therefore, should be to introduce in the early stages organisers and means of communication, but delivery of arms and equipment should not commence before the organisation has been adequately built up.

9. The target date by which these secret armies would be ready is given as the autumn of 1942. We are very doubtful whether this is in fact practicable. A better estimate will only be possible in the light of progress made in establishing the organisation.

Provided the necessary agents and wireless sets are introduced during the winter of 1941–42, the programme could well be reconsidered in the spring of 1942.

10. We regard Norway as a special case. In view of the fact that it is likely to be the scene only of a subsidiary operation, it should rank in priority below Northern France, Belgium and Holland. On the other hand, considerable progress has already been made there in the organisation of a secret army and it is feared that, unless further assistance is

made during this winter, enthusiasm will be destroyed and can never be revived. Furthermore, in Norway alone of these countries, it is possible to introduce a large proportion of the arms and equipment by sea.

11. We recommend, therefore, that in Norway a start should be made during the winter of 1941–42 in the introduction of arms and equipment for the secret army, subject to two conditions:

    (a) That they can be made available by the War Office without affecting our own armed forces.

    (b) That they can be introduced into Norway by sea.

DEMANDS ON THE ROYAL AIR FORCE

12. The plan calls for a large effort on the part of the Air Force for the period ending 1 October 1942. Subversive activities are mainly a complement to bombing and secret armies can never operate until bombing has first created suitable conditions. It would be unsound therefore to sacrifice the effectiveness of our bombing effort to these activities. Nor at present is it possible to judge how far in fact the sorties required will prove to be necessary or practicable. We recommend in paras 17–20 the machinery by which immediate needs might be met and future demands investigated. It is essential that provision of sorties for S.O.2 should not be allowed to interfere with the requirements of S.I.S.

13. In order to ensure the greatest economy in air effort, the Air Ministry should investigate with S.O.2 the provision of suitable aircraft and containers.

W/T COMMUNICATIONS

14. S.I.S. foresee no difficulties in the provision of W/T sets on the scale we understand the S.O.2 require, but the extension of this form of communication will raise demands for an increase in the W/T frequencies and the number of skilled wireless operators allotted to the S.I.S., or to S.O.2 if an independent organisation is set up under their direction. As the whole plan will depend on successful communications, and their establishment must necessarily form a commitment in the early stages, we feel that favourable consideration should be given to these demands.

SUPPLY OF MATERIAL

15. The suitability of the weapons, etc., suggested requires further investigation by the War Office and S.O.2. The provision of some of this material before the spring of 1942 can only be effected at the expense of our own armed forces. The total quantities can only be supplied after that date. If our recommendations in para. 8 are accepted the greater part of this material will not be needed before the summer of 1942 by which time the total requirements will have been more accurately estimated. We are of the opinion that provision of arms and equipment should be authorised now for the full programme of requirements for subversive activities. We suggest that only 25% of the requirements for secret armies should be provided by the spring of 1942.

APPROACH TO ALLIED GOVERNMENTS

16. We agree that the co-operation of allied governments, or their representatives in this country, should be solicited. We presume that the approach to such governments will be made through the Foreign Office and that assistance from allied armed forces will be obtained through the War Office.

CONCLUSIONS

17. Although the paper put forward by the Minister of Economic Warfare is described as an 'Outline Plan' we feel that in view of the many unpredictable factors involved, it should be regarded more in the nature of 'A target to be aimed at'. Whether or not it will be found practicable to attain this target either by the date specified or at all, will depend not only on the facilities given to S.O.2 but also on the degree of success met with in the early stages of organisation. Only when a start has been made will it be possible to judge what are the ultimate prospects of success. The essential thing, therefore, is to make a start.

18. At present a special flight is set aside for the uses of S.O.2 and S.I.S. We feel that if it were possible for the Air Ministry to make some immediate increase in these special facilities leading up during the course of the winter to a maximum of one squadron, it would be enough to enable S.O.2 to make an effective beginning both in subversive activities and in the organisation of secret armies.

19. If at any time S.O.2 needed additional facilities for some special purpose, it would be necessary for them to make application to the Air Ministry, who would have to decide whether to grant the request. It is suggested that the criteria to be applied by the Air Ministry in coming to a decision would be:

(a) The value of the particular objective.
(b) The degree of success attained by S.O.2 in the past.
(c) The availability of aircraft at the time.

20. We believe that these recommendations, if accepted, will enable S.O.2 to make an effective start. Thereafter, it will be necessary to subject the progress made and the results achieved to a periodic review in the light of which recommendations as to future development would be made. This review might be undertaken by the Joint Planning Staff in conjunction with the Foreign Office and S.O.2.

RECOMMENDATIONS

21. We recommend that the Chiefs of Staff approve the plan in principle, subject to the following qualifications:

(a) Subversive activities should be given preference over secret armies.
(b) Sabotage should be chiefly directed in accordance with the bombing policy aim.
(c) The secret armies proposed should be prepared in the following order of priority:

   Northern France
   Belgium
   Holland
   Norway (but see (e) below).

(d) That during the winter 1941/42 the preparation of secret armies in northern France, Belgium and Holland, should be limited to the introduction of essential organisers, and W/T sets.
(e) That during the winter of 1941/42 such arms and equipment as the War Office can make available without affecting our own forces should be introduced into Norway by sea.
(f) Material other than W/T sets should be provided for the full programme of subversive activities and, by the spring of 1942, for

25% of the requirements for secret armies in northern France, Belgium and Holland.
22. We further recommend that the Chiefs of Staff should:
   (a) Invite the Air Ministry to consider the possibility of increasing the special facilities now available for S.O.2 and to review any application for further facilities in the light of the considerations set out in paragraph 19.
   (b) Invite the Air Ministry to investigate with S.O.2 the provision of suitable aircraft and containers.
   (c) Invite the War Office, in conjunction with S.O.2, to consider the suitability of the proposed equipment and to arrange the necessary provision.
   (d) Instruct the Joint Planning Staff to review the progress of the plan from time to time, in conjunction with Foreign Office and S.O.2, and make recommendations as to further development.

(Signed) E. G. H. BELLARS
W. F. DICKSON
G. S. THOMPSON

Cabinet War Room,
9 August 1941

Document 6

'S.O.E. Collaboration in Operations on the Continent'.
Chiefs of Staff directive of 12 May 1942, COS(42)133(0) in
CAB 80/62.

1. The War Cabinet has approved that plans and preparations
should proceed without delay for Anglo-US operations in Western
Europe in 1942 and 1943, the intention being to develop an offensive in
stages as follows:

   (a) A series of raiding operations to be carried out during the
   summer of 1942 on a front extending from the North of Norway
   to the Bay of Biscay, coupled with
   (b) An active air offensive over north-west Europe;
   (c) A large-scale raid to bring about an air battle and/or the capture
   of a bridgehead in France within the area in which adequate
   naval and air cover can be given during the summer of 1942
   should it be decided to operate on the Continent;
   (d) A large-scale descent on western Europe in the spring of 1943.

2. *[This paragraph, dealing with allocation of responsibilities, has been
omitted—Author]*

3. SOE is required to conform with the general plan by organising
and co-ordinating action by patriots in the occupied countries at all
stages. Particular care is to be taken to avoid premature large-scale
rising of patriots.

4. To this end SOE should work in continuous collaboration with the
planning staffs of the officers referred to in paragraph 2 above, who will
keep SOE fully informed.

5. SOE should endeavour to build up and equip paramilitary organisations in the area of the projected operations. The action of such organisations will in particular be directed towards the following tasks:

CO-OPERATION DURING THE INITIAL ASSAULT

(a) Prevention of the arrival of enemy reinforcements by the interruption of road, rail and air transport.
(b) The interruption of enemy signal communications in and behind the battle area generally.
(c) Prevention of demolitions by the enemy.
(d) Attacks on enemy aircraft and air personnel.
(e) Disorganisation of enemy movements and rear services by the spreading of rumours.

6. Copies of this directive have been sent to: Commander-in-Chief, Home Forces; Air Officers Commanding-in-Chief, Fighter Command and Bomber Command; Chief of Combined Operations.

Document 7

'Special Operations Executive Directive for 1943'. Chiefs of Staff memorandum of 20 March 1943, COS(43)142(0) in *CAB 80/68*.

1. Operations by the Special Operations Executive should be carried out in accordance with the following directive for 1943 which has been prepared in conformity with the strategy decided by the Combined Chiefs of Staff.

GENERAL CO-ORDINATION

2. It is essential that subversive activity should be planned in close co-ordination with strategical policy and operational plans. Similarly, our strategy and current plans must take account of the contribution which subversive activities can make towards the military and economic offensive.

3. To this end it is important that you should keep close contact with the following authorities, to whom the substance of this directive will be communicated; they should, on their part, keep you fully informed on all matters which concern you.

The Service Departments
Foreign Office
Combined Operations Headquarters
Secret Intelligence Service
Political Warfare Executive
The Controlling Officer

Ministry of Economic Warfare

Commanders-in-Chief, Overseas, at whose headquarters S.O.E. have representatives

The Chief of Staff to the combined commanders appointed for certain operations in Europe

The O.S.S. in all theatres where O.S.S. representatives are appointed.

STRATEGICAL GUIDANCE

4. In all matters where strategical considerations are involved, you should maintain contact with the Chiefs of Staff organisation through the medium of the Joint Planning Staff.

SUBVERSIVE PROPAGANDA

5. Wherever it is necessary that your activities should be supported or accompanied by propaganda and political warfare you should obtain the assistance and co-operation of P.W.E. You should at the same time give P.W.E. the maximum assistance for their work inside the countries concerned.

INTELLIGENCE

6. You should maintain close contact with the Joint Intelligence Sub-Committee. You will continue to pass on all intelligence you may collect to S.I.S. You may undertake the collection of intelligence for S.I.S. in any areas should S.I.S. request you to so do.

The requirements of S.I.S. should in general be accorded priority over your own operations in Norway, Sweden, France and the Low Countries, and, if the appropriate Commanders-in-Chief agree, on the mainland of Italy and in Sicily. In other areas care should be taken that your activities do not clash with S.I.S. and that the latter's sources of information are not imperilled.

RESISTANCE GROUPS AND PATRIOT FORCES

7. The following definitions will be used in future:

Resistance Groups: Organised bodies operating within enemy occupied territory or behind enemy lines (this term embraces the former 'secret armies' and 'sabotage groups').

Patriot Forces: Any forces which may be embodied in areas liberated by our armies.

8. You are the authority responsible for co-ordinating sabotage and other subversive activities including the organisation of Resistance Groups, and for providing advice and liaison on all matters in connection with Patriot Forces up to the time of their embodiment into the regular forces. You will deal with these in conjunction with the General Staffs of the Allied governments whose territories are occupied by the enemy and with the General Staffs of French authorities co-operating with the United Nations.

9. You will be responsible for advising the Combined Commanders (see Paragraph 29), and such other Commanders-in-Chief as may be necessary, on questions relating to Resistance Groups and Patriot Forces, and for providing liaison officers to facilitate the organisation of Patriot Forces in any territories occupied by our troops. The actual arming and organisation of Patriot Forces will not be your responsibility but will be undertaken by the appropriate Military Authorities.

10. You will be responsible for advising the Ad Hoc Committee on Equipment for Patriot Forces (under the Chairmanship of D.D.M.O.(H), War Office) on requirements for arms for both Resistance Groups and Patriot Forces. Requirements for special sabotage equipment for use under the direction of S.O.E. will continue to be dealt with separately as at present.

11. The strategy for 1943 agreed by the Combined Chiefs of Staff and endorsed by the British and United States governments is outlined in papers No. C.C.S.155/1 and C.C.S.170/2 dated 19th and 23rd January 1943 , respectively. The contents of these papers will be communicated to you separately and you will be given information by the Joint Planning Staff regarding the planning of projected operations. Your activities should be concentrated to the maximum extent in support of this strategy and, in general, emphasis should be laid on current activities rather than on long-term preparations. Any activities which are unrelated to this strategy should be severely curtailed. In the following paragraphs examples are given of how your operations in various countries can best be co-ordinated with United Nations strategy during 1943.

12. Against this background, subversive activities should be directed on the following general lines:

(a) *Sabotage* The sabotage of industrial objectives should be pursued with the utmost vigour; sabotage of communications and other targets must be carefully regulated and integrated with our operational plans. For example, there are certain vital points in the enemy's communications which it will be desired to destroy at, but not before, the critical moment when an Allied landing is taking place. Action against these points should be studiously avoided before the moment to strike has come. The general object of sabotage is to promote economic, industrial and military disorganisation and dislocation of communications in Europe, and especially to increase the already severe strain on Germany by attacking economic and industrial objectives and their related communications in Axis and enemy-occupied territories. Sabotage directed against oil targets and enemy U-boat and air operations is of special importance.

All possible action should be taken against enemy shipping. The increasing stringency of the enemy's shipping position north of the Straits of Dover makes action to destroy or impede shipping in northern waters particularly profitable at the present time.

Sabotage should as far as possible be co-ordinated with the aims of our bombing policy, and full advantage should be taken of bombing cover for the execution of sabotage operations.

(b) *Guerrilla Activities*. These should be aimed at diverting German pressure from Russia; and hindering as far as possible the concentration and consolidation of German Forces on the Eastern Front during April, May and June. They should also aim at intensifying Germany's already severe shortage of man-power by increasing her internal security commitments in Occupied territories. Resistance Groups should be prepared to act in support of any United Nations Forces which may operate in their countries but in general the organisation of formed bodies for this purpose should not be permitted to interfere with current activities.

SOE OPERATIONS BY THEATRES

GERMANY

13. Apart from work undertaken on behalf of P.W.E., your operations in Germany must of necessity be confined mainly to sabotage, which should be directed against industrial and communication targets

and preparations for attacking specially vital points at the critical moment, to be selected in consultation where necessary with the authorities listed in paragraph 3. The fullest use should be made of the presence of foreign workers to dislocate or hamper the German industrial machine by sabotage and passive resistance.

ITALY

14. One of the first objects of our offensive strategy in 1943 is the elimination of Italy. We aim to achieve this by bombing and by offensive operations in the Central Mediterranean this summer. You should encourage revolt against the fascist government and the Germans. Sabotage in Italy itself should be mainly conducted against communications, and electric power stations, preparations being made for attacking specially vital points in the enemy's communications when the right moment to strike comes. A campaign of guerrilla activities should be encouraged in Corsica. Your detailed plans in this area should, however, be made under the direction of the Chief of the Information and Censorship Branch of Allied Force Headquarters, who is directly responsible to General Eisenhower, the Supreme Commander for operations.

THE BALKANS

General

15. An intensified campaign of sabotage and guerrilla activities in the Balkans during the spring and summer is of the first strategic importance in order to impede the concentration and consolidation of German forces on the Eastern Front. Apart from direct assistance to Russia in this way, S.O.E. operations in the Balkans must also be directed towards interrupting the despatch of oil, chrome and copper to Germany. At a later stage, they must also be co-ordinated with Allied plans. After the elimination of Italy, we must be ready to develop the maximum pressure on Germany's vital interests in the Balkans. Operations may include the establishment of our forces in the Balkans and measures to enable us to bomb communications and oilfields in Roumania and provide focal points for the activities of Resistance Groups. One of the main aims of subversive activity in the Balkans should be to encourage large-scale revolts on the approach of United Nations forces, or if a sufficiently large-scale withdrawal of Axis forces takes place.

16. We aim to bring Turkey into the war as soon as possible, and her entry will have most important results in the furtherance of our strategy

in the Balkans.

17. In the organisation of subversive activities in the Balkans, you should, throughout your preparations, maintain close contact with Commanders-in-Chief, Middle East. You should also be closely guided by the Foreign Office, in view of the dangers of entanglements with opposing political groups and the risk of action contrary to the policy of His Majesty's Government and of conflict with the Soviet Union.

Roumania

18. Your operations in Roumania should be directed in accordance with the following priority:
   (a) Sabotage of industrial installations (oil installations are of primary importance) and their communications.
   (b) The disruption of communications and the sabotage of military installations connected with German operations on the Eastern front.
   (c) The promotion of general resistance to German exploitation and control.

Bulgaria

19. You should promote resistance to German control.

Greece, Crete and the Dodecanese

20. An important function of your activities in this area is the promotion of guerrilla activities and sabotage in Greece, Crete and the Dodecanese, to create a diversion in co-ordination with our attack in the Central Mediterranean. Guerrilla activities should take precedence over sabotage. Later, special measures may be necessary in these areas, in connection with a direct attack on them but this consideration should not interfere with any activitiy that can be organised to create a diversion to our offensive operations in the Central Mediterranean. Paragraph 18 above applies particularly in the case of Greece, where it is of growing importance, now that we should build up the King and the Greek government. In your dealings with the guerrilla leaders you should let it be known that they have the King of Greece and his government to thank for the support that is being accorded to them.

Yugoslavia and Albania

21. It is of the greatest importance that all resources at your disposal should be employed to the full to strengthen guerrilla warfare and direct the efforts of all resistance groups in Yugoslavia against the enemy.

22. We attach particular importance to the dislocation of German communications in Yugoslavia and after that to interference with the principal sources of raw materials vital to the enemy.

23. It may be necessary at a later date to co-ordinate the action of all Yugoslav and Albanian guerrillas with the operations of Allied forces but this should not be allowed to detract from the fullest exploitation of guerrilla warfare from now onwards.

HUNGARY

24. Your operations in Hungary should be directed in accordance with the following priority:
   (a) The disruption of German communications with Roumania and Yugoslavia.
   (b) The promotion of revolt against collaboration with Germany.

FRANCE AND THE LOW COUNTRIES

25. With the ultimate object of invading north-west Europe, it has been decided to assemble the strongest possible forces (subject to certain prior commitments in other theatres) in the United Kingdom to be held in constant readiness to re-enter the Continent as soon as German resistance has weakened to the required extent. In the meantime, such limited operations as may be practicable will be carried out with the forces available.

26. Raids, with the primary object of provoking air battles and causing enemy losses, and certain small-scale operations, as considered desirable by the Chiefs of Staff, will be dealt with by C.C.O.

27. Planning for operations on the Continent, other than those dealt with by the C.C.O., has been placed in the hands of the Chief of Staff to the Combined Commanders appointed for the purpose.

28. You should keep in close touch with the Staffs responsible for planning any operations in France or the Low Countries. Since C.C.O. may be able to assist, or to profit by, your activities, you should keep him fully informed of all your targets in coastal districts. He will similarly keep you informed of all his operations. For the present, you should continue your campaign of sabotage against communications and military and industrial objectives. We attach the greatest importance to any action which can be taken in furtherance of the anti-U-boat campaign and against blockade-running. Where means admit you

should direct a special effort towards supplying the resistance groups in France with the means of enabling them to play an active part when they are required to do so in support of Allied strategy.

POLAND AND CZECHOSLOVAKIA

29. The sabotage of German communications to the Russian Front in these areas is of primary importance. The preparation of forces to take organised military action when the German hold is weakened has great political importance in these countries. Such forces will undoubtedly yield valuable results when the time comes, but the supply of equipment for them should not be allowed to interfere to too great an extent with the provision of material for sabotage which can be carried out now.

SCANDINAVIA

Norway and Denmark

30. Your plans for subversive activities in these countries should be closely co-ordinated with those of the Chief of Combined Operations. They should aim at sabotage coups against targets of value to Germany, German communications, transport and traffic in Swedish and Norwegian iron ore along the Norwegian coast and such industrial installations as the Ministry of Economic Warfare may, from time to time, indicate as being of particular value to the enemy.

31. Germany's security commitments in these countries should be increased to the maximum by the organisation and equipment of small guerrilla groups operating in widely separated and inaccessible areas.

Sweden

32. You should act in accordance with your existing detailed directive for Sweden until a new one has been approved.

SPAIN AND PORTUGAL

33. You should take no action in either of these countries other than the maintenance of your existing contacts and communications into Axis controlled countries, as agreed with H.M. Ambassadors at Madrid and Lisbon. You should continue discreet preparations outside both countries for action in the event, now unlikely, of a German invasion.

TURKEY

34. One of our main lines of offensive action will be to create a situation in which Turkey can be enlisted as an active Ally. Your operations in the Balkans, as described in paragraphs 16 to 25, will contribute to preparing the way for Turkey's entry into the war, by creating the maximum unrest and embarrassment to Germany in that area. No subversive activity should be undertaken inside Turkey, though you should, in consultation with the Foreign Office, make plans for the expansion of your bases in Turkey in order to intensify subversive activities in the Balkans in the event of Turkey entering the war.

FAR EAST

35. Your activities should be closely co-ordinated with the offensive plans of Commander-in-Chief, India, from whom guidance should be sought at all stages. Particular importance is attached to any action you can take against Japanese shipping and oil supplies. In consultation with Commander-in-Chief, India, you should take every step to co-ordinate your activities with those of the Dutch and Australian subversive organisations in the Far East, as well as with O.S.S., so as to establish a comprehensive plan for the organisation of subversive activities in the Indian and Pacific theatres.

PRIORITY

36. We attach importance to your operations in the following general order of priority:
  1. *The Italian Islands, Corsica and Crete*
  2. *The Balkans*
  3. *France*
  4. *Poland and Czechoslovakia*
  5. *Norway and the Low Countries*
  6. *Far East*

REPORT

37. You are invited to prepare an appreciation stating what you can do with the resources you have available for the support of United Nations strategy in 1943 in accordance with this directive. If your re-

sources are inadequate to make a reasonable contribution in any particular area, you should state how your present resources could be strengthened by withdrawals from less important theatres.

38. On 1st November, 1943, you should render a report to the Chiefs of Staff Committee through the Joint Planning Staff, showing how far you have succeeded in carrying out this Directive. You should also, in submitting your monthly progress report, correlate it with this Directive.

(Signed) C. PORTAL
DUDLEY POUND
A. E. NYE
VCIGS

Document 8

'SOE Activity in the British Zone of Austria.' Memorandum by SOE 22 November 1945, COS(45)671(0) in *CAB 80/98*.

1. Tasks of S.O.E. abroad have been agreed as follows:
   (a) To create an organisation capable of quick and effective expansion in time of war. This will necessitate maintenance of adequate clandestine contacts, collection of up-to-date information regarding potential objectives of the special types required for planning S.O.E. operations and preparation of adequate covert communications.
   (b) To serve the clandestine operational requirements of His Majesty's Government abroad by giving covert support to British national interests where threatened, but only in cases where the appropriate department of His Majesty's Government or the Chiefs of Staff may think fit, and subject always to the express approval of the Foreign Office.

2. In carrying out these tasks, S.O.E. have been directed to accord priority to those countries which are likely to be overrun in the earliest stages of conflict with Russia, but which are not, at present, under Russian domination.

3. In view of the foregoing, the following is suggested as the directive for the S.O.E. unit in Austria.

QUOTE

(a) To plan and prepare the nucleus of an S.O. organisation which will remain dormant until such time as action (by a section or whole) may be required to fulfil the clandestine operational requirements of His Majesty's Government. This nucleus to be held to an indispensable minimum, but at the same time must be within the framework of the agreed plan, which stresses the necessity for rapid expansion into a reliable resistance movement in case of war.

(b) To plan in detail a programme of clandestine activity to be applied at short notice in time of war or threat of war, as directed by the competent authorities.

(c) To collect and transmit to London information gained by clandestine means from Austria and Yugoslavia regarding specific targets and resistance movements which could be made use of in war.

(d) The greatest attention must be paid to communications. Your own official signals will be carried by S.I.S. when full integration takes place in Austria. Your plans and preparations, however, should allow for separate clandestine transmitters and courier routes.

(e) To carry out such clandestine operations as His Majesty's Government may require. In their execution you will be under the operational control of the Military Commander in Austria with a view to reducing British military commitments in Austria in accordance with the wishes of the Chiefs of Staff or other appropriate department of His Majesty's Government and subject to specific Foreign Office concurrence in every case.

(f) To maintain the closest possible liaison with S.I.S. in Austria with a view to obtaining from them details of possible objectives for special operations which they may discover. Conversely you will make available to S.I.S. such secret intelligence as the S.O.E. unit may obtain in carrying out its own authorised functions. Appointment of a single Commander of S.I.S. and S.O.E. in Austria is under consideration.

(g) Planning should commence immediately but all preparations regarding formation of nuclei should await approval from London.

UNQUOTE

4. Initially the S.O.E. unit will comprise four officers and eleven other ranks.

Notes

Introduction
 1. See J. H. Plumb's article on 'The Historian', in *Churchill, Four Faces and the Man*, pp. 148–9, for the place in Second World War British historiography of Churchill's work; for the Mediterranean strategy controversy see M. Howard, *The Mediterranean Strategy in the Second World War*, and R. Leighton, 'Overlord Revisited', in *American Historical Review*, July 1963. For Hollis, Ismay, Alanbrooke and Eden, see bibliography, and for the recent war history, see R. Parkinson, *Blood, Toil, Tears and Sweat*.
 2. *Times Literary Supplement*, 18 March 1965.
 3. Richard Deacon, *A History of the British Secret Service*, p. 343; Anthony Cave-Brown, *Bodyguard of Lies*, p. 563.
 4. Basil Liddell Hart, *Defence of the West*, pp. 53–7.
 5. C. M. Woodhouse, *Apple of Discord*, p. 39.
 6. Jasper Rootham, *Miss Fire*, p. 49.
 7. *Parliamentary Debates, Commons 1944–45*, Vol. 406, Cols. 241, 927.
 8. Quoted in Paul Addison, *The Road to 1945*, p. 255.
 9. Basil Davidson, *Partisan Picture*, pp. 342–3; and Bickham Sweet-Escott, 'SOE in the Balkans', in Auty and Clogg, *British Policy towards Wartime Resistance in Yugoslavia and Greece*, p. 14.
10. Kim Philby, *My Silent War*, pp. 6, 18–19.
11. E. Boltine, 'L'Union sovietique et la Résistance en Europe pendant la deuxième guerre mondiale', in *European Resistance Movements 1961 Milan*, p. 15.
12. Gabriel Kolko, *The Politics of War*, pp. 32–3 and passim.
13. For this view and variants of it, see the books and articles by the following authors listed in the bibliography: M. R. D. Foot, Sir Colin Gubbins, Bickham Sweet-Escott.
14. Henri Michel, *The Shadow War*, p. 358.
15. Alan Milward, 'The Economic and Strategic Effectiveness of Resistance', in Stephen Hawes and Ralph White, *Resistance in Europe 1939–1945*, pp. 186–203.

Chapter 1
 1. Quoted in Michael Howard, *The Continental Commitment; the Dilemma of*

British Defence Policy in the Era of the Two World Wars, p. 94. See also N. Gibbs, *Grand Strategy*, pp. 657–67. The labour party's wartime planning also depended heavily on economic warfare; see John Naylor, *Labour's International Policy: the Labour Party in the 1930s*, pp. 279–80.

2. W. N. Medlicott, *The Economic Blockade*, Vol. 1, xl. See also R. A. Butler, *The Art of the Possible*, p. 80.

3. K. Feiling, *Life of Neville Chamberlain*, pp. 417–18, 426.

4. Lord Gladwyn (Gladwyn Jebb), *Memoirs*, p. 96. See also Vernon Bartlett, *And Now, Tomorrow*, p. 61, and Templewood, *Nine Troubled Years*, p. 401.

5. Nicholas Bethell, *The War Hitler Won*, pp. 5–6. For régime-watching, see for example, T. Jones, *A Diary with Letters 1931–1950*, p. 429.

6. Slessor is quoted from Sir Charles Webster and Noble Frankland, *The Strategic Air Offensive Against Germany 1939–1945*, Vol. 1, p. 135, and from his own memoirs, *The Central Blue*, p. 237. For Pownall, see *Chiefs of Staff: the Diaries of Lieutenant-General Sir Henry Pownall*, edited by B. Bond, Vol. 1, p. 171, and for Harvey, *Diaries of Oliver Harvey*, edited by J. Harvey, p. 321. The statement by Cross is quoted in Medlicott, op. cit., pp. 44–6, and that by Halifax in Bethell, op. cit., p. 262.

7. See, for example, A. P. Young, *The 'X' Documents; The Secret History of Foreign Office Contacts with the German Resistance 1937–1939*.

8. *PREM 3 193/6A*, in Public Record Office, London.

9. *Dalton Diaries*, 3 and 14 June 1940. See also *King-Hall News-letter* No. 207, Nicolson's *Diaries and Letters*, p. 103, and Orwell, *War Time Diary*, p. 402.

10. *The London Journal of Raymond E. Lee 1940–1941*, pp. 13–14.

11. Dalton to Halifax, 2 July 1940, Dalton Papers.

12. James Joll, *Britain and Europe*, pp. 4–7.

13. For King George VI's statement, see M. Howard, *The Continental Commitment*, p. 143; Churchill's remark to Swinton is quoted in Swinton, *Sixty Years of Power*, p. 131. For *The Fighting Forces* and the *Journal of the Royal United Services Institute*, see the issues for August 1940. Hankey is quoted in Stephen Roskill's *Hankey, Man of Secrets*, Vol. III, p. 480, and Baldwin in Lawrence Thompson, *1940, Year of Legend, Year of History*, p. 132; see also Slessor, *The Central Blue*, p. 297.

14. See Paul Addison, *The Road to 1945: British Politics and the Second World War*, passim.

15. The information in the following paragraphs is drawn from a number of sources, and the interested reader may find fuller references in the author's article on 'The Detonator Concept: British Strategy, SOE and European Resistance After the Fall of France', in the *Journal of Contemporary History*, Vol. 10, NO. 2, April 1975. The most important sources are M. R. D. Foot, *SOE in France*, and Bickham Sweet-Escott, *Baker Street Irregular*.

16. Sweet-Escott, op. cit., p. 20; Kim Philby, *My Silent War*, p. 4; Lord Gladwyn, op. cit., p. 101.

17. For a detailed discussion of British subversive operations in the Balkans at this time, see Elisabeth Barker, *British Policy in South-East Europe in the Second World War*, pp. 28–47.

18. In addition to Medlicott, op. cit., see also Sir Llewellyn Woodward, *British*

Foreign Policy in the Second World War, Vol. 1, and J. R. M. Butler, *Grand Strategy*, Vol. 2, passim.
19. WP (40) 168 *(CAB 66/7)*, discussed at WM (40) 141 of 27 May 1940 *(CAB 65/7)*. The Cabinet discussion is recorded in the Secretary's Standard File *(CAB 65/13)*. See also J. R. M. Butler, op. cit., pp. 210–15, and P. M. H. Bell, *A Certain Eventuality*, pp. 31–52.
20. Bickham Sweet-Escott, 'SOE in the Balkans', in Auty and Clogg, *British Policy towards Wartime Resistance in Yugoslavia and Greece*, p. 5.
21. Louis de Jong, *The German Fifth Column in the Second World War*, passim.
22. H. Dalton, *The Fateful Years; Memoirs 1931–1945*, pp. 366–84.
23. Dalton to Attlee, 2 July 1940, Dalton Papers.
24. For more details on Dalton's lobbying, see the author's article 'Britain looks at Europe, 1940: Some Origins of SOE', in the *Canadian Journal of History*, Vol. X, No. 2, August 1975. For 'the European revolution', see the books by Calder and Burridge quoted in the bibliography.
25. Dalton, *The Fateful Years*, p. 368.
26. WP (40) 271, summarised by Selborne in WP (44) 570, *CAB 66/56*.
27. Churchill, *War Speeches 1938–1941*, p. 239.
28. 'SOE Assistance to Overlord', 13 October 1944, WP (44) 570, *CAB 66/56*.

Chapter 2
1. Gladwyn, *Memoirs*, op. cit., pp. 104–105.
2. Dalton Diary, 20 December 1940.
3. Foot, *SOE in France*, op. cit., p. 9. See also *CAB 123/57*.
4. Dalton, *The Fateful Years*, p. 367. His paper on *The Fourth Arm* remains classified.
5. 'Policy to France', 17 November 1940, in papers of the Political Warfare Executive (PWE), *FO 898/9*.
6. Foot, op. cit., p. 178.
7. Dalton's memorandum on meeting with Mountbatten, 9 January 1942, in *Dalton Diaries*.
8. Sweet-Escott, op. cit., pp. 47–8, and the author's interview with Gubbins, February 1974.
9. See, for example, the comments of Foreign Office officials on the 'Report on the Subversive Activities of the Czech Secret Organisations' of 7 October 1940 prepared by R. Bruce Lockhart for Dalton. F. K. Roberts (later Sir Frank Roberts) noted that while 'it may err on the side of optimism, I have little doubt that the Czechs are ahead of all our other allies in underground organisation' (C 10775/G in *FO 371/ 24392*).
10. Major-General Sir Colin Gubbins, KCMG, DSO, MC, 'Resistance Movements in the War', in *Journal of the Royal United Services Institute*, Vol. 93, 1948, p. 210. William Strang of the Foreign Office told Raczynski that, 'We in Britain regarded Sikorski as a very great man—in fact, the greatest of all the European statesmen whom the war has driven into exile' (Raczynski, *In Allied London*, p. 164).
11. Dalton, op. cit., p. 372.
12. J. Garlinski, *Poland, SOE and the Allies*, pp. 28–30; also *Great Britain*

and European Resistance, Proceedings of a Conference held at St Antony's College, Oxford, 1962, papers by Korbel and Keary on Britain and Czechoslovakia, and by H. Willetts on Poland. This source will subsequently be referred to as *St Antony's, 1962.*

13. E. H. Cookridge, *Inside SOE*, p. 26. The SOE 1940 plan for Norway, culminating in a *levée en masse*, provides a specific example; see Cookridge, p. 527.

14. Sweet-Escott, *Baker Street Irregular*, p. 49.

15. 'Factors Governing SOE operations', 21 April 1943, COS (43) 212 (0), in *CAB 80/69.*

16. Paul Addison, *The Road to 1945*, p. 122; Woodward, *British Foreign Policy in the Second World War*, Vol. V, pp. 1–63.

17. Attlee to Halifax, 30 October 1940, C 12256 in *FO 371/24378.*

18. Gubbins, op. cit., p. 212. See also Kenneth Macksey, *The Partisans of Europe in World War II*, p. 51, and WP (44) 570, *CAB 66/56.*

19. See *PREM 3 184/9*, and Dalton Diary, 27 October 1941.

20. 'Allied Governments: Incitement to Violence in Occupied Territories', in *FO 898/11.*

21. Dalton Memorandum on Propaganda Policy, 6 December 1941, in *FO 898/11.*

22. F. W. Deakin, 'Great Britain and European Resistance', essay in *European Resistance Movements 1939–1945, Proceedings of the Second International Conference on the History of the Resistance Movements held at Milan 26–29 March 1961*, pp. 98–119. Subsequently referred to as *ERM Milan 1961.*

23. For a much fuller discussion see Foot, op. cit., and Sweet-Escott, op. cit.

24. Quoted in Foot, op. cit., p. 66.

25. Major-General Sir Colin Gubbins, 'SOE and Regular and Irregular Warfare', in *The Fourth Dimension of Warfare*, edited by M. Elliott-Bateman, p. 85.

26. Churchill to Ismay, 10 February 1944, *PREM 3 185/1.* For an extended discussion of SOE–SIS wartime relations, see the author's article, 'Secret Operations versus Secret Intelligence in World War Two: the British Experience', in T. H. E. Travers and C. Archer (eds.), *War and Society* (forthcoming).

27. H. Seton-Watson in Auty and Clogg, op. cit., p. 284.

28. Sweet-Escott, op. cit., p. 56.

29. Elisabeth Barker, op. cit., pp. 71–7.

30. 'Policy to France', 17 November 1940, *FO 898/9.*

31. 'Factors governing SOE operations', annex to 'SOE activities in 1943: appreciation by SOE', COS (43) 212 (0) in *CAB 80/69.*

32. Chiefs of Staff Committee, 'Future Strategy', COS (40) 683, in *CAB 80/17.*

33. The reason for the omission is unclear. The Foreign Office were receiving regular reports from the Czechs about their secret army, and only two months after this it was claimed the force was 200,000 strong. See R. Bruce Lockhart to W. Strang, 27 November 1940, in C 10775, *FO 371/24392.*

34. DO (40) 34th of 15/10/1940, in *CAB 69/1.*

35. DO (40) 39th of 31/10/1941, in *CAB 69/1.*

36. Sweet-Escott, op. cit., p. 39.

37. Foot, op. cit., p. 149.

38. Warner to Leeper, 22 November 1940, in *FO 898/9.*

39. Chiefs of Staff Committee, 'Subversive Activities in Relation to Strategy',

25 November 1940. COS (40) 27 (0) in *CAB 80/56*.

40. Sverre Kjelstadli describes the SOE 'Norwegian Policy' document of 11 November 1940 in the following terms: '. . . the document stated that the SOE had a "long-term programme" and a "short-term programme" in Norway. The "long-term programme" aimed at building up a Secret Army, trained in guerilla *(sic)* and sabotage, coming into action in liaison with an Allied invasion some time in the future. This Army should be led, equipped and trained by the British. The "short-term programme" aimed at raids and sabotage in connection with the Directorate of Combined Operations, "tip-and-run landings and air raids"'. See his essay, 'The Resistance Movement in Norway and the Allies 1940–1945', in *ERM Milan 1961*, pp. 324–339.

41. Interview with George Taylor, January 1974, and subsequent correspondence.

42. Sweet-Escott, op. cit., p. 57.

43. Quoted in Foot, op. cit., p. 40.

Chapter 3

1. Elisabeth Barker, op. cit., p. 101.

2. See Attlee to Churchill, 7 January 1941, in Attlee Papers 2/2,1, Churchill (University College, Oxford); SOE Memorandum on 'Interference with German Oil Supplies', 8 January 1941, COS (41) 3 (0) in *CAB 80/56*; Defence Committee (Operations), 13 January 1941, DO (41) 4th in *CAB 69/2*; Frankland and Webster, op. cit., Vol. VI, p. 132; *Cadogan Diaries*, pp. 349–51.

3. Elisabeth Barker, op. cit., p. 87.

4. Sweet-Escott, op. cit., p. 21.

5. George Taylor, communication to the author, February 1975, and subsequent correspondence.

6. Elisabeth Barker, op. cit., pp. 28–78.

7. For SOE and the Belgrade *coup*, see David Stafford, 'SOE and British Involvement in the Belgrade *coup d'état* of March 1941', in *Slavic Review*, Vol. 36, No. 3, September 1977.

8. COS (41) 39th in *CAB 79/8*.

9 Howard, *Grand Strategy*, pp. 163–4; P. Kemp, *No Colours or Crest*, pp. 23–33; R. Harris Smith, *OSS*, p. 77; D. Hamilton-Hill, *SOE Assignment*, pp. 42–8. For Hoare's policy, see his *Ambassador on Special Mission*, especially pp. 128–9, 163, 173, 181, 246–8.

10. For MI9, see Airey Neave, *Saturday at MI9*, passim. For Spain and the Intelligence Service see D. McLachlan, *Room 39*, pp. 192–6.

11. For the background to Operation Savannah, see Foot, *SOE in France*, p. 153, and Passy, *Souvenirs*, Vol. I, pp. 144–6.

12. COS (41) 39th, loc. cit.

13. For the strategic background, see *Grand Strategy*, Vol. 3, Part 1, by J. M. A. Gwyer, passim. For internal morale, see Angus Calder, *The People' War*, pp. 214–16, 243.

14. Raymond E. Lee, *London Journal*, p. 251.

15. Gwyer, op. cit., p. 40.

16. For the auxiliary units and Gubbins, see D. Lampe, *The Last Ditch*, passim.

Hamilton-Hill, who was involved in auxiliary units, indicates that Gubbins gave up responsibility for them at about this time; see his *SOE Assignment*, p. 19.

17. Foot, *SOE in France*, p. 60; Sweet-Escott, op. cit., p. 67; author's discussion with Gubbins, January 1974; references in Dalton Diary, April–May 1941; Gwyer, op. cit., p. 45.

18. JP (41) 444 of 13 June 1941, in *CAB 79/12*. Gwyer, op. cit., pp. 38–48; Foot, op. cit., pp. 164–5; J. R. M. Butler, *Grand Strategy*, Vol. 2, pp. 547–51.

19. Gwyer, op. cit., p. 46.

20. Ibid., p. 46.

21. Foot, *SOE in France*, p. 13.

22. COS (41) 147 (0); not available before 1992, but reviewed by Foot, op. cit., pp. 164–5.

23. The planners' paper was discussed by the Chiefs of Staff on 16 and 24 June (see COS (41) 213rd and 223rd in *CAB 79/12*).

24. Foot, loc. cit.

25. Julian Amery, *Approach March*, p. 240.

26. Report by the Joint Planning Staff on Dalton's memorandum, headed 'Special Operations Executive', JP (41) 649 of 9 August 1941 in *CAB 79/13*.

27. COS (41) 287th and 288th, *CAB 79/13*; COS (41) 536 in *CAB 80/30* and COS (41) 309th in *CAB 79/14*. Also COS (41) 219 (0) in *CAB 80/59* and COS (41) 339th in *CAB 79/14*.

28. Memorandum of a conversation between Dalton and Gubbins on 3 November 1941 *(Dalton Papers, file marked '1941')*. This does not, however, mean that SOE had no transport problems, and in conjunction with PWE and the Foreign Office it complained bitterly to the Air Ministry in January 1942 about the lack of facilities, particularly in travel for SOE officials; they had never, for example, obtained a passage by bomber to the USA (see Eden to Sinclair, 17 January 1942, in *FO 898/11*).

29. For SO1 and PWE, see R. Bruce Lockhart, *Comes the Reckoning*; Asa Briggs, *The War of Words*, passim; Charles Cruickshank, *The Fourth Arm; psychological warfare 1938–1945*; and *FO 898/9*. For Dalton's complaints to Attlee, see Dalton to Attlee, 25 September 1941, *Dalton Papers*.

30. Quoted by F. W. Deakin in 'Britain and European Resistance', in *ERM Milan 1961*. Contrast with the extremely cautious directive to the BBC on sabotage in August 1941, quoted by Jeremy Bennett in *British Broadcasting and the Danish Resistance Movement 1940–1945*, p. 49.

31. Amery, op. cit., pp. 190–2.

32. Sweet-Escott, op. cit., pp. 117–18; FO to Sir Stafford Cripps in Moscow, 28 July 1941, in PWE papers, FO 898/9; Dalton to Churchill, 24 September 1941, in *Dalton Papers, 1941 File*. According to Elisabeth Barker, op. cit., p. 288, the Foreign Office did not know about the first parties dropped, but in December 1942 reached an agreement about them with SOE to safeguard the governments-in-exile. This appears to contradict Sweet-Escott.

33. Dalton to Churchill, 24 September 1941, in *Dalton Papers*.

34. Gubbins to Dalton, 3 November 1941, *Dalton Papers*.

35. Foot, *SOE in France*, passim. Desmond Morton to Churchill, 30 October 1941, in *PREM 3 184/9*. For the Chateaubriant shooting, see H. Noguères and others, *Histoire de la Résistance en France*, Vol. 2, pp. 150–6.

36. *PREM 3 184/9*.
37. The literature on Yugoslavia is voluminous, and only recent works concentrating on British relations with Yugoslavia are mentioned here. They are, *British Policy Towards Wartime Resistance in Yugoslavia and Greece*, edited by Auty and Clogg; Elisabeth Barker, *British Policy in South East Europe in the Second World War*; Sir Llewellyn Woodward, *British Foreign Policy in the Second World War*, Vol. 3; F. W. Deakin, *The Embattled Mountain*.
38. DO (41) 24 in CAB 69/3. For Kennedy's (DMI) comments, see *WO 193/ 768*.
39. Dalton to Churchill, 11 December 1941, in DO (41) 36 of 16 December 1941 in *CAB 69/3*.
40. See especially the works by Auty and Clogg, and Barker, quoted in footnote 37 above.
41. See the records of his conversations with top SOE officials in November 1941 in *Dalton Papers, 1941 File*.
42. Sir Arthur Bryant, *The Turn of the Tide*, p. 275; Dalton Diary, 6 and 9 January 1942, *Dalton Papers*.
43. Quoted in Elisabeth Barker, *British Policy in South East Europe*, p. 151.
44. Dalton to CEO (Jebb), 19 December 1941, *Dalton Papers*.
45. *Cadogan Diaries*, numerous references throughout February 1942.
46. Major-General Sir Colin Gubbins, 'SOE and Regular and Irregular Warfare', in M. Elliott-Bateman, op. cit., p. 87. For SOE plans for Sweden, see JP (42) 568, 3 June 1942, in *CAB 84/46*.

Chapter 4
1. JP (41) 608 in *CAB 79/13*, discussed at COS (41) 268th/269th on 31 July 1941: Final Paper in COS (41) 155 (0) in *CAB 80/59*.
2. Gwyer, op. cit., p. 143.
3. The British paper can be found in Gwyer, pp. 345–8. The final agreed Anglo-American paper (known as WW1) can be found in Appendix 1 to Vol. IV of *Grand Strategy* by Michael Howard, pp. 597–600.
4. W. S. Churchill, *The Grand Alliance*, pp. 553–4.
5. JP (42) 304, 20 March 1942, *CAB 84/43*.
6. See K. R. Greenfield, *American Strategy in World War II*, especially Chapter 2; Michael Howard, *The Mediterranean Strategy in the Second World War*, pp. 19–22; WM (42) 54th of 29 April 1942, in *CAB 65/30*.
7. COS (42) 101 (0) in *CAB 80/62*.
8. See J. Garlinski, *Poland, SOE and the Allies*, passim. In September 1941 SOE had dropped a Pole into France to investigate the possibility of building up an organisation amongst the Poles in the unoccupied zone, and Sikorski reacted strongly in the belief that this had represented an attempt to set up an independent Polish organisation behind his back. It is not clear, however, whether he knew of this in April. See Foot, *SOE in France*, p. 188.
9. For Britain and Norway, see S. Kjelstadli, 'The Resistance Movement in Norway and the Allies 1940–1945', in *ERM Milan 1961*, pp. 324–40; and the papers by Hampton and Skodvin read at the St Antony's Conference in 1962. For Televag, see E. H. Cookridge, *Inside SOE*, p. 533.
10. See G. Lovinfosse, 'La Résistance Belge et Les Alliés', in *ERM Milan 1961*,

and the same author's 'Belgium and Britain', *St Antony's 1962*.
11. It is not clear whether SOE knew in detail or even in general about the plans for the assassination. SOE trained, equipped, and transported the Czech agents, but according to both Mastny (*The Czechs under Nazi Rule*, p. 208) and Moravec (*Master of Spies*, pp. 210–11), the purpose of the operation was not known to the British. See also D. Hamilton-Hill, *SOE Assignment*, p. 39, and the essays in *St Antony's 1962*.
12. JP (42) of 1 May 1942 *CAB 79/20*; COS (42) 137th of 2 May 1942 *CAB 79/20*; COS (42) 141st of 6 May 1942 (ibid); COS (42) 274 (revised) of 26 May 1942 in *CAB 80/36*; COS (42) 166th of 1 June 1942 in *CAB 79/21*. The Poles returned to the charge in July, again unsuccessfully—see the record of their *démarche* to the Joint Planning Staff on 31 July 1942 in *CAB 84/4*.
13. JP (42) 465, *CAB 79/20*.
14. Sweet-Escott, op. cit., pp. 122–2.
15. JIC (42) 156 (0) of 29 April 1942, and JP (42) 470 (s) of 1 May 1942, in *CAB 84/45*. The final report, JP (42) 502, is unavailable before 1993. See also COS (42) 150th of 14 May 1942 in *CAB 79/20*.
16. For the Danish slowdown, see J. Haestrup, 'Britain and Denmark', in *St Antony's 1962*, who says that 'Influence from the Admiralty seems to have affected the British decisions . . .'. For the number of agents sent into Belgium, see Lovinfosse, *St Antony's, 1962*.
17. COS (42) 133 (0) of 12 May 1942 in *CAB 80/62*, approved by COS (42) 147th in *CAB 79/20*. For full text, see Appendix 6.
18. Lord Selborne to Desmond Morton, 15 May 1942, in *PREM 221/13A*.
19. JP (42) 484 of 8 May 1942 in *CAB 84/45*.
20. JP (42) 463 (0) of 30 April 1942 in *CAB 84/45*.
21. Harris Smith, op. cit., p. 42. At a meeting with the Chiefs of Staff on 16 December 1941 Nelson was instructed to step up SOE activities in North Africa (see COS (41) 423rd in *CAB 79/16*).
22. Ibid., p. 52; Sweet-Escott, op. cit., pp. 126–53; A. Cave-Brown, *The Secret War Report of the OSS*, pp. 17–19; Foot, *Resistance*, pp. 142–4; Wm. Roger Louis, *Imperialism at Bay 1941–1945*, p. 7.
23. Quoted in Howard, *Grand Strategy*, Vol. IV, p. 145; see also Woodward, *British Foreign Policy*, Vol. II, pp. 320–42.
24. Foot, *SOE in France*, p. 232; Woodward, Vol. II, pp. 343–5.
25. Foot, *SOE in France*, pp. 141, 192, 231.
26. Ibid., p. 231.
27. Ibid., pp. 204–208. COS (42) 149th (0), *CAB 79/57*.
28. Sweet-Escott, p. 111.
29. See Lovinfosse, in *ERM 1961 Milan* and *St Antony's, 1962*; and Foot, *Resistance*, pp. 254–7.
30. L. de Jong, 'The Dutch Resistance Movement and the Allies 1940–1945', in *ERM Milan 1961*, pp. 340–65, and the same author's 'Britain and Holland', in *St Antony's 1962*; Foot, *Resistance*, pp. 259–69.
31. For the material which follows, see the sources mentioned in footnote 37, Chapter 3, above.
32. Woodward, op. cit., Vol. III, p. 287.
33. Barker, op. cit., pp. 161–2.
34. Howard, *Grand Strategy*, Vol. IV, p. 387; *FRUS*, 1943, Vol. II, p 969.

35. For Mihailović's view, see Matteo J. Milazzo, *The Chetnik Movement and the Yugoslav Resistance*, pp. 34–5; Jasper Rootham, *Miss Fire*, pp. 30–1.
36. Howard, op. cit., p. 386.
37. For Greece, See Howard, op. cit., p. 387; Auty and Clogg, op. cit.; C. M. Woodhouse, *Apple of Discord*, and *The Struggle for Greece 1941–1949*; Barker, op. cit., pp. 148–73. For the quotation, see Barker, p. 97.
38. Woodhouse, op. cit., p. 26.
39. COS (42) 233 (0) in *CAB 80/64*.
40. COS (42) 274th in *CAB 79/23*.
41. COS (42) 275 (0) and COS (42) 337 (0) in *CAB 80/64* and /65.

Chapter 5

1. COS (42) 345 (0) Final, and COS (42) 354 (0) in *CAB 80/65*. See also Howard, *Grand Strategy*, Volume IV, pp. 205, 226–7, 231–3; COS (42) 466 (0) Final.
2. For the main Casablanca decisions on Anglo-American strategy for 1943, see CCS 155/1, text in Howard op. cit., pp. 621–2 and *Foreign Relations of the United States*, Casablanca Conference, pp. 749–51. For the detail on cover, see CCS 170/2, ibid., pp. 625–31.
3. For a discussion of the essentially political nature of guerrilla warfare, see Walter Laqueur, *Guerrilla*, pp. 385–96.
4. For some reason, Foot argues that 'Guerilla [sic] activities were not at this stage much encouraged by the Chiefs of Staff' [*SOE IN France*, pp. 233–34], but this is not borne out by the directive; on the contrary, it was significant that it was the first time guerrilla activities had been specifically focused on in an SOE directive, and it quite explicitly called for increased guerrilla campaigns in Greece and Yugoslavia. It did, however, seek to play down guerrilla activity *in France*. See also Sweet-Escott, p. 155.
5. The COS first discussed the 1943 directive on 4 March 1943 (COS (43) 56th in *CAB 79/26*), and again on 19 March (COS (43) 49th (0) in *CAB 79/59*). It was at this second meeting that the directive was approved (COS (43) 142 (0) in *CAB 80/68*); the Chiefs of Staff, in approving it, cancelled the 1942 directives for collaboration with operations on the Continent and in North Africa, and called for SOE to draw up new plans for the former in cooperation with COSSAC.
6. COS (43) 175 (0) in *CAB 80/68*, considered at COS (43) 90th of 12 April 1943 in *CAB 79/26*.
7. CD to AD/3 (Taylor) 2 April 1943, in *Taylor Papers*.
8. COS (43) 96th in *CAB 79/27*.
9. For the agreed Trident conclusions of 25 May 1943 see CCS 242/6, in Howard op. cit., pp. 660–7, and CCS 250/1, ibid., pp. 668–71. For the British memorandum submitted, see CCS 234 of 17 May 1943, ibid., pp. 640–50; this referred to 'up to 300,000 guerrillas [in the Balkans which] could harrass the enemy's vulnerable communications, denying him important economic resources in Yugoslavia and Greece'.
10. For Katyn and its implications for Anglo-Polish–Soviet relations in general, see Woodward op. cit., Volume II, pp. 612 et seq.
11. *PREM 3 184/9*.

12. Woodward, op. cit., Volume II, pp. 433, 450–1; Eden: *The Reckoning*, pp. 386–7; COS (43) 11th (0) in *CAB 79/61*.
13. See the Selborne–Churchill correspondence of June–July 1943 in PREM 3 184/6, 802.
14. COS (43) 230 (0) in *CAB 80/69*.
15. COS (43) 111th (0) in *CAB 79/61*. For the supplementary report, see COS (43) 267 (0) in *CAB 80/69*.
16. JP (43) 170 (Final) in *CAB 79/61*.
17. 'SOE Requirements for Air Transport', COS (43) 404 (0) Annex, 25 July 1943, *CAB 80/72*.
18. COS (43) 404 (0) in *CAB 80/72*.
19. 'Aircraft for SOE Purposes', note by CD; COS (43) 406 (0), 26 July 1943, *CAB 80/72*.
20. COS (43) 173rd (0) in *CAB 79/63*. The extracts from the SIS report, entitled 'A report on the present situation of certain groups in France', is to be found in the Joint Intelligence Committee analysis of it, headed *SOE Activities in France*, attached to the minutes of the COS meeting of 2 August 1943 (COS (43) 178th (0) in *CAB 79/63*).
21. See JIC (43) 325 (0) of 1 August 1943, in *CAB 79/63*.
22. *The Diaries of Sir Alexander Cadogan 1938–1945*, p. 549; Foot: *SOE in France*, pp. 235–6.
23. See COS (43) 240th (0) in *CAB 79/65*. And Gubbins in *The Fourth Dimension of Warfare* (ed. Elliott-Bateman), p. 95.
24. COS (43) 491 (0) in *CAB 80/73*, and COS (43) 198th (0) in *CAB 79/63*.
25. Foot, *SOE in France*, pp. 76–7 and p. 236.
26. COS (43) 508 (0) in *CAB 80/74*, discussed and approved at COS (43) 218th (0) in *CAB 79/64*.
27. The Chiefs of Staff recommendations are embodied in COS (43) 594 (0) of 30 September in *CAB 80/75*, and the results of the meeting were circulated in COS (43) 618 (0) of 11 October *(CAB 80/75)*. The background with memoranda by Oliver Lyttleton and Lord Selborne, can be followed in DO (43) 21 and DO (43) 22 in *CAB 69/5*.
28. Sir Colin Gubbins in Elliott-Bateman, op. cit., p. 100.
29. For the Québec Conference, see Howard, *Grand Strategy*, pp. 569 et seq., and 682–92; and *FRUS, Conferences at Washington and Québec 1943*, pp. 480–1, 945, 1025. SOE's report of 14 October is in COS (43) 626 (0), *CAB 80/75*, and the Combined Chiefs of Staff instructions to Eisenhower in *CAB 122/762*. See also Elisabeth Barker, op. cit., p. 117.
30. Tomasevich, op. cit., p. 231.
31. Howard, *Grand Strategy*, pp. 389–91; *Foreign Relations of the United States*, 1943, Vol. II, pp. 969–70, 976, 1009.
32. Howard, *Grand Strategy*, p. 499.
33. *FRUS*, loc. cit., pp. 1015–16, 1018.
34. Howard, op. cit., pp. 486–7.
35. See the statement by Sir Fitzroy Maclean in Auty and Clogg, op. cit., pp. 221–8.
36. Woodward, op. cit., III, p. 299; *FRUS Conferences at Cairo and Teheran*, p. 652.
37. Howard, op. cit., pp. 480–1; Myers, *Greek Entanglement*, pp. 97–109,

113–32, 189–201, 202–209.
38. Auty and Clogg, p. 263.
39. *CAB 122/742*.
40. Auty and Clogg, op. cit., p. 137; Myers, 189–90; Woodhouse, *The Struggle for Greece*, pp. 39–56.
41. Ibid., p. 187; Myers, pp. 246–65; *CAB 119/84*.
42. Auty and Clogg, p. 160; Wilson, *Eight Years Overseas*, p. 169.
43. Auty and Clogg, p. 199.
44. Ibid., p. 174.
45. An SOE memorandum on guerrilla forces in Yugoslavia, Albania and Greece of October 1943 reported that Tito's forces numbered 180,000, Mihailović's 20,000 and the guerrillas in Greece, 25,000. Whereas there were only nineteen British missions in Yugoslavia, there were fifty-three in Greece, where the guerrillas 'in general obey the orders of a joint HQ, over which the Senior British liaison officer presides . . .'. COS (43) 626 (0) in *CAB 80/75*.
46. Foot, *SOE in France*, p. 251.
47. Foot, op. cit., pp. 280–324; Cave-Brown, *Bodyguards of Lies*, pp. 319 et seq. For 'Starkey', see JP (43) 209 Final, especially paras. 40–42, and COS (43) 131st (0), *CAB 79/61*.
48. Foot, op. cit., pp. 250, 271 and Chapters IX and X, passim.
49. Ibid., pp. 240–1, 349.
50. For this exchange and related documents, see COS (43) 120 (0) in *CAB 80/68*, COS (43) 45th (0) and COS (43) 48th (0) in *CAB 79/59*, and COS (43) 70th in *CAB 79/26*.
51. Gubbins in Elliott-Bateman, op. cit., p. 90.
52. See S. Kjelstadli, 'The Resistance Movement in Norway and the Allies 1940–1945', in *ERM 1961 Milan*, pp. 324–39, and the papers in *ERM 1964 St Antony's*.
53. Joerge Haestrup, Denmark's connection with the Allied Powers during the Occupation, in *ERM 1961 Milan*, pp. 282–97, and the papers in *St Antony's, 1962*. Also John Oran Thomas, *The Giant Killers: The Danish Resistance Movement 1940–1945*, especially pp. 19–24, and J. Bennett, *British Broadcasting and the Danish Resistance Movement*, especially pp. 110 et seq.
54. 'Directive to SOE for Operations in Central Europe', JP (43) 356 (Final) of 16 October 1943 in *CAB 79/66*.
55. See Josef Garlinski, *Poland, SOE, and the Allies*, p. 52.
56. Jan Cziechanowski, *The Warsaw Uprising*, passim.
57. Sosnkowski to CIGS 21/9/43, ibid.
58. CCS to Polish Embassy, Washington, 23/9/43 in COS (43) 633 (0), *CAB 80/75*; various files in *CAB 122/923*; JP (43) 356 (Final) of 16 October 1943, *CAB 79/66*. For the Combined Intelligence Committee Report (CCS 267/3 of 17/9/43) see the extract quoted in WP (43) 439, *CAB 66/41*. See also Garlinski, *Poland, SOE, and the Allies*, pp. 175–6, and *FRUS*, 1943, Vol. III, pp. 472–89.
59. Sosnkowski to Selborne 21 October 1943, COS (43) 699 (0) in *CAB 80/76*.
60. Selborne to Churchill 21 October 1943, COS (43) 661 (0) in *CAB 80/76*.
61. WM (43) 137th, *CAB 65/40*; WP (43) 439, *CAB 66/41*. Woodward, op. cit., Volume II, pp. 638–44.

62. Eden to COS 30/12/1943 in COS (44) 1 (0) in *CAB 80/78*, and COS (44) 84 (0) in ibid.; JSM to COS London 21 September 1943, *CAB 122/923*.
63. The SOE directive on operations in Central Europe was approved by the Chiefs of Staff on 20 October at COS (43) 255th (0), in *CAB 79/66*.
64. The SOE Report itself (SOE (43) R23) is not available. For the comments and decisions of the JPS and COS, however, see JP (43) 397 (Final) in *CAB 84/58* and COS (43) 289th (0) in *CAB 79/67*.
65. COS (43) 293rd (0) (Secretary's Standard File, *CAB 79/88*).
66. See COS (43) 294th (0) (SSF, *CAB 79/88*); there are two sets of conclusions for this meeting, which differ slightly from each other.
67. COS (43) 295th (0) in SSF, *CAB 79/88*.
68. JIC (43) 517 of 22 December 1943. This is not available, but its main conclusions and some of its detailed criticisms can be deduced from the minutes of the Defence Committee meeting of 14 January 1944 (DO (44) 2nd (Final) in *CAB 69/6*), and from Lord Selborne's response to the report (DO (44) 2 in *CAB 69/6*).
69. As Foot has noted, however, the JIC clearance of F section was unjustified; several F circuits were at this time working under German control (Foot, *SOE in France*, pp. 343–4).
70. The memorandum is available as DO (44) 2 in *CAB 69/6*.
71. COS (44) 1st (0) of 3 January 1944, in SSF, *CAB 79/89*.
72. *The Times* (London) 8 November 1943; Henry Pelling, *The British Communist Party*, p. 125; E. H. Cookridge, *The Third Man*, p. 19.

Chapter 6

1. WP (44) 436, 9 August 1944, *CAB 66/53*; Woodward, *British Foreign Policy*, V, pp. 1–21, 181–191; WP (44) 304, 7 June 1944, *CAB 66/51*; Eden, *The Reckoning*, pp. 459–60; Lord Gladwyn (Gladwyn Jebb), *Memoirs*, pp. 109–47. See also 'Rankin' discussions in 1943, JP (43) 178, quoted in Sharp, *The Wartime Alliance and the Zonal Division of Germany*, p. 31.
2. WM (44) 1st, 3 January 1944, *CAB 65/45*; for hesitations by Eden, see Woodward, Vol. III, pp. 109, 115–19.
3. R. Parkinson, *A Day's March Nearer Home*, pp. 386, 395–6; and COS (43) 605 (0), 4 Oct 1944, *CAB 80/75*. See also Sir John Slessor, *The Central Blue*, p. 593, for some very blunt advice on politics to Sir Charles Portal in April 1944; Sharp, op. cit., passim.
4. See A. Cave-Brown, *Bodyguard of Lies*, passim; COS (44) 132 (0), 6 February 1944, COS (44) 44th (0), 10 February 1944, and COS (44) 232nd (0), 12 July 1944, all dealing with deception, are withheld to 1955.
5. DO (44) 2nd (Final), 14 January 1944, *CAB 69/6*; COS (44) 15th (0), 19 January 1944, *CAB 79/69*.
6. SOE (43) PLANS/350, 18 December 1943, *CAB 80/77*.
7. H. N. Sporborg, CMG, was the principal private secretary to Selborne for SOE affairs, had supervised SOE activities in northern and north-west Europe, and was vice-chief to Gubbins. For his comments on the aircraft allocation, see COS (44) 15th (0), *CAB 79/69*. Also, Sweet-Escott, *Baker Street Irregular*, p. 199.
8. CCS 319/5 in *CAB 122/780*; FRUS, Quebec, p. 945; CCS 492, in *CAB 88/*

24; COS (44) 36 (0), 16 January 1944, *CAB 80/78*.
9. For the January meeting, see COS (44) 92 (0) in *CAB 80/78*. The minutes are also quoted by d'Astier de la Vigerie in *Les Dieux et les Hommes 1943–1944*, as are accounts of other meetings on French resistance at this time with Lord Selborne. See also Foot, *SOE in France*, pp. 352–5, and SOE telegram to Washington, 31 January 1944, in *CAB 122/780*.
10. Defence Committee, 4 February 1944, *CAB 69/6*.
11. For an analysis of SOE–SIS relations during the war, see the author's essay, 'Secret Operations versus Secret Intelligence in World War Two; the British Experience', in *War and Society*, edited by T. Travers and C. Archer (forthcoming); also Foot, op. cit., p. 354.
12. The detailed correspondence between Churchill, the Chiefs of Staff, and Selborne on the French *maquis* can be found in *PREM 3 185/1*. See also Foot, op. cit., pp. 355–8; *Foreign Relations of the United States*, 1944, Vol. IV, p. 1346; 'SOE Assistance to "Overlord",' Memorandum by the Minister of Economic Warfare, 13 October 1944. WP (44) 570, *CAB 66/56*; COS (44) 208th (0), 24 June 1944, in *CAB 79/76*.
13. L. F. Ellis, *Victory in the West*, Vol. 1, pp. 122–4.
14. For SOE and 'Overlord', see in particular the following: SOE evaluation reports, COS (45) 146, COS (45) 664 and 665 (0), in *CAB 80/48 and /98*; Foot, *SOE in France*, pp. 350–418; K. Macksey, *The Partisans of Europe in World War Two*, pp. 172–205; L. F. Ellis, *Victory in the West*, Vols. 1 and 2; Gubbins, 'Resistance Movements in the War', in *Journal of the Royal United Services Institute*, Vol. 93, 1948; A. Cave-Brown, *Bodyguard of Lies*, pp. 691–782; and information on individual countries in *ERM Milan 1961*, and *St Antony's 1962*.
15. 'SOE Assistance to "Overlord",' Memorandum by the Minister of Economic Warfare, 13 October 1944, WP (44) 570, *CAB 66/56*.
16. Sverre Kjelstadli, 'The Resistance Movement in Norway and the Allies', in *ERM Milan 1961*, especially pp. 335–8. Cave-Brown, *The Secret War Report of the OSS*, pp. 311–4.
17. Major-General Sir Colin Gubbins, 'SOE and Regular and Irregular Warfare', in *The Fourth Dimension of Warfare*, edited by M. Elliott-Bateman, p. 85.
18. JRDP (45) 1, 23 January 1945, *CAB 81/47*; COS (45) 304 (0), *CAB 80/94*; COS (45) 123rd and 129th, *CAB 79/33*; 'The Value of SOE Operations in the Supreme Commanders' Sphere', COS (45) 146, 18 July 1945, *CAB 80/48*; 'Value of SOE Operations', COS (45) 665 (0), *CAB 80/98*. A report from the Commanders-in-Chief in the Middle East on SOE operations in Greece was, in contrast, extremely negative and concluded that 'as far as can be seen the strategic effect of SOE operations was negligible'. See COS (45) 664 (0), 17 November 1945, *CAB 80/98*, and also Howard, *Grand Strategy*, Vol. 4, p. 387. For a challenge to these views, see Woodhouse, *The Struggle for Greece*, pp. 106–7.
19. Woodward, Vol. III, pp. 123–31.
20. Parkinson, *A Day's March*, p. 386; FRUS, *Conferences at Malta and Yalta 1945*, p. 304.
21. Eden, *The Reckoning*, p. 448; G. Kolko, *The Politics of War*, pp. 72–3.
22. Gubbins in introduction to Haukelid, *Skis Against the Atom*, p. 23.

23. L. de Jong, *St Antony's 1962*, and *ERM Milan 1961*, p. 362.
24. Kolko, pp. 97–8.
25. Kjelstadli, *ERM Milan 1961*, pp. 331–2; Colonel C. S. Hampton, Britain and Norway, *St Antony's, 1962*, Scandinavian operations within SFHQ were almost totally British-run, the Americans playing a negligible role, except for SFHQ advanced base in Stockholm; see also Cookridge, *Inside SOE*, pp. 548–50.
26. For Denmark, see papers and discussions of Milan and St Antony's conferences of 1961 and 1962, and J. O. Thomas, *The Giant Killers: the Danish Resistance Movement 1940–1945*; A. Cave-Brown, *The Secret War Report of the OSS*, pp. 314–8; *FRUS*, 1945, Vol. IV, pp. 558–74.
27. 'Appreciation and Plan for Noah's Ark', COS (44) 54 (0), 21 January 1944, *CAB 80/78*.
28. COS (44) 54 (0), 21 January 1944, letter from Sargent to COS, *CAB 80/78*.
29. COS (44) 23rd, 27th, and 28th (0), *CAB 79/69*; COS (44) 37th (0), *CAB 79/70*.
30. PM Minute D45/4, 14 February 1944 in COS (44) 165 (0), *CAB 80/80*; JIC (44) 76 (0) (Final), 28 February 1944, *CAB 79/71*; COS (44) 199 (0), *CAB 80/81*.
31. COS (44) 68th (0), *CAB 79/71*; COS (44) 73rd (0), *CAB 79/71*.
32. Woodhouse, *The Struggle for Greece 1941–1949* p. 66; COS (44) 88th (0), *CAB 79/71*; COS (44) 101st (0), *CAB 79/72*.
33. Moyne to Churchill, 8 May 1944, *CAB 119/84*.
34. Quoted in Parkinson, *A Day's March Nearer Home*, p. 297; see also *FRUS, 1944*, Vol. V, pp. 96–8, and 112–15.
35. COS (44) 468 (0), 27 May 1944, *CAB 80/83*; and WP (44) 295, *CAB 66/50*.
36. Nicholas Bethell, *The Last Secret: Forcible Repatriation to Russia 1944–1947*, pp. 24–5.
37. Selborne to Churchill, 14 July 1944, *CAB 119/84*.
38. COS (44) 238th (L), 17 July 1944, *CAB 79/77*; JP (44) 188 (Final), 16 July 1944, *CAB 79/77*; COS (44) 238th and 241st (L) in *CAB 79/77 and /78*; SOE London to New York Tel No. 859, 20 July 1944, *CAB 122/742*.
39. COS (44) 257th (0) of 3 August 1944, *CAB 79/78*; WM (44) 103rd Confidential Annex, *CAB 65/47*. On 26 September the Chiefs of Staff were informed that the Soviet government had no objection to the despatch of British forces, and had equally no intention of sending in Soviet forces; COS (44) 318th (0), *CAB 79/81*.
40. Quoted in Newman, *March 1939*, p. 52.
41. W. S. Churchill, *Closing the Ring*, p. 282. *FRUS Conferences at Cairo and Teheran*, pp. 331, 652, 795; 'Supplies to Resistance Groups in the Balkans', Memorandum by SOE 14 February 1944, COS (44) 163 (0), in *CAB 80/80*; W. R. Roberts, *Tito, Mihailovic and the Allies 1941–1945*, p. 172.
42. Elisabeth Barker, 'Some Factors in British Decision-making over Yugoslavia 1941–1944', in Auty and Clogg, op. cit., p. 40; Deakin, *The Embattled Mountain*, pp. 261–3; Churchill, op. cit., pp. 400–402; *FRUS, 1943*, Vol. II, p. 1030, 1034; WP (44) 100, 10 February 1944, *CAB 66/64*.
43. COS (44) 8th (0), 11 January 1944, *CAB 79/69*; WM (44) 5th, 11 January 1944, *CAB 65/45*; WP (44) 19, *CAB 66/45*.
44. WM (44) 35th, 15 March 1944, *CAB 65/45*; WM (44) 48th, 13 April 1944,

   CAB 65/46; see also *FRUS, 1944*, Vol. IV, pp. 1331–3, 1337.
45. Report of 18 March 1944, WP (44) 196, *CAB 66/48*.
46. WP (44) 234, *CAB 66/49*, and Eden to Churchill, 8 May 1944, *CAB 80/83*; *CAB 119/131*.
47. See 'Statement by Brigadier Sir Fitzroy Maclean', in Auty and Clogg, op. cit., pp. 221–8; Roberts, op. cit., p. 201, 229; Sir John Slessor, *The Central Blue*, pp. 602–3.
48. For Albania and SOE, see Barker, op. cit., pp. 173–83; Sweet-Escott, op. cit., pp. 192–3; Julian Amery, *Approach March*, passim.
49. COS (44) 490 (0), *CAB 80/84*; 'Policy towards Albania; Memorandum by SOE', COS (44) 502 (0), *CAB 80/84*.
50. *FRUS*, loc. cit., p. 1383; *FRUS, 1944*, Vol. III, pp. 271–95; for an assessment of the *effectiveness* of British policy in Albania, see K. Macksey, *Partisans of Europe in World War Two*, pp. 159–60. This conflicts diametrically with Michel's judgement that 'failure here was complete', *The Shadow War*, p. 124. Certainly, the Chiefs of Staff considered in June 1944 that 'Albanian resistance has been on a very insignificant scale when compared . . . even with ELAS activities in Greece'. COS (44) 187th (0), 8 June 1944 in *CAB 79/75*.
51. *FRUS, Conferences at Cairo and Teheran, 1943*, p. 410. For much of the background for the following, see Elisabeth Barker, *British Policy in South-East Europe during the Second World War*, the official histories of British Foreign Policy by Woodward, and Sweet-Escott, *Baker Street Irregular*.
52. COS (44) 320 (0), *CAB 80/81*.
53. See COS (44) 232 (0), *CAB 80/81*; JP (44) 61 (Final), *CAB 84/61*; COS (44) 75th, 76th, and 80th (0) in *CAB 79/71*.
54. SOE Cairo to London, 13 January 1944, *CAB 119/125*.
55. COS (44) 265 (0), *CAB 80/81*, and COS (44) 113th (0), *CAB 79/73*; Sweet-Escott, p. 202.
56. Stowers Johnson, *Agents Extraordinary*, passim.
57. Barker, op. cit., pp. 225–43.
58. *FRUS, 1944*, Vol. IV, p. 147.
59. Barker, op. cit., pp. 148–90.
60. Basil Davidson, *Partisan Picture*, p. 110.
61. SOE London to New York, 31 March 1944, *CAB 122/762*; *FRUS, 1944*, Vol. III, p. 868.
62. See 'Control of SOE Operations in Hungary', COS (44) 353 (0), April 1944, *CAB 80/82*, and COS (44) 131st (0), *CAB 79/73*.
63. For much of the following, see Yehuda Bauer, *From Diplomacy to Resistance*, and his article, 'From Co-operation to Resistance: the Haganah 1938–1946', in *Middle Eastern Studies*, Vol. 2, No. 3, April 1966. Also, Sweet-Escott, op. cit., pp. 170–1.
64. Bauer claims (*From Diplomacy to Resistance*, pp. 121–2) that problems in SOE–Jewish Agency relations were caused by SOE's desire to assassinate Arab enemy agents and leaders who were receiving German money, plans with which the Agency refused to co-operate. Certainly, SOE had at least discussed the possibility of assassinating an important *German* figure in the Middle East, Otto von Hentig, who was sent on a special mission in 1941 to rally Arab support to the Germans. Gubbins, then Director of Operations

for SOE, told Dalton on 3 November 1941 that there was really no need for him (Dalton) to know about such things as the 'bumping off' of von Hentig. (See *Dalton Papers*, 1941 File).

65. COS (44) 709 (0), *CAB 80/86*; Sweet-Escott, p. 205.
66. J. Garlinski, *Poland, SOE and the Allies*, pp. 67, 85–92, 235–8.
67. WM (44) 1st, 3 January 1944, *CAB 65/45*.
68. JIC (44) 15 (0) of 13 January 1944, and COS (44) 7th (0) and 15th (0) of 10 and 19 January 1944, in *CAB 97/69*. Also JIC (44) 65 (0) of 14 February 1944, COS (44) 59th (0) of 24th February 1944 in *CAB 79/70*; COS (44) 179 (0) of 20 February 1944, *CAB 80/80*.
69. COS (44) 146th, 5 May 1944, *CAB 79/89*.
70. COS (44) 1 (0) of 1 January 1944, commenting on SOE (43) Plans/410, in *CAB 80/78*.
71. COS (44) 84 (0) of 28 January 1944, *CAB 80/79*.
72. Jan Ciechanowski, *The Warsaw Rising of 1944*, p. 47; Woodward, *British Foreign Policy in the Second World War*, Vol. III, pp. 154–83; Cabinet Minutes in *CAB 65/45–47*; Stanislaw Mikolajczyk, *The Pattern of Soviet Domination*, pp. 43–101.
73. Ciechanowski, pp. 35–48; J. Garlinski, op. cit., pp. 143–7.
74. E. Raczynski, *In Allied London*, pp. 207–8; Ehrman, *Grand Strategy*, Vol. 5, pp. 369–71; JIC (44) 204 (0) Final, 18 May 1944; COS (44) 165th (0) of 20 May, *CAB 79/74*; COS (44) 208th (0) 24 June, *CAB 79/76*.
75. Garlinski, op. cit., pp. 177–81; COS (44) 677 (0) of 31 July 1944, *CAB 80/86*; COS (44) 254th (0) and 256th (0), *CAB 79/78*; COS (44) 820 (0), 8 September 1944, *CAB 80/87*, COS (44) 303rd (0), *CAB 79/80*. See also COS (44) 868 (0) of 2 October 1944 for SOE support for daylight drops of stores and food to Warsaw, *CAB 80/87*; Sir John Slessor, *The Central Blue*, pp. 611–22; Sweet-Escott, p. 115.
76. WM (44) 130th (CA), *CAB 65/48*.
77. JP (44) 308 (Final), *CAB 84/68*; COS (44) 382nd (0) of 28 November 1944, *CAB 79/83*; Garlinski, op. cit., pp. 215–19, Raczynski, op. cit., pp. 255–6; P. Kemp, *No Colours or Crest*, pp. 247 et seq.
78. Defence Committee, 4 February 1944, *CAB 69/6*; Korbel and Keary, 'Britain and Czechoslovakia', in *St Antony's, 1962*; E. Benes, *Memoirs: From Munich to New War and New Victory*, p. 255.
79. COS (44) 805 (0) of 4 September 1944, *CAB 80/87*; COS (44) 298th (0), *CAB 79/80*; CCS 669, 669/1, *CAB 88/31*, COS (44) 317th (0), *CAB 79/81*.
80. COS (44) 880 (0), 5 October 1944, *CAB 80/88*. The SOE note is unavailable, but Ingr claimed that 'with the assistance of the SOE and SIS, Czechoslovak conspiratorial airborne parties were dropped in Bohemia and Moravia in the autumn of 1943'; Gubbins to Chiefs of Staff, 13 October 1944, COS (44) 900 (0), *CAB 80/88*.
81. F. K. Roberts to COS, 13 October 1944, COS (44) 902 (0), *CAB 80/88*.
82. F. K. Roberts to COS, 25 October 1944, COS (44) 923 (0), and Gubbins to COS, 26 October 1944, COS (44) 926 (0), *CAB 80/88*. For the nature of the US aid, see Anne Josko, 'The Slovak Resistance Movement', in *A History of the Czechoslovak Republic 1918–1949*, edited by V. Mamatey and R. Luza, pp. 380–1.
83. COS (44) 351st (0), 27 October 1944, COS (44) 366th (0) 367th (0) and 370th

(0) of 10, 13, and 15 November 1944, *CAB 79/82*; also CCS 669/2/3/4, *CAB 88/31*, and *FRUS, 1944*, Vol. III, pp. 521–3.

84. For SOE and Germany, see Foot, *Resistance*, pp. 300–304; Cave-Brown, *The Secret War Report of the OSS*, pp. 525–59; Sweet-Escott, *Baker Street Irregular*, pp. 116–7.
85. For post-surrender tasks of OSS, see Cave-Brown, op. cit., pp. 560–7.
86. Foot, *Resistance*, p. 212.
87. C8044/2802/3 in *FO 371/38839*; see also the unpublished London PhD thesis by Guy Stanley, *British Policy and the Austrian Question 1938–45*.
88. C10032/2802/3, *FO 371/38839*.
89. Cave-Brown, *Secret War Report on the OSS*, p. 554.
90. C16249/30/63 in *FO 371/38831*.
91. Cave-Brown, *Secret War Report on the OSS*, p. 556. For the transfer of operational responsibility for SOE activity in Austria from London to SACMED, see COS (45) 345th (0), 23 October 1944, *CAB 79/82*, and CCS 720 in *CAB 88/33*. For similar American attitudes to Austrian resistance, see *FRUS, 1945*, Vol. III, pp. 559, et seq.
92. C1305 in *FO 371/46603*.
93. *FRUS*, loc. cit., pp. 566 et seq.
94. See J. Stevens, 'Britain and Italy', in *St Antony's, 1962*; Sweet-Escott, p. 176.
95. Woodward, *British Foreign Policy in the Second World War*, Vol. II, p. 463; R. Parkinson, *A Day's March Nearer Home*, p. 80.
96. SOE (43) Plans/850, 18 December 1943, *CAB 80/77*; Wilson, *Eight Years Overseas*, p. 189; C. Delzell, *Mussolini's Enemies: the Italian Anti-Fascist Resistance*, pp. 312–3, 362–3, 424; N. Kogan, *Italy and the Allies*, pp. 102–3; F. Parri and F. Venturi, 'The Italian Resistance and the Allies', in *ERM Milan 1961*, pp. xxvii–xxix; F. W. Deakin, 'Great Britain and European Resistance', in *ERM Milan 1961*; R. Harris Smith, *OSS*, p. 95.
97. *FRUS, 1944*, Vol. III, pp. 1043, 1066, 1097–8, 1112–4; G. Warner, 'Italy and the Powers 1943–49', in S. J. Woolf, (ed.), *The Rebirth of Italy 1943–50*, p. 42.
98. Woodward, loc. cit., p. 538.
99. C. R. S. Harris, *Allied Military Administration of Italy 1943–1945*, p. 180; Delzell, op. cit., pp. 403–405; 'Value of SOE Operations', Report by Chief of Staff to SACMED, 18 November 1945, COS (45) 665 (0), *CAB 80/98*; Selborne to Churchill, 26 October 1944, *CAB 80/88*.
100. Delzell, op. cit., pp. 411, 479; Harris, op. cit., pp. 280–2, 355–8; Woodward, Vol. III, pp. 443–4.
101. COS (44) 933 (0), *CAB 80/88*, COS (44 352nd (0), 354th (0), 360th (0), *CAB 79/82*; WP (44) 651, 15 November 1944, *CAB 66/58*; Selborne to Churchill, 26 October 1944, *CAB 80/88*; Parri and Venturi, loc. cit., p. xxiv; Delzell, op. cit., p. 451.
102. Warner, op. cit, pp. 43–4; see also Kolko, op. cit., pp. 62–3. Neither Alexander nor his biographer (Nicolson) make a single reference to the partisans.
103. A. Cave-Brown, *The Secret War Report of the OSS*, p. 235.
104. Harold MacMillan, *The Blast of War*, pp. 670–1.
105. Harris, op. cit., pp. 308–309.

106. *CAB 119/131; FRUS*, 1944, Vol. IV, pp. 1425–6.
107. Harris, pp. 274–7; Delzell, pp. 463–9; Parri and Venturi, loc. cit. For what happened when Colonel John Stevens, a British liaison officer, attempted a too obvious strategem to cut the power of leftist groups in Piedmont, see Delzell, pp. 469–70.
108. Macmillan, loc. cit., p. 677.
109. Harris, pp. 280–2, Delzell, p. 479.
110. COS (45) 292 (0).
111. COS (44) 957 (0), *CAB 80/89*; withheld until 1995.
112. For discussions about the future of SOE, see COS (44) 381st (0), *CAB 79/ 83*, and *Cadogan Diaries* (ed. Dilks), p. 683.

Chapter 7
1. Churchill to Roosevelt, 6 December 1944, quoted in *Churchill and Roosevelt, their Secret Wartime Correspondence*, pp. 619–21.
2. W. H. McNeill, *America, Britain, and Russia, their Co-operation and Conflict*, p. 549.
3. JP (44) 308 (Final), *CAB 84/68*; COSMED 203, 207, 208, *CAB 122/1217*; COS (44) 408th (0), *CAB 79/84*.
4. COS (45) 39 (0), *CAB 122/1217*; COS (45) 54 (0), *CAB 80/91*; COS (44) 408th (0), *CAB 79/84*.
5. COS (45) 21 (0), *CAB 122/888*; Delzell, *Mussolini's Enemies*, pp. 480–2; Warner, *Italy and the Powers*, pp. 44–5.
6. Eden, *The Reckoning*, p. 523; Macmillan, *The Blast of War*, pp. 684–6.
7. Cave-Brown, *Bodyguard of Lies*, pp. 244–9; Harris Smith, *OSS*, pp. 115–22.
8. Kolko, *The Politics of War*, 379; Warner, *Italy and the Powers*, p. 45; Dulles, *Secret Surrender*, p. 147.
9. COS (45) 292 (0), *CAB 80/94*.
10. COS (45) 284 (0), *CAB 122/1217*; COS (45) 108th, *CAB 79/32*.
11. COS (45) 114th, *CAB 79/32*.
12. Parkinson, *A Day's March Nearer Home*, p. 495; COS (45) 360 (0), COS (45) 376 (0), *CAB 80/94* [still closed]; COS (45) 149th *CAB 79/34*.
13. COS (45) 198th, *CAB 79/37*; DO (45) 4th, *CAB 69/7*; COS (45) 389th, *CAB 79/42*; COS (46) 58th, *CAB 79/47*.
14. COS (45) 500 (0) *CAB 80/96*; COS (45) 572 (0), *CAB 80/97*; COS (45) 221st, *CAB 79/39*.
15. COS (45) 241st, *CAB 79/40*; COS (45) 263rd, *CAB 79/41*; COS (45) 638 (0), *CAB 80/98*.
16. *FRUS, 1944*, Vol. III, p. 279.
17. Philby, *My Silent War*, pp. 119–21; Page, Leitch and Knightley, *Philby, the Spy who Betrayed a Generation*, p. 194 (Philby makes no mention of the Albanian operation); Cave-Brown, *Bodyguard of Lies*, p. 807.

Conclusion
1. 'SOE Operations in Europe', memorandum by Lord Selborne 11 January 1944, DO (44) 2 in *CAB 69/2*.
2. A. J. P. Taylor, 'Churchill, the Statesman', in *Churchill, Four Faces and the*

Man, p. 38.

3. Jasper Rootham, *Miss Fire*, p. 44.

4. *100,000,000 Allies if We Choose* was written in July 1940 by 'Scipio', a pseudonym for R. H. S Crossman and Kingsley Martin (correspondence with the late R. H. S. Crossman). For the 'People's War', see A. Calder's book of that title, especially pp. 157–61, and Kingsley Martin, *Editor*, pp. 318–25. See also F. Lafitte, *The Internment of Aliens*, published in 1940, and T. W. Wintringham, *The People's War* (1942). For Orwell, see his essay, 'Wells, Hitler and the World State', in *The Collected Essays*, Volume 2, 1940–43, p. 169.

5. Charles Cruickshank, *The Fourth Arm*, p. 48; WP (42) 8, *CAB 66/20*.

6. Desmond Morton to Churchill, 25 February 1941, *FO 371/26466*.

7. R. W. Thompson, *Churchill and Morton*, p. 123.

8. Jebb is quoted in S. Newman, *March 1939*, p. 64; for Gubbins, see Gubbins to Selborne, 6 March 1959 (Box 22, Selborne Papers, Bodleian Library).

9. F. W. Deakin at *St Antony's, 1962*.

10. C. M. Woodhouse, *Apple of Discord*, pp. 45–8.

11. *FRUS Washington and Québec*, 1943, p. 933.

12. Memorandum by Eden on Moscow visit of December 1941, WP (42) 8, *CAB 66/20*.

13. *Parliamentary Debates, Commons, 1944–45*, Vol. 406, Col. 964.

14. Milovan Djilas, *Wartime*, p. 69.

Sources and Bibliography

UNPUBLISHED

PUBLIC RECORD OFFICE, LONDON

Hankey Papers, *CAB 63*.
War Cabinet Minutes and Memoranda, *CAB 65* and *CAB 66*.
War Cabinet, Defence Committee (Operations), *CAB 69*.
War Cabinet, Chiefs of Staff Committee, *CAB 79* and *CAB 80*.
War Cabinet, Committee on Foreign (Allied) Resistance, *CAB 85*.
War Cabinet, Combined Chiefs of Staff Committee, *CAB 88*.
Various Ministers and Official Files, *CAB 118*.
Joint Planning Staff, *CAB 119*.
British Joint Services Mission, Washington, *CAB 122*.
Lord President of the Council, *CAB 123*.
Prime Minister's Office, *PREM 3* and *PREM 4*.
Political Warfare Executive, *FO 898*.
Foreign Office, General Correspondence; selected files, *FO 371*.
Avon Papers, *FO 954*.

ELSEWHERE

Dalton Papers: British Library of Political and Economic Science at the
    London School of Economics and Political Science.
Selborne Papers: Bodleian Library, Oxford. Most of the material relating to
    SOE has been removed.
Attlee Papers: Churchill College Cambridge, and University College, Oxford.
Christie Papers, Churchill College, Cambridge.
Vansittart Papers, Churchill College, Cambridge.

PUBLISHED: SELECT BIBLIOGRAPHY

Addison, P. *The Road to 1945: British Politics and the Second World War*
    (London, 1975).
Alexander of Tunis. *The Alexander Memoirs 1940–1945* (London, 1962).

279

Amery, J. *Approach March* (London, 1973).
Amery, J. *Sons of the Eagle* (London, 1948).
Aster, S. *1939: The Making of the Second World War* (London, 1971).
Aster, S. *Anthony Eden* (London, 1976).
    Astier de la Vigerie, E. *Les Dieux et Les Hommes 1943–1944* (Paris, 1952).
Astley, J. B. *The Inner Circle* (London, 1971).
Avon, The Earl of [Anthony Eden]. *The Reckoning* (London, 1965).
Auty, P. and Clogg, R. (eds.). *British Policy Towards Wartime Resistance in Yugoslavia* (London, 1975).
Barker, E. *British Policy in South-East Europe in the Second World War* (London, 1976).
Bartlett, V. *And Now, Tomorrow* (London, 1960).
Bauer, Y. *From Diplomacy to Resistance; A History of Jewish Palestine 1939–1945* (Philadelphia, 1970).
Beesly, P. *Very Special Intelligence* (London, 1977).
Bell, P. M. H. *A Certain Eventuality* (London, 1974).
Benes, E. *Memoirs: From Munich to New War and New Victory* (Boston, nd).
Bennett, J. *British Broadcasting and the Danish Resistance Movement 1940–1945: A Study of the Wartime Broadcasts of the BBC Danish Service* (Cambridge, 1966).
Bethell, N. *The Last Secret* (London, 1974).
Bethell, N. *The War Hitler Won* (London, 1972).
Bond, B. (ed.). *Chief of Staff: the Diaries of Lieutenant-General Sir Henry Pownall* (London, 1972).
Briggs, A. *War of Words* (Vol. 3 of *The History of Broadcasting in the United Kingdom*) (London, 1961).
Britain and European Resistance 1939–1945. Proceedings of a Conference on, organised by St. Antony's College, Oxford (mimeographed) (1962).
Bruce Lockhart, R. *Comes the Reckoning* (London, 1947).
Bryant, Sir A. *The Turn of the Tide* (London, 1965).
Buckmaster, M. J. *Specially Employed: The Story of British Aid to the French Patriots of Resistance* (Batchworth, 1952).
Buckmaster, M. *They Fought Alone* (London, 1958).
Burridge, T. D. *British Labour and Hitler's War* (London, 1976).
Butler, J. R. M. (ed.) *Grand Strategy* [History of the Second World War; United Kingdom Military Series]. Vol. 1—N. H. Gibbs, 1976; Vol. 2—J. R. M. Butler, 1957; Vol. 3—J. M. A. Gwyer and J. R. M. Butler, 1964; Vol. 4—M. Howard, 1972; Vols. 5 and 6—J. Ehrman, 1956.
Butler, R. A. *The Art of the Possible* (London, 1971).
Calder, A. *The People's War: Britain 1939–1945* (London, 1969).
Cave-Brown, A. *Bodyguard of Lies* (New York, 1975).
Cave-Brown, A. (ed.): *The Secret War Report of the OSS* (New York, 1976).
Chandos, Lord (Oliver Lyttelton). *Memoirs* (London, 1962).
Churchill, W. S. *The Gathering Storm* (New York, 1948).
Churchill, W. S. *Their Finest Hour* (New York, 1949).
Churchill, W. S. *The Grand Alliance* (New York, 1950).
Churchill, W. S. *The Hinge of Fate* (New York, 1950).
Churchill, W. S. *Closing the Ring* (New York, 1951).
Churchill, W. S. *Triumph and Tragedy* (New York, 1953).

Sources and Bibliography 281

Churchill, W. S. *War Speeches 1938–1941* (London, 1945).
Ciechanowski, J. M. *The Warsaw Rising of 1944* (Cambridge, 1974).
Cookridge, E. H. *Inside SOE: The Story of Special Operations in Western Europe 1940–1945* (London, 1965).
Cooper, Duff. *Old Men Forget* (London, 1953).
Cosgrave, P. *Churchill at War, Vol. I. Alone 1939–1940* (London, 1974).
Cruickshank, L. *The Fourth Arm: Psychological Warfare 1938–45* (London, 1977).
Dalton, H. *The Fateful Years; Memoirs 1931–1945* (London, 1957).
Davidson, B. *Partisan Picture* (London, 1946).
Davies, T. *Illyrian Venture* (London, 1952).
Deacon, R. *A History of the British Secret Service* (London, 1969).
Deakin, F. W. *The Last Days of Mussolini* (London, 1962).
Deakin, F. W. 'Great Britain and European Resistance', in *European Resistance Movements*, Vol. 2 (Oxford, 1964).
Deakin, F. W. *The Embattled Mountain* (London, 1973).
Delmer, S. *Black Boomerang* (New York, 1962).
Delzell, C. F. *Mussolini's Enemies: The Italian Anti-Fascist Resistance* (Princeton, 1961).
Dennis, P. *Decision by Default: Peacetime Conscription and British Defence 1919–1939* (Durham, 1972).
Dilks, D. (ed.). *The Diaries of Sir Alexander Cadogan 1938–1945* (London, 1971).
Djilas, M. *Wartime* (New York, 1977).
Documents on International Affairs 1939–1946; Volume II, *Hitler's Europe* (edited by Carlyle, M.) (London, 1954).
Donnison, F. S. V. *Civil Affairs and Military Government: North-West Europe 1944–1946* (London, 1961).
Dulles, A. *The Secret Surrender* (New York, 1966).
Elliott-Bateman, M. *The Fourth Dimension of Warfare* (Manchester, 1970).
Ellis, L. F. *Victory in the West, Vol. 1, The Battle for Normandy* (London, 1962).
Ellis, L. F. *Victory in the West, Vol. II, The Defeat of Germany* (London, 1968).
European Resistance Movements 1939–1945. Proceedings of the First International Conference on the History of Resistance Movements, held at Liège-Bruxelles-Breendank 14–17 September 1958 (New York, 1960).
European Resistance Movements 1939–45. Proceedings of the Second International Conference on the History of the Resistance Movements held at Milan 26–29 March 1961 (London, 1964).
Feiling, K. *Life of Neville Chamberlain* (London, 1946).
Foot, M. R. D. *Resistance: European Resistance to Nazism 1940–1945* (London, 1976).
Foot, M. R. D. *SOE in France* (London, 1966).
Foot, M. R. D. 'The I.R.A. and the Origins of SOE' in *War and Society, Essays in Honour and Memory of J. R. Western* (ed. Foot) (London, 1973).
Foot, M. R. D. 'L'aide à le Résistance en Europe', *Revue d'histoire de La Deuxième Guerre Mondiale*, No. 90 (April 1973).
Foreign Relations of the United States: Diplomatic Papers 1942, Volumes II and III (Washington, 1961–62).
Foreign Relations of the United States: Diplomatic Papers 1943, Volumes II and

III (Washington, 1963–1964).

Foreign Relations of the United States: Diplomatic Papers 1944, Volumes III, IV and V (Washington 1965 and 1966).

Foreign Relations of the United States: Diplomatic Papers 1945, Volumes II, IV, and V (Washington, 1968).

Foreign Relations of the United States: The Conferences at Washington, 1941–1942, and Casablanca, 1943 (Washington, 1968).

Foreign Relations of the United States: The Conferences at Washington and Québec 1943 (Washington, 1970).

Foreign Relations of the United States: The Conferences at Cairo and Tehran 1943 (Washington, 1961).

Foreign Relations of the United States: The Conferences at Malta and Yalta 1945 (Washington, 1955).

Fuller, J. O. *The German Penetration of SOE; France 1941–1944* (London, 1975).

Garlinski, J. *Poland SOE and the Allies* (London, 1969).

Gibbs, N. *Grand Strategy* (London, 1976).

Gladwyn, Lord [Gladwyn Jebb]. *Memoirs* (London, 1972).

Greenfield, K. R. *American Strategy in World War II* (Baltimore, 1963).

Gubbins, Sir C. 'Resistance Movements in the War', *Journal of the Royal United Service Institution*, Volume 93 (May 1948).

Halifax, Earl of *Fullness of Days* (London, 1957).

Hamilton-Hill, D. *SOE Assignment* (London, 1973).

Harris, C. R. S. *Allied Military Administration of Italy 1943–1945*. (London, 1957).

Harvey, J. (ed.). *Diaries of Oliver Harvey* (London, 1973).

Haukelid, K. *Skis Against the Atom* (London, 1954).

Hawes, J. and White, R. *Resistance in Europe: 1939–1945* (London, 1975).

Hoare, Sir S. [Viscount Templewood]. *Nine Troubled Years* (London, 1954).

Hoare, Sir S. *Ambassador on Special Mission* (London, 1946).

Howard, M. *The Continental Commitment; The Dilemma of British Defence Policy in the Era of the Two World Wars* (London, 1972).

Howard, M. *Grand Strategy* (London, 1972).

Howard, M. *The Mediterranean Strategy in the Second World War* (London, 1968).

Howard, M. *The British Way in Warfare* (London, 1975).

Howarth, P. *Special Operations* (London, 1955).

Hyde, H. M. *The Quiet Canadian* (London, 1962).

Johnson, S. *Agents Extraordinary* (London, 1975).

Joll, J. *Britain and Europe 1793–1940* (Oxford, 1967).

Jones, T. *A Diary with Letters 1931–1950* (London, 1954).

Jong, L. de. *The German Fifth Column in the Second World War* (Chicago, 1956).

Kemp, P. *No Colours or Crest* (London, 1958).

Kennedy, J. *The Business of War* (London, 1957).

Kogan, N. *Italy and the Allies* (Harvard, 1956).

Kolko, G. *The Politics of War: The World and United States Foreign Policy 1943–1945* (New York, 1970).

Lampe, D. *The Last Ditch* (London, 1968).

Laqueur, W. *Guerrilla: A Historical and Critical Study* (London, 1977).

Leasor, J. *War at the Top* [Memoirs of Hollis] (London, 1959).

Lee, R. E. *The London Journal of Raymond E. Lee 1940–1941* (Boston, 1971).

Leeper, Sir R. *When Greek Meets Greek* (London, 1950).

Liddell Hart, B. H. *Defence of the West: Some Riddles of War and Peace* (London, 1950).

Louis, W. R. *Imperialism at Bay 1941–1945: the United States and the Decolonization of the British Empire* (Oxford, 1977).

Macksey, K. *The Partisans of Europe in World War Two* (London, 1975).

Macmillan, H. *The Blast of War 1939–1945* (London, 1967).

Marshall, B. *The White Rabbit* (London, 1952).

Masterman, J. C. *The Double-Cross System in the War of 1939 to 1945* (Yale, 1972).

Mastny, V. *The Czechs under Nazi Rule: the Failure of National Resistance, 1939–1942* (Columbia, 1971).

McLachlan, D. *Room 39: Naval Intelligence in Action 1939–45* (London, 1968).

McNeill, W. H. *America, Britain, and Russia; Their Co-operation and Conflict 1941–1946* (London, 1953).

Medlicott, W. N. *The Economic Blockade* (London, 1952).

Michel, H. *The Second World War* (New York, 1975).

Michel, H. *The Shadow War: Resistance in Europe 1939–1945* (London, 1972).

Mikolajczyk, S. *The Pattern of Soviet Domination* (London, 1948).

Milazzo, M. J. *The Chetnik Movement and the Yugoslav Resistance* (Baltimore, 1975).

Milward, A. S. *The New Order and the French Economy* (Oxford, 1970).

Milward, A. S. *The Fascist Economy in Norway* (Oxford, 1972).

Montagu, E. *Beyond Top Secret Ultra* (New York, 1978).

Moran, Lord. *Churchill: taken from the Diaries of Lord Moran—the Struggle for Survival 1940–1965* (London, 1966).

Moravec, F. *Master of Spies: the Memoirs of General Frantisek Moravec* (London, 1975).

Morgan, Sir F. *Overture to Overlord* (London, 1950).

Murphy, R. *Diplomat among Warriors* (New York, 1964).

Naylor, J. F. *Labour's International Policy; the Labour Party in the 1930s* (London, 1969).

Neave, A. *Saturday at M.I.9: A History of Underground Escape Lines in Northwest Europe in 1940–1945* (London, 1969).

Newman, S. *March 1939: The British Guarantee to Poland* (Oxford, 1976).

Nicolson, H. *Diaries and Letters 1939–45* (London, 1970).

Nicolson, N. *Alex, the Life of Field Marshall Earl Alexander of Tunis* (London, 1973).

Noguères, H. *Histoire de la Résistance en France* (Paris, 1967).

Orwell, S. and Angus, I. (eds.). *The Collected Essays, Journalism and Letters of George Orwell*, Volume II (London, 1970).

Parkinson, R. *Blood, Toil, Tears and Sweat: The War History from Dunkirk to Alemein, based on the War Cabinet Papers 1940–1942* (London, 1972).

Parkinson, R. *A Day's March Nearer Home* (London, 1974).

Passy [i.e. Dewavrin, A.]. *Souvenirs* (Paris, 1947).

Pelling, H. *Britain and the Second World War* (London, 1970).

Pelling, H. *Winston Churchill* (London, 1974).

Philby, K. *My Silent War* (London, 1968).

Pogue, F. C. *The Supreme Command: the European Theatre of Operations* (Washington, 1954).

Raczynski, E. *In Allied London* (London, 1962).

Roberts, W. R. *Tito, Mihailović and the Allies 1941–1945* (Rutgers University, New Brunswick, 1973).

Rootham, J. *Miss Fire; the Chronicle of a British Mission to Mihailović 1943–1944* (London, 1946).

Roskill, S. *Hankey, Man of Secrets* (London, 1974).

'Scipio' [R. H. S. Crossman and K. Martin]. *100,000,000 Allies—If We Choose* (London, 1940).

Sharp, T. *The Wartime Alliance and the Zonal Division of Germany* (Oxford, 1975).

Slessor, J. *The Central Blue* (London, 1957).

Smith, R. H. *OSS: The Secret History of America's First Central Intelligence Agency* (University of California, 1972).

Stafford, D. A. T. 'Britain Looks at Europe, 1940: Some Origins of SOE', *Canadian Journal of History*, Vol. X, No. 2 (August, 1975).

Stafford, D. A. T. 'The Detonator Concept: British Strategy, SOE and European Resistance after the Fall of France', in *Journal of Contemporary History*, Volume 10, No. 2 (April 1975).

Stafford, D. A. T. 'SOE and British Involvement in the Belgrade Coup d'État of March 1941', *Slavic Review*, Vol. 36, No. 3 (September 1977).

Stanley, G. D. D. *British Policy and the Austrian Question 1938–45*. University of London Doctoral Dissertation (1974).

Steele, R. W. *The First Offensive 1942: Roosevelt, Marshall and the Making of American Stategy* (Indiana, 1973).

Strong, Major-General Sir K. *Intelligence at the Top* (London, 1968).

Sweet-Escott, B. *Baker Street Irregular* (London, 1965).

Taylor, A. J. P., James, R. R., Plumb, J. H., Liddell Hart, B., Storr, A. *Churchill: Four Faces and the Man* (London, 1969).

Thomas, J. O. *The Giant Killers: the Danish Resistance Movement 1940–1945* (London, 1975).

Thompson, L. *1940, Year of Legend, Year of History* (London, 1966).

Thompson, R. W. *Churchill and Morton* (London, 1976).

Tomasevich, J. *The Chetniks* (Stanford, 1975).

Toynbee, A. and Toynbee, V. M. (eds.). *Hitler's Europe* (London, 1954).

Toynbee, A. and Toynbee, V. M. (eds.). *The Realignment of Europe* (London, 1955).

Warmbrunn, W. *The Dutch under German Occupation 1940–1945* (Stanford, 1963).

Warner, G. 'Italy and the Powers 1943–49' in Woolf (ed.), *The Rebirth of Italy 1943–49* (London, 1972).

Watson, M. S. *Chief of Staff: Prewar Plans and Preparations* (Washington, 1950).

Webster, C. and Frankland, N. *The Strategic Air Offensive Against Germany 1939–1945* (London, 1964).

Wheeler-Bennett, J. W. (ed.). *Action This Day* (London, 1968).

Wheeler-Bennett, J. W., and Nicholls, A. *The Semblance of Peace: the Political Settlement after the Second World War* (London, 1972).

Wilson, Field-Marshall Lord. *Eight Years Overseas* (London, 1948).

Winterbotham, F. W. *The Ultra Secret* (London, 1974).

Woodhouse, C. M. *Apple of Discord* (London, 1948).

Woodhouse, C. M. *The Struggle for Greece 1941–1949* (London, 1976).

Woodward, L. *British Foreign Policy in the Second World War*, Vols. I–V (London, 1972–76).

Woolf, S. J. *The Rebirth of Italy 1943–1950* (London, 1972).

Young, A. P. *The 'X' Documents; the Secret History of Foreign Office Contacts with the German Resistance 1937–1939* (London, 1974).

Index

Ad hoc committee on equipment for patriot forces, 106, 110, 117, 250
A.F.H.Q., 148, 169, 171, 181, 190, 194, 195, 196; evaluation of SOE, 157–8
Albania, 105–7, 119, 145, 167, 210, 218, 253–4, 270n.45, 274n.50; SOE activity in, 170–2; post-war CIA-SIS operation in, 204
Alexander, General, 96, 193–5, 201
Allied Control Commission (Italy), 193, 195
Amery, Julian, 64, 69
Anglo-Greek Co-ordinating Committee, 123–4
Anglo-Norwegian Co-ordinating Committee, 130, 161
Anglo-Soviet relations, 9, 74, 142, 204; and Mihailović, 98; and Polish resistance, 109, 183–5; and post-war planning, 144–5, 158, 197, 209–11; and resistance in eastern Europe, 172–3, 176, 178, 179, 181
Anschluss, 19, 21, 188
Antonescu, Marshal, 53
Antwerp, 155
Anvil landings, 148, 149
Ardennes counter offensive, 156, 199
Armstrong, Brigadier, 169
Arnhem landings, 155
assassination, 34, 35, 84, 267n.11, 274–5n.64
Astier de la Vigerie, Emmanuel d', 149
Athens, 167, 196, 199

Atlantic Charter, 80
Attlee, Clement, 24, 25, 34, 51, 67, 77, 91, 109, 137, 141, 194
Austria, 43, 197, 203, 204, 211, 214; SOE activities in, 188–91; SOE directive November 1945, 258–9
'Autonomous' mission, 176–7
Auxiliary Units, 30, 31, 58

Badoglio, Marshal, 191, 192
Bailey, Colonel S. W., 96, 110, 169, 174
Baldwin, Stanley, 18
Balkan Air Force, 170, 171, 181
Balkans, 14, 39, 46, 60, 64, 71, 78, 98, 100, 111, 113, 136–7, 140, 158, 180, 210, 237, 256; and Section D, 21–3; post-occupational planning, 47, 49; SOE activities 1941, 51–4; in allied strategy 1943, 103–6, 118–19, 209, 252–4; SOE activities 1944, 162–72
Balli Kombetar (BK), 171–2
Bauer, Yehuda, 181
B.B.C., 35, 67, 70, 74, 96
Beaverbrook, Lord, 45
Belgium, 44, 63, 65, 66, 70–1, 81, 84, 101, 108, 138, 153, 154–5, 159–60, 217, 241, 244–5; relations with government-in-exile, 93–4, 131–2
Benes, Eduard, 84, 185, 187
Bernhard, Prince, 88, 160
Bevan, Colonel, 147, 173, 177, 248
BK, *see* Balli Kombetar
Bohemia and Moravia, 186, 187, 202

Bomber Command, 7, 41, 59, 61–2, 65, 111–12, 116–17, 137, 149, 205
Bottomley, Air Vice Marshall, 137
Bracken, Brendan, 67, 76–8
Brooke, General Sir Alan, 3, 76, 85, 93, 97, 133, 134, 152, 163
Brossolette, Pierre, 129
Bulgaria, 52–3, 107, 145, 210, 222, 253; SOE operations in, 172–5

Cadogan, Sir Alexander, 38, 77, 116, 198, 201, 204
Cairo Conference 1943, 148, 167, 173, 174
Campbell, Mr Ronald, 53
Carinthia, 189, 195
Carte, 92–3, 128
Casablanca Conference, 104–5, 120, 122, 188
Cavendish-Bentinek, Victor, 203
Caviglia, Marshal, 191
Central Intelligence Agency (CIA), 204
Chamberlain, Neville, 11–14
Chastelain, D. A. G. de, 176, 178
Chateaubriant, 35, 72
Cherwell, Lord, 100
Chetniks, 70, 73, 74, 96, 119, 121, 168–70; *see also* Mihailović
Chiefs of Staff, 15, 26, 55, 57, 61, 63, 79, 91, 93, 108, 111, 128, 150, 152, 166, 171, 179, 181, 200, 203–4, 226; and pre-war strategy, 10; recommends special organisation for sub-version, 23; relationship to SOE, 40–1, 66, 75–6; first directive to SOE, 46–8; abandon idea of secret armies in P and C2, 66, 81; reject 'Sikorski plan', 84–5; call for closer SOE-SIS co-ordination 1942, 86–7; second directive to SOE, 87–8, *text 246–7*; directive on North Africa, 88–9; third directive, 105–6, *text 248–57*; and Mihailović, 97, 120, 122; focus on Balkan resistance at Casablanca, 104–5; give priority to Balkan over western European resistance July 1943, 114–15; recommend against fundamental reorganisation of

SOE, September 1943, 117–18; and EAM-ELAS, 126, 166; directive for central Europe 1943, 136; and German penetration of SOE, 138, 141; and Anglo-Soviet relations, 146; and aircraft for SOE in 1944, 147–9; and 'Noah's Ark', 163; and Albania, 171; and Bulgaria, 174–5; and Italy, 201; and Jewish resist-ance, 181; and Austria, 258–9; and Poland, 182–4; and Czecho-slovakia, 185–7, 200; and post-war future of SOE, 197–8, 203
Churchill, Randolph, 180
Churchill, Winston, 1, 3, 6, 14–17, 34, 45–6, 51–2, 57, 58, 59, 61, 66, 68, 69–70, 73, 77–8, 84, 88, 103, 104, 158, 159, 182, 183, 197, 199, 200, 201, 210; his *History of the Second World War*, 2; appoints Dalton as Minister in charge of SOE, 24–7; relations with Dalton, 28, 41, 68; on SOE-SIS rivalry, 38; tells Dalton that Balkans are 'acid test for SOE', 52; and Belgrade *coup d'état* March 1941, 54; resistance as 'corpus of liberating offensive', 80–1; and de Gaulle, 91, 109, 129; enthused by Steinbeck's *The Moon is Down*, 100; and Yugoslav partisans, 111–12, 120–2, 167–70; and debate on air-craft for SOE August 1943, 116; and September 1943 crisis over SOE, 117–18; on Greek resistance, 123–7, 163–5; and French *maquis*, 129–30, 149–51; favours continued existence of SOE after German pen-etration enquiry, 142; anger at SOE over 'Autonomous' mission, 177–8; and Polish resistance, 182–3; and Italy, 192, 194–6, 199, 201; romanti-cism about resistance, 206–7
CIA, *see* Central Intelligence Agency
'Claribel', 81
CLNAI, *see* Committee for the Liber-ation of Northern Italy
Clowder mission, 189–90
CNR, *see* National Council of the Re-sistance

Combined Chiefs of Staff, 119, 133, 134, 174, 248, 250
Combined Intelligence Committee, 134
Combined Operations, 248
Comintern, 68
Committee for the Liberation of Northern Italy (CLNAI), 195–6, 201
Committee on Foreign (Allied) Resistance, 208
Conseil National de la Résistance, see National Council of the Resistance (CNR)
Constanza, 51, 232–3
Controlling Officer, *see* Bevan, Colonel
Cooper, Duff, 34
Corsica, 106–11, 140, 252, 256
COSSAC, 114, 118, 127, 130, 132, 136, 142, 148, 153
counter sabotage, 155–7, 159, 196
Crete, 106, 256
Cretianu, Alexander, 176
Croatia, 120
Cross, R. H., 13
Crossman, R. H. S., 278n.4
Czechoslovakia, 43, 60, 71, 106, 108, 136, 142, 181, 202, 210, 237, 255, 256, 275n.80; secret army, 30–2, 61, 63–4, 66, 81, 181–2, 200, 214–15, 262n.9, 263n.33; assassination of Heydrich, 84; SOE operations 1944–5, 185–7, 200, 202
Czech-Soviet Treaty, 185

Dakar, 83
Dalton, Hugh, 3, 16–17, 32, 35, 38–9, 40, 50–4, 60, 73–8, 86, 91, 100, 207, 208; appointed Minister in charge of SOE, 24–6; ideas on subversion, 28–30; 1941 memorandum to Churchill on SOE, 63–4; complains of dissatisfaction to Attlee, 67–8; on SOE relations with USSR, 69; report of September 1941 on SOE, 70–1; internal SOE crisis November 1941, 75–6; and resistance in Italy, 191

Danish General Staff, 162
Danube, sabotage of traffic on, 22, 54, 227–33
Darlan, Admiral, 57, 191
Davidson, Basil, 6, 179
Davies, Brigadier E. F. ('Trotsky'), 171
Davies, Major Mostyn, 174–5
Deakin, Colonel F. W., 110, 120, 168
Defence Committee, 41, 45, 51, 67, 73, 76, 115–16, 147, 182, 185, 203; and German penetration enquiry, 138, 141–2
Delestraint, C. G. A., 129
Denmark, 44, 71, 81, 87, 108, 138, 140, 154, 156–7, 159, 217, 255; increased sabotage activity by SOE 1943, 130–1; SOE plans 1944, 161–2
Department of Propaganda ('EH'), 20, 21, 26
detonator concept, 28–49 *passim*, 50, 58, 66, 78, 80, 120, 261n.15
Dewavrin, André, 129
Dill, Sir John, 3, 55, 76
Dimitrov, G. M., 174
Djilas, Milovan, 210
Dunkirk, 16, 17, 19, 35
Dutch Forces of the Interior (NBS), 160

EAM-ELAS, 6, 99, 122, 123, 124–7, 152, 163–7, 195, 196, 209
economic warfare, 2, 11–12, 22–3, 25, 42, 60, 261
Eden, Anthony, 3, 51, 53, 77, 90, 94, 109, 124, 125, 145, 147, 148, 159, 160, 173, 176, 178, 179, 185, 192, 201; relations with Dalton, 28, 38, 76, 78; and Mihailović, 73–4, 97, 121, 168–9; and Polish resistance, 135, 182, 184; and German penetration enquiry, 141–2; and Anglo-Soviet relations, 158, 172, 185, 209; on EAM-ELAS, 163–7; bid for post-war control of SOE, 197–8
EDES, 99, 122, 123
'EH', *see* Department of Propaganda
Eisenhower, General Dwight D., 119, 120, 151, 152, 159, 160, 182, 191, 192

El-Alamein, 79
Englandspiel, 94, 132, 137, 143, 148
European communist parties, 34, 48, 68, 75

Far East, 106, 223, 256
Fatherland Front (Bulgaria-OF), 174, 175
fifth column, 23, 24
Fighting France, *see* Free French
Foot, M. R. D., 46, 92, 116
FOPS, *see* Future Operations Planning Section
Force 266, *see* SOE Bari
Foreign Ministers' meeting, Moscow 1943, 134, 135
Foreign Office, 7, 15, 24–6, 33–4, 55, 67, 75, 79, 86, 90, 103, 118, 143, 144, 175, 204, 210, 248, 253; relations with Section D, 20–1, 22; and assassinations, 35; relations with SOE, 38–9, 76–8, 125–6; SOE-Foreign Office 'Treaty' of May 1942, 77; and Mihailović, 97–8, 122; and Greece, 98–9, 123, 124–5, 163–7; and Yugoslav partisans, 120, 167–70, 190; and Polish resistance, 135, 182, 183–4; concern over post-war Anglo-French relations, 149, 158–9; ideas on post-war West European *bloc*, 158, 160; and Roumania, 176–7; and Czechoslovakia, 186–7; and Austria, 189; need to forestall communism in Italy, 193, 201
Fourth Arm, 29, 51, 67, 78, 88
France, 23, 44, 47, 48, 50, 56, 60, 62–3, 64, 65, 66, 70, 71–3, 75, 81, 88, 89, 106, 107–8, 111, 116, 136, 137, 139, 145, 153, 158–9, 175, 216–17, 237, 241, 244, 245, 254–5, 256; SOE policy towards 1942, 90–3; and de Gaulle, 91–2; and *Carte* network, 92–3; SIS activities given priority, 106; SOE activities 1943, 127–30; top priority given to *maquis*, 151; and Overlord, 155
Franco, General Francisco, 44, 55, 56, 194

Freedom Council (Denmark), 131, 157, 161, 162
Free French, 34, 56, 72, 86, 90–3, 109–10; *see also* de Gaulle, France
Free French National Committee, 72, 73, 138, 159
Front de l'Indépendance (Belgium), 160
Future Operations Planning Section (FOPS), 59, 63

Gamelin, General Maurice, 12
de Gaulle, General Charles, 35, 56–7, 62–3, 72, 75, 83, 90–3, 109–10, 127–30, 158–9; *see also* France, Free French
Gedye, G. E. R., 189
Gerbrandy, Dr., 88
Germany, 22, 43, 138, 200, 203, 211, 213–14, 221, 251–2; oil supplies, 14, 22; penetration of SOE, 137–42; SOE activities, 187–8
Girard, A., *see Carte*
Giraud, General H., 109–10, 127, 129
Glenconner, Lord, 118
Gorgopotamos viaduct, 79, 99, 101, 122
governments-in-exile, 31, 33–5, 45, 50, 61, 66, 68, 79, 82, 83–4, 86, 88, 159, 188, 207, 208, 243, 250
Grand, Colonel Lawrence, 20, 22, 30, 36
Greece, 4, 52, 63, 79, 98–100, 103, 105, 106–7, 108, 117, 119, 122–7, 145–6, 158, 162–7, 195, 209, 252, 270n.45; *see also* EAM-ELAS
GS(R), 19–20, 21; *see also* MI(R)
Gubbins, Major-General Colin, 32, 34, 37, 42, 55, 58, 59, 61, 64, 66, 71, 77, 92, 117, 152, 157, 164, 204, 208; joins SOE, 30; and secret armies, 31, 58–9; drafts MI(R) report in September 1940, 42; becomes Executive Director of SOE, 118; on counter sabotage, 159; and Polish resistance, 184; and Czechs, 186, 200, 202; on assassination, 274n.64
guerrilla warfare, 21, 32, 43, 69, 73, 79, 108, 127, 128, 137, 154, 162–3, 192,

209, 223, 268n.4; discouraged, 31, 62; plans for in Spain, 55–6; importance in 1943 Balkan strategy, 99–100, 104–6, 119, 122, 209, 251, 252; discouragement of in France 1943, 129–30
Guerrilla Warfare Committee, 25

Halifax, Lord, 13, 34, 167
Hambro, Sir Charles, 36, 69, 75, 107, 113–14, 118
Hanau, Julius, 188–9
Hankey, Sir Maurice, 18
Harris, Air Chief Marshal Sir A., 117
Harvey, Oliver, 13
Healey, Major Denis, 6
Hentig, Otto von, 274–5n.64
Heydrich, Reinhard, 84, 185, 267n.11
Hill, George, 69
Hillgarth, Alan, 56
Hitler, Adolf, 122–3
Hoare, Sir Reginald, 226
Hoare, Sir Samuel, 18, 55, 56
Hogg, Quintin, 210
Holland, 44, 63, 65, 66, 71, 81, 88, 108, 155, 159–60, 217, 241, 244–5; and *Englandspiel*, 94–5, 132, 137–40
Hollis, Sir Leslie, 3
Hopkins, Harry, 82
Horthy, Admiral, 179
House of Commons, 6, 199–200
Hoxha, Enver, 172, 204
Hudson, Major D. T., 73, 95–7, 169, 184
Hungary, 53, 107, 136, 137, 143, 145, 172–3, 178–81, 222, 228, 254

Ingr, General, 185–6, 275n.80
International Federation of Transport Workers, 188
Internationaler Sozialistische Kampfbund (ISK), 188
Iron Gates, 22, 51, 229–30
Iron Guard, 53
Ismay, Sir Hastings, 3, 226
Italian Communist Party (PCI), 192
Italy, 22, 44, 47, 48, 64, 71, 104, 136, 137, 144, 145, 148, 158, 175, 187,

210, 211, 215–16, 221, 252; SOE activities, and relations with partisans 1944–5, 191–6, 201–2

Jajce resolutions, 121, 168
Jebb, Gladwyn, 12, 20, 28, 30, 39, 46, 53, 55, 56, 76, 208
Jedburghs, 155
Jewish Agency, 179–81, 274n.64
Jewish resistance, 179–81
JIC, *see* Joint Intelligence Committee
Joint Intelligence Committee (JIC), 86–7, 115, 121, 168, 182, 183, 199, 202, 249; enquiry into German penetration of SOE, 137–43
Joint Planning Staff, 40, 58–9, 64, 80, 91, 109, 249; review of future strategy, June 1941, *text* 234–9; report on SOE, August 1941, *text* 240–5
Jouhaux, Leon, 29
July bomb plot, 188

Katyn massacre, 108
Kazan, 51, 229–33
Keble, Brigadier C. M., 118, 120
Kibbutz Mishmar Haemek, 180
King-Hall, Sir Stephen, 16, 25
King George II (Greece), 98–9, 123–5, 253
King George VI, 17
King Leopold (Belgium), 93
King Peter (Yugoslavia), 53, 121, 122, 168, 169
King Zog (Albania), 172
Koenig, General P. J., 152
Kolko, Gabriel, 7
Kupi, Major Abas, 171–2

Labour Party, 6, 25
Laval, Pierre, 90
Lawrence, T. E., 206, 210
Lebanon Charter, 165
Lee, Raymond E., 16, 57
Leeper, Rex, 36, 39
Liddell Hart, Basil, 4–5
Lidice, 84
London Controlling Section, 147
LNC, *see* National Liberation Movement (Albania)

Low Countries, 48, 60, 64, 106, 131–2, 137, 145, 237, 254–5, 256; *see also* Holland, Belgium

Macedonia, 173, 174
Maclean, Fitzroy, 121, 125, 167–70, 195, 207
Macmillan, Harold, 192–3, 195, 196
Maisky, Ivan, 95
Maniu, I., 53, 54, 177
maquis, 41, 114, 127–30, 142, 148, 149–52, 158, 159
Marshall, General George C., 82, 120
Martin, Kingsley, 278n.4
Mass Observation, 57
Masterson, Tom, 49
Menzies, Sir Stewart, 37, 92, 203, 208
Metaxas, General I., 53, 98
Michel, Henri, 7
Michelin, 153
Middle East, 47, 180, 204, 223
Middle East Defense Committee (MEDC), 117, 125, 140
Mihailović, General D., 70, 79, 105, 107, 110–11, 127, 145, 174; first SOE contacts with, 73–5; policy towards in 1942, 95–8; policy towards in 1943, 119–22; withdrawal of support, 121–2, 167–9; *see also* Chetniks
Mikolajczyk, S., 134, 183, 185
MI9, 56
Milorg, 130, 156, 161
Milward, Alan, 7
Minister of State, Cairo, *see* Moyne, Lord
Ministry of Economic Warfare, 11, 13, 67, 118, 197, 249
Ministry of Information, 26, 67
MI(R), 19, 26, 30, 47; report to Chiefs of Staff, September 1940, 42–5, *text* 213–18
Mirković, General B., 54
Molotov, V., 135, 177
Montgomery, General B., 158
Morton, Sir Desmond, 77, 109, 151, 152, 208
Moscow Conference, 1944, 158, 178, 195, 197

Moscow Foreign Ministers' meeting, 1943, 176
Moulin, Jean, 72, 128–9
Mountbatten, Lord Louis, 29, 76
Moyne, Lord, 123, 165
Muggeridge, Malcolm, xii
Mussolini, B., 191
Muus, Flemming, 131, 161
Myers, Brigadier E. C. W., 122–3, 124–5, 126, 152, 163, 170

Namier, Professor Lewis, 180
National Council of the Resistance (*Conseil National de la Résistance –* CNR), 72, 109, 110, 128, 129
National Liberation Movement (Albania – LNC), 170–2
National Peasant Party (Roumania), 53, 176
Nelson, Sir Frank, 46, 52, 92; appointed Executive Director ('CD') of SOE, 36; threatens to resign, 75
Netherlands, *see* Holland
Nicolson, Harold, 16
NKVD, 69, 70
North Africa, 88–9, 91
Norway, 44, 60, 64, 65, 71, 81, 83–4, 106, 108, 130, 137, 138, 154, 156, 159, 160–1, 217–18, 237, 241–2, 244, 255, 256, 264n.40

Office of Strategic Services (OSS), 89–90, 114, 148, 151, 188, 194, 204, 249
oil supplies, German, 14, 21, 22, 48, 49; SOE memorandum on, January 1941, 225–33
Operation Animals, 122–3, 126
Operation Barbarossa, 59
Operation Bodyguard, 146–7, 154, 163, 164, 173, 177
Operation Fortitude, 146
Operation Gymnast, 88–9
Operation Harling, 99, 101, 105, 122
Operation Neptune, 128
Operation Noah's Ark, 162–3
Operation Overlord, 128, 136, 146, 152, 153–4, 170, 183

Operation Rankin, 136
Operation Roundup, 82, 85
Operation Savannah, 55, 56
Operation Starkey, 128–9
Operation Torch, 56, 88–9, 101
Operation Zeppelin, 146–7, 173
Orde Dienst, 94
Orwell, George, 16, 207
OSS, *see* Office of Strategic Services
Osterreichische Freiheitsfront (OFF), 189–90
Oxelsund, 22

Palestine, 180
Palmach, 180
Pantelleria, 47
partisans (Yugoslavia), 95–8, 110–11, 120–2, 127, 148, 151, 167–70, 194, 200
partisan warfare, *see* guerilla warfare
Patton, General George S., 202
Pearl Harbor, 66, 75, 78
'People's War', 207
Pétain, Marshal P., 39, 91
Peugeot, 153
Philby, Kim, 6, 19, 20, 29, 30, 204, 205
Pierlot, H., 84, 93
Plaka Agreement, 125, 164
Ploesti, 226, 228
Poland/Poles, 30, 60, 71, 81, 106, 108, 111, 138, 139, 142, 145, 148, 200, 210, 214–15, 237, 255, 256; secret army, 31–2, 43–4, 61; idea of arming of abandoned by SOE, 63–4, 66; resentment at SOE, 83; Allied discussions about 1943, 132–6; development in 1944, 181–5
Polish Parachute Brigade, 184
Political Warfare Executive (PWE), 61, 67, 74, 77, 93, 174, 248
Portal, Air Chief Marshal Sir Charles, 56, 62, 63, 112–15, 150
Portugal, 48, 55–6, 145, 218, 222–3, 255
Pownall, Sir Henry, 13
Prague, 21
premature uprisings, 32, 42, 47, 68, 74, 87–8, 100, 103, 127, 222, 246
Prince Paul (Yugoslavia), 52, 53

propaganda, 65, 67, 76, 238–9, 240–1
'Prosper' circuit, 128
PWE, *see* Political Warfare Executive

Québec Conference, August 1943 ('Quadrant'), 118, 125, 126, 149, 153, 210

Reilly, Sidney, 69
Renner, Karl, 190
repatriation of Soviet citizens, 166, 178
Rjukan, 130
Roberts, F. K., 262n.9
Roosevelt, Franklin D., 80, 82, 88, 90, 104, 109, 121, 159, 210
Rootham, Jasper, 5
Roumania, 21, 22, 39, 47, 48, 49, 52–3, 54, 71, 104, 107, 145, 165, 172–3, 180, 222, 225–33, 255; SOE
Rowecki, General S., 133
activities, 175–8
Russell, Major David, 176

sabotage, 20–3, 25, 26, 32, 39, 48, 58, 60, 63, 65, 104, 106, 130, 185, 244, 250–1
SACMED, 193, 196, 200–1
Sardinia, 47, 104
Sargent, Sir Orme, 125, 126
satellite states, 172–81
Scandinavia, 144–5
Second Front, 73–4, 78, 79, 81, 82, 86, 88, 105
secrecy, xii–xiii, 1–2
secret armies, concept of, 30–6, 44–5, 48, 52, 58, 61–6, 71, 75, 78, 81, 83, 85, 95, 97, 103, 132, 182, 208–9, 241–2, 244–5
Secret Intelligence Service (SIS), xii, 1–2, 4, 7, 19–21, 26, 35, 56, 65, 77, 79, 81, 89, 103, 111–14, 115, 122, 130, 131, 143, 150, 151, 172, 174, 187–8, 208, 248, 259; relations with SOE, 86–7, 205–6; and German penetration of SOE, 137–41; Soviet penetration of, 204; special operations (post-war), 198, 203–4; *see also* Menzies, Sir Stewart

Section D, 19–23, 26, 30, 46, 52, 53, 176, 179, 187–8

Selborne, Lord, 27, 51, 78, 88, 94, 100, 147, 154, 183, 185, 202, 206, 208; replaces Dalton, 76; defends de Gaulle against Churchill, 109–10; and aircraft for SOE, 115–16, 120–1; and Mihailović, 120; and EAM-ELAS, 125; and Polish resistance, 134–5; and German penetration enquiry, 137–41; and *maquis*, 151–2; accuses Eden of appeasement, 178; and Italian partisans, 194; resigns as Minister of Economic Warfare, 198

Serbia/Serbs, 168, 169

Seton-Watson, Professor Hugh, 38

Sforza, Count C., 199

SHAEF, 151–9, 183, 202

Sharrett, Moshe, 179, 180

Sicily, 47, 104–5

Sikorski, General W., 31, 83–5, 133, 184, 262n.10, 266n.8

Simmel, Georg, xii

Simović, General D., 53, 54

Sinclair, Sir A., 150

Sinn Fein, 25

SIS, *see* Secret Intelligence Service

Slessor, Sir John, 13, 184

Slovak uprising, 185–7, 200

Slovenia/Slovenes, 120, 189, 190, 195

Smith, General W. Bedell, 151

SO1, 36, 39, 67

SO2, *see* Special Operations Executive

SO3, 36

SOE, *see* Special Operations Executive

SOE Bari, 170, 181, 182, 184

SOE Cairo, 79, 96, 98, 107, 111, 119, 120–3, 125, 151, 162–3, 170, 174

Sosnkowski, General K., 133, 134

Soviet Union, 34, 48, 50, 62–4, 68, 70, 75, 108, 133–4, 135, 144–5, 161–2, 166, 174, 176–9, 191, 192–3, 199, 203; *see also* Anglo-Soviet relations

Spaak, Paul-Henri, 94, 132, 160

Spain, 48, 49, 101, 145, 255; MI(R) recommends against using anti-

Franco elements, 44, 218; similar Foreign Office reluctance, 55–6; predominance of SIS over SOE interests in, 56; preparation for guerrilla war in, 56, 222–3

Special Forces Headquarters (SFHQ), 101, 153

Special Operations Executive (SOE), *for SOE plans and activities in individual countries, see under appropriate country entries*; origins, 10–27; formation agreed by War Cabinet, 23; Charter, 2, 26, 33, 38, 40, 77, 158; Dalton placed in charge of, 24–7; and assassination, 34–5; internal organisation, 1940, 36–7; operational capacity, September 1940, 46; first directive, November 1940, 46, 47, 55, *text* 219–24; situation at end of 1940, 49; destruction of Balkan networks 1941, 54; agreement with NKVD, 1941, 69, 76; developments 1941, 70–8; internal crisis, November 1941, 75–6; second directive, 1942, 79, 82, *text* 246–7; 'treaty' with Foreign Office, May 1942, 77; enquiry into its functioning, May 1942, 86; agreement with OSS, 89–90; relations with OSS, 101; lifting of ban on sabotage in Vichy France, 128; third directive, 1943, 87, 105–6, 122, 128, *text* 248–57; appreciation of activities, 1943, 107–9; September 1943 crisis, 117–18; report on 1943 activities, 136–7; record of losses and casualties 1943, 140; German penetration of networks, 94, 103, 114–15, 137–43, 183; fears of communist penetration, 142–3; question of directive for 1944, 136; priority list for 1944, 192; and strategic deception 1944, 146–7; contribution to Overlord, 153–8; relations with Jewish Agency, 179–81; reaches peak activity, September 1944, 197; discussion of post-war activities, 197–8, 202–3; directive for 1945, 197; directive on long-term objectives,

October 1945, 203–4, 258; directive on Austria, November 1945, 191; amalgamation with SIS, 1946, 203; aircraft supply, 32, 33, 40–1, 58, 66, 103, 106–7, 111–13, 121, 142, 147–9, 205, 243–4; French Sections (F and RF), 29, 72, 91–3, 128–9, 159; Section X (Germany), 188; communications, 22, 38, 46, 70, 87, 242; relations with Chiefs of Staff, 40–1, 115–16, 140–1; relations with Foreign Office, 38–9, 76–8, 103, 125, 197, 209; relations with SIS, 20, 22, 36–8, 65, 79, 81, 86–7, 89, 106, 115–16, 139, 140–1, 197, 205–6, 207, 209, 249, 263n.26

Sporborg, H. N., 137, 149, 164, 271n.7

Springhall, Douglas, 143, 179

Stalin, Josef, 68, 121, 158, 183, 184, 197, 200, 208, 210

Stawell, Major-General W., 195

Steinbeck, John, 100

Stevens, Colonel John, 279n.107

Stewart, Sir Findlater, 203

Stirbey, Prince B., 177

Strang, William, 262n.10

strategic bombing, 2, 11, 23, 41, 57, 59, 60, 61, 66, 80, 148–50, 242

strategic deception, 94, 105, 122, 127, 128–9, 146–7, 154, 164–5, 171, 177, 209; *see also* Operations Bodyguard, Fortitude, Starkey *and* Zeppelin

Stuart, Sir Campbell, 21

Styria, 189

Subašić, Dr. Ivan, 169

subversion, 15, 19, 20, 22–6, 29–31, 39, 42, 47–8, 59–60, 63, 65–6, 80, 104, 220–1, 235–7, 238–9, 240–1, 244

Sweden, 22, 77, 188, 255

Sweet-Escott, Bickham, xii, 20, 33, 39, 41, 46, 49, 52, 90, 93, 184

Switzerland, 47–8, 188, 191, 223

'Tabor', General, *see* Tatar, General S.

Tatar, General S. ('Tabor'), 184

Taylor, A. J. P., 206

Taylor, George, 30, 49, 52, 75, 107, 123

Teheran Conference, 121, 145, 146, 167–8

Televag, 84

Thompson, E. P., 175

Thompson, Frank, 175

Tito, Josip Broz, 41, 74, 96, 121, 122, 127, 167–170, 171, 179, 190, 194, 195, 201

Togliatti, P., 192

Tomasevich, Jozo, 119–20

Trident Conference, Washington, May 1943, 108–9, 122

Trieste, 170, 195, 201

Tripartite Pact, 53, 174

Turkey, 144–5, 158, 188, 204, 256

Ukraine, 204

'Ultra', 37, 38, 205

unconditional surrender, 187–8, 191

United States, 15, 45, 80, 210

Uren, Captain B. L., 143, 179

Vansittart, Sir Robert, 26

Varna, 51, 232–3

Venlo affair, 187–8

Veres, L., 178–9

V for Victory campaign, 67

Vichy France, 40, 76, 77, 88–9, 91–3

War Aims Committee, 19

War Cabinet, 2, 19, 23, 34, 35, 73, 82, 91, 109, 112, 135, 145, 159, 165, 166, 169, 182, 191

War Office, 24

Warsaw uprising, 64, 184, 194

Washington Conference, December 1941, 80, 82

Waugh, Evelyn, 18

Wavell, Sir A., 53, 57

western Europe, 23, 31–2, 46, 81, 88, 95, 101, 113, 114, 116, 127, 147–62, 199–200, 208, 210; concept of a post-war *bloc*, 144–5, 158–9, 196, 210

Weygand, General M., 39

Wilson, General Sir Henry Maitland, 125, 126, 164, 174, 182, 192, 193, 195, 200

Index 295

Winant, J. G., 120
Woodhouse, C. M., 5, 99, 164, 209

Yalomitza bridge, 228
Yalta Conference, 200
Yugoslavia, 48, 52–3, 63, 71, 73–5, 103, 105–8, 119–22, 126–7, 145, 167–70, 175, 195, 222, 228, 253–4, 259, 270n.45

Yugoslav *coup d'état*, 27 March 1941, 53–4, 264n.7

Zervas, Colonel N., 99, 124